Study Guide

Thomas S. O'Connor
The University of New Orleans

Contemporary Marketing
Sixth Edition

Louis E. Boone
University of South Alabama

David L. Kurtz
University of Arkansas

THE DRYDEN PRESS

Chicago   Fort Worth   San Francisco
Philadelphia   Montreal   Toronto
London   Sydney   Tokyo

ISBN 0-03-022982-0
Printed in the United States of America
012-066-9876543

Cover Source: "Marché aux Puces" by Michel Delacroix, 1977.
Courtesy of Lublin Graphics, Inc., 95 East Putnam Avenue, Greenwich, CT 06830.

Address orders:
6277 Sea Harbor Drive
Orlando, FL 32821

Address editorial correspondence:
908 N. Elm, Suite 101
Hinsdale, IL 60521

The Dryden Press
Holt, Rinehart and Winston
Saunders College Publishing

Table of Contents

To the Instructor

This Study Guide, which accompanies the sixth edition of *Contemporary Marketing*, represents a major change from the previous version. At least 75 percent of the multiple-choice and true/false questions are new. New materials have also been created for Questions for Thought, Applying Marketing Concepts, Experiential Exercises, and Computer Applications in each chapter. The Key Concepts sections have been entirely reconstructed for consistency and agreement with text materials.

A new feature of the Study Guide is the marketing plan exercise, which you will find at the end of Parts 1 through 8 in the Study Guide. "Creating a Marketing Plan" is designed to allow students to get involved with three people who start a computer service. The plan is somewhat simplified from that which might actually be necessary in an actual new-business situation, but the data on which it is based have been constructed to be as realistic as possible. In each part students are asked to complete a part of the marketing plan as outlined in the appendix to Chapter 3. By the end of the Study Guide, they will have a complete marketing plan for the company.

Each part of the Study Guide also features a Crossword Puzzle based on the key concepts contained in the chapters from that part, and three or four cases with questions for analysis.

I hope you and your students enjoy using the Study Guide and that it facilitates their learning experience and your teaching efforts. Your comments, positive or negative, will be gratefully received. And, of course, despite careful checking, a few errors may remain. I shall be equally grateful to be informed of these.

There are, of course, people to be thanked for their help with a project like this. For their unfailing support with the editorial and production aspects of this Study Guide, my thanks are extended to Jan Richardson, Doris Hill, Karen Steib, Rose Hepburn, and Gale Miller at Dryden Press. For being perhaps the best secretary in all of academics, and certainly the best that I have ever worked with, my appreciation goes to Joyce Stall. And for having put up with a husband and father that they must have thought at times during the last several months had decided to become a hermit, or at least a worshipper of word processors, my deepest, warmest thanks go out to Valerie, Brian Patrick, and Terrence Michael.

Best wishes in the use of these materials.

Thomas S. O'Connor
The University of New Orleans

To the Student

This Study Guide has been prepared with one purpose in mind: to help you gain a greater understanding of contemporary marketing. It is specifically designed to be used with *Contemporary Marketing*, sixth edition, by Louis E. Boone and David L. Kurtz. A great deal of care has been devoted to providing you with the opportunity to expand and test your knowledge as you work your way through the material in the text.

The parts of the Study Guide are coordinated with the parts of the textbook. Each part of the Study Guide is meant to be a "learning unit" covering a particular area of the discipline of marketing.

Each chapter of the Study Guide begins with a **Summary** of the text chapter. This is not meant to substitute for the material in *Contemporary Marketing*, but merely to serve as a "refresher" to help you recall significant points covered in the text as you prepare to use this guide.

The first exercise in each chapter will help to determine if you have learned the Key Concepts in that chapter. You will match the Key Concepts with their definitions, checking your answers with those at the end of the chapter. To derive the greatest benefit from this exercise, as from the other exercises, you shouldn't check your answers until you have filled in *all* the blanks.

The **Self-Quiz** contains a substantial number of multiple-choice and true/false questions. These will serve as a quick check of your understanding of the chapter material. You have available, in addition, **Questions for Thought**, which test your grasp of the major concepts of the chapter; **Experiential Exercises**, which let you examine marketing operations firsthand; **Applying Marketing Concepts**, which is designed to illustrate how the techniques and principles discussed in your text are put to use; and **Computer Applications**, which familiarize you with some of the methods of analysis that your text discusses. All of these are designed to give you, as much as is possible in an academic setting, firsthand experience at what marketing is all about. Never be afraid to do more than the minimum requirement that each exercise demands of you. As with all learning, the more you know, the more you'll want to know.

Each of the eight parts of this Study Guide contains an episode of **Creating a Marketing Plan**, a comprehensive study of the adventures of three young entrepreneurs as they develop a marketing mix "from the ground up." If you follow this exercise and use it in conjunction with the marketing plan outline from Chapter 3 of your text, you will complete the course having written a complete marketing plan for a new business. Each part also contains a **Crossword Puzzle** which is based upon the Key Concepts from the chapters in that part. I have always found crosswords to be a uniquely fun way of testing my knowledge of vocabulary. I hope you will too. Finally, each part includes **Cases** which call for you to choose from among sometimes conflicting alternatives. These are an excellent way to hone your decision-making skills.

Best of luck to you in the use of these materials.

Thomas S. O'Connor
The University of New Orleans

Part 1

The Contemporary Marketing Environment

In this section of the text, the contemporary marketing process and the environment in which it operates are introduced.

Marketing is the process of planning and executing the conception, pricing, promotion, and distribution of ideas, goods, and services to create exchanges that satisfy organizational and individual objectives. The marketing process creates time, place, and ownership utility for consumers by making the right product available at the right place, the right time, and the right price.

Marketing arises out of the exchange process. The emphasis on marketing activities increases as firms progress through the three eras of: (1) production orientation, (2) sales orientation, and (3) marketing orientation. Marketing-oriented firms define their business in terms of customer needs and wants rather than product characteristics.

Only in the recent past have the majority of U.S. organizations realized that efficient production alone will not assure long-range profitability. Long-run success cannot result unless firms adopt a company-wide consumer orientation. This realization has been called the *marketing concept*.

Marketers need to plan and coordinate the four strategic areas of product, distribution, promotion, and pricing. A comprehensive marketing mix strategy cannot be set until the needs and wants of the chosen market segment have been determined. Consumers may reject an offering because the product is not what is wanted, its price is too high, it is not available at a convenient place, or they were misinformed or remained uninformed by promotion. For marketing to take place, it is usually necessary that a firm or some combination of firms perform the eight universal functions of: (1) buying, (2) selling, (3) transporting, (4) storing, (5) standardization and grading, (6) financing, (7) risk taking, and (8) securing marketing information.

The impact of marketing activities on society is great. The cost of marketing accounts for about 50 percent of the prices paid by consumers for products and services. Marketing careers provide challenging opportunities in a number of specialties.

The marketer must be aware of the five interacting environments which affect marketing activities: the competitive, the economic, the social/cultural, the political/legal, and the technological. These environments are complex and are affected by the actions of businesses, the judiciary, nonprofit organizations, consumers, public activists, and numerous other persons and organizations within society. The dynamic nature of the environments makes it imperative that forecasting be undertaken to predict likely occurrences in each of these areas.

The competitive environment includes all those organizations competing for the purchasing power of the consumer. A firm chooses its competitive environment when it chooses its markets. Conditions in this environment usually change over time as new firms choose to enter and other firms leave the competitive arena.

Marketing strategies must be adjusted in response to changes in the political/legal environment. The Sherman Act of 1890 and other early antitrust legislation were aimed at maintaining a competitive environment. The Robinson-Patman Act and other legislation arising out of conditions which existed during the 1930s were designed to protect small competitors from discriminatory pricing practices which benefited large competitors. A number of laws passed during and since the 1950s have been designed to protect consumers from harmful marketing practices and faulty or unsafe products or services. The late 1970s and the 1980s have seen substantial deregulation of a number of industries which formerly operated under substantial government control.

Consumers' willingness to buy products depends on the economic environment. The rate of inflation, level of unemployment, and availability of critical resources all influence the likelihood of individuals parting with discretionary income. If resources are in short supply and in great demand, it becomes difficult for marketers to satisfy consumers. Marketers may, in fact, have to engage in "demarketing"—encouraging consumers to reduce their demand for scarce commodities.

Technology is changing with incredible speed. Product improvements and discoveries enable marketers to better satisfy consumer needs. There is competition in this environment, too, and technological breakthroughs by others may take market shares away from those who do not maintain the pace of activity.

The social/cultural environment has recently become more significant as a factor to be considered by marketers. This area includes all relationships marketers have with members of society, either as individuals or as members of the numerous segments which make up the societal whole. The impact of this environment is broadening because of a decline in public confidence in social institutions such as the government and major corporations. Rising educational levels and better communications have led to greater public involvement in the marketing arena.

Chapter 1

Marketing in Profit and Nonprofit Settings

Chapter Summary

Institutions exist within society because they have the ability to satisfy wants through the creation of utility of form, time, place, and ownership. In a business the production function is responsible for utility of form, while marketing creates the other three aspects of this concept. If products, services, or ideas that have form utility are made available to customers seeking those goods, at a convenient location and in such a manner that ownership may be transferred permanently or temporarily to the customers, then time, place, and ownership utility result.

Marketing, as most recently defined, is "the process of planning and executing the conception, pricing, promotion, and distribution of ideas, goods, and services to create exchanges that will satisfy individual and organizational objectives." Thus marketing is related to the concept of exchange and it is realized in this definition that customer targets are selected *before* the goods are produced. Marketing is viewed as operating within the ethical standards of society, and is useful to both profit-making and nonprofit institutions.

Historically, marketing in the United States has passed through three phases: the production era, the sales era, and the marketing era. This last phase has had as its result the formulation and adoption of the marketing concept. This concept, which is a company-wide orientation toward satisfying consumer wants and needs, implies that marketing starts the process of exchange, rather than being only the end result.

Marketing decisions are subject to a wide range of influences not under the control of the marketing institution. Competition in the marketplace, political and legal factors, the economy, technology, and social/cultural considerations are all part of the environment in which marketing decisions are made. They are usually uncontrollable as far as the specific institution is concerned. Operating within these environmental constraints, marketers control the means by which they approach their targeted consumers.

The marketing mix is the marketer's strategic tool to approach consumers. It consists of four strategies:

a. Product
b. Price
c. Distribution
d. Promotion

The product strategy includes not just the physical part of what is being offered, but also related decisions on package designs, brand names, trademarks, warranties, and even development of new products. Pricing deals with methods of setting profitable and justifiable prices. Distribution involves the physical movement of goods and also the institutional channels necessary to bring goods and consumers together. Finally, promotion links sellers and buyers by communication through salespeople, advertisement, and sales promotion.

For marketing to take place, certain activities must be performed by someone. These activities, which can be grouped into the exchange functions (buying and selling), the physical distribution functions (transporting and storing), and the facilitating functions (standardization and grading, financing, risk taking, and market information), are essential for providing target customers with the goods, services, and ideas they need when (time utility) and where (place utility) they need them.

Name _____   Instructor _____

Section _____   Date _____

Key Concepts

The purpose of this section is to allow you to determine if you can match key concepts with the definitions of the concepts. It is essential that you know the definitions of the concepts prior to applying the concepts in later exercises in this chapter.

From the list of lettered terms, select the one that best fits each of the numbered statements below. Write the letter of that choice in the space provided.

Key Terms

a.   utility
b.   marketing
c.   exchange process
d.   production orientation
e.   sales orientation
f.   seller's market
g.   buyer's market
h.   consumer orientation
i.   marketing concept
j.   marketing myopia
k.   broadening concept

l.   person marketing
m.   place marketing
n.   idea marketing
o.   organization marketing
p.   target market
q.   marketing mix
r.   product strategy
s.   pricing strategy
t.   distribution strategy
u.   promotional strategy

____   1.   An example of this would be when states, cities, and countries publicize their tourist attractions to lure vacation travelers.

____   2.   A blending together of the elements of promotion by marketers to communicate most effectively with their target market.

____   3.   Occurs when management fails to recognize the scope of its business.

____   4.   The element of marketing decision making that deals with the methods of setting profitable and justifiable exchange values for goods and services.

____   5.   Expanded view of marketing as a generic function to be performed by both profit-seeking and nonprofit organizations.

____   6.   The blending of marketing strategy elements to fit the needs and preferences of a specific target market.

____   7.   "The want-satisfying power of a good or service" is a description of this characteristic.

____   8.   A market characterized by a shortage of goods and services.

___ 9. Choosing brand names and trademarks, deciding on package design, and creating the terms of warranties are part of this.

___ 10. Marketing by mutual-benefit organizations, service organizations, and government organizations that seeks to influence others to accept their goals, receive their services, or contribute to them in some way.

___ 11. Your local public library sponsors a radio commercial telling listeners about its extended hours and special research services. How would you characterize this activity?

___ 12. This afternoon's mail brings an envelope containing a pamphlet praising a candidate for a local political office. The pamphlet, and the accompanying request for a financial contribution, is typical of this activity.

___ 13. "The strong buyer's market which appeared in this country after World War II made it necessary for business to realize that it must first market, then sell goods." What new point of view does this statement describe?

___ 14. A marketplace characterized by an abundance of goods and services.

___ 15. The philosophy that if you "build a better mousetrap the world will beat a path to your door."

___ 16. Assuring that products are shipped to the right destinations is part of this strategy.

___ 17. The objective of this company-wide consumer orientation is the achievement of long-term success.

___ 18. The process of planning and executing the conception, pricing, promotion, and distribution of ideas, goods, and services to create exchanges that will satisfy individual and organizational objectives.

___ 19. The process of trading things of value between two or more parties to satisfy perceived needs.

___ 20. When a business assumes that consumers do not wish to buy nonessential products and services and thus relies on creative advertising and personal selling to "push" its offering, it is expressing this philosophy.

___ 21. A group of people toward whom a firm markets its goods, services, or ideas with a strategy designed to satisfy their specific needs and preferences.

Name_____   Instructor _____

Section _____   Date _____

Self Quiz

You should use these objective questions to test your understanding of the chapter material. You can check your answers with those provided at the end of the chapter.

While these questions cover most of the chapter topics, they are not intended to be the same as the test questions your instructor may use in an examination. A good understanding of all aspects of the course material is essential to good performance on any examination.

True/False

Write "T" for True or "F" for False for each of the following statements.

____ 1. Domino's Pizza creates *time utility* for consumers by providing home-delivered pizza in thirty minutes or less, guaranteed.

____ 2. Marketing does not take place in underdeveloped countries because the traders who sell goods in central marketplaces cannot afford television and radio advertisements.

____ 3. Marketing activity is concerned with creating and resolving exchange relationships.

____ 4. A firm which employs creative advertising and personal selling to overcome consumer resistance is *sales oriented*.

____ 5. Production orientation is most appropriate for firms in a strong buyer's market.

____ 6. Severe weather such as deep freezes or tornadoes can tremendously reduce fruit crops like oranges. If the amount of oranges available is less than the number consumers wish to eat, a buyer's market exists.

____ 7. An example of marketing myopia is when an airline defines its main scope of business activity as providing faster service than any other airline.

____ 8. Marketing myopia is more likely to occur for firms which are customer oriented rather than production oriented.

____ 9. An example of broadening the marketing concept is the American Heart Association using a promotional campaign to encourage people to enroll for courses in cardiopulmonary resuscitation.

____ 10. If you were in charge of distribution strategy, you would be concerned with transportation, storage, and institutions such as retailers who sell to consumers.

____ 11. The marketing mix involves blending four types of marketing decisions to satisfy chosen consumer segments.

____ 12. The decision by Avi Fattal and Avi Ruimi to market their "AutoScreen" cardboard windshield screens shaped like sunglasses in red, yellow, blue, or brown is part of the company's product strategy.

____ 13. Trucking companies perform the transportation function; warehouses perform the storage function.

____ 14. Egg producers who separate their eggs into small, medium, large, and extra-large and package them separately are performing the function of securing marketing information.

____ 15. Marketing activities should be understood, but it must be remembered that they have little direct impact on job potential.

____ 16. The decision to sell "AutoScreen" cardboard windshield screens through corner drugstores, discount houses, and even to large companies to be given away as customer gifts is part of Auto-Sales' distribution strategy.

____ 17. A product built to the highest-possible quality standards will sell itself.

____ 18. If you should happen to come across a company whose chief marketing executive bore the title of "sales manager," you would have reason to suspect that the company was still in the production, rather than the sales or marketing, era.

____ 19. By focusing on the benefits resulting from the use of products or services, marketing converts wants into needs.

____ 20. The private sector of the economy has an even more diverse array of nonprofit organizations than does the public sector.

____ 21. When a community (city, state, or county, for example) launches a marketing campaign aimed at attracting new business, it is engaging in place marketing.

____ 22. A television commercial sponsored by a citizens' group stressing the necessity for your state to undertake prison reform would be an example of organization marketing.

____ 23. One characteristic more typical of nonprofit organizations than for-profit organizations is the lack of a clear organization structure.

____ 24. If you buy a set of tires, you can be sure that if the new set bears the same size markings as the old, it will fit the car. This is because tire sizes are standardized.

____ 25. Procter & Gamble's distribution of millions of free samples of Liquid Cascade to households was an interesting new approach to distribution strategy.

Multiple Choice

Circle the letter of the word or phrase that best completes the sentence or best answers the question.

Use the following information for Questions 26-29.

Assume that you and another student have started a newspaper. The purpose of the paper is to serve as an independent source of campus and community news. You have hired a secretary to type news copy with a personal computer you have bought the firm.

26. The process of changing the information you have collected into a finished product, a news-paper, would create
    a. time utility.
    b. place utility.
    c. form utility.
    d. ownership utility.
    e. marketing utility.

27. If you hire someone to deliver the finished newspapers instead of requiring your customers to pick them up at your office, you are performing the _____ function and creating _____ utility.
    a. storage, place
    b. buying, time
    c. transportation, time
    d. transportation, place
    e. risk-taking, place

28. You are in charge of contacting potential customers. You talk to students to determine who wants or needs an independent newspaper and how much they are willing to pay. In addition, after a sale is made you assign the title of the paper to the student. The function in which you are involved and the utility you create by helping transfer the title are
    a. selling function; ownership utility.
    b. buying function; ownership utility.
    c. financing function; time utility.
    d. transportation function; place utility.
    e. grading function; form utility.

29. The *marketing* efforts of your firm *will not* create
    a. form utility.
    b. time utility.
    c. place utility.
    d. ownership utility.
    e. functional utility.

30. The president of a large company recently defined marketing as the performance of business activities that direct the flow of goods and services from producer to consumer or user. This definition is too narrow because
    a. it ignores the marketing functions of transportation and storage.
    b. it does not emphasize that the role of a firm is to generate output of value to consumers.
    c. the importance of quality control is not considered.
    d. it assumes marketing only creates form utility.
    e. it does not consider the thousands of nonprofit organizations currently engaged in mar-keting activities.

31. A good marketing strategy should include
    a. high levels of market share regardless of the ethics of the marketing activities necessary to obtain that share.
    b. selection of consumer segments prior to production.
    c. establishment of the lowest-cost marketing program, regardless of customer needs.
    d. analysis of consumer needs after the product has been designed and produced.
    e. recognition that marketing does not apply to nonprofit organizations.

32. Which of the following statements best reflects a firm with a production orientation?
    a. Our company is consumer oriented.
    b. We have a first-rate sales organization which disposes of all the products we can make at a favorable price.
    c. We guarantee our customers complete satisfaction or we will refund their money.
    d. Our basic function is to produce the highest-quality product possible.
    e. Selling is only one component of marketing.

33. The marketing concept emphasizes
    a. company-wide consumer orientation.
    b. marketers running the company.
    c. a production orientation.
    d. achievement of short-run success.
    e. building retail stores in ghettos.

34. Firms facing a seller's market will tend to be concerned with
    a. producing more goods or services.
    b. convincing consumers to buy their goods and services.
    c. restricting production to meet the level of demand.
    d. hunting for new markets for their goods and services.
    e. offering consumers prices which are lower than competitors'.

35. Which of the following best exemplifies a firm which has adopted the marketing concept?
    a. Sales must increase 30 percent annually.
    b. We train our salesforce to be persuasive so it can wear down consumer resistance.
    c. Our new car was developed to satisfy the needs of young urban professionals who want a luxurious, quality mode of transportation.
    d. We do not have to worry about competitors because we have a patent on the production process for our products.
    e. Engineers plan our products and marketers sell them.

36. Which of the following would you consider to be an example of marketing myopia?
    a. telephone company—the lowest-cost phone service
    b. railroad company—transportation services to meet customer needs
    c. perfume company—hope in a bottle
    d. movie company—entertainment for all ages
    e. chicken company—nutritional dining enjoyment

37. The marketing mix includes
    a. planning the product.
    b. blending personal selling, advertising, and sales promotion tools.
    c. setting prices.
    d. establishing marketing channels.
    e. all of the above.

38. Automobile manufacturers require dealers to buy a certain number of cars each month. It is the dealer's responsibility to sell the cars; the manufacturer will not allow unsold cars to be returned. Dealers borrow money from banks and other financial institutions so they can pay car manufacturers before the cars are sold to consumers. The functions performed in this example of automobiles are
    a. dealers: risk taking; banks: financing.
    b. dealers: buying; banks: selling.
    c. dealers: securing market information; banks: grading.
    d. dealers: risk-taking; banks: buying.
    e. dealers: transporting; banks: storing.

39. An essential reason for studying marketing is
    a. there are no jobs for college students in marketing.
    b. recent governmental legislation has doubled the cost of marketing.
    c. marketing provides an opportunity to make a real contribution to society.
    d. production orientation is regaining importance in most firms.
    e. organizations refuse to hire students without any marketing background.

40. Which of the following would be considered an environmental factor impacting the marketing effort?
    a. doubling the size of the salesforce
    b. testing a new product in selected markets
    c. sharing the cost of advertisements with retailers who sell the company's products
    d. Japanese competitors offering higher quality products for the same price
    e. using prime time television advertisements to extol the benefits of the company's products

41. In which of the following situations would form utility most likely be created?
    a. A physician and his assistants use the facilities of Lakeside Hospital to study a new surgical technique.
    b. An engineer studies the feasibility of assembling particular integrated circuits, resistors, capacitors, and other electrical and mechanical components into a Sony TV set.
    c. Musicians, sheet music, instruments, and a conductor come together in Joe's Bar and Grill after a rehearsal by the Boston Symphony Orchestra.
    d. A local K-mart receives a shipment of boxed electric toasters which are priced and placed on display by employees.
    e. Ideal Cement Company places Kentucky limestone into its kilns where high temperature changes the chemical nature of the stone into Portland Cement, which is then bagged and shipped to market.

42. A Rolls-Royce executive was once heard to observe, "We have never had to worry about sales or advertising. Our cars are simply the best in the world." The chances are that Rolls Royce is
    a. an active advocate of the marketing concept.
    b. a production-oriented company.
    c. a firm with a sales orientation.
    d. unique in its analysis of marketing opportunities and target markets.
    e. operating in a buyer's market.

43. When marketing departments began to emerge during the sales era
   a.   they tended to assume a subordinate position to production, finance, and engineering.
   b.   they were often headed by an executive whose background and orientation had nothing to do with sales.
   c.   they quickly assumed a position of domination over the firm's other divisions.
   d.   marketing to specific target groups of consumers became the rule rather than the exception.
   e.   many firms returned to a strong emphasis on product quality and production techniques.

44. Nonprofit organizations
   a.   are prohibited by law from earning a profit on their operations.
   b.   are very numerous in the public sector, but seldom found in the private sector.
   c.   have as their primary objective something other than returning a profit to their owners.
   d.   seldom deal in tangible goods.
   e.   generate over $750 billion in revenues each year.

45. Efforts by nonprofit institutions to cultivate the attention, interest, and preferences of a target market toward a person are called
   a.   idea marketing.
   b.   celebrity marketing.
   c.   person marketing.
   d.   concept marketing.
   e.   personal promotion.

46. Buying, selling, transportation, and storage are known as the
   a.   exchange functions and facilitating functions.
   b.   exchange functions and normalizing functions.
   c.   facilitating functions and physical distribution functions.
   d.   exchange functions and physical distribution functions.
   e.   physical distribution functions and normalizing functions.

47. On the way home from work, John stops at a gasoline station to buy fuel. He buys unleaded regular even though he's never used this brand of gasoline, because the sign on the pump says "Minimum Octane Rating = 87" and he knows his car will perform adequately on this fuel. He pays for his purchase with his new oil company credit card. Which of the following marketing functions have most obviously facilitated John's purchase?
   a.   risk taking and securing market information
   b.   risk taking and financing
   c.   standardization/grading and financing
   d.   transportation and buying
   e.   storing and financing

48. The marketing functions of transportation and storage are most closely related to the utilities of
   a.   ownership and form.
   b.   form and time.
   c.   ownership and place.
   d.   time and place.
   e.   time and ownership.

49. Approximately what proportion of the occupations in the United States are marketing-related?
    a.   one-half to two-thirds
    b.   one-tenth to one-quarter
    c.   one-third to one-half
    d.   over one-half
    e.   one-quarter to one-third

50. The idea that customers will resist purchasing products and services not deemed essential and that the task of personal selling and advertising is to convince them to buy is typical of the
    a.   production-oriented company.
    b.   sales-oriented company.
    c.   marketing-oriented company.
    d.   types of organizations named in a and b above.
    e.   none of the above.

Name_____   Instructor _____

Section _____   Date _____

Applying Marketing Concepts

Dan Forman, a music professor at Southwestern State University, has opened a home entertainment store. The store, located near the Southwestern campus, specializes in stereo equipment, television sets, and VCRs. The brands of equipment carried include Pioneer, JVC, Magnavox, and Blue Chip. In addition to selling new equipment, Mr. Forman provides repair service for used equipment, including even the newest video specialties and compact disc players.

In a recent interview, Forman explained his business strategy: "I am mainly concerned with satisfying the at-home entertainment needs of the students, faculty, and staff of the university. Generally, I stock the products and brands that they ask for as long as I can get the product and make a profit on the sale of it. There are some manufacturers, such as Toshiba, which I have had to stop dealing with because they acted very independently, delivering equipment more than six months after it was ordered. Some of the products I stock are purchased from wholesalers because we order in small quantities. Most of our orders are shipped to us by United Parcel Service (UPS) because this ensures we get the product in a week or less after placing the order, without incurring an exorbitant freight bill. My major advertising is done in the school newspaper, where I usually offer students a discount or some free product like an equipment cover if they buy a minimum amount. My salesforce is myself and two college students. In general, the sales personnel are required to charge all customers the same price; prices are comparable to those offered by competitors. I feel it is necessary to be competitive because there are several stores nearby that offer comparable products. Overall, I have made enough to pay the bills and make a 10 percent return on my investment. My major concern is that my marketing costs seem to be too high; they are almost 25 percent of the selling price of my goods."

____ 1. Dan Forman appears to have adopted the marketing concept.

____ 2. The Toshiba Company may be production oriented.

____ 3. Forman's home entertainment store faces a seller's market.

____ 4. Forman's marketing costs are higher than the national average.

____ 5. Forman's decision to locate his store near his market created time utility for his customers.

6. Repairing VCRs and compact disc players creates
    a. form utility.
    b. place utility.
    c. ownership utility.
    d. time utility.
    e. none of the above.

7. Newspaper advertising and the three-person salesforce are part of Forman's
    a. promotional strategy.
    b. pricing strategy.
    c. product strategy.
    d. distribution strategy.
    e. target market strategy.

8. Forman's distribution strategy includes
    a. UPS.
    b. wholesalers.
    c. student discounts.
    d. free delivery to customers.
    e. UPS and wholesalers.

9. Forman's pricing strategy includes
    a. charging all customers the same price.
    b. prices comparable to competitors' prices.
    c. student discounts.
    d. free products in conjunction with minimum purchases.
    e. all of the above.

10. Forman's product strategy is best described as
    a. stock the lowest-cost products available.
    b. sell the highest-quality products.
    c. offer customers the products they want.
    d. sell only nationally known brands.
    e. none of the above.

M. J. Emerson, who recently graduated from college with a degree in business administration, has returned home to help his father run the company business, Emerson Foundry Company. Founded in 1903, the Emerson Company has long since had a reputation for casting the very finest in American architectural brasses. These brasses, usually used for door knockers and accent details, typically represent eagles with spread wings, crowing roosters, and other subjects with a traditional motif.

The first thing that M. J. did upon reporting for work was to apply his business training to an analysis of the foundry's financial records. He was surprised to learn that, during the last ten years, there had been a dramatic decline in sales of the company's architectural line. When he asked his father about this, the elder Emerson replied, "Gee, son, I don't really know why that's happening. Our brasses are the very best that can be bought. We are still making them exactly the same way we have for the last 85 years, in the same molds and with the same materials. I can't really understand why sales are off so badly. But I have taken steps to do something about it. Just last month, I hired a young man to go out and try and find us some new customers. We really do have to do something to try and increase sales volume."

M. J. was now disturbed. He knew that his father had done what he thought was the right thing, but M. J. thought that more was needed. His thinking was that the company needed to look more carefully at the marketplace. He felt that Emerson Foundry had lost touch with its customers and with architectural fashions. Though he hesitated to do it, he felt that he had to suggest to his father that they invest in some research to find out what was happening in architectural design and to adapt their products to what was currently popular. He thought it might even be possible that the firm would find it desirable to expand or even change the nature of its product line.

11. M. J.'s father, judging from his distress at the decline in his company's fortunes and the fact that he can't understand why the company's brasses aren't selling, is probably a victim of
    a. his inability to produce a product of the required quality.
    b. the "better mousetrap" fallacy.
    c. a general decline in the economy about which nothing can be done.
    d. too much of a commitment to a marketing orientation.

12. The elder Mr. Emerson's retention of a salesman may well be evidence that he has been converted to
    a. a philosophy of company-wide consumer orientation.
    b. an attitude typical of the sales era of marketing history.
    c. a mere figurehead in his son's presence.
    d. a belief that he is in a seller's market.

13. M. J.'s idea of investigating the nature of the market reveals that
    a. he is at least aware of the marketing concept.
    b. he shares his father's attitude toward the changes in the company's sales performance.
    c. his college education has been largely wasted; he should be able to analyze the problem from internal company records.
    d. he, too, is a victim of marketing myopia.

14. Marketing myopia refers to
    a. defining the scope of your business too broadly.
    b. failing to define the scope of your business.
    c. defining the scope of your business too narrowly.
    d. making comparisons between your business and businesses not at all like it.

Name_____   Instructor _____

Section _____   Date _____

Questions for Thought

The questions which follow are designed to help you become familiar with the main concepts in this chapter through interpretation in your own words. They are meant to be answered in a few sentences or a paragraph at most.

1. Discuss the role that the concept of utility plays in marketing.

2. Explain why the definition of marketing has had to be broadened in recent years.

3. Outline the three eras in the history of marketing.

4. There are four types of nonprofit marketing. Outline and discuss each one.

5. Name and define the four strategies which make up the marketing mix.

Name _____   Instructor _____

Section _____   Date _____

Experiential Exercises

1. The purpose of this exercise is to broaden your understanding by comparing the definitions of marketing provided by managers of organizations which operate near your school or home.

    a. Interview several people to find out how they define marketing. Candidates for interviews include managers of, for example, restaurants, insurance companies, department stores, charitable organizations, manufacturers, financial institutions, and university bookstores. Ask these people how they define marketing. You should also include questions about their organizations, the markets their organizations serve, and their products or services, so you can better understand their concepts of marketing.

    b. Use the results of your interviews to complete the table below.

Name of Person Interviewed	Title	Name of Organization	Definition of Marketing

c.   What are the major differences between the definitions you collected and the text definition? Some hints for finding differences in the definitions include examining which marketing mix activities are omitted, the role of the consumer in the marketing process, and the role of production.

2.   The purpose of this exercise is to enhance your understanding of the marketing concept and the extent to which nonprofit organizations have been able to adopt such a concept.

a.   Select a nonprofit organization to study. You may choose any such organization you wish; however, try to select one that is accessible, cooperative, and actively marketing some product or service.

b.   Develop a list of questions that could be used to determine if the organization you have chosen has adopted the marketing concept. Be sure to include questions about orientation, objectives, and marketing planning activities. Consider questions to extract information about the kind of nonprofit marketing the organization is doing.

List of questions:

c. Interview several people in the organization you've chosen using the questions you wrote for part b above.

d. Is the organization whose members you interviewed aware of the marketing concept? Has it been adopted by them, and, if so, to what extent? If the concept is in use, outline how it is used. Make sure you mention the kind of nonprofit marketing the organization is doing, and make suggestions about how the organization could best apply the marketing concept.

Name _____   Instructor _____

Section _____   Date _____

Computer Applications

Review the discussion of the exchange process in Chapter 1 of the text. Then use menu item 1 titled "The Exchange Process" to solve each of the following problems.

1.   A group of 76 families living in an isolated region of the Great Sandy Desert has been engaged in decentralized exchange of surplus products for several years. It is considering opening a central market that would operate every Monday in the home of a member family.

   a.   How many transactions are involved under the present decentralized exchange system?

   b.   How many transactions would be involved if the families decide to establish the central market?

   c.   What effect would the central market have on efficiency?

2. Twelve small manufacturers located in a rural part of Louisiana trade products with each other. A marketing intermediary offered to serve as a link among the firms in order to reduce the time and costs involved in the old system of decentralized exchange. However, four of the manufacturers argued that the small number of firms was insufficient to justify a marketing intermediary.

    a. How much will efficiency increase if the intermediary is used for all manufacturers?

    b. How much less efficient will the intermediary be if only eight manufacturers use it and the four dissenting manufacturers continue to trade individually with each of the other eight manufacturers and themselves?

3. Fishermen living on two adjacent islands of a Pacific atoll met recently to discuss establishment of a central market. At the present time, the fishermen are engaged in decentralized exchange, but no trade takes place between the two islands. Namu Raroia, spokesman for the 65 fishermen of Mokauea Island, proposed that each island establish its own central market. Mako Keanapua, who represents the 35 fishermen from Mokuoeo Island, has argued that one large central market should be established between the two communities. Fishermen from both Mokauea and Mokuoeo would use this central market and their original decentralized exchange systems would be eliminated.

    a. How much will efficiency increase in each community if Namu Raroia's proposal is implemented?

b. How many exchange transactions will be required if Mako Keanapua's suggestion is followed?

c. How much will efficiency increase if Mako Keanapua's proposal is implemented in place of the current decentralized system?

d. How many transactions would be necessary if each fisherman traded individually with all of the fishermen in both communities?

Chapter 1 Solutions

Key Concepts

1.	m	6.	q	11.	o	16.	t	21.	p
2.	u	7.	a	12.	1	17.	i		
3.	j	8.	f	13.	h	18.	b		
4.	s	9.	r	14.	g	19.	c		
5.	k	10.	n	15.	d	20.	e		

Self Quiz

1.	T	11.	T	21.	T	31.	b	41.	e
2.	F	12.	T	22.	F	32.	d	42.	b
3.	F	13.	T	23.	T	33.	a	43.	a
4.	T	14.	F	24.	T	34.	a	44.	c
5.	F	15.	F	25.	F	35.	c	45.	c
6.	F	16.	T	26.	c	36.	a	46.	d
7.	T	17.	F	27.	d	37.	e	47.	c
8.	F	18.	F	28.	d	38.	a	48.	d
9.	T	19.	F	29.	a	39.	c	49.	e
10.	T	20.	T	30.	e	40.	d	50.	b

Applying Marketing Concepts

1.	T	6.	a	11.	b
2.	T	7.	a	12.	b
3.	F	8.	e	13.	a
4.	F	9.	e	14.	c
5.	F	10.	c		

Chapter 2

Marketing: Its Environment and Role in Society

Chapter Summary

Environmental forces, frequently beyond the control of marketing managers, must be carefully considered when planning and executing the elements of the marketing mix. These environmental forces are of five types: competitive, political/legal, economic, technological, and social/cultural. Marketers attempt to manage these environmental forces by predicting and influencing change in them.

The competitive environment is an interactive process that occurs in the marketplace as competing organizations seek to satisfy markets. Competition may be direct, as when two firms offer the same or very similar products; indirect, in the sense that products can substitute for each other but are not alike (as, for example, when one must choose between a new TV set or a new stereo); or, very broadly, viewed as the quest after the customer's discretionary buying power. Ultimately, all firms are in this most broadly defined competitive situation. Each firm must create a viable competitive strategy for itself by deciding in which markets it will compete and how.

The political/legal environment—the body of laws and interpretations of laws that maintain competition and protect consumers—requires diligent study and a conscious effort by the marketer to successfully understand it and remain in compliance with its requirements. Federal, state, and local laws and courts may all have some jurisdiction over a particular firm's operations. Regulatory agencies, bureaucracies which interpret and enforce the laws, may also constitute a significant environmental influence, as may industry-sponsored self-regulatory groups.

The economic environment, which includes the stages of the business cycle, inflation, unemployment, resource availability, and income, has a substantial effect on marketing strategy. Prosperity, recession, depression, and recovery (the four stages of the business cycle) all have different characteristics and pose different problems to the marketer. Inflation, a condition of declining purchasing power, is a variable which tends to alter consumer behavior as its rate rises and falls, as does unemployment, which is the percent of the labor force out of work but actively looking for jobs. Resources are not in unlimited supply. This, too, affects the economy because shortages may raise prices. Finally, discretionary income, which is the money people have left to spend after necessities are paid for, directly affects what people buy. When there is a lot of discretionary income, people will spend it for luxuries. When there isn't, simpler, more utilitarian goods are bought, and fewer of them are purchased.

The technological environment, which is the application of scientific and engineering advances to marketing, results in new products and services, improved existing products, and, often, lower prices. Technology can supply the opportunity to enter a new market segment or make it necessary to change strategy as it becomes obsolete. New technology comes from research and development, almost half of which is, in the U.S., funded by the federal government.

The social/cultural environment (the interaction between marketing and the institutions of society) changes as the dynamic forces which shape society change. The United States is a culturally diverse nation, with many subcultures displaying unique characteristics. The social/cultural environment often has a stronger effect in the international market than it does domestically. Learning about social and cultural differences among countries is paramount to a firm's success abroad.

Marketing's relationship to its environment (all of the influences which affect it from the outside) is a subject of constant public scrutiny. Marketing is a materialistic thing, and many of marketing's critics say that materialism does not truly create a "quality" lifestyle. Productivity, as expressed in terms of employment and profits, may not be enough, say the social critics of the marketing philosophy. As a result, consumerism (a social force seeking to protect the consumer from unacceptable business practices), marketing ethics (defining standards of conduct and moral values), and social responsibility (the obligation to consider profit, consumer satisfaction, and social well-being of equal value in evaluating firm performance) have all become significant issues in strategy planning. Marketers must now consider their relationship to the ecology (the balance of nature) and concern themselves with issues such as pollution and the possibility of recycling used materials.

Ultimately, if marketers seek to influence the environment, they must educate consumers, seek increased government regulation, assist the marketing system to operate in a self-correcting manner, and encourage political action.

Name _____ Instructor _____

Section _____ Date _____

Key Concepts

The purpose of this section is to allow you to determine if you can match key concepts with the definitions of the concepts. It is essential that you know the definitions of the concepts prior to applying the concepts in later exercises in this chapter.

From the list of lettered terms, select the one that best fits each of the numbered statements below. Write the letter of that choice in the space provided.

Key Terms

a. environmental management
b. competitive environment
c. political/legal environment
d. economic environment
e. demarketing
f. technological environment

g. social/cultural environment
h. consumerism
i. consumer rights
j. marketing ethics
k. social responsibility

____ 1. Marketing philosophies, policies, procedures, and actions that have the enhancement of society's welfare as a primary objective.

____ 2. Interactive process occurring in the marketplace among marketers of directly competing products, marketers of substitutable products, and marketers competing for consumer purchasing power.

____ 3. Laws and interpretations of laws that require firms to operate under competitive conditions and protect consumer rights.

____ 4. Reducing consumer demand for a product or service to a level that the firm can supply.

____ 5. Application to marketing of knowledge based on discoveries in science, inventions, and innovation.

____ 6. Attainment of organizational objectives by predicting and influencing the competitive, political/legal, economic, technological, and social/cultural environments.

____ 7. The right to choose freely, to be informed, to be heard, and to be safe.

____ 8. Standards of conduct and moral values by which marketers operate.

____ 9. The relationship between the marketer and society and its cultures.

____ 10. Includes the stages of the business cycle, inflation, unemployment, resource availability, and income.

___ 11.   Aids and protects the consumer by exerting legal, moral, and economic pressure on business and government.

Name_____   Instructor _____

Section _____   Date _____

Self Quiz

You should use these objective questions to test your understanding of the chapter material. You can check your answers with those provided at the end of the chapter.

While these questions cover most of the chapter topics, they are not intended to be the same as the test questions your instructor may use in an examination. A good understanding of all aspects of the course material is essential to good performance on any examination.

True/False

Write "T" for True or "F" for False for each of the following statements.

____   1.   The marketing environment consists of a firm's product, pricing, promotion, and distribution strategy.

____   2.   The firm which uses environmental management does not try to influence the marketing environment.

____   3.   A major question in competitive strategy is how the firm should compete.

____   4.   Movies and live concert performances may be competitors because both compete for leisure-related dollars spent by the consumer.

____   5.   The Sherman Act prohibits price discrimination.

____   6.   Government regulation in the United States has passed through these four phases: protect competition, protect competitors, protect consumers, deregulate business.

____   7.   The Robinson-Patman Act protects consumers from price-gouging practices.

____   8.   Inflation, a rising price level that results in reduced consumer buying power, can occur at any stage in the business cycle.

____   9.   The Federal Trade Commission cannot do anything to stop firms from using deceptive advertisements.

____   10.   Prosperity means consumers are anxious to buy because everybody is working and prices are falling.

____   11.   Discretionary income is the amount of money people have left to spend after they've paid for food, clothing, housing, and other necessities.

____   12.   The technological environment may affect the political and legal environment.

____ 13.   The technological environment can be a source of reductions in the cost of producing and marketing products.

____ 14.   Demarketing means that firms stop trying to market any goods, services, or ideas.

____ 15.   A firm which introduces a new product such as rabbit meat or solar-powered automobiles needs to realize that the product may fail because of the social/cultural environment.

____ 16.   The United States is a mixed society composed of various submarkets, each of which displays unique cultural characteristics.

____ 17.   Consumerism is the highest expression of the philosophy that "more is better," meaning that a firm's social responsibility is limited to providing employment and generating profits.

____ 18.   President Kennedy's statement of consumer rights includes the "right to be safe." This means that products and services should be designed in such a way that they will be absolutely safe for anyone to use.

____ 19.   Competitive pressures have forced some marketers into packaging practices that may be considered misleading, deceptive, and/or unethical.

____ 20.   Marketing ethics—decisions by individuals and firms to do what is morally right or wrong—is a more easily measured concept than social responsibility.

____ 21.   The billions of tons of packaging materials that the marketing system generates every year (e.g., glass, metal, paper, and plastics) exemplify part of the ecological problem of planned obsolescence.

____ 22.   The marketing system may be influenced or controlled in four ways: by helping the competitive market system to operate in a self-corrective manner, by educating the consumer, by increasing regulation, and by encouraging political action.

____ 23.   Kevlar, DuPont's unique high-strength fiber, is a major material used in the manufacture of auto tires.

____ 24.   Even modest shifts in the environment can alter the results of marketing decisions.

____ 25.   Utilities such as those providing electricity and cable television service accept considerable regulation of their activities in return for exclusive rights to serve a particular group of customers.

____ 26.   KitchenAid's entry into the refrigerator market has created direct competition between itself and the makers of other brands of refrigerators.

____ 27.   When you choose to go to a movie rather than a concert, you are engaging in substitution.

____ 28.   Trying to answer the questions "Should we compete?" "If so, in what markets?" and "How?" is typical of socially responsible behavior.

___ 29. The four phases of government regulation have been the antimonopoly phase, the phase of protecting competitive conditions, the governmental control phase, and the phase of industry deregulation.

___ 30. The FCC, the FTC, the FDA, and the Interstate Commerce Commission are all federal regulatory agencies.

___ 31. Business cycles are characterized by conditions of prosperity followed by recovery, depression, and recession.

___ 32. Unemployment exists when there are more people looking for work than there are jobs for them to fill.

___ 33. When manufacturers make products so well that they last indefinitely and never need be replaced, they are practicing planned obsolescence.

___ 34. Processing used materials for reuse is called recycling.

___ 35. Inflation is a declining price level that increases consumer buying power.

Multiple Choice

Circle the letter of the word or phrase that best completes the sentence or best answers the question.

36. The cost of TV advertising is a part of which of the following environments of marketing?
    a. the social/cultural environment
    b. the economic environment
    c. the political/legal environment
    d. the technological environment
    e. none of the above

37. Which of the following attitudes should the marketer take toward the marketing environment?
    a. Ignore it.
    b. Realize the need to adjust a firm's marketing mix to fit environmental forces and constraints.
    c. Realize that an individual firm cannot have an effect on the marketing environment.
    d. Do not change marketing strategies until substantial losses result from environmental forces.
    e. Make sure marketing strategies satisfy legal requirements but ignore other aspects of the marketing environment because there are no legal penalties for such behavior.

38. The competitive environment
    a. is not a concern of the Cadillac division of General Motors.
    b. is becoming less important in the United States.
    c. includes all firms that are competing for a limited amount of discretionary buying power.
    d. does not include sales made in foreign markets.
    e. does not depend on the marketer's competitive strategy.

39. Major reasons why a firm may not choose to compete in a particular market include
    a.   inadequate resources.
    b.   the market does not match with objectives of the firm.
    c.   insufficient profits.
    d.   a, b, and c above.
    e.   only a and b above.

40. A correct matchup of a specific law and its objective is
    a.   Sherman Act: protect consumers.
    b.   Robinson-Patman Act: protect competitors.
    c.   Wheeler-Lea Act: protect competition.
    d.   Consumer Goods Pricing Act: protect competitors.
    e.   Consumer Product Safety Act: protect competition.

41. The economic environment includes
    a.   inflation.
    b.   unemployment.
    c.   depression.
    d.   recession.
    e.   all of the above.

42. DuPont's marketing development of Kevlar suffered from problems in the
    a.   legal/political environment.
    b.   competitive environment.
    c.   economic environment.
    d.   environments in a, b, and c above.
    e.   environments only in a and b above.

43. Which of the following statements is a correct matchup of laws and the primary element of the marketing mix impacted by the law?
    a.   Fair Packaging and Labeling Act: price
    b.   Public Health Cigarette Smoking Act: distribution
    c.   Federal Trade Commission Act: product, price, promotion, distribution
    d.   Consumer Goods Pricing Act: product
    e.   Airline Deregulation Act: promotion

44. Which of the following methods is used by the Federal Trade Commission to protect consumers?
    a.   The Commission harasses any firms believed to be violating acts.
    b.   A cease and desist order is issued, telling a firm to stop an illegal practice.
    c.   Public service announcements identifying all firms that have used deceptive selling practices are broadcast.
    d.   The officers of guilty firms are arrested and charged with a criminal act.
    e.   A closure order to shut down a guilty firm's operations is issued.

45. An example of a problem related to the question of ethics in promotional strategy would be
    a. whether an automobile dealership should be required to purchase parts from the manufacturer of the cars it sells.
    b. the portrayal of women as frivolous or the stereotype of them as housewives in advertisements.
    c. the question of whether marketers have an obligation to warn consumers of impending discount or returns policy changes.
    d. whether packages should be kept to some standard size, rather than made extra-large or odd-shaped.
    e. whether there is an obligation to serve areas where there are few users of the firm's product.

46. It is true that the
    a. Sherman Act prohibits tobacco advertising on radio and television.
    b. Clayton Act established the Federal Trade Commission.
    c. Federal Trade Commission Act prohibited price discrimination.
    d. Wheeler-Lea Act bans deceptive or unfair business practices per se.
    e. Consumer Goods Pricing Act allows resale price maintenance in interstate commerce.

47. A correct statement about the economic environment is that
    a. consumers buy more during times of inflation because prices are lower.
    b. sales may fall during a recession because of both high unemployment and declines in consumer purchasing power.
    c. frictional displacement results from recessions.
    d. cyclical unemployment is highest during times of prosperity.
    e. consumers will not alter their purchasing behavior during recessions.

48. A firm may lose its market share because consumers switch to a new product. The new product introduction is an environmental threat or opportunity which comes from the
    a. economic environment.
    b. technological environment.
    c. political and legal environment.
    d. social/cultural environment.
    e. competitive environment.

49. Which of the following is an example of a demarketing strategy?
    a. Offering a second can of paint for half price if a first can is purchased at full price.
    b. Providing consumers with tips on how to make a product last longer.
    c. Advertising the convenience of owning more than one car.
    d. Telling consumers that there is an abundant supply of the product available.
    e. Making substantial reductions in a firm's advertising budget.

50. Which of the following is an accurate statement about the social/cultural environment?
    a. The social responsibility of business is decreasing.
    b. Income statements are the best way to measure the accomplishment of socially oriented objectives.
    c. Most marketers do not need to take the social environment into consideration.
    d. Marketing strategies that are successful with one cultural segment will also be successful with other cultural segments.
    e. The social/cultural environment changes constantly.

51. DuPont's experience in marketing Kevlar has
   a.   finally made the company embrace the marketing concept of first finding out what customers want and then giving it to them.
   b.   caused the company to cease manufacturing the material entirely.
   c.   reinforced DuPont's commitment to research for research's sake.
   d.   demonstrated once and for all that a good product will sell itself.
   e.   demonstrated how little the environment of marketing affects a big company like DuPont.

52. When a firm engages in lobbying among legislative groups or enters into a joint venture with another firm whose products complement its own, it may be seeking to
   a.   avoid prosecution under the Sherman Act.
   b.   manage the environment by influencing the technological and competitive environment.
   c.   apply environmental management to the political/legal and economic environments.
   d.   manage the environment by influencing the political/legal and competitive environments.
   e.   more actively apply the marketing concept by expanding its markets.

53. Which of the following situations best reflects the competitive condition of substitution?
   a.   the availability of Tide, Cheer, Surf, Oxydol, and Fab in the detergent section of the supermarket
   b.   the availability of gypsum board, wood panelling, masonite sheet, and plaster as wall finishing materials
   c.   the choice available among rock concerts, videotape rentals, dining out, and listening to stereo tapes for an evening's entertainment
   d.   Eastern, Continental, and Air West Airlines all offering cut-rate fares between their major destinations
   e.   None of the above are examples of substitution; all represent direct competition.

54. Kimberly-Clark's decision to diversify its activities out of the newsprint field and to get into consumer markets with Huggies disposable diapers is an example of
   a.   a carefully developed and well executed competitive strategy.
   b.   an effective linking of a new product and a company's core business.
   c.   a decision to compete in a segment of the market new to the company.
   d.   all of the above.
   e.   only a and b.

55. The Robinson-Patman Act and the Miller-Tydings Resale Price Maintenance Act are examples of laws passed during
   a.   the antimonopoly period of government regulation.
   b.   the consumer protection period of government regulation.
   c.   the competitor protection period of government regulation.
   d.   the industry deregulation phase of government regulation.
   e.   the general federal power development phase of government regulation.

56. George, Howard, and Louis are the only three real estate brokers in Milledgeville. They have the habit of getting together for lunch once a month to talk things over. At their most recent meeting, George proposed that they divide the town up into sections, with each realtor taking one part as his exclusive territory. If they carry out their plan, they can be accused of violating
    a. the Consumer Goods Pricing Act.
    b. the Sherman Act.
    c. the Robinson-Patman Act.
    d. the Celler-Kefauver Act.
    e. the Federal Trade Commission Improvement Act.

57. The federal regulatory agency which monitors the rates of interstate rail, bus, truck, and water carriers is
    a. the Interstate Commerce Commission.
    b. the Federal Communications Commission.
    c. the Federal Power Commission.
    d. the Federal Trade Commission.
    e. the Transportation Regulatory Commission.

58. The Council of Better Business Bureaus is
    a. a regulatory agency of the federal government with a broad scope of powers over business.
    b. a consumer interest group which seeks to protect the rights of consumers in their dealings with big firms.
    c. a national organization of business groups devoted to consumer service and self-regulation.
    d. a media group that attempts to publicize the abuses business inflicts on the consumer.
    e. a small group of highly influential businessmen who lobby Congress against further regulation of business.

59. That phase of the business cycle during which consumers frequently shift their buying patterns to basic, functional products with low price tags from nonessential products such as convenience foods is
    a. prosperity.
    b. depression.
    c. recovery.
    d. recession.
    e. exclusion.

60. During economic recovery,
    a. consumers' ability to buy increases, but their willingness to buy often lags behind.
    b. consumer buying power declines and marketers should consider increasing promotional outlays.
    c. consumer spending is brisk, and demand for premium versions of well-known brands is strong.
    d. consumer spending reaches its lowest level.
    e. marketers may increase prices or extend their product lines to take advantage of brisk consumer spending.

Name _____ Instructor _____

Section _____ Date _____

Applying Marketing Concepts

Val Cartouche was thinking about her problems with her interior decorating business. They all began when she first decided to go into business for herself. Having found the perfect location for her store, she was dismayed when the city wouldn't give her a business license on the grounds that the local zoning ordinances didn't allow a store of that type in that location. After much effort, Val found a new location and was successful in getting a license to operate. She experienced trouble getting some minor renovations to the building made because of a building boom the city was experiencing. She also had trouble hiring salespeople and other workers because unemployment was at an all-time low and good people were at a premium.

At long last the renovations were complete, a staff had been hired, and the store was ready to open. But almost the minute the dustsheets were taken off the window displays, Val received a visit from a neighborhood committee objecting to one of her window displays. It seems the display featured a seminude mannequin in a rather suggestive pose on a sofa which was the window's central feature. In an effort to be accommodating, Val changed the display.

Soon Val was faced with two new problems. The building she had rented was equipped with an incinerator, which she intended to use to dispose of refuse and excess packing materials from the business. The first time it was lighted, however, the police appeared and presented her with a citation for violating a section of the city sanitation code. On top of that, Val discovered that the cost of the goods she was selling was going up so fast that she could barely cover the cost of replacing what she'd sold from what she was able to get for it.

The straw that broke the camel's back, however, was Val's discovery, only sixty days after she'd opened for business, that Interior Industries, a national chain of interior decorating emporiums, was about to open an outlet only two blocks away. Val knew that it could, because of its enormous buying power, undersell her by 30 percent on practically every item in her store.

Realizing that the handwriting was on the wall, Val held a sale to clear out her remaining inventory and closed her store.

____ 1. Val's difficulty in getting a business license was due to the social/cultural environment.

____ 2. Val seemed able to adapt her marketing strategy to the constraints of the environment.

____ 3. Val's problems getting a business license could have been avoided if she had checked the appropriate environmental constraints before she decided on her first location.

____ 4. The actions of a company like Interior Industries—buying in bulk and selling at low retail prices—are likely a violation of the Robinson-Patman Act.

____ 5. Val may have been shortsighted in going out of business. It's possible that she may have been able to develop an appeal to a different target market than people who would choose to shop at Interior Industries.

6. Val had problems with the
   a. economic environment.
   b. political/legal environment.
   c. competitive environment.
   d. social/cultural environment.
   e. environments in a through d above.

7. Val's citation was probably issued by the police because she
   a. was in violation of an air pollution regulation.
   b. was destroying valuable recyclable materials.
   c. used an excessive amount of natural gas firing her incinerator.
   d. had failed to get a city inspection of her store before opening.
   e. was a particular target of a "get-tough" administration.

8. Val's problems in getting her store renovated were probably due to the fact that
   a. her city was experiencing a period of recession and lots of workers had left town.
   b. the city was experiencing a prosperous period of the business cycle.
   c. she was in competition with other employment opportunities for the services of the available labor.
   d. all of the statements above are true.
   e. only the statements in b and c are true.

9. Val's inability to purchase new merchandise for what she'd paid for the old was due to
   a. her inability to manage her money so as to make sure that she'd have enough to rebuy goods.
   b. low sales volume and a high proportion of fixed costs in her store's operation.
   c. inflation which made today's dollar less valuable than yesterday's and drove up merchandise costs.
   d. unemployment at the national level which increased the cost of government services to merchants like Val.

10. From Val's point of view, Interior Industries is part of
    a. the social/cultural environment.
    b. the competitive environment.
    c. the legal environment.
    d. the economic environment.
    e. the ethnic environment.

Ann Bonzer felt really confused. When she left her home to move to Mill City, she thought she was doing the right thing. The job offer she had received had been an excellent one, and her prospective employer was a nationally known company with a fine reputation. But Mill City was another story. It was so *different* from Pastoral Falls, her hometown. For one thing, just getting around town involved fighting traffic which seemed to be totally out of control. Making left turns at divided intersections was permitted and the speed limit was 40 miles per hour even in residential neighborhoods. This didn't seem to bother the local population, nor did the fact that their lives revolved around whether or not the bus plant (Mill City's single major employer) or a Japanese firm also bidding got the order for those 300 busses from Rural Rapid Transit Company.

Ann was also disturbed at how difficult it was to make friends in Mill City. It seemed as if everyone she met had been there all their life and wasn't interested in anything or anyone not a Mill City native. All in all, though, it wasn't so bad for Ann. She was grateful that her job allowed her to use the latest in solid-state mass chromatographic analysis equipment. She felt she was on the very leading edge of scientific thought in her job at MassTech Labs, and that made up for a lot of her dislocation at having to live in Mill City.

11. Ann's perception of the traffic in Mill City being out of control was very largely due to
    a. her own rather bad driving habits.
    b. differences in the political/legal environment between Mill City and Pastoral Falls.
    c. her general dissatisfaction with Mill City itself.
    d. her dislike of her job.

12. Ann's job appears to have been deeply involved with the
    a. economic environment.
    b. social/cultural environment.
    c. competitive environment.
    d. technological environment.
    e. development of military hardware.

13. Ann's comments about Mill City people being unconcerned with anyone or anything not from Mill City is really a statement relating to the
    a. social/cultural environment.
    b. ethnic environment.
    c. competitive environment.
    d. political environment.

14. The relationship between Mill City's bus plant and the Japanese company which is also bidding on the Rural Rapid Transit contract is
    a. part of the legal environment.
    b. a condition of direct competition.
    c. a sort of indirect competition
    d. nonexistent; there is no relationship, direct or indirect, between the two firms.

Name_____   Instructor _____

Section _____   Date _____

Questions for Thought

The questions which follow are designed to help you become familiar with the main concepts in this chapter through interpretation in your own words. They are meant to be answered in a few sentences or a paragraph at most.

1. The marketing environment is comprised of five components. Enumerate and describe these.

2. Discuss some of the types of competition which marketers may face.

3. Government regulates marketing, it is true, but the process is not just one-way. Discuss how marketers may influence the political/legal environment in the context of the regulation which exists now or may exist in the future.

4. Discuss the economic factors which may affect the performance of marketing activities.

5. Technology has a profound effect on marketing activities. Give some examples of the interaction between marketing and this aspect of the environment.

Name _____   Instructor _____

Section _____   Date _____

Experiential Exercises

1. The purpose of this exercise is to enhance your understanding of the effect of the legal environment on marketing activities of business organizations. In general, the assignment consists of using secondary sources to study a recent legal case involving the marketing efforts of a company or companies.

    a. Select a recent legal case involving the marketing activities of a company or companies. Possible sources to help you locate current legal cases include *Business Periodicals Index*, *Antitrust and Trade Regulation Report*, *FTC Reporter*, *Trade Regulation Reporter*, *The Anti-trust Bulletin*, or the "Legal Developments" section of the *Journal of Marketing*. Try to select a case that has received considerable coverage in the literature.

    b. Using all the published information about the case, determine what marketing activities were involved. Was the case related to

    - product strategy?
    - distribution strategy?
    - pricing strategy?
    - promotion strategy?

    c. What laws or rules were being violated by the company?

    d. Who was being harmed by the actions of the company? Was it competition, consumers, or some other members of the public?

e.   What remedy, such as fines, imprisonment, corrective advertising, etc., was required in the case?

f.   What impact do you think this case and the remedies required will have on the company or companies involved? Will they conduct business the same as before, alter some of their marketing practices, or go out of business altogether?

2.   The purpose of this exercise is to develop an appreciation for the effect of competition on marketing activities of companies in the cigarette (S.I.C. 2111) industry.

a.   Go to the reference section of your college or university library and find *U.S. Industrial Outlook* (U.S. Department of Commerce) and Standard and Poor's *Industry Survey*. You may also wish to use other published sources including *Business Week* to gain an understanding of the cigarette industry.

b.   Who are the major competitors in this industry?

c.   What actions have the major competitors taken in the last year or so that adversely affected the performance of other companies? Which dimensions of the marketing mix have they used? Have they changed product, promotion, distribution, or price?

d. What other firms besides cigarette manufacturers should also be considered as competitors? Remember, the text definition of expanded competition suggests all firms competing for the same discretionary spending power should be included as part of the competition. Think of the product from the consumer's point of view: what might consumers consider as a substitute for cigarettes?

e. Based on what you have learned, do you feel the cigarette industry has an expanded view of competition or a myopic one (one that ignores any firms selling different products)?

Name_____   Instructor _____

Section _____   Date _____

Computer Applications

Review the discussion of decision tree analysis in Chapter 2 of the text. Then use menu item 2 titled "Decision Tree Analysis" to solve each of the following problems.

1. Nick Pisani, owner and manager of Nick's Pizza shop in a college town, is concerned about reports of a new shop opening. In fact, he estimates the likelihood of the new competitor being open for business in time for the beginning of the next school year at 70 percent. If the new shop opens at the location under consideration and Nick takes no competitive moves at this time, Nick estimates that his sales revenue projection for next year would be 40 percent lower than the $800,000 revenue forecast estimated for next year if a new competitor does not open a shop. In addition, projected earnings would probably fall from 20 percent of sales to 10 percent of sales. Nick is contemplating opening a second shop in order to build customer loyalty in case the new competitor materializes. He estimates that if he opens the second shop and the new pizza shop does not materialize, his overall sales revenue would increase to $1,000,000 and earnings would be 14 percent of sales. If he opens a second shop and the new pizza shop opens, Nick feels that his two shops will generate $600,000 in revenues and earn profits of 12 percent of sales. He would prefer to postpone his decision until he is certain of the plans of his potential competitor, but the need to plan the new shop requires him to make the decision now.

    a. Recommend a course of action for Nick Pisani.

    b. Would your recommended course of action change if Pisani estimated the likelihood of a new competitor opening at 50 percent?

2. Rachel Pritchert, vice-president of marketing of Sleepwear, Inc., a manufacturer of children's sleepwear, is concerned about a potential government ban of the fiber material used by her company in its children's sleepwear. Without such a ban, she has projected that next year her company will have sales of $20,000,000 with profits estimated at 10 percent of sales. If the government bans the materials, her company will lose about half of its sales and profits will decline to 5 percent of sales. However, Sleepwear could convert its manufacturing processes to new materials now instead of being forced to switch by the government ban. Immediate conversion would mean the company would not lose any projected sales although its profits would fall to 8 percent of sales due to increased material costs. Pritchert feels there is a 40 percent chance that the ban will be enacted.

   a. Recommend a course of action for Sleepwear, Inc.

   b. Joe Jensen, plant manager for Sleepwear, disagrees with Ms. Pritchert's estimate of immediate conversion costs. He feels that immediate conversion will result in profits of 5 percent of sales rather than 8 percent as projected by Ms. Pritchert. Would your recommended course of action for Sleepwear be different if Joe Jensen is correct?

3. Automobile dealer Millward Skrepinski is pleased with next year's $10,000,000 revenue fore-
    cast and projected earnings of 25 percent of sales. He is concerned, however, about rumors
    that a competing dealer has been negotiating for a franchise on a hot new car of Korean
    manufacture that Millward expects to compete directly with his line of Brazilian imports. If
    the rumor is true, Millward will have to cut prices substantially to achieve his sales goal of
    $10,000,000. Earnings would be reduced to only 10 percent of sales. Millward is considering
    bidding on the Korean franchise if only to prevent his competitor from getting it. The process
    of entering the bidding would cost Millward a quarter of a million dollars ($250,000) even if
    he does not receive the franchise, and he figures he has about a 40 percent chance of losing
    out. If he gets the franchise, his sales forecast and estimate of earnings would be as originally
    forecast. Should he bid on the franchise?

Chapter 2 Solutions

Key Concepts

1. k	6. a	11. h
2. b	7. i	
3. c	8. j	
4. e	9. g	
5. f	10. d	

Self Quiz

1. F	11. T	21. F	31. F	41. e	51. a
2. F	12. T	22. T	32. T	42. d	52. d
3. T	13. T	23. F	33. F	43. c	53. b
4. T	14. F	24. T	34. T	44. b	54. d
5. F	15. T	25. T	35. F	45. b	55. c
6. T	16. T	26. T	36. e	46. d	56. b
7. F	17. F	27. T	37. b	47. b	57. a
8. T	18. F	28. F	38. c	48. e	58. c
9. F	19. T	29. F	39. d	49. b	59. d
10. F	20. F	30. T	40. b	50. e	60. a

Applying Marketing Concepts

1. F	6. e	11. b
2. F	7. a	12. d
3. T	8. e	13. a
4. F	9. c	14. b
5. T	10. b	

Part One Puzzle

ACROSS CLUES

2. process by which two or more parties give value to each other and satisfy perceived needs
4. /political environment; laws and their interpretations as they affect marketing
7. want satisfying power of a product or service
8. orientation; business philosophy stressing efficiency in producing a quality product
11. companywide consumer orientation with the objective of achieving long-run success
13. group of people toward whom a firm aims a good, service, or idea to satisfy their needs
14. strategy; element of marketing mix concerned with getting product to firm's customers
17. type of marketing designed to attract people to a particular geographic area
18. element of marketing decision making involved with creating the right good for firm's customers
19. with legal, environmental factor concerned with protecting rights and maintaining competition

DOWN CLUES

1. process of creating a marketing mix to create exchanges and satisfy people's and firms' needs
3. marketplace characterized by a shortage of goods and services
5. orientation; business philosophy which assumes consumers resist purchasing nonessentials
6. result of this element of marketing decision process; setting of exchange values
9. as applied to marketing, idea that industries fail to recognize the scope of their business
10. result of blending the four strategy elements of marketing decision making
12. environmental factor involving business cycles, inflation, income, and unemployment
15. with culture, component of the environment relating marketing and society
16. type of marketing identifying and marketing a cause to chosen consumer segments

Name _____   Instructor _____

Section _____   Date _____

Cases for Part 1

1. "New" Coke—If It Wasn't Broke, Why'd They Fix It?[1]

On May 8, 1985, the Coca-Cola Company, in response to a declining share of the market and after spending $4 million and more than two years on tests designed to measure consumer response to a new formulation of its flagship soft drink, introduced "new" Coke. This sweeter, less-carbonated product, similar to Pepsi-Cola (Coke's major competitor) had beaten "old" Coke by a ratio of 53 to 47 in blind taste tests conducted with over 30,000 consumers. The "new" Coke announcement marked Coke's first major reformulation in its 99-year history.

Immediately on announcement of the new product, Coca-Cola Company stock declined in price by three points. Protests, including editorials in the nation's newspapers, soon developed, and stocks of "old" Coke on grocers' shelves rapidly disappeared, indicating that the product was being hoarded. Ninety days after the introduction of "new" Coke, "old" Coke was back—christened Coke "Classic." At that time, Roberto Goizueta, Chief Executive Officer of the Coca-Cola Company, predicted that sales of "new" Coke would far exceed those of the "Classic" brand.

By May, 1986, according to the marketing research firm A. C. Nielsen Company, sales of "Classic" Coke exceeded sales of "new" Coke by a ratio of more than 4 to 1, with "Classic" Coke capturing 14.5 percent of soft-drink sales in food stores to "new" Coke's 3.4 percent. Interestingly, both Coke brands' shares of 17.9 percent of sales as measured by Nielsen were identical with the share enjoyed by plain old Coca-Cola before "new" Coke was introduced.

Questions

a. Did Coca-Cola employ the marketing concept when changing Coke to the new formula?

---

[1] This case was based on Betsy D. Gelb and Gabriel M. Gelb, "New Coke's Fizzle—Lessons for the Rest of Us," *Sloan Management Review*, Fall 1986, pp. 71-79; and Scott Scredon, "Roberto Goizueta: One of 25 Executives to Watch," *Business Week*, April 18, 1986, p. 220.

b. Was there too much emphasis on marketing research data, or are consumers just too fickle to justify carrying out any meaningful marketing research?

c. What would you recommend Coca-Cola Company do with "new" Coke?

2.   *"Cacao Merivigliao"*[2]

Italian consumers flocked to grocery stores recently to buy "Cacao Merivigliao" (Marvelous Cocoa) only to find that the product didn't exist. A creation of the writers of Italian National TV's "Indietro Tutta" (Everything Backwards) variety show, the mythical Brazilian Cocoa began as a satire of TV sponsorship.

The satire backfired when consumers began to insist on buying the product at their local stores. The question now is whether the product ever will become available. Under Italian law, the person or company who first registers the name of a new product with the trademark office has the rights to it, and several individuals and firms claim to have been first on the scene at the trademark office. The Italian National TV Network (RAI), food marketer Buitoni (through its Perugina candy subsidiary), cocoa importer Toschi Vignola, and film distributor Shlomo Blanga all claim to have registered the "Cacao Merivigliao" name at about the same time.

If Buitoni or Vignola wins the rights, Italian consumers will soon be able to buy "Cacao Merivigliao." If, on the other hand, RAI or Mr. Blanga (who claims merely to be a fan of "Indietro Tutta") wins the rights, they have sworn that the name will not be allowed to be used on a commercial product. Complicating the issue is the fact that the law states that a trademark can be retained only if it is actively used.

"Indietro Tutta," as a show, pokes fun at other Italian TV variety offerings. The "Cacao Merivigliao" segments feature the show's host, Renzo Arbore, standing in front of a huge product logo—the face of a smiling Brazilian girl—surrounded by Las Vegas-style showgirls.

Questions

a.   How does this set of conditions relate to the application of the marketing concept in a real-world situation?

---

[2] Abstracted from "Italy Is Going Cocoa Loco for Nonexistent Product," *Advertising Age*, February 8, 1988, p. 3 *et seq.*

b.   Discuss the ethical considerations behind the actions of the four claimants to the "Cacao Merivigliao" name. Are any of their positions ethically questionable?

c.   What changes, if any, would you recommend be made to the Italian trademark law as a result of this event?

3. *Delta Bank and Trust Company*

Delta Bank and Trust Company is considering the expansion of its automatic teller machine (ATM) service. At present, the bank offers this service only at its main branch. ATMs allow banks to offer a number of services without human employees having to be present. They can accept deposits or dispense cash to customers who maintain checking or savings accounts with the bank (or even with other banks if the bank whose ATM is being used is a member of the right correspondent banking system). Customers can use ATMs to transfer money from one account to another. The machines cannot, however, open new accounts, create mortgages, or provide lock box service. To use an ATM machine, customers insert a plastic code card into a slot in the face of the machine. Then they punch in a personal code number, and the machine stands ready to accept instructions about the kind of transaction desired.

The cost of each ATM machine is currently $200,000, so bank management wants to be sure that there will be justification to expand beyond its existing level of service. There are many questions which need to be answered. One bank manager has recommended that new machines be placed next to supermarkets all over town. Another feels that the only appropriate location for these machines is at the branches of the bank because this is where people expect to find banking services. Yet another manager would like to see ATMs placed on all the college campuses in the area; she feels the convenience provided to the many faculty members and students would make them loyal depositors and customers of the bank. Another has voiced the opinion that the cost of the machines will weaken the capital position of the bank with no commensurate increase in earnings.

Question

Explain how the five marketing environments might affect the bank's decision about automatic teller machines.

4.   "Thanks to You—It's Working": The United Way

United Way of America is a nationwide organization that uses regional and statewide organizations to collect contributions from business organizations, employees, and the general public. The majority of these contributions are allocated to community agencies such as the Boy Scouts, Goodwill Industries, community day-care centers, and the YWCA. In addition, the United Way operates a community information service that provides assistance and referral to other community agencies for citizens with social, health, or related problems.

Community members generally have favorable attitudes toward the United Way, but it seems continually to fall short of raising all the money needed by the agencies it supports. In fact, its support of the operating budgets of these agencies has been declining. In recent years, the United Way has conducted marketing studies to determine what might be done to increase donations from all members of society. These studies provided the following insights:

1.   Most people are aware of the United Way and are favorably disposed toward it.

2.   Relatively few people know how much of the money United Way receives is given to community agencies or which agencies are supported.

3.   Relatively few people know that a committee of local citizens decides how to allocate the contributions among requesting agencies.

4.   Both givers and nongivers indicate they would give more if the United Way increased its support of health, medical, and social services or if contributors were allowed to designate which agencies received their contributions.

5.   Heaviest givers are white-collar, college-educated persons over 35 years of age and in the $35,000 or more annual income brackets.

6.   Noncontributors have negative attitudes toward big companies and are less likely to be encouraged by their employers to give to United Way.

Questions

a.   What environmental factors may influence the amount of contributions to the United Way?

b.   Do you think the marketing concept can be helpful to the United Way? If so, how?

Name _____   Instructor _____

Section _____   Date _____

Creating a Marketing Plan: Introduction

At this location in each section of this Study Guide, you will be presented with new facts in a continuing narrative. This ongoing exercise is designed to give you experience in gathering information, relating abilities to opportunities, and matching the needs of the marketplace to three young entrepreneurs' desire for success. You will create for this threesome a marketing plan that, if carefully followed, will pave their way to the realization of their dreams.

The narrative will outline the abilities, aspirations, and strengths of the trio as well as their shortcomings. You will be given some information about conditions in the real world, but it is expected that you will have sufficient motivation to think beyond that, especially when it is presented as an opinion of one of the participants. At the end of each of the narrative parts, questions will be posed to help you stay on the right track. Before beginning this exercise and as you are presented with new facts at the end of each section of this book, you should review the appendix to Chapter 3, "Developing a Marketing Plan," which can be found on pages 119-123 of *Contemporary Marketing*. The information you will be given in any one section of this exercise will not necessarily follow the same order as the outline of the marketing plan in your textbook, but will be designed to help you complete a particular section of the plan. By the time you have completed all of the parts of "Creating a Marketing Plan," you will have a document which should serve the needs of the three young people for whom you have prepared it and which will contain all of the essential information required for the entry of their marketing mix into the marketplace.

Meeting the Cast

Brian Patrick and Terrence O'Connor were cousins, and with their friend Laura Claire were considering their future. The three had known each other since childhood, but had not thought that their careers might bring them together until recently. After graduating together from Georgia Tech, where Terry had majored in electrical engineering and Brian in industrial management (specializing in computer applications), the two young men had decided to attend Data System Corporation's Computing Institute in Chicago to become more familiar with the hands-on side of computers and their applications in business and the home. They felt that their undergraduate education had given them an excellent preparation for dealing with computer technology, but wanted to know more about how people interacted with the "intelligent machines" of the late twentieth century. Their plan was to use this extra information to get jobs at some computer company where Terry could design new circuits which would enhance the usefulness of computing machinery and Brian could work with software and its applications to make computing systems more "user friendly."

Imagine their surprise when, on first reporting to the Institute, they met their old friend Laura. She had recently graduated with a degree in business administration from the University of Alabama and was attending the Institute because her family used a large number of computers in the operation of its wholesale food distribution business, and all of the family members had attended the Institute to learn the details of computer applications for use by the firm. Laura had not yet made a commitment to enter the family firm, and was not being pressured to do so, but her mother had pointed out to her that the information she would receive at the Institute certainly wouldn't hurt her job prospects anywhere, and should she ever decide to join the family firm she would have to attend the Institute anyway. Looking at the experience as an extension of her college training, Laura enthusiastically decided to go.

The three old friends quickly renewed their acquaintance and soon recognized that among themselves they possessed a unique combination of talents and interests that might well be put to good use. Brian and Terry had a real desire to improve computing equipment itself, Brian through improvements in software systems and Terry through improvements in the available hardware. Laura, as it turned out, really had little interest in distributing fruits and vegetables, and wanted to do something on her own, something interesting, different, and challenging.

All three of the friends did well at the Institute, mastering the details of circuit design, software development, and system applications with reasonable facility. Needless to say, each was a bit stronger than the others in his or her own specialty. Terry whizzed through the circuit design part of the course, helping the others when they found themselves in difficulty. Brian found the software logic a breeze, and Laura thrived on systems applications, particularly on applications where economy of configuration was important. Soon the course was over, and all of them received diplomas that certified them as graduates of the DSC Computing Institute.

After graduation they sat at a table in a small neighborhood restaurant they had all come to know and enjoy, relaxing over a friendly repast and discussing their plans for the future. None of them really wanted to break up the set (as they had come to think of themselves) and soon the conversation turned to the possibility of the three starting their own company in a computer-related field. Each felt that he or she could raise enough money to support one-third of the developmental cost for a firm in some aspect of the computing industry.

Questions and Instructions

There are no questions for Part 1. Read the information above two or three times and try to absorb the nature of the strengths and weaknesses of each of the three partners in this venture, whatever its nature turns out to be. In Part 2 of your text the development of the marketing plan for Latebri Enterprises will begin in earnest. (Latebri, of course, is the first two letters of Laura and Terry and the first three of Brian strung together.)

Part 2

Marketing Planning and Information

This section of the text is concerned with marketing planning and forecasting and the roles of marketing research and marketing information systems in the planning process.

The primary responsibility of any marketing manager is to create plans that will facilitate the achievement of marketing objectives. Marketing management deals with strategic issues in long-range planning and with tactical issues in the planning of shorter-run programs designed to achieve the strategic goals of the long-range plans.

Top-level managers are responsible for strategic planning; lower levels of management have a greater level of involvement in the development and implementation of tactical plans. Central to marketing planning is the idea of the strategic window—a short period of time when company resources match environmental conditions optimally.

Strategic marketing options include undifferentiated marketing, differentiated marketing, and concentrated marketing. Choices among these strategic options are based on many factors including market share and growth potential for existing products, company resources, competitors' strategies, and degree of homogeneity of competing products. The strategic business unit and market growth/market share matrix approaches are useful planning tools.

Periodic marketing audits ensure that the marketing effort of an organization is directed toward and is accomplishing the right goals. A marketing audit can uncover problems in the firm's customer philosophy, marketing organization, available marketing information, strategic orientation, and/or operating efficiency.

Forecasts of sales can be developed using quantitative or qualitative forecasting methods. Companies using the top-down process for forecasting develop their forecasts of company sales from forecasts of industry sales. Industry forecasts are based on forecasts of gross national product and other general economic indicators.

The purpose of marketing research is to provide timely, accurate, and useful information for marketing decision making. Marketing research helps marketing managers recognize problems, determine the causes of the problems, predict results of marketing mix strategies, and assess performance. The marketing research process consists of defining the problem, conducting exploratory research, formulating a hypothesis, designing the research method, collecting data, and interpretation and presentation of results.

Poor sales performance is often a symptom of problems at the managerial level. The reasons why sales performance is poor and why other symptoms of unhealthy internal conditions may appear can often be uncovered through an analysis of the company's sales records and records of other related costs using different products, territories, customers, and sales practitioners as bases. Discussions with members of the firm, wholesalers, retailers, customers, and others outside the firm may also help to identify the causes of any problems which may exist.

Generally, secondary data are used first in marketing research because they are less expensive and easier to collect than primary data. Primary data collection must be based on a research design which ensures that it is gathered without bias and is truly representative of the population from which it was taken.

Research design involves decisions about how data are to be gathered (observation, experiment, or survey methods) and who is to collect them. These decisions are usually based on the types of information needed and the resources and time available to do the primary work. Related to these decisions is that of how to select the sample from the population. Probability sampling methods such as simple random sampling or nonprobability sampling methods such as convenience sampling may be used to select samples.

Marketers are faced with a continuous need for information about their operations and activities. Day-to-day decisions are based on access to sales reports, warehouse inventory reports, and information from government and trade sources. Marketing research projects generate some of this information, but a great deal of it should come from a marketing information system containing data bases appropriate to the needs of marketing managers. Many firms have made and continue to make major resource commitments to the development of marketing information systems.

Chapter 3
Marketing Planning and Forecasting

Chapter Summary

Planning is the basis for all strategic decisions. The function of planning is to anticipate the future and determine the actions a firm must take to accomplish its objectives. Marketing planning is the implementation of planning activities as they relate to the achievement of marketing objectives.

Planning may be either strategic or tactical. Strategic plans typically focus on the long run, while tactical plans concern themselves with short-run programs that implement the activities which will achieve the long-term goals established by the strategic plan. Upper-level managers may spend as much as one-half of their time on strategic planning. Lower-level managers spend less time on this activity and concern themselves with tactical planning.

Central to marketing planning is the analysis of marketing opportunities. Organizational resources and environmental factors affect the analysis, and planners should be aware that the opportunity may be affected by a strategic window—a short period of time when company resources match environmental conditions optimally.

Three alternative strategies are available to the marketer: undifferentiated marketing, differentiated marketing, and concentrated marketing. If a firm elects to market one product to the entire market (undifferentiated marketing), offer different products to chosen segments (differentiated marketing), or offer one product to a selected segment (concentrated marketing), it has committed itself to a strategy which it believes, on the basis of an analysis of the market, to be appropriate. Undifferentiated marketing works best if consumers see competing products as homogeneous and competitors also choose an undifferentiated strategy. Differentiated marketing is the most common strategy today, typically used by marketers who seek to increase market share in a competitive marketplace where other makers also seek to differentiate. A firm with limited resources may have good success concentrating on a single product aimed at a limited market.

Breaking the business down into strategic business units helps the firm focus on customer needs. Each SBU may have its own customers, staff, and strategy. The market growth/market share matrix can be applied to each SBU to determine how it will be treated by the firm. This matrix characterizes products in terms of their market share and how rapidly the segment of the market they are in is growing. There are stars, cash cows, question marks, and dogs among products and markets.

Sales forecasts are essential to the planning, implementation, and control of marketing activities. The forecasts may be prepared either qualitatively, relying on subjective judgment, or quantitatively, using mathematical relationships as the basis for the forecast. Some of the most often-used qualitative forecasting techniques are the jury of executive opinion, the salesforce composite, the Delphi technique, and the survey of buyer intentions. Quantitative forecasting methods include trend analysis, exponential smoothing, and market testing. Forecasts may be prepared from the "top down," starting with aggregate economic projections and working down through the industry to the company and even to specific products. Forecasting is especially difficult when the product is entirely new and there is little or no previous experience with it and no historical data on which to base sales projections.

Name _____   Instructor _____

Section _____   Date _____

Key Concepts

The purpose of this section is to allow you to determine if you can match key concepts with the definitions of the concepts. It is essential that you know the definitions of the concepts prior to applying the concepts in later exercises in this chapter.

From the list of lettered terms, select the one that best fits each of the numbered statements below. Write the letter of that choice in the space provided.

Key Terms

a. planning
b. marketing planning
c. strategic planning
d. tactical planning
e. strategic window
f. marketing strategy
g. undifferentiated marketing
h. differentiated marketing
i. concentrated marketing
j. strategic business unit
k. market share/market growth matrix

l. spreadsheet analysis
m. marketing audit
n. sales forecast
o. jury of executive opinion
p. Delphi technique
q. salesforce composite
r. survey of buyer intentions
s. market test
t. trend analysis
u. exponential smoothing
v. environmental forecasting

____ 1. Technique in which a new product, price, promotional campaign, or other marketing variable is introduced in a small location to assess consumer reactions under realistic conditions.

____ 2. Directing all of a firm's marketing resources toward serving a small segment of the total market.

____ 3. Anticipating the future and determining the course of action necessary for achieving marketing objectives.

____ 4. Limited periods of time during which the "fit" between the key requirements of a market and the particular abilities of a firm is optimal.

____ 5. Determining an organization's primary objectives, allocating funds, and proceeding on a course of action designed to achieve those objectives.

____ 6. Estimate of company sales for a specific future period.

____ 7. Overall company program for selecting a particular target market and then satisfying target consumers through a blending of the elements of the marketing mix.

____ 8. Estimates of future sales based on the combined estimates of the firm's salesforce.

____ 9. Developed by the Boston Consulting Group, this identifies firms as stars, cash cows, question marks, and dogs.

____ 10. Qualitative forecasting method involving several rounds of anonymous forecasting, ending when a consensus of the participants has been reached.

____ 11. Anticipating the future and determining the courses of action necessary to achieve organizational objectives.

____ 12. Quantitative method for estimating future sales through statistical analysis of historical sales patterns.

____ 13. Thorough, objective evaluation of an organization's marketing philosophy, goals, policies, tactics, practices, and results.

____ 14. The strategy of creating different marketing mixes designed to satisfy numerous market segments.

____ 15. Used by organizations that produce only one product or service, this strategy involves marketing to all customers using a single marketing mix.

____ 16. Within a multiproduct firm, related product groupings of businesses structured for optimal planning purposes and having specific managers, resources, objectives, and competitors.

____ 17. Forecasting that focuses on the impact of external factors on the firm's market.

____ 18. Uses a decision-oriented computer program to answer "what if" questions by analyzing different groups of data provided by the manager.

____ 19. Combining and averaging the future business and sales expectations of executives from functional areas such as finance, production, marketing, and purchasing, for sales forecasting purposes.

____ 20. Implementation of activities specified in the strategic plan that are necessary to achieve the firm's objectives.

____ 21. Surveying sample groups of present and potential customers concerning their purchase intentions.

____ 22. Assigns weights to historical sales data, giving greater weight to the most recent data.

Name _____   Instructor _____

Section _____   Date _____

Self Quiz

You should use these objective questions to test your understanding of the chapter material. You can check your answers with those provided at the end of the chapter.

While these questions cover most of the chapter topics, they are not intended to be the same as the test questions your instructor may use in an examination. A good understanding of all aspects of the course material is essential to good performance on any examination.

True/False

Write "T" for True or "F" for False for each of the following statements.

_____ 1. Strategic plans focus on adoption of courses of action necessary to achieve organizational objectives in less than five years.

_____ 2. An example of a tactical plan is when a firm decides to introduce a new product next year so its sales will continue to grow 20 percent annually.

_____ 3. Supervisors should spend at least 50 percent of their time developing strategic plans.

_____ 4. Organizational objectives are the starting point for marketing planning.

_____ 5. Opportunity analysis does not involve any consideration of the marketing environment.

_____ 6. The key point of the strategic window concept is that marketing success depends primarily on good production facilities.

_____ 7. An undifferentiated marketing strategy is most effective if most competitors are using some other strategy.

_____ 8. Electronics manufacturers that produce different television sets for different market segments are using differentiated marketing.

_____ 9. A distinct advantage of concentrated marketing is that production costs are lower because longer production runs are possible.

_____ 10. A major reason to organize into SBUs is to help the company make more profitable decisions about which units need additional resources and which ones should be pruned from the company's product portfolio.

_____ 11. Successful products typically begin as cash cows and eventually develop into stars.

_____ 12. Marketing audits are a luxury which few small firms should undertake to do on a regular basis.

____ 13.   A survey of buyer intentions is a type of qualitative forecasting technique.

____ 14.   Market tests and surveys of buyer intentions can be useful for developing sales forecasts for new products.

____ 15.   An alternative to "top-down" forecasting is "grass-roots" forecasting.

____ 16.   Quantitative forecasting techniques are more subjective than qualitative techniques because they are based on opinions rather than exact historical data.

____ 17.   Fuji Photo Film's blimp was one of the significant features of the 1988 Summer Olympics at Seoul, Korea.

____ 18.   The introduction of canned and bottled Cherry Coke by the Coca-Cola Company is part of its long-term strategy of increasing availability.

____ 19.   DuPont's "Stainmaster" carpet technology created new marketing opportunities for a traditionally undermarketed product.

____ 20.   Marketing objectives and marketing strategy must be developed before environmental opportunities can be assessed.

____ 21.   The difference between undifferentiated marketing and concentrated marketing is that while undifferentiated marketing seeks to sell the same product to a wide and often unrecognized variety of market segments, concentrated marketing orients a firm's whole effort toward a single segment.

____ 22.   On the market share/market growth matrix, it is much more likely that a question mark will become a star than it is that a dog will become a cash cow.

____ 23.   An intermediate sales forecast will typically include a period of up to one year in its projections.

____ 24.   Surveys of buyer intentions are limited to situations in which customers are willing to reveal their buying intentions; they are also time-consuming and expensive.

____ 25.   The Walt Disney people used market testing as a data gathering tool in the development of their Disney Stores.

Multiple Choice

Circle the letter of the word or phrase that best completes each sentence.

26.   Strategic planning is best described as
   a.   decisions on setting the amount of this year's promotional budget.
   b.   determining primary objectives of an organization and adopting courses of action.
   c.   action based on review of monthly and quarterly sales data.
   d.   planning designed to attack and systematically solve short-term company problems.

27. Which of the following differentiates correctly between strategic and tactical plans?
    a. tactical—10-year plan; strategic—next year
    b. tactical—implementation; strategic—determination of primary objectives
    c. tactical—top management responsibility; strategic—supervisory responsibility
    d. tactical—total company budgets; strategic—unit budgets
    e. tactical—plans for new product development in the next 20 years; strategic—advertising plan for new product to be introduced next year

28. Which of the following is an example of strategic planning?
    a. Southwest Airlines refuses to raise its fares in response to an increase announced by Continental.
    b. The Seattle Seahawks offer the first 25,000 fans into the stadium at their next game a free padded seat cushion.
    c. Ford Motor Company plans to divest itself of its tractor division over the next five years and to purchase small manufacturers of consumer durables to expand its product base.
    d. JC Penney has decided to switch the bulk of this year's advertising from television to newspaper ads.
    e. Panasonic offers a $10 rebate to everyone who purchases a cordless phone of its manufacture during the next month.

29. The Standard Metal Products Company is preparing its strategic plans. Which of the following types of people should be given the greatest responsibility in this planning process?
    a. district sales managers
    b. the marketing research director
    c. the director of advertising
    d. sales representatives
    e. the vice-president of marketing

30. Marketing planning usually includes which of the following?
    a. selection of appropriate manufacturing methods
    b. determining the basic goals or objectives of the firm
    c. making decisions regarding the promotional campaign
    d. deciding whether or not to reorganize the company
    e. determining whether products meet engineering standards

31. Which of the following statements is an example of the concept of the strategic window?
    a. Videotapes of the executive committee's planning meetings are made required viewing for lower-level managers.
    b. The Harrison Brothers Hardware Company has decided to sell electric charcoal starters for barbeque pits because it has the resources to produce electric charcoal starters.
    c. Interstate Transportation Company (a bus line) has decided to offer evening bus service to the downtown area because it has done a research study which showed a need for the service. In addition, Interstate has the resources to provide the service.
    d. The Gates Tire and Rubber Company has decided to produce and market hip boots because it feels there is a market for hip boots. The company does not have adequate resources, however, to fund the production and marketing of this new product line.
    e. The Cutrell-Arbison Company has decided to lower the prices of its products by 20 percent across the board.

32. A firm selling just one product to a well defined segment of the market is using
     a. undifferentiated marketing.
     b. concentrated marketing.
     c. differentiated marketing.
     d. either concentrated or undifferentiated marketing.

33. A company like General Motors which produces several different brands of automobiles, each of which is designed to appeal to a particular group of consumers, is using _____ marketing.
     a. undifferentiated
     b. differentiated
     c. concentrated
     d. scrambled
     e. unsegmented

34. Which of the following combinations of marketing strategies and reasons for use of the strategy is correct?
     a. Undifferentiated marketing—recommend use if competitors are using differentiated marketing.
     b. Concentrated marketing—best for large companies with resources sufficient to market to all consumers.
     c. Undifferentiated marketing—good for the firm that wants to serve one market segment at the lowest possible production and marketing costs.
     d. Differentiated marketing—firm wants to serve the total market and wants to develop product loyalty in submarkets.
     e. Concentrated marketing—best if products are perceived by consumers to be relatively homogeneous.

35. General Mercantile Company is trying to organize its businesses into strategic business units. Which of the following should be considered in deciding on SBUs?
     a. Are the products of the businesses marketed to different customers?
     b. Do the businesses produce mechanically similar products?
     c. Can the businesses use the same production lines?
     d. Do the businesses use the same raw materials?
     e. Do the activities of the businesses require basically the same quality control staff?

36. If the framework provided by the Boston Consulting Group's market growth/market share matrix is used as the guideline, a firm would be most likely to drop a product which was classed as a
     a. cash cow.
     b. dog.
     c. star.
     d. question mark.
     e. skunk.

37. You are considering using the market share/market growth matrix approach to adjust your company's product portfolio. A correct action when using this approach is
    a. eliminate all question marks; they're hopeless, anyway.
    b. delete new products unless they become cash cows within six months after their introduction.
    c. find funds to finance the future growth of stars.
    d. plow money back into your cash cows; they can be made into stars if enough money is invested in them.
    e. be prepared to fund the potential growth of dogs into cash cows or maybe even stars.

38. The major purpose of a marketing audit is to
    a. satisfy the demands of the company's stockholders for accountability on the part of corporate officers.
    b. support management's perceptions that its marketing efforts are effective.
    c. evaluate the success of marketing plans and the appropriateness of philosophy, goals, and policies.
    d. keep the members of the marketing research department busy.

39. Qualitative sales forecasting methods include
    a. trend extensions of past sales results.
    b. salesforce composites.
    c. computer simulations of likely consumer reactions to a new product.
    d. levels of sales of a product in test markets.
    e. input-output models of relationships among industries.

40. The Delphi technique of sales forecasting includes
    a. use of company sales to forecast GNP.
    b. trend extensions of company sales to forecast industry sales.
    c. use of environmental forecasts as the base for industry forecasts.
    d. total reliance on juries of executive opinion for forecasts of product sales.
    e. seeking expert opinion from outside the firm in a manner similar to that used in juries of executive opinion.

41. The Coca-Cola Company's plan to boost international per capita consumption of its soft drinks by 40 percent between 1985 and 1990
    a. is a strategic plan.
    b. is probably not attainable because that's such a large increase.
    c. is tactical rather than strategic because the time frame is too short.
    d. depends on making significant changes in the international legal/political environment.
    e. is probably the responsibility of the sales department.

42. Which of the following is one of the Coca-Cola Company's identified strengths?
    a. extensive experience in the toy and fashion clothing fields
    b. a long history of success marketing wines and spirits
    c. the world's best-known trademark
    d. a conservative, noninnovative management team
    e. a high level of employee turnover

43. One of the problems inherent in using an undifferentiated marketing strategy is that
    a. mass advertising and distribution cannot be used.
    b. competitors may offer specialized products to smaller segments of the total market and satisfy each segment better than you do.
    c. it can only be used by a firm with a broad product line of similar, though not identical, products.
    d. it is difficult to achieve production efficiency because of variation in marketplace demand.
    e. it may be difficult to satisfy the specific segment of the market at which the strategy is aimed.

44. Of all the alternative marketing strategies, the one most commonly used is
    a. concentrated.
    b. undifferentiated.
    c. differentiated.
    d. standardized.
    e. matrix approach.

45. One of the strategic business units in your company's portfolio is a cash cow. The best set of actions to take with that SBU would be to
    a. allocate substantial funds for advertising and new equipment to stimulate future growth.
    b. withdraw from this market by selling or closing this SBU.
    c. reallocate resources away from this unit if it can't be converted to a star and pursue markets with greater potential, thus allowing this SBU to wither on the vine.
    d. maintain this status for as long as possible, using the funds generated by this SBU to finance the growth of other SBUs with higher growth potential.
    e. make a "go" or "no go" decision as soon as possible; then either get out of that market or aggressively pursue development of the SBU.

46. *Lotus 1-2-3*, *Visicalc*, and *Multiplan* are examples of
    a. spreadsheet software for anticipating marketing performance.
    b. marketing audit systems.
    c. decision-making tools designed on the basis of the Persian Messenger Rule.
    d. sales forecasting programs.
    e. qualitative sales forecasting techniques.

47. Which of the following is true of a marketing audit?
    a. It should be a thoroughly subjective evaluation of an organization's marketing philosophy, practices, and results.
    b. It is especially valuable in pointing out areas in which managerial perceptions and reality coincide.
    c. None follow informal procedures; elaborate checklists, questionnaires, profiles, tests, and related research are the rule.
    d. It is applicable only to large organizations—nonprofit- or profit-oriented.
    e. It should be undertaken with a clear understanding that there will be no "Persian Messengers;" truth is what is sought, and the person who tells it will never suffer for it.

48. Which of the following is a quantitative sales forecasting technique?
    a. market testing
    b. Delphi technique
    c. salesforce composite
    d. jury of executive opinion
    e. survey of buyer intentions

49. An analysis of the historical relationship between sales volume and the passage of time forms the basis of the sales forecasting technique(s)
    a. called trend analysis and exponential smoothing.
    b. of market testing.
    c. used in the Delphi technique.
    d. which are qualitative in nature.
    e. called Stanforth's Rule.

50. Which of the following would typically come first in the marketing planning process?
    a. assessment of organizational resources
    b. evaluation of environmental risks and opportunities
    c. determination of organizational objectives
    d. implementation of strategy through operational plans
    e. monitoring and assessment of strategy based on feedback

Name_____   Instructor _____

Section _____   Date _____

Applying Marketing Concepts

John Messing, general sales manager for the Western Industrial Products Company, was trying to decide what action should be taken in response to a move by the firm's major competitor, National Machine and Tool. National had just introduced a lubricant targeted specifically at users of vertical spindle planimeters. For years, Western Industrial had been the only firm which supplied a product specifically aimed at this market, and had not tried to develop products for any other market. National, on the other hand, marketed a broad line of greases and lubricants aimed at several different markets—for small tools, heavy production machinery, and high temperature equipment. The new product from National was simply a new product aimed at a new market.

1. Western Industrial was a user of which of the following strategies?
   a. undifferentiated marketing
   b. differentiated marketing
   c. concentrated marketing
   d. a mixture of concentrated and differentiated marketing

2. Which type was National's marketing strategy?
   a. undifferentiated marketing
   b. differentiated marketing
   c. concentrated marketing
   d. detailed marketing

3. If Western Industrial were to determine that its product was not limited to use in planimeters and offered it for sale to the small tool, heavy production equipment, and high temperature machinery industries without any chemical changes, it would be employing a strategy of
   a. undifferentiated marketing.
   b. differentiated marketing.
   c. concentrated marketing.
   d. unplanned distribution.

4. A decision by Western Industrial to use undifferentiated marketing would be a
   a. tactical plan.
   b. strategic plan.
   c. very unwise move.
   d. successful course of action.

5. The product that Western Industrial sells would be a _____ if it has a large market share but little growth potential.
   a. question mark
   b. cash cow
   c. dog
   d. star

The Terrence Michael Company, a manufacturer of ladies' lingerie, has been involved in a detailed process of carefully assessing its marketing philosophy, goals, plans, policies, tactics, and results. Mr. Michael, the chief executive officer of the company, has made it abundantly clear that he doesn't care how much it hurts, everyone is to make the analysis as objective as possible. The resulting report is to be used as a basic prerequisite to develop Michael's long-range plan. Part of the analysis involves a detailed look at sales by product, customer, and geographic area, and the costs associated with producing these sales.

6. Terrence Michael's management is conducting a/an
    a. marketing audit.
    b. inquisition.
    c. accounting audit.
    d. financial audit.

7. The analysis of sales and costs produced by marketing activities is concerned with which aspect of an audit?
    a. philosophy
    b. goals
    c. results

8. If the detailed history of sales is used to project sales into the future, the chances are that
    a. a jury of executive opinion will be used.
    b. trend analysis or exponential smoothing will be used.
    c. a qualitative rather than quantitative tool will be used.
    d. it will be in error; you really can't project the past into the future.

The Hawley Robinson Company has been manufacturing a broad line of clothing items for over 100 years. Its product portfolio includes men's work clothing, children's nightwear, women's coats, and even a line of trendy shirts and shorts ensembles aimed at male and female teenagers. The work clothing, which was the first product line the company entered back in 1882, remains a sound, steady performer in the marketplace, with a substantial share of a slowly growing but quite loyal market segment. In recent years, the performance of the women's coat line has been disappointing. Sales have been declining every year despite a determined effort by the company to offer a stylish, well made product at a reasonable price. A recent analysis by the Hawley marketing team indicates that both market size and Hawley's share of the market are declining in this area.

The children's nightwear line is the company's present pride and joy. The dominant brand in a rapidly growing segment, "H-R Nitees" have proved themselves the company's big profit producer for the 1980s. The results are still out on the teen ensembles. Only recently introduced, they have not yet captured a large share of the market. Hawley management feels the line is stylish and will ultimately capture a substantial share of this rapidly growing market.

9. The Hawley Robinson Company practices which type of marketing strategy?
    a. concentrated marketing
    b. differentiated marketing
    c. undifferentiated marketing
    d. mixed marketing
    e. none of the above

10. Using the market share/market growth matrix as a guide, Hawley's line of men's work clothes would be a
    a. dog.
    b. star.
    c. cash cow.
    d. question mark.

11. Hawley's new line of teen ensembles
    a. is obviously a loser and should be dropped as soon as possible.
    b. shows every evidence of being a question mark offering and should be carefully watched and nurtured.
    c. is undoubtedly a star right now and should be treated as such.
    d. will probably become a cash cow before it becomes a star.

12. If you had to make the decision to drop one of the Hawley lines of products right now, it would be
    a. the teenwear; the market is too uncertain and the risk too great to stay in it.
    b. the men's work clothes; resources could be better allocated to developing the teenwear line.
    c. the children's nightwear; sales have undoubtedly peaked and the end is in sight for this line.
    d. the women's coats; a declining share of a declining market makes this product a dog and a prime candidate for deletion.

Name _____ Instructor _____

Section _____ Date _____

Questions for Thought

The questions which follow are designed to help you become familiar with the main concepts in this chapter through interpretation in your own words. They are meant to be answered in a few sentences or a paragraph at most.

1. Define and differentiate between strategic planning and tactical planning.

2. Discuss the various factors which interact in the marketing planning process.

3. Matching products to markets may be accomplished using any one of three different strategies. Discuss.

4. Differentiate between qualitative and quantitative forecasting. Name and describe some of the methods used in each of these two types of forecasting.

5. Relate the concept of the strategic business unit to the market share/market growth matrix. Is the relationship between the two strong or weak in the planning context?

Name_____ Instructor _____

Section _____ Date _____

Experiential Exercises

1. The purpose of this exercise is to make you more familiar with sales forecasting techniques as they are applied by marketers.

   a. Pay a visit to one of your local public utilities offices—the power company, gas company, or telephone company, for example. Ask to talk to one of their planning staff and inquire how the utility projects its sales. Request information about projected use of the appropriate product/service for the rest of this year on a monthly basis, and for the next five years in yearly terms. Inquire about how they make their long-term projections.

   b. Visit your local Tourist Office, Convention Bureau, or Chamber of Commerce. If your town has none of these, go to City Hall or to the County Courthouse. Ask an appropriate official about the projections of visitors to your town. Does he or she know how many people visit there yearly, and how much money each of them spends? What are the expectations for next year? the next three years? What kinds of forecasting techniques are used to arrive at these projections?

   c. Visit the office of a local retailer, wholesaler, or manufacturer. Ask an appropriate officer of the company about the methods the company uses to project/predict sales. Ask about short-term, mid-range, and long-term projections.

   Be prepared to report to the class on the results of your visits.

2. The purpose of this exercise is to improve your understanding of the market share/market growth matrix. For each of the situations given below, categorize the product offerings as cash cows, stars, dogs, or question marks.

    a. The Universal Electric Products Company sells a portable sweeper for home use. Currently its sweeper has a five percent share of all sweeper sales. Home sweeper sales have been fairly stable over recent years. The Universal Sweeper is a _____.

    b. Scientific Products Company markets self-administered devices that allow people to test for the presence of several blood diseases. The sales of these devices are expected to grow by 50 percent over the next five years. The Scientific brand has about a 60 percent share of the market. The Scientific devices are _____.

    c. The Tomato Products Company markets a line of condiments, soups, and french fries. The company's condiments have been very successful with a market share of about 40 percent. The sale of ketchup and french fries has experienced considerable growth in the past ten years. This growth will probably continue in the near future. Mustard sales have been stable over the past few years. The Tomato Products' brand of french fries has about a ten percent share of the market.

        Tomato Products' brand of ketchup is a _____.

        Tomato Products' brand of french fries is a _____.

        Tomato Products' brand of mustard is a _____.

Name_____ Instructor _____

Section _____ Date _____

Computer Applications

Review the discussion of forecasting using trend analysis in Chapter 3 of the text. Then use menu item 3 titled "Sales Forecasting" to solve each of the following problems.

1. The Metropolitan Symphony Orchestra is concerned about its ability to meet its expenses in 1990. Management has decided that the symphony will have to raise $1,000,000 in contributions from the general public if it hopes to cover expected costs of finishing the season. Donations for the past ten years are:

1980	$370,000	1985	$600,000
1981	$406,000	1986	$650,000
1982	$450,000	1987	$720,000
1983	$500,000	1988	$800,000
1984	$540,000	1989	$880,000

a. Forecast donations for 1990 using the trend extension method.

b. Will projected contributions be large enough to meet expenses?

c. How many years will it be before the trend extension method would project more than $1,000,000 in donations? More than $1,500,000?

2. William L. Christiana, director of merchandising at Terranova and Sons Supermarket, is trying to forecast total industry food sales in his market area for 1990. Food sales in his markets for the past six years are:

1984	$ 8,000,000	1987	$16,000,000
1985	$10,000,000	1988	$18,000,000
1986	$13,000,000	1989	$20,000,000

a. Use the trend extension method to forecast food sales for 1990.

b. William's boss, the vice-president of marketing, argues that William should have based his forecasts on eight years of past sales data rather than six. Yearly sales were $8,000,000 for both 1982 and 1983.

How much would the sales forecast for 1990 change if it were based on sales for the eight-year period 1982-1989?

3. Jane Pepper, director of the Hunting, Fishing, and Outdoor Show, is in charge of making arrangements to handle the crowds who attend this week-long event held every March in Harbor City. Attendance for the past seven years is shown below:

1983	3,000,000	1987	5,000,000
1984	3,500,000	1988	5,000,000
1985	4,000,000	1989	5,000,000
1986	4,500,000		

a. Forecast show attendance for 1990 using the trend extension method.

b. Why might attendance for 1990 differ substantially from the trend extension method forecast?

Chapter 3 Solutions

Key Concepts

1. s	7. f	13. m	19. o
2. i	8. q	14. h	20. d
3. b	9. k	15. g	21. r
4. e	10. p	16. j	22. u
5. c	11. a	17. v	
6. n	12. t	18. l	

Self Quiz

1. F	11. F	21. T	31. c	41. a
2. T	12. F	22. T	32. b	42. c
3. F	13. T	23. F	33. b	43. b
4. T	14. T	24. T	34. d	44. c
5. F	15. T	25. T	35. a	45. d
6. F	16. F	26. b	36. b	46. a
7. F	17. F	27. b	37. c	47. e
8. T	18. T	28. c	38. c	48. a
9. F	19. T	29. e	39. b	49. a
10. T	20. F	30. c	40. e	50. c

Applying Marketing Concepts

1. a	5. b	9. b
2. b	6. a	10. c
3. a	7. c	11. b
4. b	8. b	12. d

Chapter 4

Marketing Research and Information Systems

Chapter Summary

The critical task of the marketing manager is decision making. Marketing research aids the decision maker by presenting pertinent facts, analyzing them, and suggesting possible action. All marketing decision areas are candidates for marketing research activities. Most often, marketing research efforts are directed toward determining market potential, market characteristics, and market share.

Marketing research has a short but interesting history. Started in the United States in 1879 by N. W. Ayer, the field rapidly expanded and in 1911 Charles C. Parlin founded the first commercial research department at Curtis Publishing Company. At the present time, there are over 1,000 marketing research firms operating in the U.S., and over 85 percent of the nation's leading manufacturing firms have their own marketing research departments. Marketing research companies may be characterized as syndicated services (comprised of specialists who provide a standard set of data on a regular basis), full-service research suppliers (companies who will undertake complete marketing research projects for their clients), and limited service research suppliers (firms that specialize in only certain activities, such as field interviewing or data processing).

The starting point of all marketing research is the need for certain information in order to make a decision. The marketing research process consists of six stages: (1) defining the problem; (2) exploratory research; (3) formulating a hypothesis; (4) research design; (5) collecting data; and (6) interpretation and presentation. In following this process, it is important not to confuse problems with their symptoms. Exploratory research often allows the marketer to more accurately understand the problems the firm faces and to focus on specific areas for study in seeking solutions. The use of interviews with informed people within the firm and with wholesalers, retailers, and customers, as well as the analysis of internal data, is typical of exploratory research. Once exploratory research has provided some insights into the firm's situation, a more formal research project may be undertaken. A hypothesis (a statement of a tentative explanation for some specific event) is advanced and a method is designed to test that hypothesis.

It may be necessary to gather data to carry forward the test of the research hypothesis. This data may be primary (gathered by the researcher specifically for this one use) or secondary (previously published by someone else). Secondary data are often found within the company doing the research, though a large number of external sources are also available. The widespread use of computers makes databases attractive for many firms. These collections of data that are retrievable by computer greatly simplify the search for usable information.

If it is necessary for the researcher to collect data from primary sources, three methods are available: observation, survey, or controlled experiment. Observation involves actually viewing, either physically or mechanically, the actions of subjects. A survey, which may be conducted by personal interview, telephone interview, or mail, is the most often used of the primary data gathering techniques. The experiment, the last and the least-used method of gathering primary data, is costly because its use requires that the environment be controlled while the experiment is under way.

Since the populations which researchers need to investigate are usually large, some method had to be found that would allow the researcher to learn about the population without having to gather data from each member of it. This method is called "sampling" and consists of selecting a representative group from the population. Samples may be probability samples chosen so that every member of the population has an equal chance of being selected, or they may be nonprobability samples selected by some arbitrary method. Among the types of probability samples are the simple random, the stratified, and the cluster. Nonprobability samples include the quota and the convenience.

Once data have been gathered, they must be interpreted and presented to those who will use them. The basic rule of presentation is that it be clear, concise, and nontechnical. The marketing information system, a planned, computer-based method of providing managers with a continual flow of information relevant to their decision-making needs, uses the results of marketing research as well as other sources to provide up-to-the-minute information that allows problems to be corrected before they adversely affect operations.

Name_____   Instructor _____

Section _____   Date _____

Key Concepts

The purpose of this section is to allow you to determine if you can match key concepts with the definitions of the concepts. It is essential that you know the definitions of the concepts prior to applying the concepts in later exercises in this chapter.

From the list of lettered terms, select the one that best fits each of the numbered statements below. Write the letter of that choice in the space provided.

Key Terms

a. marketing research
b. exploratory research
c. sales analysis
d. sales quota
e. iceberg principle
f. marketing cost analysis
g. hypothesis
h. research design
i. primary data
j. secondary data
k. database
l. focus group interview
m. experiment

n. population (universe)
o. census
p. probability sample
q. simple random sample
r. stratified sample
s. cluster sample
t. nonprobability sample
u. convenience sample
v. quota sample
w. data
x. information
y. marketing information system

____ 1.   Data relevant to the marketing manager in making decisions.

____ 2.   In-depth evaluation of a firm's sales.

____ 3.   Arbitrary sample in which most standard statistical tests cannot be applied to the collected data.

____ 4.   Total group the researcher wants to study.

____ 5.   Nonprobability sample based on the selection of readily available respondents.

____ 6.   Series of advanced decisions that, when taken together, comprise a master plan or model for conducting marketing research.

____ 7.   Probability sample constructed so that randomly selected subsamples of different groups are represented in the whole sample.

____ 8.   Sample in which every element of the population has an equal chance of being selected.

____ 9.   Information function that links the marketer and the marketplace.

____ 10. Information-gathering procedure in marketing research that typically brings eight to twelve people together in one location to discuss a given subject.

____ 11. Basic type of probability sample in which every item in the relevant universe has an equal opportunity to be selected.

____ 12. Previously published data.

____ 13. Scientific investigation in which a researcher controls or manipulates a test group and compares its results with those of a group that did not receive the controls or manipulations.

____ 14. Probability sample in which geographical areas or clusters are selected and all of or a sample within them become respondents.

____ 15. Evaluation of such items as selling costs, billing, and advertising to determine the profitability of particular customers, territories, or product lines.

____ 16. Collection of data that are retrievable through a computer.

____ 17. Collection of data from all possible sources in a population or universe.

____ 18. Statement about the relationship among variables, including clear implications for testing it.

____ 19. Information or statistics collected for the first time during a marketing research study.

____ 20. Level of expected sales against which actual results are compared.

____ 21. Nonprobability sample that is divided such that different segments or groups are represented in the total sample.

____ 22. Theory suggesting that collected data in summary form often obscure important information.

____ 23. A planned, computer-based system designed to provide managers with a continuous flow of information relevant to their specific decision areas.

____ 24. Statistics, opinions, facts, or predictions categorized on some basis for storage and retrieval.

____ 25. Discussing a marketing problem with informed sources within the firm as well as with outside sources such as retailers and customers.

Name_____ Instructor _____

Section _____ Date _____

Self Quiz

You should use these objective questions to test your understanding of the chapter material. You can check your answers with those provided at the end of the chapter.

While these questions cover most of the chapter topics, they are not intended to be the same as the test questions your instructor may use in an examination. A good understanding of all aspects of the course material is essential to good performance on any examination.

True/False

Write "T" for True or "F" for False for each of the following statements.

_____ 1. The amount and sophistication of marketing research have increased greatly since its beginnings in 1879.

_____ 2. Charles C. Parlin founded the first commercial marketing research department in the early part of the twentieth century.

_____ 3. Exploratory research has as its goal the determination of what data are needed for testing hypotheses.

_____ 4. One of the drawbacks to using secondary data is often the time and expense which must be expended to get it.

_____ 5. The marketing vice-president of the Miramar Boat Company has said that sales of his product would double if the number of retailers selling it were increased by 20 percent. This statement is an example of a hypothesis.

_____ 6. A study of the traffic patterns of consumers in shopping malls would be secondary data for the firm which did the study.

_____ 7. Internal secondary data are data collected by the U.S. government; external secondary data are data collected by foreign governments.

_____ 8. Experimentation is the least-used of the primary data gathering methods because it is so expensive to control all the variables in a real-life situation.

_____ 9. By 1990, the U.S. government plans to have on line a computerized mapping database which will combine features such as railroads, highways, and rivers with census data.

_____ 10. Mall intercept interviews generally take longer to complete and are more costly than door-to-door personal interviews.

____ 11. A marketing researcher trying to decide whether to use a telephone survey which will cost $20 per completed interview or a mail survey which will cost $15,000 to print and mail 1,000 questionnaires should select the mail survey as long as it receives an average response rate.

____ 12. Simple random sampling and quota sampling are two types of probability sampling.

____ 13. Stratified sampling assures that members of different groups, such as large and small companies, are included in the sample.

____ 14. Marketing information systems are restricted to providing only detailed analyses of the buying behavior of specific consumer market segments for specific time periods; marketing research, on the other hand, involves the continuous collection and analysis of marketing information providing a systematic and comprehensive study of areas that deviate from established goals.

____ 15. Marketing information systems have grown in sophistication and importance as evidenced by increasing levels of resources committed to their development.

____ 16. Despite an increasing recognition of the importance of marketing research as a decision-making tool, less than 50 percent of the nation's leading manufacturing firms have marketing research departments.

____ 17. The use of functional accounts in marketing cost analysis requires that traditional accounts be reallocated to the purpose for which the expenditure was made.

____ 18. A database is any collection of data which are retrievable from public records.

____ 19. The most important source of marketing data in the United States is the federal government.

____ 20. *Sales and Marketing Management* magazine's annual "Survey of Buying Power" is an excellent source of data on the audiences reached by various advertising media.

____ 21. "People meters" are part of the new technology of the experimental method in marketing research.

____ 22. Telephone interviews account for an estimated 55 to 60 percent of all primary marketing research.

____ 23. While focus groups are flexible in use and provide immediacy of information, they suffer, because of their size, from a lack of statistical reliability.

____ 24. Since marketing research reports are directed to management, the technical details of the research should be presented in the body of the report; it is important that the reader understand the statistical and mathematical complexities of the analysis.

____ 25. Of all the methods of collecting marketing research information, the one least used is observation.

Multiple Choice

Circle the letter of the word or phrase that best completes the sentence or best answers the question.

26. Marketing research consists of generating information to
    a. identify and define marketing opportunities.
    b. evaluate marketing actions.
    c. monitor marketing performance.
    d. improve understanding of marketing as a process.
    e. do all of the above.

27. Marketing research efforts commonly center on which of the following activities?
    a. analysis of gross national product for various countries
    b. creating budgets for the firm's operating divisions
    c. development of effective advertising copy and layout
    d. gauging the performance of existing products
    e. studying the impact of federal deficits on product sales

28. If a marketing research organization provides a standardized set of data on a regular basis to all customers, it is
    a. a full-service supplier.
    b. a captive data supplier.
    c. a contract research firm.
    d. a syndicated service.
    e. none of the above.

29. The first task of the marketing researcher when conducting a research investigation is to
    a. conduct exploratory research.
    b. go to the library.
    c. define the problem.
    d. do a sales and cost analysis.
    e. plan a research design.

30. During an exploratory investigation, a researcher may
    a. discuss the problem with members of the salesforce.
    b. conduct a sales analysis.
    c. discuss the problem with wholesalers and retailers.
    d. do a marketing cost analysis.
    e. do any or all of the above.

31. The marketing research process should follow the sequence of
    a. problem definition, research design, hypothesis, exploratory research, data collection, interpretation and presentation.
    b. problem definition, interpretation and presentation, data collection, research design, hypothesis, exploratory research.
    c. problem definition, exploratory research, hypothesis, research design, data collection, interpretation and presentation.
    d. interpretation and presentation, problem definition, exploratory research, research design, data collection, hypothesis.
    e. hypothesis, interpretation and presentation, problem definition, exploratory research, research design, data collection.

32. Compared to secondary data, primary data have the advantage of being
    a. almost always less expensive to collect.
    b. less time-consuming to acquire.
    c. tailored to the specific needs of the marketer.
    d. readily available from the U.S. government.
    e. all of the above.

33. The purpose of a sales analysis is to
    a. eliminate accountants' jobs.
    b. obtain meaningful information from accounting data.
    c. evaluate such items as selling costs, warehousing, advertising, and delivery expenses.
    d. analyze the company's achievement of market share objectives.
    e. acquire external secondary data to make decision making more successful.

34. It is true that
    a. the personal interview method is limited to very simple, basic questions.
    b. administering interviews by computer is more time-consuming than using human interviewers, but misunderstood questions are more easily handled by the machine.
    c. test markets are a type of experiment.
    d. mail surveys normally achieve the highest response rates of any survey methodology.
    e. focus groups are usually composed of at least 50 people.

35. Which of the following correctly matches the type of survey to the reason for choosing it?
    a. focus group—can interview many people, one at a time, at very low cost
    b. mall intercept—wish to contact people where they work
    c. mail survey—want to receive a response from everyone in the universe
    d. personal interview—want to contact people living all over the world at the lowest possible cost
    e. telephone interview—want to gather small quantities of impersonal information cheaply and quickly

36. Which of the following correctly matches the type of sample with an appropriate example?
    a. cluster sample—interview all residents of six cities selected from all U.S. cities
    b. quota sample—interview 100 students selected randomly from a list of all students
    c. stratified sample—interview the first 35 men and the first 35 women who enter the Lakeside Shopping Mall
    d. simple random sample—interview anybody you can find on the street
    e. convenience sample—call every tenth name in the telephone directory

37. An advantage of probability sampling over nonprobability sampling is
    a. probability sampling is usually less costly.
    b. standard statistical techniques can be applied to probability samples.
    c. probability sampling requires less time for sample selection.
    d. probability sampling will produce samples whose characteristics are identical to those of the population.
    e. probability samples are easier to select than nonprobability samples.

38. Marketing information systems
    a. provide a continual flow of information.
    b. are needed by companies that have marketing research departments.
    c. require the full support of top management for success.
    d. must be matched to the level of sophistication of the organization.
    e. do all of the above.

39. A key difference between marketing research and marketing information systems is:
    a. marketing research is wider in scope.
    b. marketing information systems involve the continuous collection and analysis of marketing information.
    c. marketing research focuses daily on the marketplace, providing up-to-the-minute information on market conditions.
    d. marketing research uses more different types of data.
    e. marketing information systems are restricted to providing information about competitors.

40. Marketing information systems
    a. should be left to the technical staff for development and implementation.
    b. do not depend on clear definition of marketing managers' responsibilities for their effective use.
    c. depend on a careful review and appraisal of the marketing organization and its policies for their effectiveness.
    d. are, for many small- to medium-sized firms, a real waste of time and effort.
    e. are only a more costly way to handle clerical tasks than alternative methods would be.

41. The critical task of the marketing manager is
    a. planning and implementing the marketing research function.
    b. developing a useful and effective marketing information system.
    c. interpreting research results.
    d. making effective decisions that will enable his/her firm to solve problems as they arise and prevent future problems.
    e. reducing the cost of information gathering for his/her firm.

42. It has been said that marketing research
    a. need not be closely linked with the other elements of the marketing planning process.
    b. costs 50 to 60 percent more for firms that lack a strategic marketing plan.
    c. has been an organized marketing activity for so long that there's little new to learn by doing it.
    d. has benefited little from recent advances in computer technology.
    e. should only be done by specialists hired from outside the firm seeking to use the research results.

43. The decision of whether to conduct a marketing research study through an outside agency or internally
    a. is usually based on the cost.
    b. may be affected by the reliability and accuracy of the information the outside organization is able to collect.
    c. could be affected by the size of the firm; many smaller firms routinely use outside agencies to do their studies.
    d. could be affected by the suspicion that the internal researcher is conducting the study only to test a favorite personal theory.
    e. may depend on all of the above.

44. A marketing research firm that contracts with a client to conduct a complete marketing research project is called
    a.   a syndicated service.
    b.   a captive research source.
    c.   a limited-service research supplier.
    d.   a full-service research supplier.
    e.   either b or d.

45. A sudden decline in market share for a popular consumer product would be
    a.   a real problem to be solved as soon as possible.
    b.   typical of situations that happen all the time when the consumer market is involved.
    c.   a symptom that there may have been changes in the target market or the environment or that changes need to be made in the marketing mix.
    d.   an obvious indication that promotional strategy is not succeeding as expected.
    e.   nothing to worry about; these kinds of things are self-correcting over the long run.

46. In exploratory research, collection of data within the firm is often referred to as
    a.   informal investigation.
    b.   financial analysis.
    c.   marketing analysis.
    d.   research sourcing.
    e.   situation analysis.

47. Marketing cost analysis requires a new way of classifying accounting data. This new approach requires that accounts be classified
    a.   arbitrarily.
    b.   functionally.
    c.   traditionally.
    d.   randomly.
    e.   naturally.

48. Which of the following is an example of secondary data from an external source (external secondary data)?
    a.   company sales records
    b.   salesforce activity sheets
    c.   records of product performances in the marketplace
    d.   marketing cost analyses for the firm's products
    e.   government publications summarizing economic conditions

49. Of all of the sources of primary research data, the one which accounts for the majority of all such data is
    a.   observation.
    b.   mail surveys.
    c.   telephone interviews.
    d.   experimentation.
    e.   personal interviews.

50. If your supervisor in the marketing research department of the Southern States Life, Health, and Accident Insurance Company told you that he wanted you to take a sample in which participants were equally divided among people under the age of 35, between 35 and 55, and over 55, you would take a
   a. simple random sample.
   b. convenience sample.
   c. stratified sample.
   d. systematic sample.
   e. quota sample.

Name _____   Instructor _____

Section _____   Date _____

Applying Marketing Concepts

Carol Hellman, marketing research analyst for Colquitt Chemical Corporation, was told to find out why "Bovita," the company's new vitamin supplement for cattle, wasn't doing as well as expected and to report her findings in two weeks.

She decided that the first thing to do was to gather primary data from all the 10,000 customers who had bought "Bovita" in the past year. The main thing she wanted to determine was why cattle raisers weren't making repeat purchases of the product. After reviewing bids from three outside marketing research suppliers, she chose the AKG Research Corporation because its bid was the lowest. Ms. Hellman directed AKG to design and conduct the study of all "Bovita" customers without talking to any Colquitt management personnel. After the primary research study was commissioned, she started talking with Colquitt's salesforce and wholesalers to determine the cause of "Bovita's" lackluster sales performance. Finally, Ms. Hellman reviewed the records that were available in the company's marketing information system. These records included breakdowns of sales and marketing costs for "Bovita" in each sales territory. This analysis showed:

Territory

	East Actual*	East Quota*	West Actual*	West Quota*	North Actual*	North Quota*	South Actual*	South Quota*
Sales	$500	$400	$300	$200	$400	$300	$600	$500
Cost of Sales	300		180		120		180	
Gross Margin	200		120		280		420	
Marketing Expenses	400	120	90	60	240	90	500	150
Contribution	(200)		30		40		(80)	

*thousands of dollars

____ 1. Ms. Hellman was collecting primary data before secondary data.

____ 2. A census of customers was taken.

____ 3. Outside marketing research organizations should conduct research projects without talking to the users of the research information.

____ 4. Very few organizations purchase outside marketing research services.

____ 5. Colquitt Chemical should not need marketing research if its marketing information system is effective.

6. The best way to gather the information Ms. Hellman wanted from customers in two weeks would be by means of
   a. observation.
   b. telephone interviews.
   c. personal interviews.
   d. focus group interviews.
   e. a mail survey.

7. The sales and expense analysis suggests that
   a. sales in all territories were below expectations.
   b. the East territory was the only problem market.
   c. marketing expenses were above expected levels in all territories.
   d. the salesforce is incurring excessive travel and entertainment expenses.
   e. customers do not like the products.

8. Ms. Hellman's decision to do primary research before sales and expense analysis was based on the conclusion that answers about the causes of "Bovita's" problems could be obtained from
   a. dealers.
   b. customers.
   c. the salesforce.
   d. government publications.
   e. company management.

9. The results of her investigation should be
   a. discarded.
   b. reviewed by management and then discarded.
   c. stored in Colquitt's marketing information system for future use.
   d. acted on immediately.

10. The major reason why Ms. Hellman chose AKG Research is that
    a. it was the cheapest.
    b. it had the desired expertise.
    c. it was intellectually detached.
    d. it was a subsidiary of the Colquitt Chemical Corporation.
    e. the AKG people had done many similar projects for other companies.

Janice Albertson, local services director for the Cogburn Cable Communications system, was perturbed. She knew that the government charter under which her company provided cable television service to Mirkheim City required her to provide a public access channel to the community. Though the charter said that access to the production facilities and distribution system of Cogburn Cable for purposes of producing and sending out public access programming should be free, there was nothing in the charter which said that the cable company could not sell commercial time on the public access channel. Ms. Albertson wondered if selling commercial time on the public access channel would be worthwhile. Since TV and radio stations and cable channels generally price their commercial time on the basis of the number of people who watch their shows, she knew she would have to get some estimate of how many people watched "Mirkheim at Home," as the public access channel was known. She also felt that she should get the information just as soon as possible, for she knew that Cogburn was soon to go before the city council to plead for a renewal of its charter to provide service, and even if it didn't prove possible to sell commercial time on the access channel, it would be good to have the information about "watchership" for the council hearings on renewal.

____ 11. Ms. Albertson's project is in the nature of an exploratory study.

____ 12. Most of the data for this project must be gathered from primary sources.

____ 13. A major source of secondary information for this study would be Cogburn's logs of public access use of its production facilities.

14. The most appropriate definition of Ms. Albertson's problem is
a. Ms. Albertson does not know how many homes are served by Cogburn Cable's system.
b. Ms. Albertson does not know the size of the audience which watches "Mirkheim at Home."
c. Ms. Albertson does not know who is using the production facilities of Cogburn Cable to produce shows for "Mirkheim at Home."
d. Ms. Albertson is unaware of the legal implications of public access television.

15. Since Ms. Albertson needs her information in a short period of time, the best way to get it would be
a. by use of the experimental method.
b. through use of a mail survey.
c. over the telephone; use telephone interviews.
d. by stopping people on the street and asking them questions about "Mirkheim at Home."

16. Which of the following might be an acceptable hypothesis upon which Ms. Albertson might develop her research?
a. Viewers want to see more entertainment shows and fewer educational offerings on their public access channel.
b. The quality of production for the public access channel is inferior to the quality of production on other channels.
c. Public access television is a waste of time and should be disallowed as a service to the viewership.
d. Public access television has an audience sufficiently large for advertisers to be willing to pay enough to make it profitable for the cable company.

17. If Ms. Albertson does decide to use primary research and to design a sample-based method, which of the following would you suggest to her as most appropriate?
a. Ms. Albertson should randomly sample customers from Cogburn Cable's list of current subscribers.
b. Ms. Albertson should conduct depth interviews with highly placed executives at Cogburn to get the benefit of their expertise and knowledge about how people watch TV.
c. Ms. Albertson should systematically draw a sample from the pages of the local telephone directory.
d. Ms. Albertson should carefully analyze the location characteristics of Cogburn's subscribers and assume an audience from what she finds there.

Name_____   Instructor _____

Section _____   Date _____

Questions for Thought

The questions which follow are designed to help you become familiar with the main concepts in this chapter through interpretation in your own words. They are meant to be answered in a few sentences or a paragraph at most.

1.   Outline and discuss the steps in the marketing research process.

2.   Differentiate between primary and secondary data and mention at least two different sources of each.

3.   Outline the three methods by which a survey can be conducted.

4.   Why are samples used in marketing research and how may these samples be chosen?

5.   How does marketing research differ from a marketing information system?

Name_____ Instructor _____

Section _____ Date _____

Experiential Exercises

1. The purpose of this exercise is to help you understand how marketers can use the marketing research process to gain an understanding of their markets.

    Assume you are considering opening a new business that would be primarily directed toward local college students. Select a type of business—the choice is yours. Some possibilities might be a restaurant, book store, videotape rental store, health spa, or hair care salon.

    a. Determine how many students might be in the market for your product or service. Obtain these numbers from college publications such as admissions brochures or from interviews with records personnel. If there are several schools in your town, get this information for all of them. The number you arrive at may include all students or just a part of the student population, depending on your service or product. You may not restrict the market for your product to commuters, members of specific classes, or persons of a particular sex.

        Size of market (persons) _____.

    b. Using a telephone directory, city directory, student newspaper advertisements, or other sources including observation, determine the names and locations of firms currently providing the products or services you plan to market to college students.

    Name of Competitor   **Location**

    _____   _____

    _____   _____

    _____   _____

    _____   _____

    _____   _____

    (If extra space is needed, make your own table like this.)

c. What do you think are the marketing strengths and weaknesses of these competitors? For each competitor, prepare a chart like that below:

Competitor: _____

Marketing Mix Element	Strengths	Weaknesses
Product		
Price		
Distribution		
Promotion		

d. Interview at least five students who would be in the market for your product or service to determine

- where they go to buy the products or services your store will sell;

- what they like about the places where they now buy;

- what they don't like about these competitive businesses.

e. Based on this exploratory research, do you feel that there is sufficient evidence of business potential to support a more formal marketing research project or do you think that your exploratory evidence indicates that there is not need for another business of this type and no more research can be justified?

2. The purpose of this exercise is to show the different types of marketing information available for a retail trade area. It will help you to identify the difference between primary and secondary research and recognize that the value of information in making decisions is sometimes different from the cost.

You are the owner/developer of a chain of women's specialty stores called *Career Path*. You are interested in the possibility of opening four new stores in a city of 600,000 people that is located 1,000 miles from your current concentration of 14 stores. You know nothing about the area except that it seems to be a good place for expansion. You contact a market research firm in the area in order to get information about the city, about the competition, and so on. It gives you the information in Table 1, which includes both primary and secondary research and their prices.

a. In the space provided in Table 1, indicate what *type* of research you feel each point would involve (P = primary, S = secondary). Be able to justify your decisions.

b. Rank the 10 types of information listed in the order you think they should be handled when making decisions about the new market area. Rank them in descending order from 1 to 10, with 1 being most important. Be able to justify your ranking.

c. If you were limited to the following dollar amounts in obtaining the market information listed in Table 1, which of the listed projects would you purchase? Be able to justify your answers.

Dollar amounts	Which Projects to Do (Write in numbers only)
$ 4,000 maximum	_____
$ 8,000 maximum	_____
$12,000 maximum	_____
$16,000 maximum	_____

Table 1

Type	Rank	Cost
_____	_____	_____

1. List of the gross sales figures of all current women's specialty stores in the area for the last two years (cost = $400)

2. Map of the area showing major traffic routes, current shopping centers and types of stores, and locations of department and women's specialty stores (cost = $1,500)

3. Color-coded map of the area showing home and commercial property values (cost = $1,000)

4. Telephone survey of 500 randomly selected households in the area designed to determine the consumers' familiarity with your store name, interest in specialty stores of this type, and awareness of other specialty stores and their advertising (cost = $5,000)

5. Demographic breakdown of the area by sex, age, gross income, education, disposable income, family size, and occupation (cost = $2,000)

6. Mail survey of 300 subscribers to female-oriented magazines, questioning about their awareness of styles, need for complete services in specialty women's clothing, amount of money spent on clothing annually, frequency of patronage of specialty shops (cost = $5,000)

7. Report of 15-year summary of economic trends in the area, shopping centers, occupations, disposable income, clothing sales, and specialty shops (cost = $1,800)

8. Focus group report of 12 people concerning attitudes toward prices of clothing and specialty shops, services expected, appropriate atmosphere, type of salespersons, and seasonal changes (cost = $2,800)

9. List of all organizations, clubs, and organizations that cater to the in-crowd and their manager's names (cost = $800)

10. List of all current retail space openings in the area with price per square foot, turnover rate for those spots and shopping centers, population within one square mile, with income ranges, housing values, occupations, ages, and family sizes (cost = $2,400)

3. The purpose of this exercise is to familiarize you with the process of sample selection. It will help you to understand some of the practical problems faced by the sample designer.

You have been approached by the head of your major department at school. She is concerned because enrollments in the department have recently begun to decline and is wondering if perhaps the department has an "image problem." She feels that a survey of a representative sample of the student body will help to get a better handle on the true state of affairs, and knowing of your interest in sampling theory, she has asked you to help in the process of sample design.

a. Design a process for selecting a simple random sample of the student body of your college or university. CAUTION! Remember that each member of the population must have an exactly equal chance of being chosen for the sample to be truly random.

b. How might a cluster sample be chosen from among the same population?

c. Discuss some of the ways you might sample the student body in a nonprobabilistic fashion. What are the drawbacks to this type of sampling scheme?

Name _____   Instructor _____

Section _____   Date _____

Computer Applications

Review the discussion of sales analysis in Chapter 4 of the text. Then use menu item 4 titled "Sales Analysis" to solve each of the following problems.

1. Northwestern Business Supply Company uses outside sales representatives to sell its broad line of business forms in the states of Washington, Oregon, Idaho, Utah, and Montana. Each state is a sales territory and has its own sales representative. Last year's salaries and expenses for each of the five representatives were:

State	Salaries	Expenses
Washington	$45,000	$15,000
Oregon	$75,000	$15,000
Idaho	$60,000	$30,000
Utah	$52,500	$ 7,500
Montana	$90,000	$45,000

All were assigned sales quotas 20 times their salaries (the representative servicing Idaho, for example, is expected to sell $1,200,000).

Actual sales of Northwestern's products were:

Washington	$ 750,000
Oregon	$1,450,000
Idaho	$1,275,000
Utah	$ 795,000
Montana	$2,250,000

a.   Calculate the cost/sales ratio for each of the five states.

b.   Calculate the performance-to-quota ratio for each of Northwestern's sales representatives.

c.   Overall, what is the performance-to-quota ratio for all of Northwestern's salesforce?

2.   Debbie Gibson, a marketing consultant, has been hired to analyze the sales of Eastern Shore Industries of Daphne, Alabama. The company sells fiberglass boats nationally, and is organized into four sales regions: the Northwest, Southwest, Northeast, and Southeast. Average salaries of sales representatives in these regions are $90,000, $70,000, $85,000, and $110,000, respectively. Average levels of sales are $1,800,000 in the Northwest, $2,000,000 in the Southwest, $1,400,000 in the Northeast, and $2,400,000 in the Southeast.

a.   Calculate the cost/sales ratio for each of the four regions.

b. Following Ms. Gibson's recommendation, Eastern Shore has decided to examine the sales performances of the four sales representatives in the Northeast. Each sales representative is assigned a $400,000 quota. Their actual sales are:

Aubert $600,000
Kidd $250,000
Lambert $400,000
Nicholls $150,000

Calculate the performance-to-quota ratio for the Northeast and each of the sales representatives in the region.

Chapter 4 Solutions

Key Concepts

1.	x	6.	h	11.	q	16.	k	21.	v
2.	c	7.	r	12.	j	17.	o	22.	e
3.	t	8.	p	13.	m	18.	g	23.	y
4.	n	9.	a	14.	s	19.	i	24.	w
5.	u	10.	l	15.	f	20.	d	25.	b

Self Quiz

1.	T	11.	F	21.	F	31.	c	41.	d
2.	T	12.	F	22.	T	32.	c	42.	b
3.	F	13.	T	23.	T	33.	b	43.	e
4.	F	14.	F	24.	F	34.	c	44.	d
5.	T	15.	T	25.	F	35.	e	45.	c
6.	F	16.	F	26.	e	36.	a	46.	e
7.	F	17.	T	27.	d	37.	b	47.	b
8.	T	18.	F	28.	d	38.	e	48.	e
9.	T	19.	T	29.	c	39.	b	49.	c
10.	F	20.	F	30.	e	40.	c	50.	e

Applying Marketing Concepts

1.	F	6.	b	11.	F	16.	d
2.	T	7.	c	12.	T	17.	a
3.	F	8.	b	13.	F		
4.	F	9.	c	14.	b		
5.	F	10.	a	15.	c		

Part Two Puzzle

ACROSS CLUES

1. the information function that links the marketer and the marketplace
7. sales forecasting method that asks executives for their opinions; of executive opinion
10. related product groupings of businesses within a multiproduct firm
11. in-depth evaluation of a firm's sales
12. planned, computer-based system designed to give managers continuous decision information
15. theory that suggests that summarizing data often obscures important information
17. type of data which has previously been published
18. type of probability sample in which every element of population has equal chance of inclusion
19. type of research design involving use of controlled and manipulated test groups
20. in marketing, thorough, objective evaluation of philosophy, goals, policies, tactics, and so forth

DOWN CLUES

2. research based on discussing a problem with informed sources inside the firm and out
3. collection of data retrievable through a computer
4. tentative explanation of some specific event; statement about the relationship of variables
5. probability sample composed of randomly selected subsamples of different groups
6. collection of data from all possible sources in a population or universe
8. applied to sales, is level expected against which results are compared
9. total group that a researcher wants to study
13. data being collected for the first time during a marketing research study
14. qualitative sales forecasting technique that involves several rounds of anonymous forecasting
16. probability sample in which geographic areas are selected from which people are polled

Name _____   Instructor _____

Section _____   Date _____

Cases for Part 2

1. *The Manustat Corporation*

The Manustat Corporation is a medium-sized producer of ballpoint, roller-tip, and hard felt-tipped pens located in Squamus, New Jersey. Management has recently become concerned because sales have declined from $2,000,000 last year to $1,600,000 this year. In an effort to find the source of the decline in sales, it has performed a sales and costs analysis of company field operations. The firm maintains three regional salesforces: the northern force, the middle force, and the southern force, each of which calls on 16 of the contiguous United States. The northern force also handles Alaska and the Aleutian Islands, the middle force represents the company in the Hawaiian Islands and other U.S. Pacific territories such as Guam and American Samoa, and the southern force handles Puerto Rico and the Virgin Islands. The results of the company's sales and cost analysis appear in Table P2-1.

Table P2-1: The Manustat Corporation

Sales Performance by Salesforce Area: Last Year versus This Year

	Northern		Middle		Southern		Total	
	Last Year	This Year	Last Year	This Year	Last Year	This Year	Last Year	This Year
Sales*	$1000	$1160	$600	$200	$400	$240	$2000	$1600
Cost of Sales	600	920	360	120	240	120	1200	1080
Gross Margin	400	240	240	80	160	120	800	440
Marketing Exp.	280	200	200	20	120	80	600	240
Area Contrib.	120	40	40	60	40	100	200	200

Product Sales by Area

	Northern		Middle		Southern		Total	
Ballpoint Pens	300	500	100	100	100	100	500	700
Roller Pens	200	600	300	80	0	120	500	800
Felt-Tips	500	60	200	20	300	20	1000	100
Totals	1000	1160	600	200	400	240	2000	1600

*All numerical values are in thousands (x 000)

After examining the information contained in Table P2-1, answer the following questions:

Questions

a.   What are the problems facing the Manustat Corporation?

b.   What other information, if any, would you need prior to suggesting action to correct the problems?

2.   *The Four Wise Men*[1]

Once upon a time, in a faraway land, there lived four wise and learned men who were, unfortunately, blind. And one day there came to them a traveler who had been to an even more distant land where he had acquired a handsome elephant. Now this stranger knew that the four wise men had the ear of the king and if they were to go to his majesty and extol the virtues of his wondrous beast, his fortune would assuredly be made. Accordingly, he appealed to the wise men to come and examine his new acquisition so they could go forth and tell the king what they found the animal to be like. The wise men agreed, but being wise, they did not wish to hear a sales talk from the elephant's owner. He was allowed to leave with the elephant only a voiceless keeper to hold the animal's rein while the wise men conducted their examination. The wise men, meanwhile, had agreed to keep their own counsel (mouths shut) about their opinions of the new animal, even among themselves.

---

[1] This story, in one or another of its many forms, appears either in the *Rubyiat of Omar Khayyam* or the *Tales of a Thousand and One Nights*, or possibly in both.

The first wise man approached the elephant, and, feeling about, encountered the animal's facile and active trunk. Grasping it and feeling it writhe about in his hands, he thought, "A-ha; this animal is very like a snake." And so thinking, he withdrew and allowed the second wise man to approach the animal. The second wise man promptly collided with one of the elephant's massive legs. Feeling the rough, craggy skin of the animal and the huge girth of its leg, this wise man thought, "So! This animal is very like a tree." The third wise man, after nearly being knocked from his feet by the movement of the elephant's ear and feeling its leathery yet plastic texture, concluded that elephants must be some species of giant bat, and the fourth, encountering the side of the animal, concluded that "This animal must surely be some kind of giant horse."

And each wise man, thinking his own thoughts, left the elephant's stall to report to the king.

Questions

a. If the elephant as a whole reflected the population the four wise men were to sample, how representative of that population do you suppose their four samples are?

b. What sort of sample did each wise man take? Answer in the context of the descriptions of sampling methods in your text.

c.   What changes in the method of sampling and the analysis of the information gained from the samples would you advise the wise men to use the next time they are called upon to describe some innovation to the king (provided their credibility and their heads survive this experience)?

3.   *Wheat Shipments to Europe: The Data Look Good but How About the Interpretation?*

As part of a Federal Faculty Fellowship[2] assignment with the Foreign Agricultural Service (FAS) of the U.S. Department of Agriculture (USDA), a marketing researcher interviewed officials of grain importing and processing firms in several European countries. These interviews, which were completed during the middle 1980s, were designed to field-test two survey questionnaires which, it was hoped, would improve the process of evaluating FAS foreign market development programs.

The FAS is a USDA agency with the responsibility of promoting the export sales of U.S. agricultural commodities, including both animal feeds and foodstuffs for humans. With a network of agricultural attachés and assistants in more than 60 foreign service posts around the world —in addition to a support and administrative staff in Washington—FAS cooperates with major U.S. trade and commodity organizations to develop these foreign markets.[3]

Many of the European officials with whom the Federal Faculty Fellow discussed the questionnaires took advantage of the opportunity to bring up a problem with which they were concerned. They lamented what they reported was the deteriorating quality of U.S. grain shipments to their part of the world. Their specific complaints were that the shipments contained excessive quantities of dirt and other foreign matter. The researcher was urged to report this problem to USDA officials in order to reinforce the foreign officials' previous requests that grain shipments be brought up to U.S. domestic standards.

---

[2] The Federal Faculty Fellowship Program is jointly sponsored by the Sears Roebuck Foundation and the American Assembly of Collegiate Schools of Business.

[3] See *What Is the Foreign Agricultural Service?*, Foreign Agricultural Service, United States Department of Agriculture, July, 1970, p. 2.

Before departing for home, the researcher discussed the problem with an official at the U.S. Embassy. The embassy staff member replied, "Oh, you've got to watch out for these buyers; they're shrewd. The grain they're receiving now was bought under cash grain contracts for future delivery at prices that are higher than the spot market price today. These guys are just looking for an excuse to get out of these costly contracts. Don't worry about their complaints. It often happens that when grains have been contracted for future delivery at a high price and the market falls, we get lots of complaints about quality. We have to be careful to separate *real* quality problems from attempts to deal with market fluctuations."

Not long after the researcher's return to the United States, newspapers broke the first story about the bribery of federal grain inspectors at the port of Houston; two months later, a similar situation was reported in New Orleans. It should be noted, however, that grain inspectors would be well aware that the likelihood of detection of substandard shipments would be much higher at ports in advanced, industrialized countries than in a developing nation. It would be much more risky to take a bribe for upgrading shipments to Europe than to some third world countries.

Questions

a. Is this a common type of problem—field-level interpretation and filtering of information affecting the adequacy of the home office data base?

b. What might have been done by the embassy official in Europe to determine whether the problem was real or the European buyers were trying to take advantage of a situation affecting primarily third world destinations?

c.   What control measures might be incorporated into a marketing information system to protect against the possibility of field-level misinterpretation and excessive filtering of data flows?

4.   *City Center Cultural Complex*

Janelle Van Dortmund, Executive Director of the City Center Cultural Complex in Springfield, is working on a five-year marketing plan. Part of the planning process involves deciding whether the complex should adopt an undifferentiated marketing strategy, a concentrated strategy, or a differentiated strategy. The Cultural Complex has been in existence for some ten years, and its entire history has been one of financial struggle.

The problem lies, in part, in the fact that within ten miles of the Cultural Complex there are two similar facilities with very distinct images. *Country Heritage, USA*, appeals to people with an interest in music, art, and crafts activities typical of the development of this country as a rural, individually oriented nation of small farmers and dwellers in small towns. *The Twenty-first Century*, on the other hand, features cultural activities of the most modern sort, from exhibits of the most innovative art to concerts by orchestras and groups so innovative that their names change weekly. Ms. Van Dortmund is well aware that audience studies conducted at cultural centers all across the country have shown that people have very definite likes and dislikes in their cultural pursuits; culture is a very personal thing.

Approximately 20 percent of the residents of Springfield participate in cultural activities of one sort or another on a regular basis. The population has remained stable over the last ten years and will probably not vary much over the next five.

Question

What marketing strategy would you recommend to Ms. Van Dortmund? Should she adopt a concentrated, differentiated, or undifferentiated strategy? Explain your choice.

Name _____ Instructor _____

Section _____ Date _____

Creating a Marketing Plan: Getting Started

The information you will receive in this part will help you to complete Parts I.A. and I.B. of your marketing plan for Latebri Industries.

Episode Two

In episode one, we learned of the decision by Laura, Terry, and Brian to get together and start a company called Latebri Industries. For reasons of simplicity, and because of their families, the three ultimately decided to return to their hometown, a city of some 1.3 million people located in the Southeast. After careful consideration of their resources, they decided that they could not possibly afford to enter the highly competitive computer sales market, as there were already more than 160 vendors in the local market. They also discovered that custom software was available from not fewer than 75 local sources. Having absorbed the marketing concept and still wishing to match their abilities and resources with some untapped pool of demand, they cast about a little further and discovered that although 160 firms sold computers and 75 developed software for them, only 42 companies were equipped to repair them. A few hours in the library revealed that the market for repair of computers was expected to reach $46 billion in potential for the current year,[1] increasing at a rate of some 14 percent per year into the foreseeable future. Of the $46 billion current potential in the computer repair market, some $3.5 billion was expected to be derived from repair of personal computers, with the remainder coming from business repairs.[2] It was further predicted that the market for service of office automation equipment, mainly PCs used for word processing and spreadsheet analysis, would grow at a rate of 33 percent per year, leading all other computer-related service fields.

Environmentally, analysis revealed that a computer service company faced no special inhibitions in law. A business license would be needed and a sales tax account would have to be opened (sales taxes were collected on physical goods sold, but not on pure services). There was, of course, competition in the local market, but it seemed to be divided along very specific lines: some firms serviced large-scale mainframes and others the lines of computers which they sold; the local economy was simply a miniature of the national economy. Projections made for the national scene could be scaled down to fit the local. The influence of the social environment on the firm would be minimal, except of course that people who use computers and own them for business or pleasure tend to be the more affluent and leaders of the community. Finally, the technological environment offered perhaps the greatest risk and complication to Latebri Industries. Changes in computer technology could conceivably lead to the "disposable computer." In other words, the pace of change in this industry has been such that it may soon become more cost-effective to replace a computer that breaks down, rather than repair it; mitigating this possibility, however, is the fact that the computer industry has for some years been building their machines with the capacity for internal upgrades at minimal expense.

---

[1] "Makers' Share of Service Mart Seen Shrinking," *Computer World*, 1 October 1984, p. 83.

[2] "A New Industry is Fixing to Fix Your Personal Computer," *Fortune*, 18 March 1985, pp. 150-156.

A research project conducted by the partners acquired additional information about the local market. This information is summarized in Table P2-2.

Table P2-2: Characteristics of the Local Market

Total Population: 1,300,000
Proportion of National Population: 0.52%
Number of Households: 335,000
Proportion of Households Owning Computers: (Est.) 35.5%

Businesses in the Market:

	Total	By Number of Employees				
		1-4	5-9	10-19	20-49	50 up
Central Area	23,521	12,597	4,548	2,976	2,059	1,341
Suburbs	2,374	1,294	481	278	186	135
Total	25,895	13,891	5,029	3,254	2,245	1,476
Percent Using PCs*	95	93	97	99	99	100
Avg. No. Per Firm*	3	1	2	3	9	15

*(Est.)

The partners, who, by the way, are going to incorporate their firm for reasons of taxation and personal liability, have on hand at the present time $150,000 in cash. $60,000 of this is their own, the remainder having been borrowed from various friends and relatives.

Guidelines

a. In the context of part I.A. of the outline of the marketing plan in the appendix to Chapter 3 of your text, how would you characterize the likely nature of this firm?

b. On the basis of the information presented, complete part I.B. of the marketing plan. Basically, the points to be considered should relate, first, to the segments available for penetration, which segments may appear feasible for these people, and which you think they should choose.

Part 3

Buyer Behavior and Market Segmentation

This section of the text focuses on understanding buyers in the consumer and organizational environments and on the process of selecting market targets.

A key consideration in the design of marketing mixes is consumer behavior. The acts of consumers as they obtain and use products and services depend on personal and interpersonal influences. The family, reference groups, social classes, and culture are important interpersonal determinants of consumer behavior. The influence of these groups varies with the individual's status and role within the group. It is possible that an individual may be an opinion leader and influence the buying behavior of others; alternatively, an individual may not be a formal member of the group but instead may use that group as a reference point for consumption behavior. The influence of groups such as the family and culture changes as the individual's situation and the values of society change.

Important personal determinants of consumer behavior are needs, motives, perceptions, attitudes, and learning. Consumers do not act until a need is demonstrated to them. Motivation depends on which needs have already been satisfied and the consumer's perception of those stimuli which have passed through perceptual filters. The product bought, store patronized, or price paid to satisfy an aroused need will depend on attitudes and the extent to which previous purchases have provided reinforcement of learned behaviors.

The amount of time and effort spent on consumer decision making varies for the three categories of (1) routinized response behavior, (2) limited problem solving, and (3) extended problem solving.

The organizational market is made up of four components: (1) the industrial (producer) market, (2) trade industries (wholesalers and retailers), (3) governments, and (4) institutions. The size and importance of these markets make specific analysis of their buying techniques and practices necessary. Several characteristics differentiate organizational markets from consumer markets. These include geographic concentration, a relatively small number of buyers, and a unique classification system—the Standard Industry Classification Codes. Demand in organizations is different from consumer demand due to such influences as derived demand, joint demand, inventory adjustment, and demand variability.

The buying practices of most organizations result in more complex buying situations than are usually the case with consumers. Multiple buying influences are common in organizational purchasing because many individuals may be involved in the purchase of a single item. Government markets are becoming more difficult to serve because of the increased attention being given to purchasing. Government's desire to shift business risk to goods providers has made supplying the government more expensive and subject to unforeseen costs.

Market segmentation is predicated on the existence of markets, which are composed of people with purchasing power and the authority to use it. Consumer markets, those involving people who purchase products and services for ultimate consumption, are frequently segmented on the bases of geography, demographics, psychographics, and benefits desired from products. The consumer markets of the United States are shifting geographically to the states of the Sunbelt, to seacoast states, and to the West. A majority of the U.S. population lives in urbanized areas. Between now and the turn of the twenty-first century the U.S. population is expected to grow to almost 300 million people, with the fastest-growing segments being the 30- to 45-year-olds and those over age 65.

The buying patterns of families depend on their stage in the family life cycle.

Engel's laws suggest relationships between level of income and percent of income spent on food, housing, clothing, and other items.

The activities, interests, and opinions of consumers usually serve as the basis for psychographic segmentation.

Industrial markets must be analyzed differently than consumer markets because of differences in purposes and characteristics of purchases and purchasing behavior. Industrial markets may be segmented on the bases of geography, type of product, or end use to which a product is to be put.

Chapter 5
Consumer Behavior

Chapter Summary

People who are the same age, who earn the same amount of income, and who are otherwise demographically similar may not exhibit the same consumer behavior patterns. Consumer decisions are based on complex personal and interpersonal influences which differ from individual to individual. In general, the interpersonal influences which affect consumer behavior may be categorized as cultural, societal, and familial; that is, they grow out of the culture, out of the particular society of which the person is a member, and out of the person's experiences with family. Of the three interpersonal influences, culture is the broadest and refers to the behavioral values that are created and inherited by a society. Cultural bases can change over time, but only slowly. The influence of culture, particularly of cultural differences, is most strongly felt in the international market, but may be present even within a domestic market. In the United States, the black, Hispanic, and Asian subcultures represent a substantial proportion of the population whose history, backgrounds, and values differ from the mainstream.

Social influences represent nonfamily group influences on the individual. They include the class system and reference groups as primary features. In addition, social influences reflect the activities of opinion leaders. The family influences the individual in a very pervasive way. His or her role in this most intimate of reference groups has a significant effect on how the group functions.

The personal determinants of consumer behavior are needs and motives, perceptions, attitudes, learning, and self-concept. A need is the lack of something useful, while a motive is an inner state which directs the individual to satisfy needs. Perception is the process by which people interpret stimuli received through the senses. Most stimuli are screened out of conscious perception, so the marketer's task is to overcome these screens to effectively present his or her message. People express their orientation toward an object or idea through their attitudes. Every attitude has a cognitive component expressing knowledge, an affective component measuring the individual's feelings, and a behavioral component expressing a tendency to act in a certain way. Attitudes are learned phenomena; that is, we are not born with them but develop them over a period of time through experience.

Consumers usually decide what they're going to buy in an orderly, though often unrecognized, way. First, they recognize that they have a problem, then, they search for problem solutions, evaluate the alternative solutions they've discovered, make a decision to buy something, buy it, and evaluate their action afterward. The consumer's involvement in this process, from the point of view of the time consumed and the effort expended in doing it, may be categorized as routinized response behavior, limited problem solving, and extended problem solving. In routinized response behavior, all the alternatives are known and the only activity is making the choice. When a new alternative appears, limited problem solving may take place. And finally, if a new type or brand of product appears which is difficult to categorize, extended problem solving may have to be undertaken.

Name_____   Instructor _____

Section _____   Date _____

Key Concepts

The purpose of this section is to allow you to determine if you can match key concepts with the definitions of the concepts. It is essential that you know the definitions of the concepts prior to applying the concepts in later exercises in this chapter.

From the list of lettered terms, select the one that best fits each of the numbered statements below. Write the letter of that choice in the space provided.

Key Terms

a. consumer behavior
b. culture
c. subculture
d. status
e. roles
f. Asch phenomenon
g. reference group
h. opinion leader
i. need
j. motive
k. perception
l. perceptual screen

m. subliminal perception
n. attitudes
o. learning
p. drive
q. cue
r. response
s. reinforcement
t. self-concept
u. evoked set
v. evaluative criteria
w. cognitive dissonance

____ 1.   Inner state that directs a person toward the goal of satisfying a felt need.

____ 2.   In consumer decision making, these are the features considered in a consumer's choice of alternatives.

____ 3.   A discrepancy between a desired state and the actual state; lack of something useful.

____ 4.   A group with which an individual identifies to the point where it dictates a standard of behavior for him or her.

____ 5.   The complex set of values, ideas, attitudes, and other meaningful symbols that helps people to communicate, interpret, and evaluate as members of society.

____ 6.   All the acts individuals commit in obtaining, using, and disposing of economic goods and services, including the decision processes that precede and determine these acts.

____ 7.   Behavior that members of a group expect of individuals who hold a specific position within the group.

____ 8.   Object existing in the environment that determines the nature of the response to a drive.

____ 9. One's enduring favorable or unfavorable evaluations, emotional feelings, or pro- or con-action tendencies.

____ 10. Individual in a group who serves as an information source for other group members.

____ 11. Changes in behavior, immediate or expected, that occur as the result of an experience.

____ 12. Occurrence, first documented by the psychologist after whom it is named, that illustrates the effect of a reference group on individual decision making.

____ 13. Perceptual filter through which messages must pass.

____ 14. In consumer decision making, the number of brands that a consumer actually considers before making a purchase decision.

____ 15. The real self, self-image, looking-glass self, and ideal self; mental conception of one's self.

____ 16. Relative position of any individual in a group.

____ 17. Individual's reaction to cues and drives.

____ 18. Manner in which an individual interprets a stimulus; the often highly subjective meaning that one attributes to an incoming stimulus or message.

____ 19. Subgroup of a culture with its own distinct mode of behavior.

____ 20. A strong stimulus that impels action.

____ 21. Receipt of information at a subconscious level.

____ 22. Postpurchase anxiety that results when an imbalance exists among an individual's cognitions (knowledge, beliefs, and attitudes).

____ 23. Reduction in drive that results from an appropriate response.

Name _____   Instructor _____

Section _____   Date _____

Self Quiz

You should use these objective questions to test your understanding of the chapter material. You can check your answers with those provided at the end of the chapter.

While these questions cover most of the chapter topics, they are not intended to be the same as the test questions your instructor may use in an examination. A good understanding of all aspects of the course material is essential to good performance on any examination.

True/False

Write "T" for True or "F" for False for each of the following statements.

____   1.   The core values of a culture are slow to change.

____   2.   Combining ethnic minorities such as Asians, blacks, and Hispanics and treating them as a single, homogeneous market segment is usually a wise strategy.

____   3.   Culture is the broadest environmental determinant of consumer behavior.

____   4.   The interpersonal determinants of consumer behavior include attitudes, learning, and perception.

____   5.   Despite all the changes which have taken place in U.S. society in recent years, almost nine out of ten Americans still regard their family as one of the most important parts of their lives.

____   6.   Blacks and Hispanics are of particular importance to marketers of name brand products.

____   7.   The average family incomes of Japanese, Chinese, and Filipino residents of the U.S. are higher than those of white residents.

____   8.   The Asch phenomenon suggests that most consumers are individualists; their decisions are not affected by groups.

____   9.   Consumers may be influenced by groups they belong to, groups they desire to associate with, and groups with which they do not want to be identified.

____   10.   The two-step process of communication suggests that information flows from mass media such as newspapers and television to opinion leaders, and then from opinion leaders to the masses of the population.

____   11.   Important demographic differences between the white population and the ethnic subcultures of blacks and Asians are that the black population is younger and Asians are not as well educated.

___ 12.   Consumer behavior is the result of the interaction between interpersonal and personal determinants.

___ 13.   One's role in a group is the relative position which one occupies in that group.

___ 14.   A person's social class is determined by the person's income, level of education, family background, and type of dwelling in which he or she resides.

___ 15.   Opinion leaders can be particularly important in the introduction of new products.

___ 16.   The percentage of U.S. households containing a married couple is increasing.

___ 17.   Within the household, syncratic decision making occurs when an equal number of decisions is made by each partner.

___ 18.   Teenage boys and girls do not play important roles in their families' grocery purchases.

___ 19.   Motives are inner states that direct a person toward the goal of satisfying a felt need.

___ 20.   A person who buys a yacht so that he or she will be admired and respected by his or her friends is satisfying a social need.

___ 21.   Attitudes have cognitive, affective, and behavioral dimensions.

___ 22.   Product samples and discount coupons can be effective devices in shaping consumer behavior.

___ 23.   Doubling the size of a print ad increases its attention value by about 80 percent.

___ 24.   The statement "My friends see me as an outstanding coach and manager" is an example of the component of self-concept known as the *ideal self*.

___ 25.   A food shopper who makes an unplanned purchase of a magazine displayed at a checkout counter is engaged in routinized response behavior.

Multiple Choice

Circle the letter of the word or phrase that best completes the sentence or best answers the question.

26.   Consumer behavior includes
   a.   purchasing goods and services.
   b.   shopping at stores which carry goods likely to satisfy the felt need.
   c.   putting goods and services to use.
   d.   awareness of a need for a product.
   e.   all of the items in a through e above.

27. Cultural influences
    a. are the same within a single country.
    b. do not affect consumer behavior.
    c. are inherited; people are born with cultural ideas and values.
    d. can be different for different ethnic groups within the same society.
    e. can be easily modified by marketing activity.

28. Which of the following generalizations about the black, Hispanic, and Asian-American sub-cultures in the U.S. is correct?
    a. They account for more than 25 percent of the total U.S. population.
    b. The black population is more affluent than the white population.
    c. Both blacks and Hispanics are very brand-loyal.
    d. Asian-Americans, on the average, are not as well educated as whites.
    e. Blacks spend more on tobacco, alcohol, entertainment, and personal care than whites do.

29. For a reference group to significantly influence a person's behavior
    a. the person must belong to the group.
    b. the group must be composed of opinion leaders.
    c. the product purchased must be in common use; it must not be conspicuous or different.
    d. the product purchased must be one that can be seen by others.
    e. the person has to have daily physical or electronic contact with the group.

30. Social class influences consumer behavior. Which of the following correctly matches social class to a consumer behavior characteristic of families?
    a. lower class—head of household is a small business owner
    b. upper middle class—purchases home in prestigious neighborhood
    c. lower middle class—buys new car early in model year, every year
    d. upper middle class—kitchen full of appliances as symbols of family security
    e. lower class—likely to join an exclusive social club

31. An important trend which has affected the U.S. family and, as a result, has altered consumer behavior, is
    a. a decline in the number of single-person households.
    b. growth in the number of women employed outside the home.
    c. a decline in the influence of children on family purchases.
    d. a decline in the number of single-parent households.
    e. the increased influence of parents on their children's purchases.

32. It is true that
    a. one need not be aware of a need for motivation to take place.
    b. perception is an objective phenomenon based solely on stimuli.
    c. attitudes never change, they only accumulate.
    d. perception is the interaction of stimuli and individual factors.
    e. there are no such things as perceptual screens.

33. Which of the following is a correct description of a specific need?
    a. safety need—purchasing a bulletproof vest for protection from physical harm
    b. social need—joining an exclusive club to achieve recognition and respect
    c. self-actualization need—taking a sea cruise to be with your friends
    d. physiological need—enrolling in an adult education class to develop unrealized potential
    e. esteem need—enrolling in a local health club to increase personal longevity

34. Which of the following is a good way to ensure that customers will receive an advertising message?
    a.   Increase the size of ads in newspapers and magazines.
    b.   Use color rather than black and white for newspaper ads.
    c.   Create ads that leave it to the imagination of the reader or viewer to fill in missing words or to complete the concept.
    d.   Add an additional physical sense, like the sense of smell, to the ad presentation.
    e.   All of the above are good ways to penetrate perceptual screens.

35. Which of the following is an example of a comment reflecting the affective component of attitude?
    a.   "I heard that K-mart is having a sale."
    b.   "Billy's Supermarkets have the best values in this area."
    c.   "I intend to buy a BMW 735i when I receive my next promotion."
    d.   "My friend, Janet, told me that she knows of three stores that sell Godiva Chocolates."
    e.   "I bought a Coke yesterday."

36. Jahn Hankammer ate dinner at the Bon Ton Cafe because he wanted to use the 20 percent discount coupon he had clipped from a newspaper ad. He was so impressed with the food and the service that he plans to return to the Bon Ton tomorrow night. Which of the following is a correct description of a component of the process of learning in this example?
    a.   cue—restaurant service
    b.   response—clip coupon
    c.   reinforcement—cheap price
    d.   cue—newspaper coupon
    e.   drive—desire for money

37. The way one would like to be is
    a.   the ideal self.
    b.   the real self.
    c.   the looking-glass self.
    d.   the utopian self.
    e.   none of the above.

38. Which of the following correctly describes a stage in the consumer decision-making process?
    a.   postpurchase evaluation—read newspaper ads to find dealers who sell the desired product
    b.   problem recognition—discover that any of several brands would be satisfactory for your intended use
    c.   search—buy the desired product at the nearest store
    d.   evaluation of alternatives—decide which of the available products offers the best array of benefits
    e.   purchase act—discover that you don't have any toothpaste

39. The marketing implications of cognitive dissonance are that
    a.   buyers do not evaluate their purchases after they've paid their money.
    b.   postpurchase evaluation only occurs for low-value products.
    c.   it may be desirable to provide information that supports the chosen alternative.
    d.   dissatisfied customers will not change their behavior in the future.
    e.   consumers will be dissatisfied regardless of the quality or price of the product.

40. Which of the following would be a likely factor on which a subculture might be based?
    a. nationality of a group of individuals
    b. geographical area in which a group of people lives
    c. religious affiliation of a group of people
    d. whether a group of people lives in a rural or an urban area
    e. All of the above are valid bases for a subculture.

41. Which of the following statements most accurately represents characteristics of the Hispanic subculture?
    a. Hispanics are the nation's largest and second-fastest growing subculture.
    b. Hispanics already represent a majority of the populations in Miami, San Antonio, and El Paso.
    c. The majority of U.S. Hispanics are natives of Puerto Rico.
    d. Hispanics, as a group, are less likely to be brand-loyal than other ethnic subcultures.
    e. The Hispanic subculture is older than the U.S. population as a whole, with a median age of 32 years as compared to the national average of 23.6 years.

42. You are attending a party at the home of a friend and are introduced to "Lieutenant Samuel Jones of the Coast Guard." From this introduction, you know
    a. Mr. Jones' role within a formal aspirational group.
    b. Mr. Jones' status within a formal membership group.
    c. Mr. Jones' social class position in society.
    d. Mr. Jones' role within an informal membership group.
    e. very little about Mr. Jones; certainly none of the above.

43. Being an opinion leader
    a. goes with the territory—a person who is an opinion leader in one situation will probably be an opinion leader in all situations.
    b. makes one product and service specific—knowledge of and interest in the item under consideration motivate leadership.
    c. tends to induce one to delay purchasing new products so as not to make mistakes which will be visible to his or her followers.
    d. is generally a role that goes with high visibility and upper social class status.
    e. means that your followers expect you to take information from them and use it to make decisions for them.

44. When the flow of information about products, retail outlets, and ideas passes from the mass media to opinion leaders and from those opinion leaders to the population,
    a. you have an example of Katz and Lazarsfeld's two-step process of communication.
    b. the flow is what is known as *direct*.
    c. the process can be characterized as a "hypodermic needle" communications system.
    d. you have a typical multistep flow of communications.
    e. none of the above is a good description of what's happening.

45. Social class has proven to be superior to income as a segmentation variable for consumers' choices of
    a. major appliances and alcoholic beverages.
    b. clothing.
    c. soft drinks and mixes.
    d. foods and evening television programs.
    e. none of the above.

46. When an individual opens a savings account, buys life insurance, or joins a health club to improve his/her physical condition, he/she is probably seeking to satisfy his/her
    a. social needs.
    b. esteem needs.
    c. safety needs.
    d. self-actualization needs.
    e. physiological needs.

47. If a marketer were to seek to shape a consumer's response pattern to the marketer's product, a good program to follow might be
    a. to distribute cents-off coupons of moderate value and then, if a purchase resulted, to include a higher-value coupon in the bought goods.
    b. to distribute free samples of the product accompanied by a substantial cents-off coupon and then, if a purchase resulted, to include a coupon of lower value in the bought goods.
    c. to advertise the product heavily to the target market and then, if a purchase resulted, to offer free merchandise by mail to responding buyers.
    d. to redesign the product package and then promote heavily to a new, untapped market segment.
    e. to require all retailers who wished to stock the product to buy at least ten cases in their first order and then insist that stock levels be maintained at least at that level in all subsequent orders.

48. Which of the following is the most common cause of problem recognition by consumers?
    a. dissatisfaction with the brand or type of good which one is presently using
    b. routine depletion of one's stock of a product
    c. realization that one's stock of goods on hand is inadequate to the job one has set oneself; that a broader assortment of goods is needed
    d. changed financial status; because of a raise in pay, one recognizes there is no longer a need to postpone buying a new car
    e. boredom with what one is doing or how one is doing it

49. In the problem solving process, the evoked set includes
    a. all brands and types of product which may be capable of doing the intended job.
    b. only those brands and types of product with which the consumer may have had previous experience suitable for the job.
    c. those brands and types of product of which the consumer is aware and which have not been excluded because they are too costly, have been unsatisfactory in prior use, or have a negative image because of advertising or word-of-mouth communication.
    d. only one product—the one that's ultimately chosen.
    e. the various problems which the consumer seeks to solve with some scheme to prioritize them.

50. Mel Jacobsen has decided it's time to buy a new car. To help his efforts along these lines, he has bought several issues of *Car and Driver* magazine, visited several automobile dealerships, and carefully read all the sales literature he received from the dealers. He is ready to make his choice from the four models which meet his needs. Mel's problem-solving behavior has been
    a. routinized response.
    b. limited problem solving.
    c. extended problem solving.
    d. extreme problem solving.
    e. excessive problem solving.

Name_____   Instructor _____

Section _____   Date _____

Applying Marketing Concepts

Chang Deng was glad, in a way, to be coming home. After eight years away, first at college in the northeast, then for graduate study at a large southeastern university, it was nice to know she'd soon be seeing her parents, grandparents, and great-grandparents again. To herself she admitted, though, that she was going to have to readjust herself to her family's way of doing things. During her time away from home, she'd gotten used to doing things pretty much her own way, keeping her own hours, and making decisions for herself. She knew some of that would have to change.

One of the first things that she knew was going to cause difficulty was her desire to have her own apartment near the medical facility where she was to be employed. She knew that even if Great-grandfather Chang approved, he was going to want to go with her (and probably bring along all the rest of the family) when she went apartment hunting. And she was concerned that he would try and bargain with the landlord over the rent or as to who would pay for the utilities. Deng had even seriously considered taking a position far away from home, being quite concerned about the levels of influence she was sure her family was going to bring to bear on her, but she had always felt comfortable in San Jacinto and, after all, there certainly were a lot more young Chinese-Americans there than there had been in Pottstown or Atlanta.

Wondering a little bit about how long it would take for her to brush up on her Chinese and then breathing a sigh, Deng gathered up her possessions and left the plane.

_____   1.   Part of Chang Deng's interest in the number of Chinese-Americans in San Jacinto may have had something to do with the fact that ethnic Chinese like to operate in an environment that preserves their ethnic identity.

2.   Deng's thoughts about there being "more young Chinese-Americans in San Jacinto than in Pottstown or Atlanta" reflects the fact that
   a.   Orientals who live in the east and south have tended to be assimilated into the general population.
   b.   the Oriental population of the United States is concentrated primarily on the west coast.
   c.   Deng didn't really know where to look to find persons of her own ethnic group. Pottstown and Atlanta have large Oriental populations.
   d.   Deng was an unusual young woman, having a much higher level of education than is typical of Asian-Americans.

3.   Deng's worries about apartment hunting stemmed from the Chinese custom(s)
   a.   of shopping as a family group.
   b.   of allowing buying decisions to be made by a family elder.
   c.   of bargaining over almost any purchase.
   d.   All of the above were part of her concern.

4. Deng realized she'd have to brush up on her Chinese because
    a. her family, like most Chinese-American families, spoke the language at home and when dealing with other ethnic Chinese.
    b. it's always a good idea to have working knowledge of a second language.
    c. she knew that her work would require her to use that language a lot.
    d. Chinese is such a complex language that it must be used constantly or you forget it.

For several years, Adele Cressy has been a successful amateur bicycle racer. She had long favored the Peugeot "Trans/sportif" model for her racing activities, but recent problems with her veteran two-wheeler led her to consider investing in a new cycle. Her successful business consulting practice meant that she could afford the best equipment for this special hobby, so she started looking for the best bike she could find.

She spoke with fellow racers about their preferences in cross-country wheels and became convinced that she would be more credible and have a psychological advantage if she switched to the SEAT "Sierra Nevada" bike. Her father, who doesn't race bikes but who has always watched his daughter's progress with interest, opposed the change because, in his opinion, the SEAT bike was not as durable as the Peugeot. Adele continued to read biking magazines, talk to friends, and check advertisements for this type of machine. Ultimately, she decided to buy the SEAT.

Next, she had to decide where to buy her new bike. The alternatives available to her were two local dealers and a mail-order firm located only 100 miles away. All three of these dealers were offering the bike she wanted, but the mail-order house's bike was substantially less expensive than those from the other two outlets. Adele finally ordered her SEAT from the mail-order house, Wheels Unlimited.

The following week, her SEAT arrived by express. She decided to ride over to her father's house to show him her acquisition and convince him she'd made the right decision. Unfortunately, the SEAT broke down halfway to his house and she had to call him to help her get it home in his pickup truck. Adele suffered considerable doubt about her purchase. She would have liked to tell the mail-order house what to do with its bike . . . keep it!

____ 5. Adele was mainly concerned with her ideal self.

____ 6. Need arousal occurred because of her dissatisfaction with the bike she already owned.

____ 7. Adele bought her bike because of subliminal perception.

____ 8. Adele is probably a member of the lower class.

____ 9. Adele's search for alternatives was affected by both personal and interpersonal factors.

10. Adele's decision to buy the SEAT because of her friends' influence helped satisfy her _____ needs.
    a. physiological
    b. safety
    c. social
    d. esteem
    e. self-actualization

11. If Maslow's theory of needs is true for Adele, she has at least partially satisfied her
    _____ needs.
    a. physiological
    b. safety
    c. social
    d. all of the above
    e. none of the above

12. For this purchase, the most important influence on Adele was
    a. social class.
    b. reference group.
    c. culture.
    d. attitude.
    e. family.

13. Adele's postpurchase doubt about her purchase is
    a. cognitive dissonance.
    b. subliminal perception.
    c. psychotic imbalance.
    d. psychographic influence.
    e. status loss.

14. Adele may have learned not to buy SEAT bikes because
    a. reinforcement did not take place.
    b. no drive was present.
    c. her response was inconsistent with her drive.
    d. the cues were correct.

Name_____ Instructor _____

Section _____ Date _____

Questions for Thought

The questions which follow are designed to help you become familiar with the main concepts in this chapter through interpretation in your own words. They are meant to be answered in a few sentences or a paragraph at most.

1. Outline the method usually used to classify behavioral influences in consumer decisions.

2. Identify and define the interpersonal and personal determinants of consumer behavior.

3. Outline and discuss the steps in the consumer decision process.

4. Discuss the differences among routinized response behavior, limited problem solving, and extensive problem solving.

Name _____ Instructor _____

Section _____ Date _____

Experiential Exercises

1. The purpose of this exercise is to help you improve your understanding of consumer behavior by examining the process you used in making a recent purchase. Select a major purchase you made in recent months: a car, clothing, luggage, an appliance, or an item of home entertainment electronics. Use this purchase experience to answer the following questions.

    a. How did you become aware of the need to make this purchase?

    b. What sources of information did you use to determine the alternatives that were available to satisfy your needs?

    c. List the brands of product that you considered as alternatives for this purchase.

        My evoked set included:

    d. Circle the brand listed above that you purchased. What factors led you to buy this brand in preference to the others? Was it price, quality, size, performance, color, or some other characteristic or combination of characteristics?

    e. Where did you buy the product? What criteria led you to buy from that place?

f.   Did you experience any cognitive dissonance after this purchase? Do you wish, for example, that you had bought a different brand, or from a different store, or had postponed your purchase altogether?

g.   Now make the assumption that you are a marketer of the type of product you purchased. If you wished to market your product to consumers who behave like you, what would you include in your marketing mix?

Price strategy:

Product strategy:

Promotion strategy:

Distribution strategy:

2.   The purpose of this exercise is to analyze the effect which reference groups have on individual consumer behavior. For the purposes of this exercise, your family will be considered a membership group, though your membership in it is involuntary.

You are using this Study Guide presumably because you are taking an introductory course in marketing at a college or university. Of interest is how you happen to be at this particular school, taking this particular course.

a.   How did you make the decision to attend college? List the people who influenced your decision.

b. Who, of the people listed above, are members of your family? (Remember, family includes spouses and children, as well as parents, siblings, aunts, uncles, cousins, et cetera.) List the names and relationships below.

c. Were any of the people who influenced you members of the profession or practitioners of the art in which you hope to receive your degree? List the members of this aspirational group.

d. Did you base your decision to attend this school on whether or not any members of your high school class or other group of which you are/were a member were going to attend this school? If so, list the members and the membership group.

Closing note: It is a rare individual, indeed, who is able truthfully to leave blank any of the categories in the above exercise. If you have, you might consider the following question:

e. List below the names of people who influenced you to attend college so you *wouldn't* turn out like they did. I hope the number of members of this dissociative group is smaller than the number of members of groups b, c, and d.

Name _____   Instructor _____

Section _____   Date _____

Computer Applications

Review the discussion of evoked set and evaluative criteria in Chapter 5 of the text. Then use menu item 6 titled "Evaluation of Alternatives" to solve each of the following problems.

1. Wayne McLemore is faced with the prospect of choosing carpeting for his dining room. Being a less-than-domestic type, he has decided to approach the problem systematically. He has established that there are four criteria which the new carpet must satisfy: it must be durable, it must be the right color (one which will harmonize with McLemore's existing decor), it must be affordable, and it must be easy to maintain. McLemore is considering four brands of carpet: Everdure, Eleganza, Majeste, and Valuta. He has assigned to each brand of carpet a score ranging from 1 (poor) to 5 (excellent) on each of the evaluative criteria. These scores are shown below:

Evoked Set Brand	Durability	Evaluative Criteria Color	Price	Maintenance
Everdure	5	3	2	4
Eleganza	4	5	3	3
Majeste	5	2	5	3
Valuta	4	4	1	3

a. Which brand would Wayne select using the overall scoring method?

b. If Wayne thinks that color and price are 50 percent more important than any of the other evaluative criteria, which brand will he select?

c. If Wayne arbitrarily decides that any carpet scoring less than 3 on any criterion is unacceptable, which carpet will he select using the overall method?

d. If Wayne decides to apply the weighted scoring method to the answer to c (above), will his decision change?

2. John and Cynthia Albertson are trying to decide where to buy a new refrigerator. They've already decided that Kelvinator is the brand they want, and the problem now is to determine whether they should buy it from Appliance Mart, Smith's Department Store, Discount Appliances, National Furniture Company, or The Warehouse. The Albertsons' evaluative criteria are: convenience of store location, price, credit terms, trustworthiness of sales personnel, and installation. They decide to use a 10-point rating scale in making their assessment. Scores range from 1 (unacceptable or not offering the feature) to 10 (perfect). The scores assigned jointly by the Albertsons are shown below:

| Evoked Set | | | Evaluative Criteria | | |
Store	Location	Price	Credit	Trust	Installation
Mart 8	5	4	5	4	
Smith's	5	8	9	10	7
Discount	5	9	4	4	3
National	8	8	8	9	7
Warehouse	3	9	4	3	2

a. Using the overall scoring method, which store would the Albertsons choose?

b. Suppose the Albertsons decide that trust and installation are twice as important as the other criteria. Which store would they then select?

c. If, after some discussion, the Albertsons change their minds and decide that price and credit are 50 percent more important than any other criteria, which store will they then select?

d. If the Albertsons decide that they will not buy from a store that receives a rating of less than 5 on price, credit, trustworthiness, or installation, which store will they select using the overall scoring method?

3. Theophile Boudreaux, a native of Thibodeaux, Louisiana, is considering purchasing a new fishing boat in which to roam the byways of the Bayou LaFourche. He is considering five models: Bateau Splendide, Bateau Rapide, Bateau Speciale, Pirogue Grande, and Skiff Lafitte. He has decided to evaluate the boats on the basis of price, engine size, reliability, fuel economy, and how comfortable his old dog, Pheideaux (pronounced Fido), will be riding in the bow. Theophile has rated each model using 4 for excellent, 3 for good, 2 for fair, and 1 for poor. The ratings are shown below:

Evoked Set Model	Price	Engine	Evaluative Criteria Reliability	Economy	Comfort
Splendide	2	4	2	1	3
Rapide	3	4	1	2	2
Speciale	4	3	3	2	3
Grande	3	3	3	1	3
Lafitte	2	2	2	1	4

a. Which model will Theophile select using the overall scoring method?

b. Suppose M. Boudreaux considers price twice as important as engine size, reliability, and fuel economy. Comfort is 50 percent more important than engine size, reliability, and fuel economy (Pheideaux is an *old* dog). Which model will M. Boudreaux choose?

c. Monsieur Boudreaux, using the overall scoring method, also has decided that he will not accept a boat that is rated "poor" on reliability or fuel economy. Which model should he select?

d. If Monsieur Boudreaux had used the weighted scoring method in c, would his decision have changed?

Chapter 5 Solutions

Key Concepts

1. j	6. a	11. o	16. d	21. m
2. v	7. e	12. f	17. r	22. w
3. i	8. q	13. l	18. k	23. s
4. g	9. n	14. u	19. c	
5. b	10. h	15. t	20. p	

Self Quiz

1. T	11. F	21. T	31. b	41. b
2. F	12. T	22. T	32. d	42. b
3. T	13. F	23. F	33. a	43. b
4. F	14. F	24. F	34. e	44. a
5. T	15. T	25. T	35. c	45. d
6. T	16. F	26. e	36. d	46. c
7. T	17. F	27. d	37. a	47. b
8. F	18. F	28 c	38. d	48. b
9. T	19. T	29. d	39. c	49. c
10. T	20. F	30. b	40. e	50. c

Applying Marketing Concepts

1. T	8. F
2. b	9. T
3. d	10. d
4. a	11. d
5. F	12. b
6. T	13. a
7. F	14. a

Chapter 6
Organizational Buying Behavior

Chapter Summary

The organizational market is composed of four segments: the industrial or producer's market; trade industries, including wholesalers and retailers; governmental bodies; and institutions. The industrial segment of the organizational market purchases goods and services for use in the production of other goods and services. This use may be direct, in the sense that the goods and services bought become part of something being produced, or indirect, facilitating production but not becoming part of the product. The trade industry segment of the organizational market is composed of resellers who purchase goods and services for resale to others. Governmental bodies buy with the intent of rendering a public benefit, while institutions, of which the most typical examples are hospitals, museums, and schools, operate primarily as service providers. Some institutions are nonprofit in nature, while others are operated for a profit.

The industrial market includes some 80 percent of the whole membership of the organizational market and employs about two-thirds of all organizational employees. Among the major characteristics of the industrial market are the tendency for members of its various segments to be geographically concentrated and for there to be relatively few buyers in each segment. Members of the industrial market may also be identified by their Standard Industry Classification Codes. These Department of Commerce codes inform the user about which segment of the industrial market a particular firm is a member of. Demand in the industrial market possesses some unusual properties. First, it is *derived*; that is, it is linked to demand in other markets, such as the consumer market. Second, it is often *joint*; that is, the demand for one product depends on the demand for another product that is a complement of the first. Third, the industrial market, unlike the consumer market, intentionally accumulates inventories to provide for variations in supplies of raw materials and demand for finished goods. And finally, demand in the industrial market exhibits wide swings in volume; this occurs because even small changes in consumer demand affect the inventory requirements of producers.

Buying by organizations is a more complex process than buying by individuals. The process tends to involve more participants and follows procedures dictated by company policy. Consideration may be given to such decision-affecting factors as price, service, certainty of supply, and product efficiency. Organizations typically face one of three situations when seeking to make a purchase. The first, the *straight rebuy*, is merely the repurchase of an item known to give satisfactory service; the second, the *modified rebuy*, is a situation where the alternative choices are, to at least some extent, reevaluated in the buying process; and finally, there is the *new-task buy*, a condition wherein goods or services are being bought for the first time and considerable investigation and evaluation of alternative choices must be undertaken.

Organizational buying may be looked at in terms of the *buying center*, a term which identifies all those people who are involved in a buying action. Buying center roles fall into five categories: users, who actually apply products to their end use; gatekeepers, who either allow or disallow the passage of information to other buying center members; influencers, whose provision of information for evaluation or writing of specifications has a strong influence on what is done; deciders, who actually make the decision of what is to be bought; and buyers, the people who place the actual order. The organizational buying process actually parallels the same process undertaken by consumers, being characterized by need recognition, search for information, delineation of vendors, solicitation of sales proposals, review of proposals, and the purchase decision. This two-stage process usually follows set guidelines reflecting the nature of the buying task and the importance of the particular purchase to the organization.

The government market is basically quite similar in its behavior to the rest of the organizational market. Some major points of difference are that in the government market regulations are usually quite specific as to what must be done and how, and the government is often the only purchaser of certain goods and services.

Name _____ Instructor _____

Section _____ Date _____

Key Concepts

The purpose of this section is to allow you to determine if you can match key concepts with the definitions of the concepts. It is essential that you know the definitions of the concepts prior to applying the concepts in later exercises in this chapter.

From the list of lettered terms, select the one that best fits each of the numbered statements below. Write the letter of that choice in the space provided.

Key Terms

a. industrial (producer) market
b. trade industries
c. value added by manufacturing
d. Standard Industry Classification (SIC)
e. derived demand
f. joint demand
g. value analysis
h. vendor analysis

i. straight rebuy
j. modified rebuy
k. new task buying
l. buying center
m. reciprocity
n. bids
o. specification

____ 1. Written sales proposals by vendors.

____ 2. Demand for an industrial product that is linked to demand for a consumer good.

____ 3. Component of the organizational market consisting of individuals and firms that acquire goods and services to be used, directly or indirectly, to produce other goods and services.

____ 4. Situation in which purchasers are willing to reevaluate available options in a repurchase of the same product or service.

____ 5. Written description of a product or service needed by a firm. Prospective bidders use this description first to determine whether they can manufacture the product or deliver the service, and then to prepare bids.

____ 6. Highly controversial practice of extending purchasing preference to suppliers that are also customers.

____ 7. Demand for an industrial good as related to the demand for another industrial good necessary for the use of the first item.

____ 8. Systematic study of the components of a purchase to determine the most cost-effective way to acquire the item.

____ 9. Recurring purchase decision occurring when the item has performed satisfactorily and is purchased again by a customer.

____ 10. Difference between the price charged for a manufactured good and the cost of the raw materials and other inputs.

____ 11. First-time or unique purchase situations that require considerable effort on the decision maker's part.

____ 12. Participants in an organizational buying action.

____ 13. Component of the organizational market composed of retailers or wholesalers that purchase goods for resale to others.

____ 14. Numerical system developed by the U.S. government that subdivides the industrial marketplace into detailed market segments.

____ 15. Assessment of a supplier's performance in areas such as price, back orders, timely delivery, and attention to special requests.

Name _____   Instructor _____

Section _____   Date _____

Self Quiz

You should use these objective questions to test your understanding of the chapter material. You can check your answers with those provided at the end of the chapter.

While these questions cover most of the chapter topics, they are not intended to be the same as the test questions your instructor may use in an examination. A good understanding of all aspects of the course material is essential to good performance on any examination.

True/False

Write "T" for True or "F" for False for each of the following statements.

_____ 1. Value added by manufacturing in the United States each year is well in excess of a trillion dollars ($1,000 billion).

_____ 2. Geographical concentration in the industrial market greatly influences the marketing strategy used in serving it.

_____ 3. Capital items are short-lived business assets that require a large initial cash outlay.

_____ 4. Buying center participants play different roles in the purchasing process.

_____ 5. Gatekeepers control the flow of information to other members of the buying center.

_____ 6. The primary motivation of the government market is to create and expand a civil bureaucracy.

_____ 7. Most purchases by government must, by law, be made on the basis of bids (written sales proposals) from potential vendors.

_____ 8. Nonprofit institutions can be included in the government market.

_____ 9. Depreciation is the accounting concept of charging a portion of a capital item's cost as a deduction against annual revenues for purposes of determining a company's net income.

_____ 10. The government market is viewed as unprofitable by many suppliers.

_____ 11. Demand in the industrial market is often derived from demand in the consumer market.

_____ 12. Organizational buyers are influenced only by rational needs like cost, quality, and reliability of delivery.

_____ 13. Value analysis is an ongoing analysis of a vendor's performance on such features as price, back orders, delivery time, and attention to special requests.

___ 14.   Inventory adjustments are not usually a major determinant of organizational demand.

___ 15.   The Standard Industrial Classification system is of little use to sales representatives.

___ 16.   Buying centers are not part of a firm's formal organizational structure, but instead are informal groups whose composition varies with the decision being made.

___ 17.   Reverse reciprocity is the practice of extending supply privileges to firms that provide you with needed supplies.

___ 18.   Life cycle costing involves computing the cost of using a product over its lifetime rather than considering just the original bid price.

___ 19.   Haloid Corporation once made photographic papers. Now it manufactures an extensive line of specialty carbon papers.

___ 20.   Some firms sell only to the organizational market, a different group sells only to consumers, and nobody sells to both organizations and consumers.

___ 21.   When General Mills buys wheat to make cereal, it is making a purchase in the industrial market.

___ 22.   Producers include manufacturing firms, farmers and other resource industries, construction contractors, and providers of such services as transportation, public utilities, finance, insurance, and real estate.

___ 23.   Though the number of buyers in any segment of the industrial market is usually quite large, geographical concentration makes it easy to serve them all.

___ 24.   The accelerator principle refers to the disproportionate impact which changes in consumer demand have on industrial market demand.

___ 25.   While nonprofit organizations are considered to be a part of the institutional market, not all the members of the institutional market are nonprofit organizations.

Multiple Choice

Circle the letter of the word or phrase that best completes the sentence or best answers the question.

26.   The organizational market is made up of four major segments. Of the following, which is one of the segments?
   a.   the foreign sector
   b.   the institutional market
   c.   exchange markets
   d.   the development market
   e.   the social market

27. The ratio of retail organizations to manufacturers in the United States is approximately
    a. 4:1
    b. 5:1
    c. 3:1
    d. 10:1
    e. 2:1

28. Bauxite and electricity are both required for the production of aluminum. If the supply of electricity is reduced, there will be an immediate effect on the demand for bauxite. What concept does this represent?
    a. derived demand
    b. joint demand
    c. demand variability
    d. inventory adjustments
    e. specific demand

29. Because industrial buyers are geographically concentrated and relatively few in number,
    a. the marketing channel for industrial goods is typically much longer than for consumer goods.
    b. wholesalers are more frequently used to handle their business than they are in the consumer goods field.
    c. some companies have set up national accounts sales organizations to deal solely with buyers at national headquarters.
    d. advertising plays a much larger role in the industrial market than it does in the consumer market.
    e. personal selling is seldom used as the promotional tool of choice by vendors to this market.

30. The largest single source of information to aid marketers in gaining access to the organizational market is
    a. advertising.
    b. trade listings.
    c. a buying center.
    d. the federal government.
    e. distributors' guides.

31. Which of the following properly matches SIC codes and industry groups?
    a. book printing: 27; books: 2732; printing, publishing, and allied industries: 273
    b. book printing: 273; books: 2732; printing, publishing, and allied industries: 27
    c. book printing: 2732; books: 273; printing, publishing, and allied industries: 27
    d. book printing: 27; books: 273; printing, publishing, and allied industries: 2732
    e. book printing: 2732; books: 27; printing, publishing, and allied industries: 273

32. If a buyer was content with his purchase of low-cost products like pencils and decided to continue buying them, the situation would be an example of
    a. a modified rebuy.
    b. a constant rebuy.
    c. a new-task buying situation.
    d. a straight rebuy.
    e. a standardized purchase.

33. Which of the following would you expect to affect an organizational buyer?
    a.   the needs of the users of the products being bought
    b.   information received from an "influencer" in the buying center
    c.   the buyer's own emotional needs
    d.   the need for reliability, low cost, and quality from suppliers
    e.   All of the above will have some effect on the organizational buyer.

34. Value analysis may be defined as
    a.   securing needed products at the best possible price.
    b.   using a professional buyer to systematize purchasing.
    c.   examining each component of a purchase in an attempt to delete the item or replace it with a more cost-effective substitute.
    d.   convening a committee charged with all the buying responsibility for the firm.
    e.   evaluating suppliers' performance in categories such as price, back orders, delivery time, and attention to special requests.

35. Marketers who find themselves servicing accounts in the straight rebuy category should concentrate on
    a.   maintaining a good relationship with the accounts by providing adequate service and delivery.
    b.   trying to assess factors that would make the accounts willing to reconsider their decisions.
    c.   providing the accounts with enough substantive information about the product so that direct comparisons with competing products can be made more easily.
    d.   selling other accounts; these accounts are in the bag and really don't need any service.
    e.   developing the accounts; if they're buying one thing from you on a regular basis, there must be other items they need that you can supply.

36. In the buying center, the role filled by technical people such as engineers, quality control specialists, and R & D staff personnel is usually that of
    a.   the user.
    b.   the gatekeeper.
    c.   the influencer.
    d.   the decider.
    e.   the buyer.

37. Most government purchases, by law, must be made on the basis of
    a.   written sales proposals.
    b.   book value of the item needed.
    c.   estimates prepared by government personnel.
    d.   cost/benefit studies of the goods required.
    e.   availability of the most graft to the greatest number.

38. Purchase behavior by organizations tends to be more complex than purchase behavior by consumers largely because
    a.   organizations are more geographically spread out.
    b.   organizational buys require the approval of more people.
    c.   the item(s) being purchased is/are always more complex.
    d.   there aren't enough sales representatives.
    e.   big organizations are very bureaucratic and slow.

39. Which of the following is typically a part of Stage II of the industrial buying process?
    a. the triggering event
    b. a search for information about potential suppliers
    c. a detailed analysis of alternative proposals
    d. identification of potential suppliers
    e. product demonstrations and sales proposals

40. A buying center includes everyone in the organization who participates in an organizational buying action. How many buying center roles are there?
    a. 3
    b. 20
    c. 5
    d. 10
    e. 4

41. Which of the following organizations would typically be a member of the institutional sector of the market?
    a. Metropolitan Life Insurance Company
    b. Merchants Trust and Savings Bank
    c. The American Red Cross
    d. National Stock and Bond Trading Corporation
    e. Rubenstein Men's Clothing Store

42. Which of the following characteristics is typical of the industrial sector of the organizational market?
    a. more money spent on personal selling than advertising
    b. geographical dispersion of members
    c. large number of buyers
    d. purchases made for resale, not production use
    e. providing a public benefit is primary motivation

43. Which of the following is typical of the trends which have been evident in the federal government market during the last several years?
    a. a requirement that each government agency create its own procurement regulations regardless of the red tape involved
    b. implementation of an executive order which requires that all vehicles owned by the federal government have some military usefulness in the event of war
    c. more purchases of off-the-shelf goods rather than special order merchandise
    d. development of unit-system costing techniques to reduce the cost of particular government operations
    e. allocation of resources to departments which have shown the greatest ability to spend their budget allotment

44. Which of the following firms would be a member of the industrial segment of the organizational market?
    a. Bloomingdale's, the well-known department store chain
    b. National Switch and Signal Company, makers of railroad signaling equipment
    c. the Delgado Museum of Art, an endowed public institution
    d. the Training and Development Command of the U.S. Army
    e. the University of Arkansas at Fayetteville

45. When a firm is trying to move a potential customer from a straight rebuy situation to a modified rebuy posture by correctly assessing the factors that would make buyers reconsider their decisions, it is an example of
    a. gatekeeping.
    b. purchase agency.
    c. sales management.
    d. competition.
    e. engineering management.

46. A good definition of the organizational market should include
    a. recognition that nonprofit organizations are not members.
    b. mention of retailers, producers, and wholesalers.
    c. selection of organizational segments prior to production.
    d. a set of guidelines for those who are allowed to join.
    e. a managerial philosophy oriented toward heavy industry.

47. A company is seeking a supplier for a new type of gasket to be installed on the self-launching lifeboats now required to be carried on all U.S. flagships. The whole concept of the self-launching lifeboat is new. The purchasing process would most likely be
    a. a modified rebuy.
    b. a straight rebuy.
    c. a relative standard.
    d. a new-task buy.
    e. an experimental purchase.

48. Which of the following would be an example of a member of the trade industries?
    a. the Texas Highway Patrol
    b. Lumber Products Company (wood products wholesale and retail)
    c. National Metal Stamping Co. (produces steel parts)
    d. Memorial Stadium (a football stadium)
    e. the Missouri School of Mines (an engineering school)

49. In which of the segments of the organizational market is the average number of employees per organization the greatest?
    a. government—federal, state, and local
    b. trade industries
    c. industrial producers
    d. institutions
    e. agricultural production

50. A substantial majority of shipments of manufactured goods from plants with 20 or more employees is accounted for by relatively few states. Which of the following correctly states the facts?
    a. 57 percent from 21 states
    b. 73 percent from 14 states
    c. 91 percent from 12 states
    d. 66 percent from 19 states
    e. 77 percent from 24 states

Name _____   Instructor _____

Section _____   Date _____

Applying Marketing Concepts

George Herrin, director of marketing for Commercial Laundry Equipment Company, was pondering two reports which had just arrived in his office. Both were somewhat disturbing because they told him that his firm had lost sales to competition for reasons he considered less than fair. In the first instance, Commercial had lost out on a contract to supply transmissions to Longley Washer Company because Longley had decided to buy from Western Gear Corporation. Mr. Herrin felt that the decision had been based not on the quality of Western's product, but on the fact that Western owned General Sales, Ltd., the big operator of laundromats that bought all its coin-operated washing machines from Longley. In the second case, it appeared as though Commercial had lost out on a U.S. Navy contract for stainless steel spinner tubs to a German firm because the Germans could supply the needed parts at a lower price. The Navy ignored Commercial's arguments that the German product would cost substantially more in the long run because of heat treatment inferior to that of Commercial's product.

____ 1.   In all likelihood, Commercial Laundry Equipment had to supply a written sales proposal for the Navy contract.

____ 2.   These two episodes involved purchases by members of the industrial and government segments of the organizational market.

3.   The case of Longley favoring Western Gear over Commercial was most likely caused by
   a.   bribery.
   b.   reciprocity.
   c.   derived demand.
   d.   threats of force or violence.

4.   The Standard Industry Classification code for Longley Washer Company would lie between
   a.   01-09; agriculture, forestry, and fishing.
   b.   10-14; mining.
   c.   20-39; manufacturing.
   d.   40-49; transportation and other public utilities.
   e.   70-89; services.

5.   The main reason Commercial lost the Navy contract was because
   a.   its price was too high.
   b.   its product was of inferior quality.
   c.   the Navy thought it might be an uncertain source of supply.
   d.   it was unable to provide the needed service.
   e.   somebody got bribed.

6. Commercial might well have gotten the Navy contract if
   a. international politics hadn't tainted the decision.
   b. the German product hadn't been vastly superior in design.
   c. life-cycle costing had been used by the Navy.
   d. Western Gear hadn't interfered with the sale.

Until its recent acquisition by Chrysler Corporation, American Motors Corporation occupied a unique place in the U.S. automotive market. Though it was not widely publicized by American Motors (or by anybody else, for that matter), it was quite possible that a given American Motors product might have an engine built by General Motors, a transmission from Chrysler, any of a variety of rear axles, and electrical and mechanical components from any or all of the other American auto manufacturers.

7. If demand for American Motors products declined in the consumer market, demand for General Motors engines would also decline. This is a case of
   a. derived demand.
   b. joint demand.
   c. reciprocity.
   d. supply variability.

8. In deciding to buy engines, transmissions, and mechanical parts from outside suppliers rather than make them themselves, and in choosing the sources from which those parts would be bought, the American Motors people probably based their decision on
   a. value analysis.
   b. vendor analysis.
   c. a combination of value analysis and vendor analysis.
   d. their desire to be innovative and to be leaders in domestic automotive engineering.

9. Suppose that the management of American Motors had decided that a two-month inventory of parts was not enough to have on hand to assure that production would continue in the event of a curtailment of the availability of transmissions, and had increased its stock-on-hand to four-months' worth. This would have been an example of
   a. demand variability.
   b. conservative thinking.
   c. an inventory adjustment.
   d. derived demand.

10. The Standard Industry Classification for American Motors would lie between
    a. 01-09; agriculture, forestry, fisheries.
    b. 10-14; mining.
    c. 20-39; manufacturing.
    d. 40-49; transportation and other public utilities.
    e. 70-89; services.

Name_____   Instructor _____

Section _____   Date _____

Questions for Thought

The questions which follow are designed to help you become familiar with the main concepts in this chapter through interpretation in your own words. They are meant to be answered in a few sentences or a paragraph at most.

1. Define and discuss the major components of the organizational market.

2. Discuss the nature and importance of the industrial market in some detail, giving examples where appropriate.

3. Industrial market demand possesses several unusual characteristics when compared with the consumer market. Discuss these.

4. How does organizations' buying behavior differ from individuals' buying behavior?

5. Buying centers are important to organizations. How does one recognize a buying center and what sort of roles do their participants play?

6. How do government markets differ from other organizational markets and how are they the same?

Name _____   Instructor _____

Section _____   Date _____

Experiential Exercises

1. The purpose of this exercise is to help you understand the complexity of the industrial buying process. The fiberglass utility pole example discussed in Chapter 6 of your text is used as the basis for this example.

    a. List in the table below the members of the utility who were involved in the decision to purchase the fiberglass utility pole.

    b. Using a scale of 1 (not at all influential) to 10 (very influential), rate the participants in the buying process as to how much influence each had in making the decision to purchase the fiberglass pole offered by supplier B. Record your answer in the table.

    c. What factors do you think were most important to each of these people in deciding about the utility pole? Were they

        Durability?
        Cost?
        Dependability of the supplier?
        Something else?

Name or Title of Influential Member	Relative Influence (Scale: 1 to 10)	Factors This Person Considered Most Important
1.		
2.		
3.		
4.		

d. In view of the purchase process described, what marketing mix strategy would you recommend to a firm selling fiberglass utility poles?

2. The purpose of this exercise is to familiarize you with the marketing of goods to the government. Visit the office of a government agency located near your campus. You may select from among federal, state, or local organizations. Some agencies whose offices might be convenient for you to visit could include the local school district, your local police or sheriff's department, or city, county, or state administrative offices. Once you have made an appointment to visit, tell your contact person that you'd like to know how that organization buys its equipment and supplies.

a. Ask about the methods the organization uses to purchase. Is it the job of an individual, a committee, or a higher agency? Record the information below.

b. Ask about the process of requesting bids and getting contracts. Are there any special rules that apply to this agency? Record the response below.

c. Ask about the "bid list." Does the agency have one and how is it used, if at all? Record the response below.

Name_____   Instructor _____

Section _____   Date _____

Computer Applications

Review the discussion of the expected net profit (ENP) concept in Chapter 6 of the text. Then use menu item 7 titled "Competitive Bidding" to solve each of the following problems.

1. Melvil Dewey, manager of Smith and Jones, a manufacturer of industrial goods, is considering offering a certain product to a local buyer at one of two possible prices. Alternative A is $35,000 and Alternative B is $38,000. Dewey believes that there is a 60 percent chance of the customer buying the item at the lower price, but only a 40 percent chance that the good will be bought at the higher price. Cost of the product to Smith and Jones is $30,000. What should Mr. Dewey do in this case?

2. Allison Industrial, Inc., of Tulsa, Oklahoma, has spent $500 million developing a new shale oil extraction pump. The company expects eventually to sell 2,500 of these units, but knows that the market could evaporate if the leading firm in the targeted segment does not buy the pump. One of the company's executives has proposed a price of $650,000 for each unit, while another has suggested that $720,000 would be more appropriate. The marketing research department has assigned a 30 percent probability to the likelihood of the lead customer buying at the higher price and a 70 percent probability to the likelihood of purchase at the lower price. What should Allison Industrial do in this situation?

3. Cemented Armor Corporation has finally perfected its newest product, the ultimate in light-weight military armor plate. The problem now is to convince the right Pentagon officials of the product's superiority. Cemented Armor estimates that if its product is bought by the military, it will ultimately become part of 1,000 of the new M-89 battle tanks soon to be produced. The cost to the company of the armor's installation is $120 million. Management is considering two possible bids to submit for this armor: $280,000 and $320,000 per tank. The executive board thinks that the probability of the Army accepting the first price is 65 percent, while the probability of its accepting the higher price is 35 percent. Use the ENP formula to determine which of the prices Cemented Armor should bid.

4. Kawakatsu Export Company would like to penetrate the U.S. market with its line of mini-tractors. Developed primarily for use in truck gardens, the K-10 and K-15 units cost the company $1,000 and $1,500, respectively, when delivered in the U.S. Hideki Takata, Kawa-katsu's "man in Los Angeles," has been authorized to negotiate any price above $1,300 for the model K-10 and anything above $1,800 for the K-15. Takata will receive a sales commission of one-third of the difference between the sales price of each tractor and its cost. Takata has assessed the probability of making a sale at each of several alternative prices. He'd very much like to sell at least one unit before the month's end and thinks that the best way to go about it would be to make a proposal on a single unit at a reasonable price. His list of prices and probabilities of sale is:

Price	Probability of Sale
$1,650 for a K-10	30 percent
$2,100 for a K-15	35 percent
$1,750 for a K-10	15 percent
$2,250 for a K-15	25 percent
$1,850 for a K-10	5 percent
$2,400 for a K-15	15 percent

What model and price should Takata propose to the contractor?

Chapter 6 Solutions

Key Concepts

1. n	5. o	9. i	13. b
2. e	6. m	10. c	14. d
3. a	7. f	11. k	15. h
4. j	8. g	12. l	

Self Quiz

1. F	11. T	21. T	31. c	41. c
2. T	12. F	22. T	32. d	42. a
3. F	13. F	23. F	33. e	43. c
4. T	14. F	24. T	34. c	44. b
5. T	15. F	25. T	35. a	45. d
6. F	16. T	26. b	36. c	46. b
7. T	17. T	27. a	37. a	47. d
8. F	18. T	28. b	38. b	48. b
9. T	19. F	29. c	39. c	49. a
10. T	20. F	30. d	40. c	50. b

Applying Marketing Concepts

1. T	6. c
2. T	7. b
3. b	8. c
4. c	9. c
5. a	10. c

Chapter 7

Market Segmentation

Chapter Summary

Markets consist of people and organizations with the necessary purchasing power, willingness, and authority to buy. Goods may be classified according to the intentions of the buyer. Thus, consumer goods are goods bought by consumers for personal use, while industrial goods are products purchased for use directly or indirectly in the production of other goods and services.

Market segmentation is the process of dividing the total market into groups whose members possess a sufficient number of shared characteristics to differentiate them from members of other groups. Such groups are said to be homogeneous. It is then possible to target products to specific groups. In the consumer area, the usual bases for segmentation are geography, demography, psychography, and the benefits offered by the product or service. Geographic segmentation involves subdividing the market into homogeneous groups on the basis of where the population is located. Segmenting demographically breaks down the overall population into groups based on such factors as age, sex, religious preference, and level of income. Psychographic segmentation uses the behavioral characteristics arising out of a group's activities, opinions, interests, and life-styles to identify shared characteristics. Finally, benefits segmentation offers potential for being the most powerful consumer market segmentation tool of all because it identifies market segments based on the perceived benefits consumers expect to receive from the purchase of a product or service. Industrial markets are usually segmented geographically (especially for concentrated industries), by the types of products bought, or on the basis of the end uses for which products are purchased by industrial buyers.

The actual process of segmentation requires several steps, carefully carried out. First, a determination of the bases on which the segmentation is to be undertaken must be made; then, user profiles must be drawn for the selected market segments; an assessment of the overall potential for the chosen segments must be compiled; estimation of market share and the cost versus benefits of entering each segment based on existing competition and the selected marketing mix must be prepared; and finally, a segment or segments must be selected to become the firm's target market. These five steps are often facilitated by using a tool called *target market decision analysis*. This tool involves developing a grid which names the various possible target market segments and isolates their distinguishing characteristics. Any basis for market segmentation may be used in target market decision analysis, and the tool is appropriate for both consumer and industrial markets.

Name _____   Instructor _____

Section _____   Date _____

Key Concepts

The purpose of this section is to allow you to determine if you can match key concepts with the definitions of the concepts. It is essential that you know the definitions of the concepts prior to applying the concepts in later exercises in this chapter.

From the list of lettered terms, select the one that best fits each of the numbered statements below. Write the letter of that choice in the space provided.

Key Terms

a. market
b. consumer goods
c. industrial goods
d. market segmentation
e. geographic segmentation
f. Consolidated Metropolitan
    Statistical Area (CMSA)
g. Primary Metropolitan
    Statistical Area (PMSA)
h. Metropolitan Statistical
    Area (MSA)

i. demographic segmentation
j. family life cycle
k. Engel's laws
l. life-style
m. psychographic segmentation
n. AIO statements
o. benefit segmentation
p. product segmentation
q. end-use application segment
r. target market decision analysis

_____ 1. Dividing a population into homogeneous groups based on behavioral and life-style profiles developed by analyzing consumer activities, opinions, and interests.

_____ 2. Process of family formulation and dissolution that includes five major stages: young single, young married without children, other young, middle age, and older.

_____ 3. Major urban area within a CMSA.

_____ 4. Three general statements on spending behavior: as a family's income increases, a smaller percentage goes for food; the percentage spent on housing, household operations, and clothing remains constant; and the percentage spent on other items increases.

_____ 5. Evaluation of potential market segments by dividing the overall market into homogeneous groups using cross-classifications which may be based on variables such as type of market, geographic location, frequency of use, or demographic characteristics.

_____ 6. Dividing an industrial market into homogeneous groups on the basis of product specifications identified by industrial buyers.

_____ 7. Products purchased by the ultimate consumer for personal use.

___ 8. Process of dividing the total market into several relatively homogeneous groups with similar product or service interests based on such factors as demographic or psychographic characteristics, geographic location, or perceived product benefits.

___ 9. The way people decide to live their lives, including family, job, social activities, and consumer decisions.

___ 10. Products purchased for use directly or indirectly in the production of other goods and services.

___ 11. A group of people who possess purchasing power and the authority and willingness to purchase.

___ 12. Dividing an industrial market into homogeneous groups on the basis of how different industrial purchasers will use the product.

___ 13. Major population concentration, including the 25 or so urban giants.

___ 14. Collection of statements in a psychographic study to reflect activities, interests, and opinions of respondents.

___ 15. Dividing a population into homogeneous groups based on characteristics such as age, sex, and income level.

___ 16. Dividing a population into homogeneous segments on the basis of location.

___ 17. Dividing a population into homogeneous segments on the basis of benefits consumers expect to receive from a product or service.

___ 18. Large, freestanding urban area for which detailed marketing-related data are collected by the Bureau of the Census.

Name _____   Instructor _____

Section _____   Date _____

Self Quiz

You should use these objective questions to test your understanding of the chapter material. You can check your answers with those provided at the end of the chapter.

While these questions cover most of the chapter topics, they are not intended to be the same as the test questions your instructor may use in an examination. A good understanding of all aspects of the course material is essential to good performance on any examination.

True/False

Write "T" for True or "F" for False for each of the following statements.

____ 1. *Commercial goods* is a term some marketers use to identify industrial goods not directly used in producing other goods.

____ 2. It is always possible to segment a market; some are just more difficult to segment than others.

____ 3. A market requires only people or institutions; there are no additional requirements.

____ 4. Light bulbs sold to lamp manufacturers are industrial goods. Light bulbs sold to consumers to replace ones in their home fixtures are consumer goods.

____ 5. To determine the number of people who are in the automobile market, you would count people who want to buy a car and have the purchasing power to do so.

____ 6. The 25 largest metropolitan areas in the country account for about one-half of the country's population.

____ 7. Automobile tires are classed as consumer goods, not industrial goods.

____ 8. Population is growing more rapidly in the midwest than in any other part of the country, according to the most recent census.

____ 9. Moorhead, Minnesota would be an example of a Primary Metropolitan Statistical Area.

____ 10. Market segmentation is the process of dividing the market into several homogeneous groups.

____ 11. Geographic market segmentation of consumers is useful when tastes vary among regions.

____ 12. The role of market segmentation is to allow marketers to design one marketing mix that will satisfy all customers of a product.

____ 13. One of the reasons demographic variables are used in market segmentation is because they are easy to identify and measure.

____ 14. Industrial markets may be segmented geographically, by types of products used and uses to which products are put.

____ 15. The most common approach to market segmentation in the consumer market is benefits segmentation.

____ 16. It is a violation of the Equal Rights Act to segment a consumer market on the basis of race, color, nationality, religion, sex, or age.

____ 17. A firm that uses market segmentation assumes that different types of customers can best be served with different marketing mixes.

____ 18. The proportion of elderly persons in the population is increasing and it is estimated that by the year 2030 persons over the age of 65 will account for 20 percent of the population.

____ 19. In terms of the family life cycle, young marrieds with small children tend to be early purchasers of new fashion items and are recreation oriented.

____ 20. Women who live alone spend less than half as much on medical services, prescription drugs, and health insurance than do men living alone.

____ 21. Benefit segmentation of the toothpaste market might produce segments concerned with price, tooth decay, taste, or brightness.

____ 22. Over one-third of all Americans move every year.

____ 23. Firms which use target market decision analysis ignore the differences in needs and wants among market segments.

____ 24. As defined by the President's Commission on Americans Outdoors, "get-away actives" use outdoor recreation as a chance to be alone and experience nature.

____ 25. Segments which have been identified by psychographic analysis can be expected to behave differently from each other.

Multiple Choice

Circle the letter of the word or phrase that best completes the sentence or best answers the question.

26. Markets require people, a willingness to buy, and
    a. engineering personnel.
    b. purchasing agents.
    c. purchasing power.
    d. authority to buy.
    e. only c and d above.

27. The major difference between consumer and industrial markets is
    a. the size of the average purchase.
    b. the reasons for which purchases are made.
    c. the types of goods which are bought.
    d. the educational levels of the buyers.
    e. the length of time spent in negotiation.

28. A basic reason why marketers elect to segment markets is
    a. that it simplifies their decision making enormously.
    b. that they need some means of simplifying the task of finding buyers for their products.
    c. that the world is too large and filled with too many diverse people and firms for any one marketing mix to satisfy everyone.
    d. so that when the production line goes into operation, it can turn out the millions of items necessary to secure economies of scale.
    e. so that competition will find it difficult to determine what is going to happen next.

29. Under which of the following conditions may it be impossible to segment the market?
    a. It is possible to measure the market in terms of both purchasing power and size.
    b. It appears feasible to promote to the market segment.
    c. The various segments of the market seem large enough to be adequately profitable.
    d. There are no apparent problems in providing the segments of the market with adequate service.
    e. The number of segments in the market is greater than the capacity of the firm to serve them.

30. Which of the following is one of the major population shifts of the last two decades?
    a. to the north from the south and southwest
    b. from interior states to states with a seacoast
    c. from the northeast to the north central and midwest areas
    d. to the plains states from the west coast
    e. from the southern U.S. to Canada

31. At the present time, the proportion of the population which can be expected to move in any given year is about
    a. one-fourth.
    b. one-fifth.
    c. one-sixth.
    d. one-seventh.
    e. one-eighth.

32. A freestanding urban area with an urban center population of 50,000 which exhibits social and economic homogeneity and has a total population of 100,000 or more would be defined by the U.S. government as a(n)
    a. PMSA.
    b. MSA.
    c. CMSA.
    d. SSMA.
    e. OGPU.

33. Which of the following is a demographic variable?
    a.   an individual's musical preference
    b.   the attitude one has toward conservative government
    c.   the rate at which one uses a particular product
    d.   one's occupation, craft, or trade
    e.   an individual's aspirations for the future

34. Which of the following is an example of market segmentation?
    a.   An appeal is developed which hopefully will reach all consumers, regardless of income.
    b.   Residents of urban areas and residents of rural areas are approached with exactly the same marketing mix.
    c.   An automobile company separates its markets into economy buyers and luxury buyers.
    d.   A firm markets its products to all residents of the U.S. with the same single-product marketing mix.
    e.   General Foods considers all residents of the United States members of its market.

35. The most notable current trend in the U.S. population is the
    a.   "coming of age of America," as the new baby boomers of the Sixties reach their adulthood and become productive members of society.
    b.   "maturing of America," as the people in the 50 to 65 year-old age group become a majority of the population.
    c.   "graying of America," as the 76 million people now 25 to 44 years old move on into later-middle and old age.
    d.   "stagnation of America," as the birth rate approaches zero and population begins actually to decline.
    e.   "rejuvenation of America," as the rate of new family formation and birth rate increase.

36. A market segment based on the family life cycle concept includes
    a.   the high-income segment.
    b.   heavy users of full-sized cars.
    c.   swingers.
    d.   residents of large eastern metropolitan areas.
    e.   middle-aged married persons without children.

37. According to Engel's Laws, an increase in family income should bring
    a.   fewer dollars expended for food.
    b.   fewer dollars expended for housing.
    c.   fewer dollars expended for education and recreation.
    d.   a higher percentage of income spent for housing.
    e.   a lower percentage of income spent for food.

38. This group, which according to the President's Commission on Americans Outdoors comprises about ten percent of all adults, participates in outdoor activities mainly to keep fit. It is called the
    a.   excitement-seeking competitives.
    b.   get-away actives.
    c.   health-conscious sociables.
    d.   fitness-driven.
    e.   unstressed and unmotivated.

39. If you had to draw a psychographic profile of the typical owner of a Mercedes-Benz auto-mobile, the person described would be
    a. someone who likes to feel in control of his/her life and his/her vehicle and prefers muted shades of tan, gray, or silver.
    b. someone who demands performance over luxury and prefers red as the color for his/her vehicle.
    c. someone who is personally rather austere and has a taste for elegance and darker colors.
    d. someone who desires comfort, wants to be chauffeured, and is concerned about the impression his/her car makes on others; color and mechanical features are unimportant.
    e. someone with a high level of income, of upper-middle age, and possessing a professional or technical education.

40. Marketers who want to aim their marketing mix at the segment of the population who are single people living with members of the opposite sex are interested in the government's classification of
    a. MSAs.
    b. SSWDs.
    c. CMSAs.
    d. empty-nesters.
    e. POSLSQs.

41. If you were to segment a market into categories such as "don't wants," "weight-conscious," "moderates," and "hedonists," you would be using
    a. geographic segmentation.
    b. demographic segmentation.
    c. benefit segmentation.
    d. psychographic segmentation.
    e. heavy-user segmentation.

42. Melrose Specialty Company designs and markets to wholesalers of fruits and vegetables a special package of computer software specifically designed to help these firms keep inventory at the peak of condition at all times. Melrose has applied
    a. geographic segmentation.
    b. end-use segmentation.
    c. product segmentation.
    d. marginal segmentation.
    e. demographic segmentation.

43. The stage of the segmentation process which involves describing the life-style patterns, attitudes toward product attributes and brands, brand preferences, product-use habits, and similar characteristics of typical members of each segment is called
    a. developing relevant profiles for each segment.
    b. forecasting market potentials.
    c. selecting specific market segments.
    d. forecasting probable market share.
    e. selecting market segmentation bases.

44. It would be normal to segment an industrial market on the basis of
    a. customers' hours of operation.
    b. customers' names.
    c. purchasing agents' age.
    d. uses to which customers put your products.
    e. customers' nearness to good beaches.

45. Which of the following is an appropriate example of the indicated type of market segment?
    a. geographic—people living within 1 1/2 miles of a particular shopping center
    b. psychographic—young marrieds with children
    c. demographic—people looking for the lowest-cost watch
    d. benefits segmented—people interested in sports events
    e. demographic—people with a positive attitude toward education

46. The Holt Caterpillar Tractor Company was originally very successful because it developed models of its basic tractor specifically adapted to farming, road-building, earth-moving, and military uses. It applied which of the following types of segmentation?
    a. product
    b. end-use
    c. perceived benefits
    d. geographic
    e. melodramatic

47. Target market decision analysis
    a. is useful only after market segments have been identified.
    b. is restricted to geographic segmentation.
    c. is a tool used to develop market segments with distinguishing characteristics.
    d. can be used for consumer markets but is too expensive to be used for industrial markets.
    e. is generally done with just one population characteristic, such as age.

48. The states expected to gain the greatest number of residents by the year 2000 are
    a. California, Florida, Texas, and Arizona.
    b. California, Oregon, Washington, and Nevada.
    c. Florida, Georgia, Alabama, and South Carolina.
    d. Mississippi, Louisiana, Arkansas, and Texas.
    e. Montana, Wyoming, and North and South Dakota.

49. When a manufacturer creates a product such as Chevrolet's "Beau Jacques" pickup truck (which was sold in Louisiana some years ago; the same truck was sold in surrounding states as the "Gentleman Jim" model), it is using
    a. benefits segmentation.
    b. psychographic segmentation.
    c. end-use segmentation
    d. geographical segmentation.
    e. arbitrary segmentation.

50. Which of the following would be more likely to be a basis for segmenting the industrial, rather than the consumer, market?
    a. behavioral profiles of people
    b. age, sex, and other demographic characteristics of people
    c. benefits desired by people
    d. location of dense populations of people
    e. the intended use of the product

Name_____   Instructor _____

Section _____   Date _____

Applying Marketing Concepts

The Wolverine Manufacturing Company has developed a line of disposable work clothing. The clothing can be sold profitably for about half the price charged for conventional garments. The items are durable enough to withstand several washings if desired, but can be easily disposed of simply by treating them with a special chemical solution. Large manufacturing companies are expected to be a major market for these clothes, with people in the firms' procurement departments expected to have the authority and purchasing power to buy. The company expects the most interest in its products to come from firms in heavy manufacturing, where the rigors of the production line destroy clothes at a rapid rate. Executives at Wolverine also foresee a market for their product among individuals who like to undertake do-it-yourself projects but don't like to have old, oily, scruffy work clothes lying around the house.

____ 1.   By definition, the real market for disposable clothing is factory production-line workers.

____ 2.   According to Engel's Laws, the percent of income spent on clothing stays the same over all levels of consumer income.

____ 3.   Products sold to people who want to use them for their do-it-yourself projects would be classed as commercial goods.

4.   The Wolverine Manufacturing Company is selling disposable clothing as
     a.   industrial goods.
     b.   consumer goods.
     c.   both industrial and consumer goods.

5.   The segmentation method most appropriate to Wolverine's attempt to reach the industrial market is probably
     a.   geographical.
     b.   end use.
     c.   product.
     d.   psychographic.

6.   If benefit segmentation is used by Wolverine, it should direct its efforts toward people who want
     a.   durability.
     b.   high fashion.
     c.   convenience in use.
     d.   lowest-cost clothes.

7. By selecting heavy production-line manufacturing as a main target market for its disposable work clothing, Wolverine has
   a. automatically limited itself geographically to those places where that kind of industry exists.
   b. made it more difficult to segment the market on a geographical basis. Heavy industry is more or less uniformly distributed throughout the country.
   c. placed no limitations on itself from the point of view of market segmentation.
   d. restricted itself to only that market for the foreseeable future.

On a trip to Central City Park one day, you notice that the people in the park seem to fall into several different categories based on the kinds of things they are doing and the way they're doing them. Some folks seem to be having a great time playing volleyball. They really work hard at it, and each point is well fought and hard won. Others are using the park by jogging the perimeter paths; a surprising number of these people seem to be women. A third group is having a barbecue. The traditional hamburgers and hot dogs are in evidence, but so are a lot of salad greens and diet root beer. The thrust of this gathering seems to be the outdoor air and pleasant conversation.

8. Your excursion through the park has shown you three different groups of park users (excluding yourself). How would you characterize your analysis of them, assuming it to be correct?
   a. demographic
   b. geographical
   c. psychographic
   d. benefits segmentation

9. The people who are having the barbecue would probably be classed as
   a. excitement-seeking competitives.
   b. fitness-driven.
   c. unstressed and unmotivated.
   d. health-conscious sociables.

10. Which class of the President's Commission on Americans Outdoors would the volleyballers fall into?
    a. get-away actives
    b. excitement-seeking competitives
    c. fitness driven
    d. health-conscious sociables

Name_____   Instructor _____

Section _____   Date _____

Questions for Thought

The questions which follow are designed to help you become familiar with the main concepts in this chapter through interpretation in your own words. They are meant to be answered in a few sentences or a paragraph at most.

1. When one speaks of a market, what does one really mean?

2. How is market segmentation used in the development of a marketing strategy?

3. Describe the four bases for segmenting consumer markets and contrast them with the bases for segmenting industrial markets.

4. Outline the process by which market segmentation should be done.

5. Explain how target market decision analysis can be used in segmenting markets.

Name_____   Instructor _____

Section _____   Date _____

Experiential Exercises

1. The purpose of this exercise is to help you understand the importance of market segmentation studies in isolating and evaluating markets. You will apply the four types of segmentation (geographic, demographic, psychographic, and benefits) to an existing retail store in your hometown or in the town where your college or university is located. Make sure you know each of the four types of segmentation before starting this exercise. Select a store with which you are familiar.

    a. Indicate the type of retail outlet you have chosen. (Examples: restaurant, supermarket, clothing store, discount house, home entertainment outlet, et cetera.)

    b. How far from the store do you think most of the patrons live?

    c. What are the demographic characteristics of the people you see shopping in the store?

    Age?

    Sex?

    Family life cycle status?

    Education?

    Income?

d.   Do you think that the people who shop regularly at this store have a different psychographic profile from other residents of this city or town? Are there differences in

Activities, such as work or entertainment?

Interests, such as recreation or food?

Opinions about themselves or culture?

e.   How well do you feel the marketing mix of the store fits with the needs and wants of the regular patrons?

Price?

Promotion?

Product and service?

Distribution?

2.   The purpose of this exercise is to provide insight into the importance of population studies in marketing mix planning and in understanding future trends in the marketplace.

a.   Go to your college or university library and find the most recent *Sales and Marketing Management Magazine* "Survey of Consumer Buying Power." Look up the information for the county in which your hometown is located. You should be able to find total population, median age of the population, number of households, retail sales, and personal income figures for the area. Acquire the same data for the county in which your college or university is located. Using a common base (per capita = per unit of population is typical), compare the two locations. If your hometown is also your college town, use the town in which your school's biggest nonlocal rival is situated as the other location. How do the two places differ?

Total population?

Age distribution of the population?

Personal income (per capita)?

Retail sales?

Other sales?

b.   Discuss the factors which may lie at the root of these differences.

3. List three items you think most often appear for sale at garage (or yard or carport) sales when people are moving. What service, pricing method, or other marketing strategy can you create to provide these people with an alternative to the quick sale/lose money situation they seem usually to face? (Suggestion: a two-year sell-back policy on furniture and appliances, or monthly use of a parking lot for group sales.)

Yard Sale Item	Service, Pricing Method, Strategy
1.	
2.	
3.	

Name _____   Instructor _____

Section _____   Date _____

Computer Applications

Review the discussion of Engel's Laws in Chapter 7 of the text. Then use menu item 5 titled "Engel's Laws" to solve each of the following problems.

1. The Tyrrell and Richard families have just prepared their 1990 household budgets. Both families expect salary increases at the beginning of the year. The general categories of the families' budgets are shown below.

Budget Category	Tyrrell Family Budget 1989	1990	Richard Family Budget 1989	1990
Clothing	7%	7%	11%	15%
Housing	34%	34%	25%	25%
Food	24%	26%	18%	17%
Other	35%	33%	46%	43%

Do either of these two budgets conflict with Engel's Laws? If so, how?

2. Ivgeny Yaroslavl is a professional dancer. Since his defection from the National Ballet Company of Turkestan he has established a fine reputation for himself in the United States. His agent has just negotiated contracts for 1990 that should boost his income to $300,000, up from the $200,000 he made in 1989. His CPA has also developed a personal budget that reflects his expected income increase in 1990.

Budget Category	1989 Expenses	1990 Expenses
Clothing	$13,200	$ 19,000
Food	$22,000	$ 28,000
Entertainment	$20,000	$ 30,000
Travel	$ 6,000	$ 9,000
Housing	$34,000	$ 40,000
Professional Fees	$20,000	$ 30,000
Taxes	$60,000	$100,000
Savings and Investments	$24,800	$ 44,000

After subtracting taxes and the agent's fees from Yaroslavl's gross income to determine net income for 1989 and 1990, determine whether the CPA's proposed budget coincides with Engel's Laws.

3. Rob and Rosalie Lakey recently consulted their financial advisor to assist them in planning their 1990 spending plans. The advisor, observing that Rosalie's plans to return to full-time employment will increase the family's income by 20 percent in the upcoming year, told the couple they could afford to increase their clothing expenditures by 30 percent as long as increases in their food spending were held to 15 percent. The advisor also suggested that the couple purchase a new home. Though their monthly housing costs would rise by 20 percent, most of the increase would be tax deductible as an interest expense.

Do the financial advisor's suggestions about clothing, food, and housing conflict with Engel's Laws?

Chapter 7 Solutions

Key Concepts

1. m	5. r	9. l	13. f	17. o
2. j	6. p	10. c	14. n	18. h
3. g	7. b	11. a	15. i	
4. k	8. d	12. q	16. e	

Self Quiz

1. T	11. T	21. T	31. c	41. d
2. F	12. F	22. F	32. b	42. b
3. F	13. T	23. F	33. d	43. a
4. T	14. T	24. T	34. c	44. d
5. T	15. F	25. T	35. c	45. a
6. T	16. F	26. e	36. e	46. b
7. F	17. T	27. b	37. e	47. c
8. F	18. T	28. c	38. d	48. a
9. F	19. F	29. e	39. a	49. d
10. T	20. F	30. b	40. e	50. e

Applying Marketing Concepts

1. F	5. c	9. d
2. T	6. a	10. b
3. c	7. F	
4. a	8. c	

Part Three Puzzle

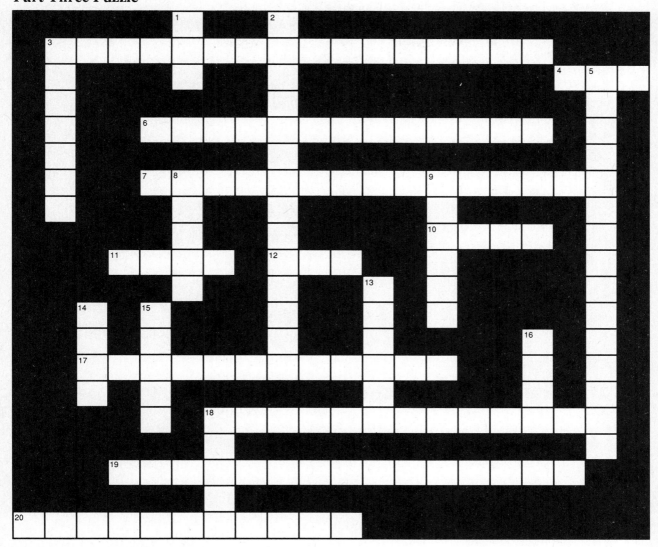

ACROSS CLUES

3. acts of individuals in getting, using, and disposing of goods and services
4. numerical system that subdivides the industrial marketplace into detailed market segments
6. products purchased by the ultimate consumer for personal use
7. retailers and wholesalers who purchase goods for resale to others
10. psychologist who documented the phenomenon that illustrates the effect of reference groups on us
11. lack of something useful; difference between desired and actual states
12. statements used in a psychographic study to reflect attitudes, interests, opinions
17. dividing the whole market into homogeneous groups with similar product or service interests
18. demand for an industrial product that is linked to demand for a consumer good
19. process of family formation and dissolution including five major stages
20. demand for an industrial good related to demand for another industrial good it complements

DOWN CLUES

1. any object which determines the nature of the response to a drive
2. individuals and firms that buy goods and services to produce other goods and services
3. complex of values, ideas, etc., that helps people to function together as members of society
5. products purchased for use in the production of other goods for resale
8. behavior that members of a group expect of individuals who hold a position within the group
9. relative position of any individual in a group
13. inner state that directs a person toward the goal of satisfying a felt need
14. major population concentration, including the 25 or so urban giants
15. proposed statements on spending behavior related to changes in family income
16. major urban area within a CMSA
18. strong stimulus that impels action

Name_____   Instructor _____

Section _____   Date _____

Cases for Part 3

1. *Warrior Chemical Company*

Warrior Chemical Company has developed a new formulation of household cleaning compound which offers a significant improvement in ease of use and cleaning power over products previously available. Its immediate problem is to decide on an appropriate target market so as to maximize profits. The company has been able to acquire a substantial amount of information to aid in making the decision.

The two variables usually used by firms selling this sort of product are income and stage of family life cycle. The levels of income used are low (up to $29,999 annual income), medium ($30,000 to $60,000 annual income), and high (more than $60,000 annual income). The stages of the family life cycle usually considered are the bachelor, newly married, full nest, empty nest, and solitary survivor.

Four other firms sell products which could be considered similar to Warrior's new formulation. A sample of the members of each of the income/life-cycle segments was selected and each member of the sample was asked to try Warrior's product and the four competitive products. These people were then asked to express their preference for the five products by ranking the most preferred as 1 and so on. The average rank assigned to WarChem (the interim name assigned to the Warrior product) is shown in Table P3-1.

Table P3-1: Relative Preference for WarChem

	Family Life-Cycle Stage				
Income	Bachelor	Newlywed	Full Nest	Empty Nest	Solitary
Low	5	5	5	5	5
Medium	3	4	2	3	3
High	1	2	3	4	5

The estimated total unit sales for WarChem's competitors for last year are shown in Table P3-2.

Table P3-2: Last Year's Sales (in Thousands of Units) for Four Competitive Products

	Family Life-Cycle Stage				
Income	Bachelor	Newlywed	Full Nest	Empty Nest	Solitary
Low	10,000	8,000	20,000	10,000	2,000
Medium	14,000	12,000	16,000	14,000	10,000
High	6,000	6,000	10,000	12,000	6,000

Finally, the company has estimated the costs of producing one million gallons of WarChem and marketing it to each segment. The selling price has been set at $4.50 per gallon. The cost breakdown is shown in Table P3-3.

Table P3-3: Production and Distribution Costs for Each Segment (in Millions of Dollars)

	Family Life-Cycle Stage				
Income	Bachelor	Newlywed	Full Nest	Empty Nest	Solitary
Low	$1.2	$1.0	$2.0	$0.8	$1.0
Medium	0.8	1.0	2.2	0.7	1.2
High	0.9	1.0	2.5	0.6	1.5

Questions

a.   Given this information, which target market should the firm choose?

b.   What additional information do you feel is necessary to make this target market decision?

c.   It may be difficult to actually get the data in quantitative form as presented in these three tables. Which information would be the most difficult to gather? The easiest?

2.   *Middlebrook Homes, Inc.*

Middlebrook Homes, Inc., is in the process of subdividing a tract of land in western Georgia. Although the area is essentially rural in nature, it is located within ten miles of a city of 100,000 and within 60 miles of Atlanta. The company desires to focus in on a target market but is unsure of the consumer characteristics to use in its segmentation.

Middlebrook has hired a newspaper-clipping firm to provide information about recent advertising by other property developers. Typical headlines taken from recent ads for similar single-family, detached-dwelling developments read: "Country-Style Living with Every Modern Convenience," "The Home-Buying Opportunity of the Year FOR ONLY $2,500 DOWN!" and "Total Privacy and a Carefree Life-Style."

The decisions Middlebrook wants to make include the precise location of the dwellings within the subdivision; whether or not to include recreational features such as a golf course and swimming pool; whether or not to include a small shopping center in its development plans; the size of homes (in square feet) to build; and what sorts of exterior design plans to adopt for the homes it will build.

Question

What characteristics do you think Middlebrook Homes should use when determining the target market?

3.   *John Huddleston, Househusband*

John Huddleston was beginning to wonder if he had truly become a househusband. Though fully employed, the nature of his work (he was a sales engineer for a manufacturer of milling machines in an area of the country densely covered by factories) was such that, unless an emergency occurred, he could schedule his calls at his own convenience. His wife, who was a commodities broker for a large, Chicago-based commodity trading house, had to be in the office when the Chicago Board of Trade opened at 8:00 AM, and usually couldn't get away until at least two hours after it closed at 2:00 PM. (The Chicago Board of Trade is the equivalent of the New York Stock Exchange for Commodities—trading in wheat, frozen orange juice, pork bellies, and the like.)

This put most of the household chores squarely back on John. It was he who woke the kids in the morning, made them breakfast, and drove them to school, his wife having long since left for work. He shopped at the supermarket between calls on customers, and if he had a slack day on his hands, often did laundry and cooked meals. When 3:00 in the afternoon rolled around, John picked up the kids at school, took them to Little League or soccer practice, and got dinner on the table before Susan, his wife, stumbled in the door.

In the evenings and on weekends, husband, wife, and kids pitched in and kept things on an even keel, Susan often cooking and freezing several days' worth of meals on an assembly line basis. Recently, however, there had been less emphasis on cooking and more on all of them having family fun together whenever possible. John was the first to admit, though somewhat sheepishly, that this had become possible because his cooking had become good enough to rival that of his wife.

Questions

a.   In what ways does John Huddleston's situation mirror the changes that have taken place in our society in the last 30 years?

b. Of what significance to marketers are scenarios such as the one represented by John and his role as consumer?

c. How have the changes evidenced in this case affected the segmentation process for consumer goods?

Name _____   Instructor _____

Section _____   Date _____

Creating a Marketing Plan: Who's Out There?

The information you will receive in this part will help you to complete Part I.C. of your marketing plan for Latebri Industries, Incorporated.

Episode Three

Having performed the appropriate rituals and filled out the proper forms, Latebri Industries was now duly and properly incorporated under the laws of the state in which it was domiciled. The officers of the corporation were Laura Claire, President; Brian Patrick, Executive Vice President for Systems Analysis; and Terrence O'Connor, Executive Vice President for Circuit Design and Repair. Having gotten themselves organized, the three partners decided they needed more information about the nature of the competitive environment if they were to reduce the risk of business failure. They accordingly turned to that standard research volume which the telephone company thoughtfully provides to all of us—but which few of us use to its logical extent—the *Yellow Pages*. Searching through the current *Yellow Page* listings for New Essex, their home city, they discovered 62 firms listed under "Computers—Service and Repair." A telephone survey of these 62 firms revealed that the telephones of 4 were no longer in service, 6 were actually located outside the New Essex metropolitan area, and 10 repaired only industrial mainframes and did not work on PCs. This left 42 firms remaining active in the market as direct competitors of Latebri.

The partners were aware, however, that a number of computer sales firms serviced computers. Accordingly, they checked their *Yellow Pages* once again, and determined that, of the 164 firms which survived the sort of culling process outlined above, 121 (75 percent) offered repair service, but only 102 (62 percent) serviced PCs, and only 29 (18 percent) repaired brands which they did not sell. When asked if they repaired peripherals (printers, modems), 120 (80 percent) responded in the affirmative. One hundred twenty-one (74 percent) of the firms offered service contracts to their customers.

Forty-one computer vendors (25 percent) indicated that they did not repair computers, and 24 of these indicated that they did not make any recommendations to their customers about where they should take their computers should they fail in service. None of the 42 service-only companies received a recommendation from more than two computer dealers.

The partners, who conducted the two surveys themselves, remarked to each other on an aspect of their work which the raw statistics didn't reveal. As Brian put it, "These computer store people don't seem to care about service work at all. In fact, one guy I called said he knew they *sold* computers, but he wasn't sure about repairing them."

Laura responded, "You know, I noticed that even when I was talking to the places that didn't sell computers—you know, the service and repair companies. At eight of the firms I talked to, and I did all the service and repair places, they put me on hold when I asked if they repaired personal computers."

"You know something else," piped up Terry, "there are over 50 display ads in the Computers—Dealers section of the *Yellow Pages*, but only five in the service and repair section. I wonder why that is?"

Guidelines

There are both objective and subjective components to the analysis of competition. Apply both quantitative and qualitative analysis to the information presented above to complete Part I.C. of your marketing plan.

Part 4

Product and Service Strategy

This section of your text focuses on the first of the four elements of the marketing mix to be analyzed—product strategy. The decisions and the problems involved with developing a viable product to offer to the firm's target market are examined.

The planning of the marketing mix begins with the product concept. Pricing structures, selection of marketing channels, and promotional plans are all based on the product plan. A firm must take a marketing view of its product to be successful in today's highly competitive markets. The product must be viewed as a bundle of physical, service, and symbolic attributes designed to satisfy wants. Firms planning to introduce new products must concern themselves with the various stages through which the product will pass from the time it is introduced until sales begin their final decline. The adoption process which individuals follow in their acceptance of a new product and the factors which influence the rate of adoption must also receive attention if the new product is to be accepted by consumers.

Products may be classified as either industrial or consumer goods. Industrial goods are further classified into the five categories of installations, accessory equipment, component parts and materials, raw materials, and supplies, while consumer goods are usually referred to as convenience, shopping, or specialty goods.

Our examination of product strategy begins with product line planning. Firms market a series of related products to ensure corporate growth and optimum use of resources. Next, new-product planning is considered. This ongoing activity is subject to a number of influences which affect the decision to develop a line of products rather than concentrate on a single product. The stages in the new-product development process and four methods of organizing for new-product development are reviewed to ensure a thorough knowledge of this subject. Criteria for the deletion of existing products from the product line are also considered.

Very important to product strategy decisions are the availability and use of brand names, symbols, trademarks, and packaging by companies to identify their products. Consumer knowledge and acceptance of brands also constitute important considerations in the formulation of strategy. In today's litigious society, product safety has become another important component of strategic decision making.

Chapter 8
Product Strategy

Chapter Summary

Over the years, many systems to classify consumer goods have been developed. The one which seems to have stood the test of time, however, divides consumer goods into three categories: convenience goods, shopping goods, and specialty goods. Convenience goods are those products which consumers purchase frequently, need immediately, and wish to spend a minimum of effort buying. Shopping goods are items which are purchased after an extensive investigation of alternative styles, qualities, colors, and prices. Specialty goods have unique features which cause the buyer to actively seek them out.

Interestingly, industrial goods are classified not on the basis of the behavior of individuals or organizations in acquiring them, but rather on the basis of the uses to which they are put. Thus industrial goods are classed as installations (usually major capital items such as new factories and heavy machinery), accessory equipment (capital items with shorter lives than installations and usually of substantially lower cost), component parts and materials (items of inventory which actually go into the finished product), raw materials (products of farms, mines, and forests which will undergo further processing before being used in the final product), and supplies (regular expense items necessary to daily operations, which do not become part of the final product).

The product life cycle describes the sales behavior of a product from the time it is introduced into the marketplace until the time it finally ceases being offered. Each of the four stages of the cycle has its own set of characteristics which require adaptation of the marketing mix in order to properly function. During *introduction*, people must be made aware of the product's existence. During the *growth* phase, promotion of specific brands of the product becomes common and competition intensifies. As the product enters *maturity*, sales continue to grow, but profits decline. Available product often exceeds demand, and prices may be cut in an attempt to win market share. Finally, the product enters the stage of *decline*. In this stage, there is an absolute decline in industry sales, and eventually the product leaves the market. Decline is usually the result of a change in consumer preferences or an innovation which makes the existing product obsolete. It is often possible to extend the life cycle of a successful product by getting people to use it more often, increasing the number of users, finding new uses for the product, or changing packaging, labelling, or product quality.

When a new product is introduced into the marketplace, it does not usually become an immediate success. It takes time for consumers to adopt new product offerings: first, they must become aware of the new product; then, they must become interested in it; they must evaluate it; a trial purchase must take place; and finally, the product must be accepted (adopted) or rejected. People who tend to be adoption leaders are often younger, better educated, and more mobile than the average. They usually have higher incomes and more social status than later adopters.

The rate at which products are adopted depends on five factors: (1) the degree to which the innovation possesses *relative advantage* over the existing offering; (2) *compatibility* of the innovation with the value systems of potential purchasers; (3) *complexity* of the innovation; (4) the *divisibility* of the innovation (how easy it is to try out); and (5) *communicability* of the innovation's points of advantage to potential buyers. Marketers who are aware of these facts take pains to overcome the weaknesses of their offerings and stress their strong points. Complex products are promoted using informative messages that explain how they work. Emphasis is placed on the advantages which products offer over the competition and sampling of them is used whenever possible to increase early trials. The design process recognizes the need for compatibility with existing practice and thinking. Recognition of the need to deal with an innovation's characteristics can often result in increased sales through earlier adoption.

Name _____   Instructor _____

Section _____   Date _____

Key Concepts

The purpose of this section is to allow you to determine if you can match key concepts with the definitions of the concepts. It is essential that you know the definitions of the concepts prior to applying the concepts in later exercises in this chapter.

From the list of lettered terms, select the one that best fits each of the numbered statements below. Write the letter of that choice in the space provided.

Key Terms

a. product
b. convenience goods
c. shopping goods
d. specialty goods
e. installations
f. accessory equipment
g. industrial distributor
h. component parts and materials

i. raw materials
j. supplies
k. MRO items
l. product life cycle
m. adoption process
n. consumer innovator
o. diffusion process

____ 1. Finished industrial goods that actually become part of the final product.

____ 2. Wholesaling marketing intermediary that operates in the industrial goods market and typically handles small accessory equipment and operating supplies.

____ 3. Products purchased only after the consumer has made comparisons of competing goods in competing stores on the basis of price, quality, style, and/or color.

____ 4. Acceptance of new products and services by the members of a community or social system.

____ 5. Products with unique characteristics that cause the buyer to prize them and make a special effort to obtain them.

____ 6. Major capital items, such as new factories and heavy machinery, that typically are relatively expensive and long-lived.

____ 7. The four stages through which a successful product passes: introduction, growth, maturity, and decline.

____ 8. First purchaser of a new product or service.

____ 9. Industrial goods, such as farm products (wheat, cotton, soy beans) and natural products (coal, lumber, iron ore), used in producing final products.

____ 10. Supplies for an industrial firm, categorized as maintenance items, repair items, or operating supplies.

____ 11. Series of stages in the consumer decision process regarding a new product, including awareness, interest, evaluation, trial, and rejection or adoption.

____ 12. Capital items, usually less expensive and shorter-lived than installations, such as typewriters, hand tools, and calculators.

____ 13. Regular expense items necessary in the firm's daily operation but not part of the final product.

____ 14. Bundle of physical, service, and symbolic attributes designed to enhance consumer want satisfaction.

____ 15. Products that consumers want to purchase frequently, immediately, and with a minimum of effort.

Name_____ Instructor _____

Section _____ Date _____

Self Quiz

You should use these objective questions to test your understanding of the chapter material. You can check your answers with those provided at the end of the chapter.

While these questions cover most of the chapter topics, they are not intended to be the same as the test questions your instructor may use in an examination. A good understanding of all aspects of the course material is essential to good performance on any examination.

True/False

Write "T" for True or "F" for False for each of the following statements.

____ 1. A broad definition of the word *product* focuses on the physical or functional characteristics of a good or service.

____ 2. An unsought good is one for which the consumer does not yet recognize a need.

____ 3. Products purchased on the spur of the moment or out of habit when the supply is low are referred to as impulse goods.

____ 4. The burden of promoting convenience goods falls largely on the wholesaler and retailer.

____ 5. Homogeneous shopping goods are shopping goods that the consumer considers essentially similar to each other, such as refrigerators.

____ 6. Price is an important factor in the purchase of heterogeneous shopping goods, while styling and quality are more significant in the purchase of homogeneous goods.

____ 7. Specialty goods can usually be found in fewer retail outlets than either convenience or shopping goods.

____ 8. Consumer goods are classified as convenience, shopping, or specialty goods on the basis of the behavior patterns of individual buyers.

____ 9. The classification system for industrial goods is based on product uses rather than on consumer buying patterns.

____ 10. Installations can be called the shopping goods of the industrial market.

____ 11. Price is often the deciding factor in the purchase of installations.

____ 12. The useful life of a piece of accessory equipment is usually much shorter than that of an installation.

____ 13.   Wholesalers and advertising are more likely to be used by manufacturers of accessory equipment than by manufacturers of either installations or component parts and materials.

____ 14.   Supplies are often called MRO items because they include manufacturing, required, and on-site materials.

____ 15.   The majority of firms in a particular market enter during the maturity phase of the product life cycle.

____ 16.   Successful products have a life cycle of three stages.

____ 17.   During the introduction phase of the product life cycle, companies attempting to increase their sales and market share must do so at the expense of competitors.

____ 18.   Fashions are currently popular products that tend to follow recurring life cycles.

____ 19.   One strategy for extending the product life cycle is to increase the overall market size by attracting new customers who previously have not used the product.

____ 20.   First adopters of a specific product can usually be relied upon to be first adopters of other products and services.

____ 21.   The degree to which an innovation appears superior to previous ideas is called its *divisibility*.

____ 22.   The first stage of the adoption process is awareness.

____ 23.   First adopters of innovative products are more mobile than later adopters and change their jobs and home addresses more often.

____ 24.   The diffusion process is the acceptance of new products and services by the members of a community or social system.

____ 25.   Using the normal distribution as a basis, innovators account for about 16 percent of the population.

Multiple Choice

Circle the letter of the word or phrase that best completes the sentence or best answers the question.

26.   From a marketer's point of view, what people buy when they purchase a product or service is
   a.   a group of physical or functional characteristics.
   b.   satisfaction of a want.
   c.   often nothing more than advice.
   d.   something they cannot do for themselves.
   e.   an absolute necessity for the maintenance of life and limb.

27. When a consumer sets out to purchase convenience goods he or she
    a. often visits numerous stores before making a purchase.
    b. makes comparisons of competing goods on the basis of price, style, and/or color.
    c. often lacks complete information about what is sought.
    d. may be willing to travel a substantial distance and spend a lot of time to get what is wanted.
    e. rarely visits competing stores or compares price and quality.

28. Products purchased on the spur of the moment or when the supply happens to be low are referred to as
    a. impulse goods.
    b. demand goods.
    c. specialty goods.
    d. shopping goods.
    e. staple goods.

29. Shopping goods would typically include
    a. Coca-Cola and Dixie Beer.
    b. bread, milk, and gasoline.
    c. clothing, furniture, and appliances.
    d. Rolex watches and BMW automobiles.
    e. candy, cigarettes, and newspapers.

30. Of the following, which would have the greatest influence on the decision to purchase a homogeneous shopping good?
    a. the good's styling
    b. the store's name and reputation
    c. the brand name which the product bears
    d. the price of the good
    e. the quality of the product

31. Which of the following is characteristic of the market for specialty goods?
    a. unwillingness of the buyer to accept substitutes
    b. buyers have little information about the product they seek
    c. numerous retail outlets serving each geographical area
    d. low-priced goods often lacking a brand name
    e. trial purchases of competing brands made with little financial risk

32. The burden of promoting convenience goods falls largely on
    a. the retailer; it is his desire to stimulate sales.
    b. the wholesaler; retailers don't have the money to promote these goods efficiently.
    c. the manufacturer; retailers often carry competing brands and can't be relied upon to devote effort to one of them.
    d. the government; if more people buy more goods, the economy grows.
    e. a partnership between the manufacturer and wholesaler; they can work together efficiently to get the job done.

33. Consumers often put very little effort into comparing price and quality when they're buying
    a. convenience goods or specialty goods.
    b. shopping goods or convenience goods.
    c. impulse goods or shopping goods.
    d. convenience, shopping, or specialty goods.
    e. specialty goods or shopping goods.

34. The major problem with the convenience, shopping, and specialty good classification of consumer goods is that
    a. many goods are so different that they fall totally outside the scope of the classification.
    b. the system cannot be used in terms of the majority of buyers; it must be applied to a specific individual.
    c. some products fall into the gray areas between categories; they cannot fit neatly into one or another of the classifications.
    d. consumers differ in buying patterns; an item that's a shopping good for one person may be a specialty good for someone else.
    e. the system no longer works; human behavior has changed so radically during the last ten years that the system is out of date.

35. The category of industrial goods whose purchase may involve negotiations lasting over a period of several months, the participation of a large number of decision makers, and the provision of technical expertise by the selling company is
    a. raw materials.
    b. accessory equipment.
    c. installations.
    d. component parts and materials.
    e. supplies of various types.

36. Which of the following would generally be classed as component parts and materials?
    a. eggs, milk, and potatoes
    b. flour, chocolate chips, and baking powder
    c. coal, copper, and lumber
    d. hand tools and word processors
    e. brooms, floor-cleaning compound, and stationery

37. Operating supplies are often called *MRO items*. The letters MRO stand for the words
    a. manufacturing, research, and organizational.
    b. multiple, random, and obvious.
    c. many, ridiculous, and outrageous.
    d. manual, required, and out-of-stock.
    e. maintenance, repair, and operating supply.

38. The specialty goods of the industrial market are called
    a. MRO items.
    b. raw materials.
    c. accessory equipment.
    d. installations.
    e. supplies.

39. In the industrial market, finished goods that become part of the final product are called
    a. accessory equipment.
    b. component parts and materials.
    c. maintenance items.
    d. repair items.
    e. mechanical attachments.

40. The firm's objective in the introductory stage of the product life cycle is to
    a. extend the cycle as long as possible.
    b. improve warranty terms and service availability.
    c. emphasize market segmentation.
    d. stimulate demand for the product.
    e. price competitively.

41. Efforts to extend the product life cycle should begin
    a. toward the end of the introductory stage.
    b. early in the maturity stage.
    c. toward the middle of the growth stage.
    d. in the latter part of the maturity stage.
    e. as the product enters the decline stage.

42. The activities of the Louis Rich Company to make turkey an "anytime meal" are an example of extending the product life cycle by
    a. increasing the frequency of use of the product.
    b. finding new uses for an existing product.
    c. increasing the number of users of turkey.
    d. changing package size, labels, or product quality.
    e. physically modifying the product for a new market.

43. Which of the following is a common occurrence during the introductory stage of the product life cycle?
    a. Word-of-mouth and mass advertising induce hesitant buyers to make trial purchases.
    b. Losses are common due to heavy promotion and extensive research and development expenditures.
    c. Competitors are attracted to enter the market.
    d. Competitors discover the product and promotional characteristics most preferred by the market.
    e. Shifting consumer preferences may cause a decline in sales.

44. The stage of the adoption process which has been reached when an individual becomes sufficiently involved with a new product to begin to seek information about it is
    a. awareness.
    b. evaluation.
    c. interest.
    d. trial.
    e. rejection.

45. The 34 percent of adopters who wait to adopt new products until after half of those who are going to adopt have done so are the
    a. early adopters.
    b. innovators.
    c. laggards.
    d. early majority.
    e. late majority.

46. People who purchase a new product almost as soon as it's available in the market are known as
    a. traditional shoppers.
    b. barefoot pilgrims.
    c. members of the late majority.
    d. laggards.
    e. consumer innovators.

47. First adopters of new product innovations tend to be
    a. older than those who adopt later.
    b. less mobile than those who adopt later.
    c. better educated than those who adopt later.
    d. more likely to rely on word-of-mouth than later adopters.
    e. people who change jobs very seldom.

48. The stage of the adoption process during which consumers consider whether or not the product is beneficial is
    a. adoption/rejection.
    b. interest.
    c. trial.
    d. evaluation.
    e. awareness.

49. Excluded from the model of the diffusion process for new products are
    a. children and other persons not of legal age.
    b. persons not of U.S. citizenship.
    c. people who never adopt the product.
    d. people who adopt the product very early or very late.
    e. nonhuman beings such as dogs, cats, and elves.

50. The degree to which the superiority in use of a new product is observable by others is a measure of the product's
    a. relative advantage.
    b. communicability.
    c. complexity.
    d. divisibility.
    e. compatibility.

Name_____   Instructor _____

Section _____   Date _____

Applying Marketing Concepts

Mosca Tancredi was very busy. It was a nasty day outside, and the bad weather had stimulated him to analyze his company's sales records. He was both pleased and confused by what he saw there. Mosca's firm, Tancredi Enterprises, manufactured products which were used by both consumers and industry. From its new plant in Richland, Washington, it shipped "Tancredi Trous," a line of high fashion men's pants, all over the United States. The pants were in such demand, Mosca knew, that people would literally drive a hundred miles to a store that sold them in order to buy a pair. The firm's other soft goods line, a coverall widely used by service firms, had long been a satisfactory performer in the industrial marketplace. One of the firm's hard lines, the TanJar Therapeutic Chair, seemed to have fallen on hard times. Developed five years before, sales had grown slowly for three years, then rapidly for another two years. Now, however, things were not so rosy. Competitors had begun to appear and Mosca felt that prices and profits from the chair were being squeezed by their activities. The other hard line in the Tancredi stable, the Tantic Precipitator, a device used to remove dust from "clean rooms" in electronics factories and laboratories in hospitals and pharmaceuticals plants, continued to do well. Mosca was glad he'd had the good luck to realize that hospitals and pharmaceutical companies could use the precipitator just when the electronics market for the thing seemed to be peaking out. He wondered if perhaps he could do the same thing with the therapeutic chair. So far most sales had been made to chiropractors and physical therapists for use in treating their patients, but Mosca knew that, because of all the adjustments that could be made to it, the chair could also be used as a very convenient workstation for people doing clerical work. He began to think about the possibilities.

1. Into which category of consumer goods could "Tancredi Trous" best be placed?
   a. convenience
   b. homogeneous shopping
   c. heterogeneous shopping
   d. specialty
   e. impulse

2. Tancredi's line of workman's coveralls is probably treated by industry as
   a. installations.
   b. shopping goods.
   c. accessory equipment.
   d. supplies.
   e. raw materials.

3. The TanJar chair is in which stage of the product life cycle?
   a. introduction
   b. growth
   c. maturity
   d. decline
   e. death

4. Mosca's deliberations about development of the TanJar chair into a workstation for clerical employees
   a. reveal his desperation; the idea is obviously ludicrous.
   b. have definite possibilities; it would extend the product life cycle by finding a new use for the product.
   c. would offer the possibility of extending the product life cycle by adding new users to the product's market.
   d. could conceivably extend the product life cycle by increasing the frequency with which the chair is used.

5. From Tancredi Enterprises' point of view, its new plant is
   a. a specialty good.
   b. an installation.
   c. accessory equipment.
   d. a convenience good.
   e. none of the above.

6. Mosca's development of the hospital and pharmaceutical industry market for the Tantic Precipitator was
   a. a good example of extending the product life cycle by finding new users for the product.
   b. pure luck; he couldn't do that again in a thousand years.
   c. an example of product life cycle extension through a change in product packaging or quality.
   d. a very astute example of how a product can be changed from a shopping good to a specialty good by advertising.

John Millstone, general sales manager for Lanier Hose and Tube Company, was checking sales figures for a type of industrial tubing his company had introduced three years before. Sales of the product had increased the two years following introduction but began to decline in the last quarter of the current year. Several competitors had introduced similar tubing a year after Lanier's new-product introduction. When Millstone lowered prices, its sales had recovered, and total industry sales continued to increase but at a slower rate than during the previous year.

7. This product is in which stage of the product life cycle?
   a. introduction
   b. growth
   c. maturity
   d. decline
   e. death

8. If Millstone were to discover that this tubing could be used to make novel and decorative lighting fixtures, there might be a good chance that
   a. he could extend the product life cycle by finding new users for the product.
   b. he could extend the product life cycle by developing this new use for the product.
   c. he could forget about making industrial tubing and go strictly into the lighting fixture business.
   d. he could repackage the tubing and sell it to hobbyists for use in their aquariums and fish tanks.

Name _____   Instructor _____

Section _____   Date _____

Questions for Thought

The questions which follow are designed to help you become familiar with the main concepts in this chapter through interpretation in your own words. They are meant to be answered in a few sentences or a paragraph at most.

1. Identify the classifications into which consumer goods can be placed and briefly discuss each.

2. Identify and define the various types of industrial goods. Clearly state the basis on which the types are defined.

3. Outline the product life cycle, discussing the characteristics of each stage and outlining how the cycle can be extended.

4. What characteristics determine how fast an innovation will diffuse through the marketplace? What actions can a marketer take that will accelerate this process?

Name_____   Instructor _____

Section _____   Date _____

Experiential Exercises

1. The product life cycle consists of four stages: introduction, growth, maturity, and decline.

    a. Name a consumer product that you believe to be in the introduction stage of its product life cycle. What characteristics of the market for the product led you to place it in this stage?

    b. Name a consumer product that you believe to be in the growth stage of its product life cycle. What characteristics of the market for the product led you to place it in this stage?

    c. Name a consumer product that you believe to be in the maturity stage of its product life cycle. What characteristics of the market for the product led you to place it in this stage?

    d. Name a consumer product that you believe to be in the decline stage of its product life cycle. What characteristics of the market for the product led you to place it in this stage?

2. Indicate whether the product is a convenience, shopping, or specialty good for each of the products you listed in Exercise 1 of this section. Give reasons for your choice of product classification.

    a. Product:

        Classification:

        Reasons:

    b. Product:

        Classification:

        Reasons:

    c. Product:

        Classification:

        Reasons:

    d. Product:

        Classification:

        Reasons:

3. How would each of the products you listed in Exercise 1 be classified if they were sold in industrial markets?

   a.   Product:

        Classification:

        Reasons:

   b.   Product:

        Classification:

        Reasons:

   c.   Product:

        Classification:

        Reasons:

   d.   Product:

        Classification:

        Reasons:

4. The pace of technology is such that products are often introduced, developed through a portion of what might be their natural growth, and sent into early decline as new products take their place. Sometimes, though, a product seemingly obsolete will suddenly experience a renewal as some previously unperceived advantage gives it a new lease on life. For each of the products or concepts mentioned below, examine the product's initial introduction to the marketplace, subsequent events, and the current status of this particular technology. Use the product life cycle and the concept behind its extension as the basis for your analysis.

a. Laserdiscs

b. Tube-type electronic equipment (especially sound amplifiers)

c. Electric automobiles

d.   Outdoor cooking

e.   Miniaturization

Name_____   Instructor _____

Section _____   Date _____

Computer Applications

Review the discussion of return on investment (ROI) in Chapter 8 of the text. Then use menu item 8 titled "Return on Investment" to solve each of the following problems.

1. Brian's Company (Pty.), Ltd., of Alice Springs, Northern Territory, Australia, is engaged in the development of a new feeding system for sheep. It is estimated that it will cost $6 million to develop the new system. The firm expects to sell $30 million worth of the systems, producing a profit of $3 million. What is the ROI for this product? (All figures are in U.S. dollars.)

2. Laissez le Bon Temps Roulez!, Inc., franchises its new pub concept internationally. The company projects that a franchisee will earn $150,000 in the first year of operation based upon $750,000 in sales. The total investment for a franchise owner is $1,200,000, which includes franchise fees, building, equipment, and operating capital. What is the typical first year's ROI for a new Laissez le Bon Temps Roulez! outlet? (By the way, "Laissez le bon temps roulez!" means "let the good times roll!")

3. Methods and Systems, Inc., of New Rochelle, New York, has a patent on the high resolution system for the television of the future. It estimates that it would have to spend a total of $36 million to successfully develop the product. Royalties are expected to bring in about $240 million, but costs of research and development, legal fees, taxes, and general expenses are expected to reduce the firm's net income to about $9 million. What is the expected ROI on this item?

4. The Merlman Company produces replacement parts for obsolete automobiles. It has been approached by the DeSoto Collectors' Club of America to discuss the feasibility of Merlman producing parts for the Club's particular make of car. Merlman executives estimate that they could sell $45 million worth of DeSoto parts over the life of their investment. However, tooling would cost $6 million, and the flow of profits would be about $900,000 per year from sales. Calculate the ROI for the proposed DeSoto parts.

Chapter 8 Solutions

Key Concepts

1. h	6. e	11. m
2. q	7. l	12. f
3. c	8. n	13. j
4. o	9. i	14. a
5. d	10. k	15. b

Self Quiz

1. F	11. F	21. F	31. a	41. b
2. T	12. T	22. T	32. c	42. a
3. T	13. T	23. T	33. a	43. b
4. F	14. F	24. T	34. c	44. c
5. T	15. F	25. F	35. c	45. e
6. F	16. F	26. b	36. b	46. e
7. T	17. F	27. e	37. e	47. c
8. F	18. T	28. a	38. d	48. d
9. T	19. T	29. c	39. b	49. c
10. F	20. F	30. d	40. d	50. b

Applying Marketing Concepts

1. d	5. b
2. d	6. a
3. c	7. c
4. b	8. b

Chapter 9

Product Mix Decisions and New-Product Planning

Chapter Summary

The assortment of product lines and individual offerings available from a marketer comprises that marketer's product mix. A product line is a series of related products, while an individual offering is a product which stands alone. Product mixes can be talked about in terms of their length, width, and depth of assortment. Length has to do with the number of different products in the mix, width is the number of different product lines the firm offers, and depth alludes to the degree of difference among the products in the marketing mix.

A product line, rather than a single product, is usually chosen as the preferred alternative when a firm wishes to grow, use company resources optimally, increase the firm's importance in the market, and exploit the product life cycle. A large number of ideas must be generated to ultimately result in the creation of one commercially successful product. The success of a new product depends on a multitude of factors, not the least of which is the product-development strategy chosen by the firm. Four different such strategies are available: (1) product improvement, in which existing products are modified to meet consumer needs; (2) market development, wherein the effort is made to find new markets for established products; (3) product development, a strategy which introduces new products into established or identifiable markets; and (4) product diversification, which calls for the creation of new products for new markets.

In most larger firms, new product development is handled by a new-product committee, a new-product department, product managers, or venture teams. New-product committees review new-product ideas originating both inside and outside the firm. New-product departments are set up for the express purpose of developing new products. Product managers have broad-scale responsibility for determining product strategies for a specific product, brand, or product line. Venture teams are temporary groups set up to develop a specific product or product line. New-product ideas evolve through six stages on the way to market introduction: idea generation, screening, business analysis, product development, market testing, and commercialization.

Branding, packaging, and customer service are three components of product strategy which can provide an additional competitive edge for a firm which manages them astutely. A brand is a name, term, sign, symbol, design, or some combination of these used to identify the products of a firm and to differentiate them from the competition. The brand name is the vocalized part of a brand. A trademark is a brand that has been given legal protection, reserving its use exclusively for the brand's owner. Trademarks include both the product's brand name and the pictorial parts of the brand design. Packaging is designed to protect products against damage, spoilage, and pilferage; to assist in marketing the product; and to be cost effective. Customer service, which refers to the way marketers deal with their customers, has become a major factor in the competitive environment of the late 1980s. The major aspects of customer service are customer relations, delivery, repair service, and warranties.

In recent years, product safety has come to be increasingly important as a component of the total product concept. Product designers have made voluntary attempts to reduce hazards, a number of laws have been enacted calling for stricter safety standards for various industries, and, in 1972, Congress passed the Consumer Product Safety Act. This law established the Consumer Product Safety Commission, which has jurisdiction over every consumer product except food, automobiles, and a few items already regulated by other federal agencies. The CPSC can force the recall of products for safety reasons or ban them outright without a court hearing. The Commission can inspect factories and bring criminal charges against persons and companies that violate its rules. Safety is an important consideration when dealing with the concept of product liability (the producer's or marketer's legal responsibility for injuries or damages caused by a defective product). This concept as well is assuming new importance in modern marketing.

Name_____   Instructor _____

Section _____   Date _____

Key Concepts

The purpose of this section is to allow you to determine if you can match key concepts with the definitions of the concepts. It is essential that you know the definitions of the concepts prior to applying the concepts in later exercises in this chapter.

From the list of lettered terms, select the one that best fits each of the numbered statements below. Write the letter of that choice in the space provided.

Key Terms

a. product mix
b. product line
c. cannibalizing
d. line extension
e. product positioning
f. product manager
g. venture team
h. concept testing
i. test marketing
j. brand
k. brand name
l. trademark
m. generic name
n. brand recognition

o. brand preference
p. brand insistence
q. brand extension
r. family brand
s. individual brand
t. manufacturer's (national) brand
u. private brand
v. generic product
w. label
x. Universal Product Code (UPC)
y. customer service
z. warranty
aa. product liability

____ 1. Stage of brand acceptance at which consumer is aware of the existence of a brand but does not prefer it to competing brands.

____ 2. Brand name that has become a generally descriptive term for a product.

____ 3. The manner in which marketers treat their customers.

____ 4. Brand that has been given legally protected status exclusive to its owner.

____ 5. Brand name owned by a wholesaler or retailer.

____ 6. Various related goods offered by a firm.

____ 7. Assortment of product lines and individual offerings available from a marketer.

____ 8. Food or household item characterized by a plain label, little or no advertising, and no brand name.

____   9.   Organizational strategy for identifying and developing new-product areas by combining the management resources of technological innovation, capital, management, and marketing expertise.

____   10.   Stage of brand acceptance at which the customer will accept no alternatives and will search extensively for the product or service.

____   11.   Strategy of giving an item in the product line its own brand name rather than identifying it by a single family brand name used for all products in the line.

____   12.   Special code on packages read by optical scanners.

____   13.   Measuring consumer attitudes and perceptions of a product idea prior to its actual development.

____   14.   Stage of brand acceptance at which the customer will select one brand over its competition based on previous experience with it.

____   15.   Decision to use a popular brand name for a new product entry in an unrelated product category.

____   16.   Guarantee to the buyer that the manufacturer will replace a product or refund its purchase price if the product proves defective during a specified time period.

____   17.   Consumer's perception of a product's attributes, use, quality, advantages, and disadvantages.

____   18.   New product that is closely related to other products in the firm's existing product line.

____   19.   Process of selecting a specific city or television coverage area considered reasonably typical of a new total market and then introducing the product with a marketing campaign in this area.

____   20.   Name used for several related products such as the Johnson and Johnson line of baby care products.

____   21.   Concept that manufacturers and marketers are responsible for injuries and damages caused by their products.

____   22.   Brand name owned by a manufacturer or other producer.

____   23.   Individual in a manufacturing firm assigned a product or a product line and given complete responsibility for determining objectives and establishing marketing strategies.

____   24.   Name, term, sign, symbol, design, or some combination of these used to identify the products of one firm and differentiate them from the competition.

____   25.   Descriptive part of a product's package, listing brand name or symbol, name and address of the manufacturer or distributor, ingredients, size or quantity of product, and/or recommended uses, directions, or serving suggestions.

_____   26.   Part of a brand consisting of words or letters that comprise a name used to identify and distinguish the firm's offerings from those of competitors.

_____   27.   Refers to a product that takes sales from another offering in a product line.

Name _____   Instructor _____

Section _____   Date _____

Self Quiz

You should use these objective questions to test your understanding of the chapter material. You can check your answers with those provided at the end of the chapter.

While these questions cover most of the chapter topics, they are not intended to be the same as the test questions your instructor may use in an examination. A good understanding of all aspects of the course material is essential to good performance on any examination.

True/False

Write "T" for True or "F" for False for each of the following statements.

_____   1.   "Depth of assortment" refers to the number of product lines in a firm's product mix.

_____   2.   An established firm initiates product planning by first assessing its current product mix.

_____   3.   If a new product takes sales away from an existing product in the same line, it is said to be cannibalizing the line.

_____   4.   A recent survey has revealed that only about 15 percent of new-product ideas were truly "new."

_____   5.   A product improvement strategy concentrates on finding new markets for existing products.

_____   6.   New products introduced into markets where the introducing firm already has an established position are called *flanker brands*.

_____   7.   New-product committees usually make decisions quickly and have very liberal viewpoints toward the development of novel concepts.

_____   8.   Product ideas that survive the development stage are subjected to a thorough business analysis.

_____   9.   Test marketing often suffers from the flaw that occurs when competitors reduce the selling price of their products in the test market area during the period of the test.

_____ 10.   Test marketing of consumer durables such as dishwashers, refrigerators, and stereo equipment is often a long, drawn-out process because of the possible losses a company may suffer if the testing is not thorough enough.

_____ 11.   Phased development of new products works well for firms that dominate mature markets and develop variations on existing products. It works less well for firms affected by rapidly changing technology.

____ 12. The decision to prune old, marginal products from the product line usually should be made during the late maturity or early decline stage of the product life cycle.

____ 13. Trademark protection can be secured only for the pictorial or design portion of a product's brand.

____ 14. More than 700,000 trademarks are currently registered in the United States.

____ 15. Effective brand names are easy to pronounce, recognize, and remember.

____ 16. The Lanham Act of 1946 says that in order for a brand name to be legally registered as part of a trademark it must contain words in general use.

____ 17. If the brand name of a trademarked product becomes the name by which that class or type of product is known in general, the original owner may lose the exclusive right to use it.

____ 18. During the stage of brand acceptance called *brand recognition*, consumers will choose a product over its competitors if it is available.

____ 19. Coca-Cola Company's marketing of a line of clothing bearing the Coca-Cola name is an example of brand extension.

____ 20. Family brands are more expensive to market than individual brands because a new promotional campaign must be developed to introduce each new product to its target market.

____ 21. Individual brand names should be used for products which are dissimilar and family brand names for those which are similar in quality and use.

____ 22. Food and household products characterized by plain labels, little or no advertising, and no brand names are called *private brands*.

____ 23. The use of colors such as black, gold, and maroon and design features such as borders and crests help promote a product's premium image.

____ 24. Packaging plays a very small role in product safety; after all, most products aren't used until after they have been removed from the package.

____ 25. Product liability refers to the concept that beyond making sure that their products will do the job they have been advertised to do, manufacturers and marketers have no responsibility for injuries and damages caused by those products.

Multiple Choice

Circle the letter of the word or phrase that best completes the sentence or best answers the question.

26. The number of product lines a firm offers defines
    a. the width of assortment within its product mix.
    b. the length of assortment within its product mix.
    c. the depth of assortment within its product mix.
    d. the length of assortment within its product line.
    e. the width of assortment within its product line.

27. When a firm's product development orientation is toward developing new products for new markets, it is practicing a strategy of
    a. product positioning.
    b. market development.
    c. product development.
    d. line extension.
    e. product diversification.

28. Once they have made it to store shelves, approximately what proportion of new products fails?
    a. one-quarter
    b. one-third
    c. one-half
    d. two-thirds
    e. three-quarters

29. Church and Dwight's strategy of finding new markets for its baking soda by promoting it as a refrigerator cleanser is an example of
    a. a product improvement strategy.
    b. a market development strategy.
    c. a product development strategy.
    d. a product positioning strategy.
    e. a product diversification strategy.

30. The most common organizational arrangement for new-product development is the
    a. new-product department.
    b. product manager system.
    c. new-product committee.
    d. venture team arrangement.
    e. idea-generation concept.

31. That part of the product development process designed to determine consumer reactions to a product under normal conditions is called
    a. idea generation.
    b. concept testing.
    c. screening.
    d. business analysis.
    e. test marketing.

32. Which of the following is a drawback of test marketing?
     a. If the test is carefully controlled, consumers will not be aware that it is taking place.
     b. After the test has been going on for a few months, the firm can estimate the product's likely performance in a full scale introduction.
     c. Test marketing can cost $250,000 to $1 million depending on the size of the test market city and the cost of buying media to advertise the product.
     d. The residents of the test market should represent the overall population in such characteristics as age, sex, and income.
     e. Test market locations are typically chosen so that they are of a manageable size.

33. The primary reason why long-lived durable goods are seldom test marketed is because
     a. of the major financial investment required for their development, the need to establish a distribution network for them, and the parts and servicing required.
     b. the act of test marketing communicates company plans to competitors prior to introduction of the product.
     c. competitors who learn about the test market often cut prices in the test area, distribute cents-off coupons, or take other actions to disrupt the experiment.
     d. firms are afraid their competitors will "pirate" their ideas and rush into production with copycat products.
     e. test market locations are so difficult to find.

34. The approach to development of a new product using teams of design, marketing, manufacturing, sales, and service people who are involved with the product from idea generation to commercialization is called
     a. phased development.
     b. parallel development.
     c. the Program Evaluation and Review Technique.
     d. the Critical Path Method.
     e. sequential scheduling.

35. Monsanto sold *All* detergent to Lever Brothers because
     a. of shortages of raw materials which made the product no longer profitable to manufacture and sell.
     b. the product had gone into the decline stage of its product life cycle and the company's executives felt it should be "pruned" from the product mix.
     c. the only reason it had added it to its product mix in the first place was to provide a complete line of goods for its customers, but it no longer felt this obligation.
     d. the product did not really fit into a product mix largely composed of industrial goods.
     e. the company had only been acting as agent for Lever Brothers in the first place.

36. The right of exclusivity granted the owner of a brand by trademark registration
     a. includes any pictorial designs used in the brand.
     b. covers the brand name of the product.
     c. includes brand name abbreviations such as "Coke" for "Coca-Cola."
     d. preserves the brand owner's right to slogans such as "It's Miller Time."
     e. extends to all of the conditions mentioned in a through d.

37. When a company uses the same brand name for several related products, it is practicing
    a. family branding.
    b. individual branding.
    c. national branding.
    d. private branding.
    e. institutional branding.

38. Which of the following is more true of individual branding than family branding?
    a. A promotional outlay benefits all of the products in the product line.
    b. It is easier to introduce a new product to retailers and the consumer.
    c. It can be used when products are of dissimilar quality without harming the firm's product image.
    d. Consumers who have a good experience with one of the firm's products will be more likely to purchase another.
    e. It should be used for products which are generally similar in use and in market characteristics.

39. Which of the following most correctly describes generic products?
    a. They are products offered by wholesalers and retailers which bear those middlemen's brands.
    b. The most popular products among them are cigarettes and paper products such as towels and tissues.
    c. They account for more than 4 percent of total store sales.
    d. Their market share has been steadily increasing since 1982.
    e. They are products offered by manufacturers which bear those firms' brands.

40. The competition between manufacturers' brands and private brands has been called
    a. "the siege of the marketplace."
    b. "the battle of the big boys."
    c. "the war between the worlds."
    d. "the polarization of the American consumer."
    e. "the battle of the brands."

41. The main purpose of oversized packaging, such as the plastic or paperboard boxes in which prerecorded audio tapes are sold, is to
    a. provide extra physical protection to the contents.
    b. prevent spoilage of the product by tampering.
    c. assist in marketing the product by providing convenient access to it.
    d. reduce pilferage by shoplifters by making the product too bulky to fit conveniently into a pocket or purse.
    e. be a cost-effective way of facilitating goods handling.

42. Which of the following is a good example of using a package to assist in marketing a product?
    a. packaging beer in brown or green bottles
    b. providing tamper-resistant seals on food and medicine containers
    c. designing the package so that it can be put to some other use after the product it contains has been expended
    d. designing the package so that the product will not be deformed or crushed in shipment
    e. choosing from various alternative package designs the one which will adequately protect the contents at least cost

43. Of the following, which is the only country other than the United States which has not either already adopted conversion to the metric system of measurement or mandated it for the future?
    a. Burma
    b. the Union of Soviet Socialist Republics
    c. Bahrain
    d. Great Britain
    e. East Yemen

44. The Universal Product Code
    a. is a device which allows consumers to determine how long it has been since the product they are buying was produced.
    b. is a circular emblem displayed on many packages certifying that the product is manufactured to "universal standards."
    c. is a code read by optical scanners that print the item and its price on the cash register receipt.
    d. is a law that specifies that the labels on packages all over the world contain the same type and quantity of information.
    e. is a standard of ethics for the manufacturers of consumer goods that sets forth their customer relations policy.

45. The major components of customer service are
    a. customer satisfaction, customer interaction, personal service, and detailed attention.
    b. customer relations, delivery, repair service, and warranties.
    c. custom delivery, custom service, custom pricing, and custom design.
    d. customer assistance, complaint resolution, sales information, and adjustment policy.
    e. assistance, resistance, reaction, and submission.

46. General Electric's "Satisfaction Guaranteed" program is an excellent example of
    a. a packaging program which has generated substantial goodwill for the company in the consumer market.
    b. a warranty program which has been effective in stimulating demand for a product line.
    c. a situation where a company has had to protect itself from consumer lawsuits by allowing returns of merchandise on a very liberal basis.
    d. a customer service policy which guaranteed delivery of merchandise when and where the customer wanted it.
    e. how important product safety is in the minds of the executives of even so large a company as General Electric.

47. The federal law which has had the greatest impact on product safety has been
    a. the Toxic Substances Act of 1968.
    b. the Fair Packaging and Labelling Act of 1966.
    c. the Product Safety Standards Act of 1987.
    d. the Consumer Product Safety Act of 1972.
    e. the Magnusson-Moss Consumer Products Warranty Act of 1973.

48. The concept that manufacturers and marketers may be responsible for injuries and damage caused by their products is called
    a. corporate social responsibility.
    b. the premise of extended warranty.
    c. customer relations.
    d. the rule of individual responsibility.
    e. product liability.

49. Which of the following was a brand name but has become generic through common usage over the years?
    a. Nylon
    b. Jell-O
    c. Xerox
    d. Hoover
    e. Frigidaire

50. Creating a package design which features a gold crest with a heavy maroon accent assists in marketing the product by
    a. making the product more convenient to use.
    b. producing a package which can be easily reused.
    c. evoking the product's image through package design.
    d. producing a package which is cost effective.
    e. protecting the product against damage, pilferage, or spoilage.

Name_____ Instructor _____

Section _____ Date _____

Applying Marketing Concepts

Riverside Candy Company has been in business for over fifty years. The company was founded in 1934 to manufacture and distribute *Riverside Ramps*, a hard caramel confection in bar form which the company still carries in its product mix. Over the years, the company has added to its line of candies and now sells *Riverside Rollers* (round, hard candies), *Riverside Ripples* (a bar candy with alternating vanilla/chocolate stripes), and *Riverside Rapids* (a fast-dissolving candy specially designed for use by joggers and runners "for quick energy on the go"). Each Riverside candy item is packaged in a distinctive brown and cream wrapper featuring the Riverside trademark.

1. The type of branding which Riverside has traditionally used is
   a. individual branding.
   b. family branding.
   c. dealer branding.
   d. generic branding.
   e. indeterminate branding.

2. Just recently, Riverside was approached by a large supermarket chain which wants to buy *Riverside Rapids* to be packaged in its own wrappers and sold under its name. The supermarket brand is a
   a. generic brand.
   b. national brand.
   c. individual brand.
   d. family brand.
   e. private brand.

3. Riverside has just received notice of an action against it by a federal agency. It seems that it failed to show the required nutritional information on a product label. The agency which has taken the action against Riverside is the
   a. Federal Energy Commission.
   b. Consumer Product Safety Commission.
   c. Food and Drug Administration.
   d. Interstate Commerce Commission.
   e. Commission on Trade with Developing Nations.

4. If Riverside's product had been an electrical appliance which was suspected of having a dangerous design flaw, the acting agency would have been the
   a. Federal Energy Regulatory Commission.
   b. Bureau of Alcohol, Tobacco, and Firearms.
   c. Consumer Products Safety Commission.
   d. Directorship of the Federal Reserve System.
   e. National Electrical Products Purchasing Commission.

5. If Riverside decided to branch out into the production of flavored syrups for use by sellers of snow cones, and decided to create a new brand, such as "Best Taste," for that line, it would be
   a. developing a new family brand for the syrup line.
   b. individually branding the syrups.
   c. making a serious mistake; users of Riverside candies aren't going to be interested in snow cone syrups.
   d. in violation of the law; each food product must bear the brand name most closely associated with its maker.

Max Logancamp sat back in his chair, adjusted his headset, and prepared to answer his fortieth phone call of the day. "Hello," he said. "Logancamp here. How may I help you?" Listening carefully to the voice on the other end of the line, Max clucked (some would say he "tsk-tsked") occasionally, and finally said, "I see, ma'am. You say that the model 2021 dishwasher you bought from us isn't working properly. When you set it to the 'fill' cycle, no water enters the machine. Is that right?" Max gave another careful listen. "OK, then, how long ago did you buy the machine?" The caller responded. Max replied, "Fine, then there's no problem. I'll just have shipping send you out another one. When would you like us to get it to you? Yes, we can get it to you at nine tomorrow morning. You have my promise on it. My name? Max Logancamp. Just ask for me if you have any problems at all. It's been a pleasure talking to you, too, ma'am. Good-bye." Max then prepared to talk to the forty-first caller of the day.

6. Judging from the context of the above paragraph, Max is probably a(n)
   a. telephone operator for some communications company.
   b. executive of the company that makes these products.
   c. customer contact person in the customer relations department of the firm.
   d. scheduler for the repair department of his firm.
   e. very confused and disorganized individual.

7. Why do you suppose Max wanted to know when the lady had purchased her dishwasher from the firm?
   a. so he could determine which model in the line it was
   b. so he could determine if the product was still under warranty
   c. so he could decide whether to handle this customer nicely or as a real pain in the neck
   d. just because he was a curious sort of person
   e. for no apparent reason

8. The firm for which Max works, judging from his end of the conversation, has
   a. a real commitment to customer service.
   b. many, many problems in the repair department.
   c. real difficulty in getting along with delivery people.
   d. people handling customer complaints who don't seem to care.
   e. problems with the quality of its product offering.

9. The only component of the customer service process which Max didn't handle or deal with in this call is
   a. customer relations.
   b. warranties.
   c. delivery.
   d. repair service.
   e. price adjustments.

Name_____ Instructor _____

Section _____ Date _____

Questions for Thought

The questions which follow are designed to help you become familiar with the main concepts in this chapter through interpretation in your own words. They are meant to be answered in a few sentences or a paragraph at most.

1. Why is it more common for a firm to develop a line of related products than a single product?

2. Discuss the major new-product development strategies and the factors which affect the success or failure of each.

3. Outline and explain the various organization structures for new-product development.

4. List and discuss the stages in the new-product development process.

5.   How may brands, trademarks, and brand names be used in a marketing strategy?

6.   Discuss customer service and outline its various components.

Name_____ Instructor _____

Section _____ Date _____

Experiential Exercises

1. The purpose of this exercise is to help you understand the requirements of package design. You are being asked to design a package for a new product. This package must bear the information required by law, have visual appeal, protect the product, and be cost effective. Dimensions will be limited, for reasons of distribution, to a rectangular configuration 6 inches long by 2 inches wide by 3/4 inch deep. You may use any material you choose so long as it satisfies the requirements above. The package need not be rigid so long as those specifications are met.

    Choose *one* of the following products:

    a. A family cereal called *Mountain Nuggets*, an all-natural product containing nuts and dried pears, lightly sweetened with dark molasses.

    b. A snack food called *Tri-Pro*, whose basic ingredients are dried beef, sunflower seeds, and cheese solids, and which contains three times the protein of any other snack food on the market.

    c. An instant dessert called *Fudge a Little*, a creamy, low-calorie dish with a bottom layer of brownies and a top layer of pudding.

    Your package will contain 3-3/4 ounces of the product. The first two products can be eaten as is, but the *Fudge a Little* must be mixed with 8 fluid ounces of skim milk.

    Don't be afraid to let your creative juices flow, but realize that practical considerations must also govern your design.

2. Using library sources such as *The Wall Street Journal*, *Advertising Age*, and *Marketing News*, investigate sources for the last year or so for news of new-product introductions into the market. Continue until you have found at least one example of each of the following strategies.

   a. *Product improvement*

      Nature of product:

      Name of company:

      Why is this an example of product improvement?

   b. *Market development*

      Nature of product:

      Name of company:

      Why is this an example of market development?

c. *Product development*

Nature of product:

Name of company:

Why is this an example of product development?

d. *Product diversification*

Nature of product:

Name of company:

Why is this an example of product diversification?

Name_____ Instructor _____

Section _____ Date _____

Computer Applications

Review the discussion of alternative approaches to evaluating alternatives in Chapter 9 of the text. Then use menu item 5 titled "Evaluation of Alternatives" to solve each of the following problems.

1. Standard Coffee Company is considering one of three package designs for its ground coffee. The firm has identified three major factors to consider in making this decision: product protection, promotional appeal, and ease of storage. Standard's management has scored each of the package designs on a scale of 1 (poor) to 5 (excellent) for each of the three decision factors. These scores are shown below:

| | | Decision Factors | |
Package Design	Protection	Appeal	Storage
A	4	3	2
B	2	5	3
C	4	3	4

a. Which package design would the company select using the overall scoring method?

b. Suppose that management considers ease of storage to be 100% more important than any other decision factor. Which package design would be selected?

c. Suppose that management, using the overall scoring method, also decides that it will not accept any package design that scored less than 3 on any factor. Which package design would be selected?

d. Would your response to Question c change if management used the weighted scoring method?

2. California Clothing Company, a firm located in Fresno, is trying to select a brand name for a new line of clothes aimed at toddlers. The legal department has cleared five names for possible use by the firm. Research has determined that the impact of the names varies among audiences such as parents, grandparents, and even the children themselves. Each brand name has been evaluated for each group on a 5-point scale ranging from 1 (poor) to 5 (excellent). The rankings are as follows:

Brand Names*	Marketing Impact with		
	Children	Parents	Grandparents
A	3	3	3
B	3	4	5
C	4	2	2
D	5	4	4
E	2	3	2

*The names have been hidden to prevent bias.

a. Which brand name would be selected using the overall scoring method?

b. Suppose that management considers the brand name's impact with parents and grandparents to be 100% more important than its impact with children. Which brand name would be selected?

c. Suppose that management, using the overall scoring method, decides that it will not accept a brand name rated less than 4 by any group. Which brand name would be selected?

d. Would your decision in Question c change if the weighted scoring method were used?

3. Alabama Book Company, a distributor of paperback books in Huntsville, is considering five new retail display racks. There are three major factors to be considered in making the decision on the new rack: promotional appeal; maximum display inventory; and cost. Management has scored each of the display designs on a scale of 1 (poor) to 5 (excellent) for each of the decision factors. These scores are shown below:

Display	Promotional Appeal	Maximum Inventory	Cost
A	5	3	5
B	4	4	1
C	3	5	2
D	3	4	3
E	5	4	4

a. Which display would the firm select using the overall scoring method?

b. Suppose that management considers cost the least important decision factor. Promotional appeal and maximum inventory are considered 100% more important than cost. Which display would be selected?

c. Suppose that management, using the overall scoring method, also decides that it will not purchase any display scoring less than 4 on any decision factor. Which display would be selected?

d. Would your response to Question c change if management used the weighted scoring method?

Chapter 9 Solutions

Key Concepts

1.	n	7.	a	13.	h	19.	i	25.	w
2.	m	8.	v	14.	o	20.	r	26.	k
3.	y	9.	g	15.	q	21.	aa	27.	c
4.	l	10.	p	16.	z	22.	t		
5.	u	11.	s	17.	e	23.	f		
6.	b	12.	x	18.	d	24.	j		

Self Quiz

1.	F	11.	T	21.	T	31.	e	41.	d
2.	T	12.	T	22.	F	32.	c	42.	c
3.	T	13.	F	23.	T	33.	a	43.	a
4.	F	14.	T	24.	F	34.	b	44.	c
5.	F	15.	T	25.	F	35.	d	45.	b
6.	T	16.	F	26.	a	36.	e	46.	b
7.	F	17.	T	27.	e	37.	a	47.	d
8.	F	18.	F	28.	d	38.	c	48.	e
9.	T	19.	T	29.	b	39.	b	49.	a
10.	F	20.	F	30.	c	40.	e	50.	c

Applying Marketing Concepts

1.	b	6.	c
2.	e	7.	b
3.	c	8.	a
4.	c	9.	d
5.	a		

Part Four Puzzle

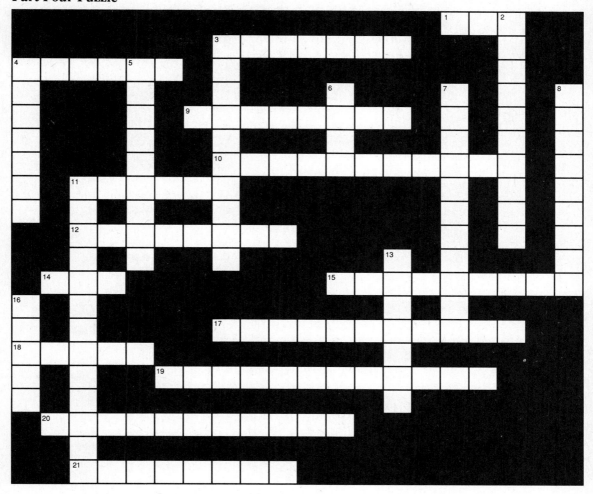

ACROSS CLUES

1. acronym for term describing stages through which a successful product passes
3. bundle of attributes designed to enhance consumer want satisfaction
4. the consumer who selects a brand over the competition based on prior experience _ _ _ _ _ s it
9. process which includes awareness, interest, evaluation, trial, and adoption or possibly rejection
10. class of goods purchased frequently, immediately, and with minimum effort
11. when customers will accept no substitute for the desired product, they _ _ _ _ _ on it
12. goods purchased only after extensive comparisons of price, quality, style, and color
14. materials such as farm products and natural products used in producing finished goods

15. goods with unique characteristics that make them prized and worth a special effort to get
17. strategy for new product development which brings together expertise from many fields
18. name, term, sign, symbol, design, or combination used to identify the products of a firm
19. industrial goods such as wheat, cotton, soybeans, coal, lumber used in producing final goods
20. consumer's perception of a product's attributes, use, quality, and other features
21. expense items used in the operation of the business but not entering the final product

DOWN CLUES

2. finished industrial goods that actually become part of the product

3. assortment of product lines and individual items available from a marketer
4. brand name owned by a wholesaler or retailer
5. new product that is closely related to existing products in the firm's product line
6. in relation to products, various related goods offered by a firm
7. what happens when one product takes sales from another product in a firm's product line
8. type of industrial capital good of which typewriters, hand tools, and adding machines are examples
11. major capital items such as factories and heavy machinery with long life expectancy
13. products characterized by plain labels, little or no advertising, and no brand name
16. descriptive part of a product's package, usually conveying much information

Name_____   Instructor_____

Section _____   Date _____

Cases for Part 4

1.   *Ontario Chemicals and Coatings, Ltd.*

Louis Sherbrooke, product manager for Ontario Chemicals and Coatings, was wondering what to do with one of the firm's new products, Tempadhere. Tempadhere, an adhesive designed for use as a temporary "tacking agent" to hold large sheets of steel in alignment for final assembly by welding, had recently been developed by OCC as a by-product of one of its major chemical processes. The product had tremendous holding power, which was its major advantage over other tacking agents used in the metal fabrication industry.

The product had been on the market only a couple of weeks when complaints began to pour in from dissatisfied users. The apparent problem was that the product worked too well! Users found that it was exceedingly difficult to remove from their weldments once fabrication had been completed, interfering with further processing and assembly. "Well, it looks like we're going to have to pull Tempadhere off the market," said Richard Hartmann, vice president of production for OCC. "Surely we can find other uses for such a product."

Question

What was this company's definition of a product? How does this differ from the definition with which you have become familiar in this course?

2.   *Little People Toys*

Little People Toys are high quality products marketed throughout the United States and Canada. They are usually sold in specialty toy shops and in a few of the best department stores.

Since prices in toy shops are normally higher than prices in the usual toy outlets, big people who shop in toy shops are usually more interested in quality and service than in price. Research evidence gathered by Little People suggests that most people who have made a purchase of a Little People toy will continue to buy the Little People brand when they purchase toys in the future.

Question

What kind of consumer goods are represented by the Little People line of toys? Why do you suppose this is so?

3.   *Maldinado Manufacturing Company*

In recent years there have been a number of financial crises at Maldinado Manufacturing because the company seems to be unable to introduce new products in a timely fashion. Competitors always seem to introduce the innovations and Maldinado ends up copying these products. By the time Maldinado has a product ready to go into the marketplace, competitors are already well established with their innovations and Maldinado is forced to compete mainly on a price basis.

In the past, Vito Maldinado, the company's president, had depended on the sales and production staffs to come up with new-product ideas. Those who had ideas got temporary relief from some of their other duties to see their ideas through actual development and marketing.

This procedure had caused problems. Not only did it move workloads around, it also resulted in no one having the ultimate responsibility for developing new products. Vito knows something must be done soon, so he is trying to create a better way to assign the responsibility for new-product development within his organization.

Question

How can Mr. Maldinado ensure that someone is responsible for developing new products?

4.   CBS, Incorporated[1]

In October 1987, CBS, Incorporated, in cooperation with the U.S. Product Safety Commission, announced a voluntary recall and replacement of the plastic bodies of its "Clippety Clop," "Comanche," and "Colt" ride-on toy "Wonder" horses because the plastic body might break during use.

CBS had received 105 complaints that the body of the toy had broken without warning while being ridden, causing the rider to fall suddenly. Forty of these incidents resulted in injuries such as cuts, scrapes, and bruises.

Over 114,000 of these ride-on toys, produced and distributed to retailers between March 1984 and May 1986, had been sold nationally for approximately $60 each. The defective toys had been produced prior to June 1986 by the Wonder Unit of CBS Toys. Only toys with control numbers (stamped on the belly) of 86206 or less were affected.

Consumers were warned to immediately stop using the toy and retailers were warned to remove affected toys from sale. A toll-free number was provided for questions concerning replacement of the product and identification of potentially defective items.

A statement from the Consumer Products Safety Commission, attached to the recall document, read in part "an estimated 325 million potentially hazardous products have been called back from the marketplace and consumers since 1973 (when CPSC was created). Most of these were voluntarily recalled by manufacturers, who established programs to repair or replace the products, or to refund the purchase price."

---

[1]   Abstracted from "CBS 'Wonder' Spring Ride-on Horses Recalled," A *Consumer Product SAFETY ALERT* (Washington: U.S. Consumer Product Safety Commission), October 1987.

Questions

a.   What is the significance of the voluntary recall of these products by CBS, Inc.? Relate product liability to the recall.

b.   How significant do you suppose pressure by the CPSC was in causing CBS to issue the recall?

Name _____   Instructor _____

Section _____   Date _____

Creating a Marketing Plan: Where Do We Go from Here?

The information you will receive in this part will help you to complete all of Part II of your marketing plan for Latebri Industries, Incorporated.

Episode Four

As episode four begins, the young entrepreneurs are discussing their long-term plans for the company. They are examining their resources and attempting to match the potential in the marketplace to their own potentials and abilities. They quickly recognized that the potential for the kind of service they planned to offer was quite substantial. If the information they had was correct, then the potential in the local market could be as much as $18,200,000 per year, growing at a rate of somewhere between 14 and 33 percent per annum. Their resources, on the other hand, were limited to the $150,000 they had on hand, plus their own educations and talents.

Meanwhile, there were already 42 potentially active competitors in the market, with some 102 other companies who might someday pose a threat. On the other hand, many of these potential competitors had displayed little marketing "savvy" to the partners when they had conducted their market survey.

Laura was the first to speak. "Listen, guys," she said, "we have to set some kind of goals for ourselves or we won't have anything to work toward. What do you say we start with the long run and work our way back to the present? I figure that, if we play our cards right, we can hold onto at least 1 percent of the market in five years. What do you think? That would be at least $300,000 in volume by then. Do you think we can get that big a market share? We'd have to do at least $100,000 this year and grow by at least 32 percent a year to get there in five years."

"Do you think that's aiming high enough?" asked Terry. "We've got to get this operation going, which we know is going to cost at least $110,000 if we do it right. We're sure to lose money unless we get a pretty big chunk of the market pretty quick."

"On the other hand," said Brian, "if we aim too high and don't achieve our goals, we may think we've failed when we're really doing well. I figure that we'd be better off looking at bottom line profits rather than share of the market. I think we ought to look to make at least 10 percent profit on sales."

"Look," said Laura, "I'll agree with both of you. I sure hope we can latch onto 1 percent of this market. I hope we can make 10 percent on sales. But remember, we have to do this the customer's way. I think we should be open 24 hours a day, seven days a week. That should give us a real advantage over the other companies in the market. Sure, it'll cost a little more at first, but we'll build customer loyalty and probably generate more up-front money from maintenance contracts that way. Besides, I think we're all being too conservative. Remember, we're going *after* this market, not just giving it lip service. We really should expect to lose money for the next couple of years. But we'll be offering people what they need, and it's sure to pay off in the long run."

Guidelines

a. Where are Laura, Terry, and Brian getting the figures they are using in these discussions?

b. Remember that a lot of what happens depends on how actively the three pursue their business. Enthusiasm and dedication do count if the market offers sufficient potential in the first place. Summarize their objectives and complete Parts II.A., II.B., and II.C. in your marketing plan.

Part 5

Pricing Strategy

This section of your text contains an analysis of the pricing component of the marketing mix.

Price is the component of the marketing mix most universally affected by the legal environment. The antitrust legislation outlined in Chapter 2 provides the basic foundation for the regulation of price, amplified by the Robinson-Patman Act which prohibits a broad range of price-discriminatory actions.

Pricing objectives can be related to profitability, sales volume, meeting the competition, and creating a prestige image for one's product or firm. Price elasticity, which is the degree of responsiveness of demand to changes in price, is another factor which must be considered in the pricing of a product.

Two basic factors, price theory and cost, provide the rational framework for pricing. Price theory, which suffers from problems associated with its assumption that firms attempt to maximize profits and from the difficulty of estimating demand in the real world, is relatively seldom used in the setting of actual prices. Costs, on the other hand, are the most commonly used basis for setting prices today. The typical cost-plus approach to pricing attempts to set a price for the product which will recover the cost of producing and distributing it and allow for some margin of profit. Two methods of applying cost-plus pricing exist, the full-cost method and the incremental cost method.

Breakeven analysis is a technique which is often used to help marketing executives decide whether required sales levels to achieve profitability are a realistic goal. The model is, however, cost (not demand) based, and so does not directly answer the question of whether consumer demand will be sufficient to actually reach the breakeven point. A modified breakeven model, which superimposes an estimated demand curve over the cost and revenue curves of the breakeven chart, helps identify the range of feasible prices and provide a more realistic base for deciding on the price to actually ask in the marketplace.

The making of pricing decisions is a two-step process which involves the setting and administering of pricing structure. Alternative pricing strategies include a skimming strategy, a penetration pricing strategy, and a competitive strategy. Competitive conditions have a significant effect on which of these strategies is chosen by a particular firm.

Quoting prices to potential customers may involve considerations of cost structures, traditional practices in the industry, and the firm's own policies. There are numerous possibilities which influence price quotes, among them being the discounts and allowances which may prevail in a particular industry. Shipping costs often figure prominently in the pricing of goods. These costs represent a part of price, and it is important to know whether they will be paid by the vendor or the purchaser of the goods.

Pricing policies include psychological pricing, unit pricing, and flexible pricing. The way a good is priced may affect the consumer's perception of its quality. Price limits often relate the price/quality relationship in the consumer's mind.

Prices in the industrial market are often subject to negotiation. Alternatively, they may be negotiated in talks between buyer and seller. In large corporations, the necessity to set transfer prices when goods are transferred among profit centers of the same firm is a major decision problem. The setting of such prices can have a direct effect on the profitability of the centers involved.

Pricing of public services has become something of an issue in recent years. The issue concerns which costs to assign to which public service provider as a basis for price setting and whether such prices should be cost based at all or should be instruments for achieving social or civic objectives.

Chapter 10

Price Determination

Chapter Summary

Pricing is perhaps the most regulated of the components of the marketing mix. The antitrust legislation which you studied in the material on the legal/political environment provides the foundation on which this regulation is based. The Robinson-Patman Act amended the Clayton Act to prohibit price discrimination in sales to wholesalers, retailers, and other producers that is not based on a cost differential. The states have also enacted laws which have an effect on pricing decisions. Unfair trade laws, as they are usually known, require sellers to maintain minimum prices for comparable merchandise. In recent years, these laws have diminished in importance. Fair-trade laws, once found in 44 states, no longer exist. The Consumer Goods Pricing Act banned the use of fair trade in interstate commerce.

Pricing objectives, just as any other business decision, should be the result of overall organizational goals as interpreted in the firm's more specific marketing goals. These pricing objectives can be classified into four major groups: (1) profitability objectives; (2) volume objectives; (3) meeting competition objectives; and (4) prestige objectives. Elasticity of demand is an important element in the determination of price. The degree to which consumers respond to changes in price is affected by such factors as the availability of substitute or complementary goods, whether a product or service is a necessity or a luxury, the proportion of a person's budget spent on the item, and the importance of time to the decision on whether or not to buy.

Price theory, the economic explanation of the behavior of prices and demand, has certain flaws when applied in practice. Though it assumes that all firms operate on the basis of a profit-maximizing set of goals, not all firms seek to maximize profits. In addition, it is often difficult, if not impossible, to measure demand in the real world. Finally, inadequate training of managers and poor communications between economists and managers put obstacles in the way of real-world application of the theory of price.

One of the facts of life about prices is that whatever price is set for a product or service, it must ultimately cover the cost of producing and distributing that product or service. Thus cost-plus pricing is the most common approach to setting price in use today. This method of setting price uses a base-cost figure per unit of product and adds a markup to cover unassigned costs and to provide a profit. *Full-cost* pricing uses all relevant variable costs in setting a product's price, while *incremental cost* pricing attempts to use only those costs directly attributable to a specific output as a basis in setting price for that output. This procedure overcomes the arbitrary allocation of fixed expenses. Cost-based pricing does not, however, directly consider product demand.

Breakeven analysis is a technique for determining the number of products or volume of services that must be sold at a stated price to generate enough revenue to cover total costs. A simple technique, it is easily understood by all executives and can help them decide whether the necessary sales levels for a given price are within the range of possibility. Breakeven analysis does have its shortcomings, however. The model assumes that all costs are either fixed or variable and ignores the fact that some costs have traditionally been allocated arbitrarily; in addition, it assumes that per-unit variable costs remain stable at all levels of operation, ignoring the possibility of quantity discounts, better uses of labor, and other economies of scale; finally, this model does not consider demand. Based on costs alone, it does not directly address the question of whether or not consumers will actually buy the product at the price selected for the analysis and in the quantities necessary for breakeven to occur. In order for the model to be made meaningful, it must be modified. In the modified breakeven model, consumer surveys, analyses by marketers and channel participants, and actual field tests are used to assess consumer reaction to different prices. Superimposing these data onto a breakeven chart can then identify a feasible range of prices for consideration by the marketer.

Name_____   Instructor _____

Section _____   Date _____

Key Concepts

The purpose of this section is to allow you to determine if you can match key concepts with the definitions of the concepts. It is essential that you know the definitions of the concepts prior to applying the concepts in later exercises in this chapter.

From the list of lettered terms, select the one that best fits each of the numbered statements below. Write the letter of that choice in the space provided.

Key Terms

a. price
b. Robinson-Patman Act
c. unfair-trade laws
d. fair-trade laws
e. profit maximization
f. target return objectives
g. Profit Impact of Market
    Strategies (PIMS) Project
h. customary prices
i. demand

j. supply
k. pure competition
l. monopolistic competition
m. oligopoly
n. monopoly
o. elasticity
p. cost-plus pricing
q. breakeven analysis
r. modified breakeven analysis

_e_ 1. In pricing strategy, point at which the additional revenue gained by increasing the price of a product equals the increase in total cost.

_p_ 2. The practice in pricing strategy of adding a percentage or specified dollar amount (the markup) to the base cost of product or service to cover unassigned costs and to provide a profit.

_q_ 3. Pricing technique used to determine the number of products or services that must be sold at a specified price in order to generate sufficient revenue to cover total cost.

_n_ 4. Market structure involving only one seller of a product or service for which there are no close substitutes.

_r_ 5. Pricing technique used to evaluate consumer demand by comparing the number of products or services that must be sold at a variety of prices in order to cover total cost.

_F_ 6. Short-run or long-run pricing objectives of achieving a specified return on either sales or investment.

_M_ 7. Market structure involving relatively few sellers and significant entry barriers to new competitors due to high start-up costs.

_L_ 8.   Market structure involving a heterogeneous product and product differentiation among competing suppliers, allowing the marketer some control of price.

_O_ 9.   A measure of responsiveness of purchasers and suppliers to a change in price.

_b_ 10.   Federal legislation prohibiting price discrimination not based on a cost differential; also prohibits selling at an unreasonably low price to eliminate competition.

_C_ 11.   State laws requiring sellers to maintain minimum prices for comparable merchandise.

_K_ 12.   Market structure characterized by homogeneous products for which there are so many buyers and sellers that none has a significant influence on price.

_a_ 13.   Exchange value of a good or service.

_I_ 14.   Schedule of the amounts of a firm's product or service that consumers will purchase at different prices during a specified time period.

_J_ 15.   Schedule of the amounts of a product or service that a firm will offer for sale at different prices during a specified time period.

_g_ 16.   Major research study that discovered a strong positive relationship between a firm's market share and its return on investment.

_d_ 17.   Statutes enacted in most states that permitted manufacturers to stipulate a minimum retail price for a product.

_h_ 18.   In pricing strategy, the traditional prices that customers expect to pay for certain products and services.

Name _____   Instructor _____

Section _____   Date _____

Self Quiz

You should use these objective questions to test your understanding of the chapter material. You can check your answers with those provided at the end of the chapter.

While these questions cover most of the chapter topics, they are not intended to be the same as the test questions your instructor may use in an examination. A good understanding of all aspects of the course material is essential to good performance on any examination.

True/False

Write "T" for True or "F" for False for each of the following statements.

_F_   1.   Marketers' decisions in setting the price for a product are influenced only by consumer demand.

_T_   2.   The value of an item is what it can be exchanged for in the marketplace.

_T_   3.   Rents on homes, fees paid to physicians, fares on airlines, tolls to use bridges, and premiums paid to get insurance coverage are just prices under other names.

_F_   4.   The Robinson-Patman Act is sometimes called the "Anti-P & G Act," because it was designed to curb pricing abuses by large consumer-goods manufacturers like Procter and Gamble.

_F_   5.   The Robinson-Patman Act absolutely prohibits price discrimination in sales to wholesalers, retailers, and other producers.

_F_   6.   Unfair-trade laws are federal laws requiring sellers to set prices at cost plus some modest markup.

_T_   7.   The Miller-Tydings Resale Price Maintenance Act of 1937 exempted interstate fair-trade contracts from compliance with antitrust requirements.

_T_   8.   Price serves as a means of regulating economic activity; employment of any or all of the factors of production depends on the price each factor receives.

_T_   9.   A recent study of marketing executives revealed that they now rank price as the single most important marketing mix variable.

_T_   10.   In another recent survey of American businessmen, "meeting competitors' prices" was the pricing goal most often mentioned by respondents.

_F_   11.   A measure of Americans' devotion to their pets is the fact that expensive gourmet cat foods accounted for 22 percent of the 2 billion pounds of cat food sold in 1987.

T   12.   The amount of profits a firm makes may be computed from the equation: Profits = Price x Quantity Sold − Expenses.

F   13.   If a firm raises its prices 10 percent and sales decline by 11 percent, the firm's revenues will increase.

F   14.   In marginal analysis, profit maximization is achieved as long as the addition to total revenue caused by selling one more unit exceeds the increase in total cost caused by producing that unit.

T   15.   The most commonly reported primary pricing objective among American businessmen, according to a recent survey, was a specified rate of return on investment.

F   16.   Economic theory assumes that all businesses strive to maximize sales; the truth, however, is that many of them seek to maximize profits, perceived to be a more realizable goal.

T   17.   The share of the market a company possesses is a frequently used indicator in court evaluations of cases involving alleged monopolistic practices.

F   18.   The PIMS study revealed that two of the most important factors influencing profitability were markup percentages and market location.

T   19.   Research has shown that brands ranked number one or two in their market generally earn satisfactory returns on investment for their firms, while weaker brands, on average, fail to earn adequate returns.

F   20.   It appears that the most astute segmentation strategies may be those seeking to obtain small shares of larger markets rather than those seeking to gain larger shares of small markets.

T   21.   The fact that Joy perfume is advertised as "the costliest perfume in the world" indicates that its maker is seeking to achieve a prestige pricing objective.

T   22.   The division of the U.S. beer market into premium and popular-price segments is an example of a traditional approach to pricing often called *customary pricing*.

F   23.   Pure competition is a market structure with large numbers of buyers and sellers of heterogeneous products in which product differentiation exists, allowing the marketer some control over prices.

F   24.   The price set for a product or service in the marketplace must be sufficient to cover the variable cost involved in producing and marketing the product or service.

F   25.   The elasticity of demand is the percentage change in the price of a product or service divided by the percentage change in the quantity of the product or service which is demanded.

Multiple Choice

Circle the letter of the word or phrase that best completes the sentence or best answers the question.

C 26. The law (typical of Depression-era legislation) which was inspired by price competition from developing grocery store chains and prohibits price discrimination in sales to wholesalers, retailers, and other producers is
   a. the Clayton Act.
   b. the Miller-Tydings Act.
   c. the Robinson-Patman Act.
   d. the Consumer Goods Pricing Act.
   e. the McGuire-Keogh Act.

b 27. Udell's survey of marketing executives, taken a quarter of a century ago to determine the relative importance of price as an element of the marketing mix, found that
   a. price was ranked most important of all the elements.
   b. price was the third most important elements of the marketing mix, ranking only above distribution.
   c. price was considered less important than product, distribution, or promotion in the marketing mix.
   d. price was considered second only to product as an element of the marketing mix.
   e. all of the elements of the marketing mix were ranked of equal importance by the responding executives.

a 28. The objective ranked first among primary pricing objectives in a recent study of U.S. businesses was
   a. a specified return on investment.
   b. meeting competitors' prices.
   c. maximizing profits.
   d. increasing total profits above previous levels.
   e. serving the greatest number of market segments.

d 29. Which of the following is a volume pricing objective?
   a. seeking a 20 percent annual rate of return on investment
   b. matching the prices of the established industry price leader
   c. establishing relatively high prices to develop and maintain an image of quality and exclusiveness
   d. seeking to capture and retain a specific market share
   e. attempting to assure a specific dollar profit in the current year

b 30. The typical end result of volume pricing objectives is
   a. a stable marketplace with numerous successful producers.
   b. growth of the firm using this type of objective.
   c. strong differentiation among producers, leading to industry domination by only one firm.
   d. a confusion of objectives and strategies, creating a class of chaos seldom seen elsewhere.
   e. a marketplace where a price change by one producer will always lead to price changes by the others.

e 31. The most commonly mentioned primary or secondary pricing objective in a recent survey of
       U.S. businesses was
       a. achievement of a specified level of total profit.
       b. significant growth in market share.
       c. maximization of profits.
       d. creating an image of quality and exclusivity.
       e. meeting competitors' prices.

d 32. Which of the following would more likely be a pricing objective of a nonprofit organization
       than a for-profit organization?
       a. meeting competitors' prices
       b. achieving a target return on investment
       c. generating a specific dollar sales volume
       d. seeking to discourage consumption of a product
       e. maximizing sales volume

a 33. The producer of which of the following products follows a prestige pricing policy?
       a. Baccarat crystal
       b. Seiko watches
       c. Budweiser beer
       d. Ken-l Ration dog food
       e. Coca-Cola soft drinks

c 34. One of the most significant studies of pricing strategies and objectives of the last twenty
       years was the PIMS Project. For what does the acronym PIMS stand?
       a. Project to Investigate Marketing Scientifically
       b. Polish Institute of Marketing Studies
       c. Profit Impact of Marketing Strategies
       d. People Investigating Marketing Studiously
       e. Palmolive Investigation of Marketplace Situations

e 35. When a nonprofit organization follows a lower-than-average pricing policy or even offers a
       service free, it is probably following a strategy of
       a. cost recovery pricing.
       b. market suppression.
       c. profit maximization.
       d. seeking a target return on investment.
       e. providing market incentives.

b 36. Retail prices that customers expect as a result of custom, tradition, and social habit are called
       a. residual prices.
       b. customary prices.
       c. day-to-day prices.
       d. unusual in today's market.
       e. standard prices.

d 37. A schedule of the amounts of a product or service that will be offered for sale at different prices during a specified time period is
   a.   a demand schedule.
   b.   competition in the marketplace.
   c.   a description of market structure.
   d.   a supply schedule.
   e.   an equilibrium schedule.

c 38. A market structure characterized by relatively few sellers, each of which may affect the market (though none may control it), is called
   a.   pure competition.
   b.   monopolistic competition.
   c.   oligopoly.
   d.   monopoly.
   e.   perfect competition.

e 39. The market structure typical of most retailing and featuring large numbers of sellers of heterogeneous and differentiated products is
   a.   pure competition.
   b.   modified competition.
   c.   perfect competition.
   d.   oligopolistic competition.
   e.   monopolistic competition.

c 40. The market structure characterized by homogeneous product and ease of seller entry due to low start-up costs is
   a.   oligopoly.
   b.   monopolistic competition.
   c.   pure competition.
   d.   modified competition.
   e.   monopsonistic competition.

a 41. A condition of monopoly exists when
   a.   there is only one seller in a market and no close substitute for the product being sold.
   b.   sellers in the market are few but large and the product is undifferentiated.
   c.   there are few buyers in a market, and sellers have to scramble to keep them supplied.
   d.   there are numerous buyers and sellers in the market but communication among them is imperfect.
   e.   buyers refuse to purchase what sellers have to offer.

b 42. Costs which remain stable regardless of the level of production achieved are called
   a.   variable costs.
   b.   fixed costs.
   c.   average total costs.
   d.   marginal costs.
   e.   average revenue.

d 43. In the analysis of revenue and cost curves, profit maximization occurs when
    a.   average total cost equals average revenue.
    b.   marginal cost equals average revenue.
    c.   average revenue equals average total cost.
    d.   marginal cost equals marginal revenue.
    e.   average total cost equals marginal cost.

b 44. The most commonly used method of setting prices today is
    a.   marginal analysis pricing.
    b.   cost-plus pricing.
    c.   full-cost pricing.
    d.   incremental-cost pricing.
    e.   breakeven pricing.

e 45. The approach to pricing which uses only those costs directly attributable to a specific output in setting prices for that output is
    a.   cost-plus pricing.
    b.   customary pricing.
    c.   full-cost pricing.
    d.   breakeven pricing.
    e.   incremental-cost pricing.

c 46. Modified breakeven analysis differs from traditional breakeven analysis in that
    a.   breakeven occurs when total revenue equals marginal revenue, instead of when average revenue equals total cost.
    b.   no consideration is given to the required profit when making the analysis.
    c.   consideration is given to the characteristics of consumer demand as well as to prices and costs.
    d.   breakeven no longer occurs when total profit equals total variable cost, but rather when total variable cost equals marginal revenue.
    e.   calculations are made using computer programs, rather than manually.

a 47. Basic breakeven analysis
    a.   identifies when a company's costs will exactly equal its revenues at a certain price for the product, assuming that costs can be assumed to be divisible into fixed and variable parts.
    b.   is useless as a pricing tool because it is based on assumptions which are always untrue.
    c.   has become less sophisticated in recent years because there has been a tendency to abandon it in favor of more useful tools.
    d.   is an effective way of recognizing marketplace variables and preparing for them in advance.
    e.   is not described by any of the above choices.

C 48. Price elasticity of demand may be identified as
  a. the quantity change in demand for a product or service divided by the quantity change in its price.
  b. the quantity change in the price of a product or service divided by the quantity change in demand for it.
  c. the percentage change in the quantity of a product or service demanded divided by the percentage change in its price.
  d. the percentage change in the price of a product or service divided by the percentage change in the quantity of it demanded.
  e. the percentage change in the price of a product or service divided by the percentage change in the quantity of it supplied.

a 49. Demand for a product or service is considered to be elastic when the numerical value of the elasticity calculation is
  a. greater than one (1.0).
  b. less than one.
  c. equal to one.
  d. greater than one-half (0.5).
  e. less than one-half.

b 50. The Melvin Manufacturing Company makes metal castings for the plumbing industry. It is planning to introduce a new manhole cover assembly and is wondering how many units it'll have to sell to break even on the deal. Fixed costs to tool up to make this assembly have been $100,000. Variable costs for each unit produced will be $20. At a price of $45 per assembly, how many units must be sold to break even?
  a. 2,500
  b. 4,000
  c. 5,000
  d. 8,000
  e. 7,500

Name_____   Instructor _____

Section _____   Date _____

Applying Marketing Concepts

Southern Michigan Packing Company processes and sells canned fruit under the Southern Miss label. Noel Campbell, director of marketing for the packing company, was planning a speech to be delivered before the student marketing club at the local university. Noel knew the students would want to know about his company's marketing mix in general, but he figured that pricing was sure to be an exceptionally hot issue because of a big price-fixing case which had been getting a lot of publicity lately. He also knew that it would be difficult to explain the company's pricing policies since the firm did not aggressively use price to generate more sales. As one of three firms processing and selling canned fruit in a five-state area, Southern Michigan was satisfied with its third of the market and really didn't want to rock the boat unnecessarily. Prices were set at the beginning of the selling year, as the harvest was brought in. Those prices were then maintained till the next harvest, subject only to special promotional activities.

In general, prices were set by first estimating supply and demand for the company's products. Next, the cost of buying and canning the fruit was computed. Costs that could not be assigned to a particular fruit item were not included in the calculations. Once costs were determined, an amount sufficient to cover selling expenses and provide a reasonable profit was added to determine list price. Since the other two firms in the area used the same method of determining price, initial prices were usually quite close, often identical. Differences that existed in the early part of the season "ironed themselves out" by midyear.

____ 1.   Southern Michigan Packing Company's pricing objective would be classified as profit maximization.

____ 2.   The company would benefit from using modified breakeven analysis.

____ 3.   Southern Michigan Packing is constrained by customary prices and thus cannot change prices from year to year.

____ 4.   The company's prices do not take into account demand for its products.

____ 5.   If Mr. Campbell were to apply modified breakeven analysis to his problem, he would have to use a method that assumes that variable cost would be a constant amount per unit.

6.   Southern Michigan Packing Company's pricing objective is
   a.   profit maximization.
   b.   meeting competition.
   c.   a target rate of return on investment.
   d.   to maximize sales.
   e.   to secure market share.

7. Mr. Campbell's talk is really about setting prices in a
    a.   purely competitive market.
    b.   monopolistically competitive market.
    c.   oligopolistic market.
    d.   monopsonistic market.
    e.   market characterized by highly differentiated products.

8. The pricing mechanism which the company uses is
    a.   the cost-plus approach.
    b.   based on breakeven analysis.
    c.   basically a modified breakeven process.
    d.   based on analysis of demand elasticity.
    e.   probably aimed at arriving at a customary price.

9. Mr. Campbell's method of determining costs for pricing purposes was to apply
    a.   full costing.
    b.   breakeven analysis.
    c.   markup on selling price.
    d.   incremental costing.
    e.   differential costing.

10. If we had been told that the Southern Miss brand was strongly preferred over competing brands in two of the five states where it was sold, we could have concluded that, in those states, Southern Miss' market was probably
    a.   purely competitive.
    b.   monopolistically competitive.
    c.   oligopolistic.
    d.   poligopolistic.
    e.   monopolistic.

Marcelin Plauche is in an enviable position. Qualified as architect, civil engineer, and interior designer, Mr. Plauche (pronounced ploe-shay) is in such demand as both designer and contractor of private homes that he can literally name his own price. People will (almost) literally kill to own a Plauche-built home. Mr. Plauche realizes that such popularity probably will not last forever and has publicly stated that his fees are going to be high enough so that when things taper off, he, his wife, and their twelve children can live comfortably for many, many years. As a result, the cost of a home built by this man now averages $200 per square foot, while the average house built in the area costs around $50 per square foot. Though livid with envy, other contractors continue to build homes because, even though they would love to be able to, not many people can afford a home that costs $200 per square foot.

11. Mr. Plauche is well aware that his work possesses an image of quality and exclusivity that appeals to status-conscious people, and is pricing according to
    a.   a prestige objective.
    b.   a target return objective.
    c.   a volume objective.
    d.   an objective of meeting competition.
    e.   an objective of maximizing sales.

12. The structure of the supply side of the home building market in Mr. Plauche's part of the country right now is probably
    a. purely competitive.
    b. monopolistically competitive.
    c. a monopoly.
    d. oligopolistic.
    e. monogamous.

13. If we assume that the actual cost of construction of a Plauche-built home is no greater than that of a home built by a "lesser" contractor and we take seriously Plauche's comments about "living comfortably for many, many years," we might conclude that his pricing objective would be
    a. profit maximization.
    b. target return on investment.
    c. meeting competition.
    d. securing market share.
    e. serving a selected market segment.

14. If Mr. Plauche collects money from his clients by submitting to them the invoices from his subcontractors and suppliers after he adds sums for his own costs and efforts, then the pricing method he is using is
    a. breakeven pricing.
    b. incremental cost pricing.
    c. modified breakeven pricing.
    d. customary pricing.
    e. cost-plus pricing.

Name_____   Instructor _____

Section _____   Date _____

Questions for Thought

The questions which follow are designed to help you become familiar with the main concepts in this chapter through interpretation in your own words. They are meant to be answered in a few sentences or a paragraph at most.

1. How is the process of pricing constrained by laws?

2. Discuss the major objectives served by pricing strategies.

3. Discuss the concept of supply and demand elasticity. Enumerate the factors which determine the degree of price elasticity for a good or service.

4. While price theory gives us a sound basis for the discussion of price, it does have its short-comings. Discuss some of the practical problems involved in applying price theory to actual pricing decisions.

5. Discuss the major advantages and shortcomings of using breakeven analysis in pricing decisions. How does modified breakeven improve on the basic model?

Name_____ Instructor _____

Section _____ Date _____

Experiential Exercises

1. This exercise allows you to obtain first-hand knowledge of the perceived importance of price from the marketing manager of a selected firm.

   Interview the marketing manager (whose title may be product manager, division manager, or general marketing manager) of a manufacturing, processing, or service firm. Talk with this individual about the nature of the firm's marketing operation. When you have a good grasp of it, hand the manager four cards, each containing the name of a variable of the marketing mix: price, product, promotion, or distribution.

   a. Ask the marketing manager to rank the variables in order of importance to the product line that you have been discussing. List these variables in the spaces below.

   Ranking of importance of marketing variables for (name of product or service):

   Ranked first:

   Ranked second:

   Ranked third:

   Ranked fourth:

   b. Ask the manager to explain why these variables have been ranked as they were. Why, for example, is the first-ranked variable more important than the second-ranked variable? Try to get some measure of relative importance from the manager. How *much* more important is the first-ranked variable than the second, and so forth?

c.   How do these rankings compare with the rankings from a recent study reported on in your text? If there are differences, explain.

2.   A common price-setting technique among small retailers is "keystoning." Visit several retail establishments—stores such as independent hardware stores, small pharmacies, and home-owned sporting goods stores are suggested—and ask them about their use of "keystoning." (Warning: some may not know it or use it, but most do.)

a.   Outline the process of pricing by the "keystoning" method.

b.   What sort of pricing method is "keystoning"?

Name_____ Instructor _____

Section _____ Date _____

Computer Applications

Review the discussion of breakeven analysis in Chapter 10 of the text. Then use menu item 16 titled "Breakeven Analysis" to solve each of the following problems.

1. Pickering Products Company has been offered manufacturing and distribution rights to the Wainwright Walker, a therapeutic device which facilitates the healing of broken bones in the lower torso and legs. The current proprietor of the product, Bill Wainwright, has been unsuccessful in developing it and so would be willing to sell out for only $20,000. Jan Sexton, the executive vice-president of Pickering Products, believes that the product can be successfully marketed at a price which will return $6.48 per unit to the company after all outside costs are paid. Examination of Wainwright's records indicates that the variable cost of manufacture for the walkers is $1.80 per unit. Fixed costs to Pickering to get underway with this product would be $56,000.

   a. What is the breakeven point in units?

   b. If Pickering wanted to recover the cost of acquiring rights to the walker during the first year of operations, what would the breakeven point be?

   c. Pickering's president has mandated that every new product the company acquires must produce a $5,000 profit in the first year. How many units must the firm sell to break even if both acquisition costs and the mandated profit must be earned?

   d. There is some question as to whether the variable costs that show on Wainwright's books are totally accurate. How would your answers to a, b, and c be affected if variable costs were 20 percent higher than expected?

2. McInnis Field Services Company, an oil-field supply and development outfit, is working on its marketing plan for the next fiscal year. Lauren Pauli, director of operations, has prepared the following estimates.

Fixed costs $1,092,000
Average variable cost per job   8,000

The table below summarizes the company's capacity to handle jobs. Each line represents maximum capacity.

Price of Jobs	Number of Jobs
$ 20,000	48
$ 40,000	32
$ 60,000	21
$ 80,000	16
$100,000	12
$160,000	10

a. Which average contract size would generate the most profit for the company?

b. In order to bid and win contracts over $90,000, additional equipment costing $160,000 must be obtained. How would the change in fixed costs affect the company's profitability?

Chapter 10 Solutions

Key Concepts

1. e	7. m	13. a
2. p	8. l	14. i
3. q	9. o	15. j
4. n	10. b	16. g
5. r	11. c	17. d
6. f	12. k	18. h

Self Quiz

1. F	11. F	21. T	31. e	41. a
2. T	12. T	22. T	32. d	42. b
3. T	13. F	23. F	33. a	43. d
4. F	14. F	24. F	34. c	44. b
5. F	15. T	25. F	35. e	45. e
6. F	16. F	26. c	36. b	46. c
7. T	17. T	27. b	37. d	47. a
8. T	18. F	28. a	38. c	48. c
9. T	19. T	29. d	39. e	49. a
10. T	20. F	30. b	40. c	50. b

Applying Marketing Concepts

1. F	6. b	11. a
2. T	7. c	12. b
3. F	8. a	13. a
4. T	9. d	14. e
5. T	10. b	

Chapter 11

Managing the Pricing Function

Chapter Summary

Pricing decisions must be made in any organization which provides goods and/or services to the consuming public. In order for these decisions to be made, someone must be responsible for administration of the pricing structure and an overall price structure must be in place. In the average organization, there are three possibilities with respect to who will be doing the administration: a pricing committee composed of top executives, the president or chief executive officer of the company, or the chief marketing officer. A recent study has revealed that, in 51 percent of the firms surveyed, the chief marketing officer was responsible for administration of the price structure, while in 68 percent of the cases marketers, by whatever title they might be called, were administering prices.

There are, of course, alternative pricing strategies available to the firm. These can, in general, be classified into three categories: a skimming strategy; a penetration strategy; and a competitive strategy. Skimming pricing is usually used as a market-entry strategy for distinctive products with little or no initial competition. Penetration pricing is used when there is a wide array of competing brands in the marketplace. Competitive pricing is often the choice when marketers wish to concentrate their competitive efforts on marketing variables other than price.

How prices are quoted depends on such considerations as cost structures, traditional practices in the industry, and policies of individual firms. Price quotes can involve list prices, market prices, cash discounts, trade discounts, quantity discounts, and allowances such as trade-ins, promotional allowances, and rebates. Shipping costs often figure heavily in the pricing of goods. There are a number of alternative methods for dealing with shipping costs. Among these are FOB plant (the price includes no shipping charges), freight absorption (allows the buyer to deduct the cost of transportation from the bill), uniform delivered price (all buyers, regardless of location, are charged the same price), and zone pricing (prices are set by regions).

Pricing policies are general guidelines whose foundations are in the firm's pricing objectives, which are intended for use in making specific pricing decisions. Pricing policies include psychological pricing, unit pricing, price flexibility, product line pricing, and promotional pricing. The relationship between price and the consumer's perception of the quality of a product has been the subject of considerable research. In the absence of other cues, price is an important measure of how consumers view the quality of a product. A significant concept is that of price limits, where the perception of product quality varies directly with price. The concept of price limits suggests that extremely low prices may be considered "cheap," indicating inferior or unacceptable quality.

Negotiated prices and competitive bidding are pricing techniques used primarily in the industrial sector, the government, and institutional markets. Prices may be established by either method. Competitive bidding occurs when several suppliers are asked to provide price quotes on the same service or good. Buyer specifications are the basis on which the bids are prepared. Negotiated contracts are used in other industrial procurement situations. The exact terms of the contract are set through talks between representatives of the buyer and the seller.

Large corporations which have adopted the "profit center" concept often have the problem of charging themselves for goods transferred from one profit center to another. A profit center is any part of the organization to which revenue and controllable costs can be assigned. The transfer prices on these goods moving within the firm have a direct impact on the cost and profitability of the output of both profit centers involved.

The pricing of public services involves a complex of decisions somewhat different from those involved in pricing products and services to be delivered by firms owned by private interests. In the public sector, decisions must be made concerning which costs to assign to a particular action or service, the relationship between direct and indirect prices (such as taxes on a service), and whether price should be an instrument for recovering cost or a device for accomplishing social or civic objectives. The public sector, which was traditionally a user of full-cost pricing, has in recent years tended to use incremental pricing.

Name_____ Instructor _____

Section _____ Date _____

Key Concepts

The purpose of this section is to allow you to determine if you can match key concepts with the definitions of the concepts. It is essential that you know the definitions of the concepts prior to applying the concepts in later exercises in this chapter.

From the list of lettered terms, select the one that best fits each of the numbered statements below. Write the letter of that choice in the space provided.

Key Terms

a. skimming pricing strategy
b. penetration pricing strategy
c. competitive pricing strategy
d. list price
e. market price
f. cash discount
g. trade discount
h. quantity discount
i. trade-in
j. promotional allowance
k. rebate
l. FOB plant
m. freight absorption
n. uniform delivered price

o. zone pricing
p. basing point system
q. pricing policy
r. psychological pricing
s. odd pricing
t. unit pricing
u. price flexibility
v. product line pricing
w. promotional pricing
x. loss leader
y. escalator clause
z. transfer price
aa. profit center

_Z_ 1. Cost assessed when a product is moved from one profit center in a firm to another.

_h_ 2. Price reduction granted for large-volume purchases.

_L_ 3. "Free on Board" price quotation that does not include shipping charges, for which the buyer is responsible; also called _FOB origin_.

_a_ 4. Pricing strategy involving the use of a price that is high relative to competitive offerings.

_b_ 5. Pricing strategy involving the use of a relatively low entry price as compared with competitive offerings; based on the theory that this initial low price will help secure market acceptance.

_I_ 6. Credit allowance given for an old or used item when a customer purchases a new item.

_J_ 7. Advertising or sales promotional funds provided by a manufacturer to other channel members in an attempt to integrate promotional strategy within the channel.

_X_   8. Product offered to consumers at less than cost to attract them to retail stores in the hope that they will buy other merchandise at regular prices.

_P_   9. System for handling transportation costs used in some industries during the early twentieth century in which the buyer's costs included the factory price plus freight charges from the basing-point city nearest the buyer.

_n_ 10. System for handling transportation costs under which all buyers are quoted the same price, including transportation charges.

_y_ 11. In industrial pricing, component of a bid that allows the seller to adjust the final price based on changes in the costs of the product's ingredients between the placement of the order and the completion of construction or delivery of the product.

_v_ 12. Practice of marketing different lines of merchandise at a limited number of prices.

_u_ 13. Pricing policy permitting variable prices for goods and services.

_d_ 14. Established price normally quoted to potential buyers.

_r_ 15. Pricing policy based on the belief that certain prices or price ranges are more appealing to buyers than others.

_b_ 16. General guidelines based on pricing objectives and intended for use in specific pricing decisions.

_e_ 17. Price a consumer or marketing intermediary actually pays for a product or service after subtracting any discounts, allowances, or rebates from the list price.

_aa_ 18. Any part of an organization to which revenue and controllable costs can be assigned.

_0_ 19. System for handling transportation costs under which the market is divided into geographic regions and a different price is set in each region.

_F_ 20. Price reduction offered to a consumer, industrial user, or marketing intermediary in return for prompt payment of a bill.

_t_ 21. Pricing policy in which prices are stated in terms of a recognized unit of measurement or a standard numerical count.

_w_ 22. Pricing policy in which a lower-than-normal price is used as a temporary ingredient in a firm's marketing strategy.

_c_ 23. Pricing strategy designed to deemphasize price as a competitive variable by pricing a product or service at the general level of comparable offerings.

_K_ 24. Refund for a portion of the purchase price, usually granted by the product's manufacturer.

_S_ 25. Pricing policy based on the belief that a price with an uncommon last digit is more appealing than a round figure, such as $9.99 rather than $10.00.

_g_ 26. Payment to a channel member or buyer for performing marketing functions; also known as a functional discount.

_m_ 27. System for handling transportation costs under which the buyer may deduct shipping expenses from the costs of the goods.

Name _____   Instructor _____

Section _____   Date _____

Self Quiz

You should use these objective questions to test your understanding of the chapter material. You can check your answers with those provided at the end of the chapter.

While these questions cover most of the chapter topics, they are not intended to be the same as the test questions your instructor may use in an examination. A good understanding of all aspects of the course material is essential to good performance on any examination.

True/False

Write "T" for True or "F" for False for each of the following statements.

F   1. One benefit of a penetration pricing strategy is that it allows the firm to quickly recover its research and development costs.

T   2. Ballpoint pens, television sets, digital watches, and pocket calculators were all introduced into the market using a skimming pricing strategy.

F   3. During the late growth and early maturity stages of the product life cycle, the price is typically raised because of the desire to control the size of the product's market.

T   4. The one chief disadvantage of a skimming pricing strategy is that it attracts competition into the market.

T   5. Consumer products such as toothpaste and detergent are frequent targets of a penetration pricing policy.

F   6. Penetration pricing is often called a "market-plus" approach to pricing because it is based on the premise that a higher-than-market price will attract buyers and move the brand from the "unknown" category to at least the brand recognition stage.

T   7. Since in many instances the firm intends to increase the price in the future, large numbers of consumer trial purchases are critical to the success of a penetration strategy.

F   8. Penetration pricing is likely to be used when the demand for the product or service is highly inelastic.

T   9. A competitive pricing strategy shifts the emphasis to nonprice competition by concentrating marketing efforts on the product, distribution, and promotional elements of the marketing mix.

T   10. The basis on which most price structures are built is the list price—the rate normally quoted to potential buyers.

F   11.   The sticker price on the window of a new automobile shows the market price for the basic model of that car and then adds the prices of all options that are included.

F   12.   Originally instituted to improve the liquidity position of sellers, trade discounts may be legal as long as they are offered to all customers on the same terms.

T   13.   If a trade discount were quoted as "35 percent, 10 percent off list" to wholesalers, this would mean that wholesalers would pay the manufacturer of the good the list price less the 35 percent that they were to discount the list price to retailers, less another 10 percent of the discounted price to compensate them for their costs, profits, and services.

F   14.   Noncumulative quantity discounts are reductions in price determined by purchases over a stated time period.

F   15.   The major categories of allowances are price reductions and trade-offs.

F   16.   "FOB origin" pricing provides a price that includes all shipping costs.

T   17.   The method of quoting prices called "uniform delivered pricing" is sometimes also known as "postage-stamp pricing."

F   18.   The often-used term "FOB" is really an abbreviation for "Free of Bond."

T   19.   Both zone and uniform delivered pricing have the drawback that some customers (in the case of uniform delivered pricing those near the shipping point and in the case of zone pricing those near the inner boundary of the zone) will be paying "phantom freight."

T   20.   Originally, odd pricing was used as a cash-control device within the firm, forcing clerks to make change.

T   21.   Studies of the use of unit pricing have typically discovered that when the technique is used shoppers pay less or save money and store brand purchases increase.

F   22.   The use of variable pricing is more common in retailing than in the industrial market because retailers are not bound by the provisions of the Robinson-Patman Act.

T   23.   Product-line pricing is really a combination of product and price strategies which allows the shopper to pick a price range and then devote his or her attention to the other features of the product such as color, style, or material.

T   24.   Promotional pricing may be used recurrently or on a one-time only basis; in either case, it is considered to be a temporary ingredient in a firm's selling strategy.

F   25.   An escalator clause in a purchase contract allows the buyer to adjust the final price paid, based on changes in costs and needs that occur between the time the order is placed and the time the product is completed or delivered.

Multiple Choice

Circle the letter of the word or phrase that best completes the sentence or best answers the question.

b 26. The pricing strategy used by Blue Chip Electronics is best characterized as a
   a. skimming strategy.
   b. penetration pricing strategy.
   c. competitive strategy.
   d. "market-plus" strategy.
   e. functional strategy.

c 27. Which of the following is one of the advantages of a penetration pricing strategy?
   a. It allows the firm to quickly recover its research and development costs.
   b. It is effective in segmenting the overall market on a price basis.
   c. It discourages competition, since the prevailing price does not suggest attractive financial returns.
   d. It permits the marketer to control demand in the introductory stages of the product's life cycle and to adjust productive capacity to meet demand.
   e. It largely negates the price variable in the marketing strategy.

d 28. When a skimming strategy is used, the product's price is typically reduced during the late growth and early maturity stages of the product life cycle because
   a. volume of production is sufficiently high to reduce the average per-unit cost of the product.
   b. competition has been effectively stifled and the product can now be allowed to sell at its "natural" price.
   c. the profits earned during the introductory and early growth stages of the cycle may be plowed into new productive technology, making lower prices possible.
   d. of the pressure of competition and the desire to expand the product's market.
   e. the product's proprietors have achieved their target objective and can now afford to take less off the top for contributions to profit and overhead.

a 29. Though the one chief disadvantage of a skimming pricing policy is its tendency to attract competition, it may still be used effectively for a long period of time if
   a. the firm marketing the product has patent rights over its design or can retain a proprietary ability to keep out competition (such as by keeping production methods a trade secret).
   b. research and development costs are small and the amounts to be recovered can be realized very early in the product life cycle.
   c. production facilities are developed to satisfy all potential demand which may develop from any source.
   d. financial pressure can be brought to bear on potential competitors, making them fearful of entering the market.
   e. inventories of goods are kept larger than any potential demand for the product.

e 30. When a penetration pricing strategy is used,
   a. prices are set at a level well above the prices of competing products.
   b. the price of the product is adjusted as necessary to keep it competitive with similar products in the market.
   c. the product is usually in the decline stage of its life cycle and price manipulation is a normal feature of this stage.
   d. it is almost necessary that there be no preexisting competition; otherwise, the strategy won't work.
   e. products or services are priced noticeably lower than competing offerings.

d 31. A penetration pricing policy is likely to be used when
   a. the demand for the product is highly inelastic.
   b. the demand for the product is only moderately inelastic.
   c. the demand for the product is somewhat elastic.
   d. the demand for the product is highly elastic.
   e. the supply of the product is highly elastic.

a 32. In industries where competitors' offerings are relatively homogeneous, a common pricing strategy is
   a. competitive pricing.
   b. skimming pricing.
   c. penetration pricing.
   d. pricing based solely on costs.
   e. market-plus pricing.

c 33. Pricing at the level of comparable products was used as a primary pricing strategy by what proportion of the firms responding in a recent survey?
   a. one-third
   b. one-half
   c. two-thirds
   d. three-quarters
   e. nearly all the respondents used this strategy

c 34. Which of the following most closely represents the list price of a product?
   a. the amount of money you and your next door neighbor's son both agree is fair to pay him to cut your lawn
   b. the amount of money you ask for when you decide to sell your 1973 Ford Torino
   c. the manufacturer's "suggested retail price" on a new RCA television set
   d. the advertised price of a home for sale by the owner in a classified newspaper advertisement
   e. the price you pay for an article after all discounts and allowances are subtracted from the original price

b 35. Reductions in price offered to consumers, industrial users, or channel members for prompt payment of a bill are known as
   a. trade discounts.
   b. cash discounts.
   c. quantity discounts.
   d. cutback discounts.
   e. "off price" discounts.

b 36. If the payment terms on an invoice are shown as 3/10, net 45, then
    a.   the full amount must be paid within 10 days and legal action will be taken after 45.
    b.   the full amount is due in 45 days but if you pay the invoice in 10 days you can deduct 3 percent from the total.
    c.   3 percent of the invoice must be paid in 10 days, and the rest in 45 days.
    d.   10 percent of the amount due must be paid in 3 days, with the rest due at the end of 45 days.
    e.   three-tenths of the amount billed is due in 45 days.

d 37. Trade discounts are also known as
    a.   cash discounts.
    b.   seasonal discounts.
    c.   incremental discounts.
    d.   functional discounts.
    e.   quantity discounts.

e 38. If a trade discount of 50 percent, 15 percent off list, was offered to a wholesaler by a manufacturer, then the wholesaler would pay which of the following prices for a good whose usual retail price to the consumer was $100?
    a. $32.50
    b. $35.00
    c. $37.50
    d. $41.00
    e. $42.50

a 39. If a discount is offered on the basis of the dollar value or the number of units of product bought by a purchaser over a stated period of time, it is a
    a.   cumulative quantity discount.
    b.   noncumulative quantity discount.
    c.   cash discount.
    d.   promotional discount.
    e.   trade status discount.

c 40. Allowances are similar to discounts in that they are
    a.   justifiable on the grounds that larger customers deserve to pay less per unit for the materials they buy.
    b.   based on the operating expenses of each level in the channel of distribution.
    c.   deductions from the price the purchaser must pay.
    d.   the rate normally quoted to potential buyers.
    e.   used uniformly across the consumer and industrial segments of the market.

d 41. A refund by the seller of a portion of the purchase price paid for a product is a
    a.   functional discount.
    b.   trade-in.
    c.   promotional allowance.
    d.   rebate.
    e.   cash discount.

e   42.   When a seller quotes all potential buyers the same price for goods, transportation included, regardless of where the potential purchasers are located, that seller is using
   a.   FOB plant pricing.
   b.   freight absorption pricing.
   c.   zone pricing.
   d.   all-for-one pricing.
   e.   uniform delivered pricing.

a   43.   Uniform delivered pricing is also known as
   a.   postage-stamp pricing.
   b.   pricing to the market.
   c.   zone pricing.
   d.   basing point pricing.
   e.   standard industry pricing.

d   44.   Pittsburgh-plus pricing was
   a.   a variety of zone pricing once used in the meatpacking industry.
   b.   a type of FOB origin—freight-allowed pricing typical in the fresh produce (fruits, vegetables, and like goods) industry.
   c.   widely used by manufacturers of parts for automobiles during the 1960s and 1970s.
   d.   the long-standard method of quoting prices in the steel industry in the United States.
   e.   a method of determining how much it would cost to ship anything to Pittsburgh.

b   45.   When a retailer prices merchandise in terms of some standard unit of measure (ounce, liter, pound, gram), that retailer is using
   a.   promotional pricing.
   b.   unit pricing.
   c.   odd pricing.
   d.   psychological pricing.
   e.   average-cost pricing.

a   46.   The use of a variable-price policy by a seller is characterized by
   a.   the necessity of having to bargain with the seller over the price of every item in the store.
   b.   prices which end in numbers not ordinarily used in price quotations, such as 97, 98, or 99.
   c.   placing goods into "price lines" to simplify the customer's decision-making process.
   d.   lower-than-normal prices used temporarily to generate traffic through the store.
   e.   none of the above.

c   47.   When a retail firm prices goods below cost to attract customers whom it hopes will then buy other, regularly priced merchandise, the firm is using
   a.   bait and pull pricing.
   b.   bull and bear pricing.
   c.   loss leader pricing.
   d.   product-line pricing.
   e.   multiple-unit pricing.

d 48. The concept of *price limits* basically says that
   a. people consciously limit their spending to goods not affecting their consumption patterns.
   b. a firm may encounter legal opposition if the prices of its products exceed certain limits.
   c. the relationship between price and sales volume is limited to values greater than 2.
   d. consumers have limits where their product-quality perceptions vary directly with price.
   e. reasonable individuals expect to be able to limit spending to necessities and a few luxuries, even in bad times.

b 49. In the governmental and industrial markets, when there is only one supplier of a good or service or where extensive research and development work is called for by a contract,
   a. competitive bidding may nonetheless be required by law.
   b. negotiation is likely to be the basis on which the contract is awarded.
   c. an escalator clause is typically included in the contract to protect the buyer from price increases.
   d. transfer pricing may be used to reduce the process of contracting to a comprehensible level.
   e. specifications must be carefully written so that breach or abrogation of the contract will be easy to prove in court.

e 50. If a public-sector price is set so that people will be encouraged to use or discouraged from using a particular product or service, then price is being used as a
   a. cost-recovery device.
   b. means of passing the indirect cost of the product or service on to the public.
   c. measure of the ability of the public to pay.
   d. device to transfer costs from one sector of the market to another.
   e. means of achieving a social or civic objective.

Name_____ Instructor _____

Section _____ Date _____

Applying Marketing Concepts

Eckdahl Corporation manufactures a range of microwave ovens distributed throughout the United States. Sold primarily through specialty outlets, Eckdahl products are recognized to be of excellent quality. Sales volume and profits have both increased dramatically over the last five years. The company sells through its own salesforce, but also uses wholesalers in parts of the country where sales volume isn't large enough to justify maintenance of a company sales representative.

Eckdahl is a respected name in its industry. Retailers often feature in their advertising the fact that they carry the Eckdahl line. The company encourages this activity and gives dealers who do this sort of thing price reductions to help them pay their advertising costs. Eckdahl also has a somewhat unusual pricing approach for its industry. Prices on Eckdahl products are the same to any dealer anywhere in the country. Transportation is always included in any price quote.

The company's product line includes ovens in three sizes. The smallest, or "micro" units, average .4 cubic feet in capacity and sell in the $225 to $275 range, depending on special features. The medium-sized ovens, of "standard" size, average .7 cubic feet in capacity and sell in the $325 to $400 range. The large units, whose capacity averages 1.3 cubic feet, sell for $600 to $800. Eckdahl publishes manufacturer's suggested retail prices (MSRPs) whose dollar amounts always end in a 98, and encourages dealers to stick with that ending even if they discount the product off the MSRP. It is management's firm belief that the 98 ending helps sales.

____ 1. Eckdahl's pricing policies encourage retailers to sell Eckdahl products as loss leaders.

____ 2. When Eckdahl quotes the same price to all buyers of its products it is using a unit pricing policy.

____ 3. The company is encouraging retailers to use psychological pricing.

____ 4. If Eckdahl were to institute a trade-in program, it would be encouraging retailers to sell the company's products at less than list price.

____ 5. By pricing its products in different ranges, the company is attempting to establish definite price/quality relationships in the consumer's mind.

6. The discount which Eckdahl Corporation gives wholesalers who sell to retailers is called a
    a. cash discount.
    b. trade discount.
    c. quantity discount.
    d. promotional discount.
    e. rebate.

7. What type of allowance was described in this case?
   a. a rebate
   b. a trade-in
   c. a promotional allowance
   d. an allowance for returned goods
   e. a sales representative's field allowance

8. Eckdahl's geographic pricing policy is
   a. FOB plant.
   b. FOB plant—freight allowed.
   c. zone pricing.
   d. basing point pricing.
   e. uniform delivered pricing.

9. The company's general pricing policy is one of
   a. product line pricing.
   b. unit pricing.
   c. skimming pricing.
   d. penetration pricing.
   e. price fixing.

10. The firm encourages its retailers to engage in
    a. skimming pricing.
    b. penetration pricing.
    c. unit pricing.
    d. odd pricing.
    e. unusual pricing.

Fred Lee Motor Company is a multi-brand new car dealership in Stuttgart, Arkansas. The company sells two domestic makes, one German, and two Japanese. Advertising strongly suggests that potential new-car buyers "shop Fred Lee for best prices," but specific prices are never advertised and each retail customer bargains with the company for his or her own selling price on a car.

The company is also on the state's "bid list," so it periodically receives requests to bid on providing automobiles for the highway patrol, game and fish department, and other state agencies. These bid requests are carefully read, and if what is needed is clearly enough described, the company may enter a bid. Occasionally, the fleet manager may have to call Little Rock to find out exactly what is meant by certain wording of the request sent out by the state agency.

All cars sold by the Lee dealership are delivered in Stuttgart. If the buyer doesn't want to take delivery in Stuttgart, the company can make arrangements to have the car delivered by another dealer from his stock for the amount of money it would cost to ship the car from Stuttgart to that dealership.

When asked about his pricing policies, Mr. Lee said, "One thing we know is that we never want to be the cheapest dealer around, nor do we want to be the highest priced. People don't like you to be either one of those things. We just want to sell cars at a reasonable price, one that people think represents good value for the money."

____ 11.   Though all consumer prices are subject to negotiation at Lee's, the company's advertising suggests that its pricing strategy is a competitive one.

____ 12.   When a supplier such as Lee's enters a bid on a state request for bids, he or she is really opening the process of negotiation to supply those vehicles.

13.   Lee Motor Company's basic pricing policy appears to be a
   a.   fixed-price policy.
   b.   variable price policy.
   c.   list price policy.
   d.   product line policy.
   e.   zone pricing policy.

14.   When the fleet sales manager calls Little Rock to get additional information on bid requests, he is probably trying to clarify the bid request's product
   a.   specifications.
   b.   end use.
   c.   price limits.
   d.   function.
   e.   user name.

15.   The geographical pricing policy the company uses for delivery of cars at locations other than Stuttgart is
   a.   zone delivered pricing.
   b.   freight absorption pricing.
   c.   postage-stamp pricing.
   d.   basing point pricing.
   e.   FOB destination.

16.   Mr. Lee's comments about not wanting to be too cheap or too expensive suggest that he is aware of
   a.   how fickle the consumer can really be.
   b.   price limits.
   c.   the uses of odd pricing.
   d.   the essence of the automobile-buying experience.
   e.   how difficult it is to make money.

Name _____   Instructor _____

Section _____   Date _____

Questions for Thought

The questions which follow are designed to help you become familiar with the main concepts in this chapter through interpretation in your own words. They are meant to be answered in a few sentences or a paragraph at most.

1.   Identify and discuss the alternative pricing strategies available to a firm.

2.   Describe the various methods a firm may use to quote prices to potential customers.

3.   Examine in some detail the various pricing policies which marketers may use. When do you think each is most appropriate?

4. Discuss some of the relationships between money price and consumer perceptions of the quality of goods.

5. Why is transfer pricing an important consideration in the industrial market? What is the reasoning behind the use of this particular pricing technique and where might a firm encounter difficulty using it successfully?

Name_____   Instructor _____

Section _____   Date _____

Experiential Exercises

1. This exercise is designed to familiarize you with the psychological concept of price limits. You will visit various retail stores and investigate the range of prices for selected products.

    a. For each of the products listed below, determine the range of prices charged for that product in two stores.

		Store Name	Price Range Low	Price Range High
Flowering plants	#1	_____	_____	_____
	#2	_____	_____	_____
Women's suits	#1	_____	_____	_____
	#2	_____	_____	_____
13-inch color TV sets	#1	_____	_____	_____
	#2	_____	_____	_____
16-ounce curved claw nail hammers	#1	_____	_____	_____
	#2	_____	_____	_____
Personal computers	#1	_____	_____	_____
	#2	_____	_____	_____

    b. Discuss the price ranges you have discovered with the manager of one of the stores you investigated. How do these price ranges relate to what you've read about price limits? How does the store manager feel about his prices and price limits?

2. This exercise is designed to give you a greater understanding of the discounting process in the industrial market.

Visit a local manufacturer or wholesaler. After identifying yourself as a college student, ask to speak with whoever is in charge of the accounts payable and the accounts receivable ledgers. This person may be the head of the bookkeeping department or some other individual. Once contact has been made, request the following information:

a. What kinds of discounts are granted and what are the terms on which these discounts are granted? (Don't be surprised if they're called something you haven't seen in your text. Trade terms often differ from academic ones.) Determine the types and terms of these discounts and enter below.

1. Trade (functional):

Terms:

2. Quantity:

Terms:

3. Cash:

Terms:

b. What are the types and terms of discounts are offered by the suppliers? Determine the types and usual terms and enter below.

1. Trade (functional):

Terms:

2.   Quantity:

Terms:

3.   Cash:

Terms:

c.   Ask the person you're talking to if it is his/her company's policy to take cash discounts or to pay the invoice only when it's due.

The cost to a firm of granting a cash discount or of failing to take one when it's offered in terms of an equivalent rate of interest may be computed as follows:

Equivalent rate of interest = the stated percentage of the cash discount multiplied by 365 divided by the difference between the number of days when the invoice comes due less the last day to take the discount. Thus, if terms of 3/15, net 45 are offered, the equivalent rate of interest becomes:

$$Ei = 3 \times 365/(45-15) = 36.5\%$$

Determine the cost to the company of granting or not taking cash discounts.

Name_____   Instructor _____

Section _____   Date _____

Computer Applications

Review the description of the expected net profit (ENP) approach to competitive bidding in Chapter 11 of the text. Then use menu item 7 titled "Competitive Bidding" to solve problems 1 and 2.

1. Underwood Construction Company has received a request for bids from the City of Camden, New Jersey, for the design and construction of a new water purification plant. Underwood's estimating department has concluded that the cost to complete the project will be $1,920,000. Miller McDermott, Underwood's president, has prepared two bids based on this estimate, a low bid of $2,320,000 and a high bid of $3,040,000. McDermott estimates that there is a 40 percent chance that the higher bid will be successful and a 55 percent chance of winning the contract with the lower bid.

    a. Which of the two bids would provide the higher expected net profit?

    b. If new information, such as the decision by a major Underwood competitor not to bid, increases the probability of acceptance of the high bid to 60 percent and the low bid to 70 percent, which bid now provides the higher expected net profit?

2. The Brandon Consulting Group, an engineering development company specializing in making prototypes of new consumer garden equipment, has been asked to build the design prototype of a new device called a "StumpJumper." This machine would use hydraulic pressure to bounce stumps out of the ground. Gunilde Brandon, the company's president, would like to make $11,000 on the job. She estimates the cost to actually build the machine at $4,250.

    a. What is the probability of acceptance required to earn a net of $11,000 if Gunilde submits a bid of $19,500?

    b. Suppose she decides to bid $24,500 for the job. What would the probability of acceptance become?

Chapter 11 Solutions

Key Concepts

1.	z	7.	j	13.	u	19.	o	25.	s
2.	h	8.	x	14.	d	20.	f	26.	g
3.	l	9.	p	15.	r	21.	t	27.	m
4.	a	10.	n	16.	q	22.	w		
5.	b	11.	y	17.	e	23.	c		
6.	i	12.	v	18.	aa	24.	k		

Self Quiz

1.	F	11.	F	21.	T	31.	d	41.	d
2.	T	12.	F	22.	F	32.	a	42.	e
3.	F	13.	T	23.	T	33.	c	43.	a
4.	T	14.	F	24.	T	34.	c	44.	d
5.	T	15.	F	25.	F	35.	b	45.	b
6.	F	16.	F	26.	b	36.	b	46.	a
7.	T	17.	T	27.	c	37.	d	47.	c
8.	F	18.	F	28.	d	38.	e	48.	d
9.	T	19.	T	29.	a	39.	a	49.	b
10.	T	20.	T	30.	e	40.	c	50.	e

Applying Marketing Concepts

1.	F	6.	b	11.	T	16.	b
2.	F	7.	c	12.	F		
3.	T	8.	e	13.	b		
4.	F	9.	a	14.	a		
5.	F	10.	d	15.	d		

Part Five Puzzle

ACROSS CLUES

1. acronym for the Profit Impact of Marketing Strategies project
3. relative to pricing, stating prices in terms of recognized units of measure
7. discounts offered in return for prompt payment of a bill
9. exchange value of a good or service
11. one of the authors of a major federal law prohibiting price discrimination activities
12. pricing objectives which seek to achieve a specified return on sales or investment
13. state laws requiring sellers to maintain minimum prices for comparable merchandise
17. amounts of product which will be bought at different prices during a specified time period
18. allowances given for old items when customers buy new items
21. acronym for "free on board," a price quotation that usually does not include shipping charges
22. in relation to pricing, general guidelines based on pricing objectives for use in decisions

23. market structure with only one seller of a product or service with no close substitutes
26. market structure with relatively few sellers and significant entry barriers to new competition
27. a bid component that allows the seller to adjust the price if costs change during the contract
28. measure of the responsiveness of buyers and sellers to a change in price
29. price used when a product is moved from one profit center in a firm to another

DOWN CLUES

2. pricing strategy involving the use of a high initial price relative to competition
4. discount offered for the performance of marketing functions
5. price purchaser actually pays for a product after discounts, allowances, and rebates
6. established price normally quoted to potential buyers

8. discounts granted to buyers who purchase a significant amount of a product from a vendor
10. traditional prices that customers expect to pay for certain products and services
11. pricing strategy using a relatively low entry price compared to competition
14. refunds of a portion of the purchase price, usually granted by a product's manufacturer
15. type of competition with homogeneous product and many buyers and sellers
16. pricing policy based on the belief that an unusual last digit makes a price more appealing
19. quantities of product that will be offered for sale at different prices over period of time
20. practice of adding percentage or fixed dollar amount to cost to arrive at selling price
24. in product pricing, practice of marketing lines of products at a limited number of prices
25. handling transportation costs by dividing the market into regions for pricing that service

Name _____   Instructor _____

Section _____   Date _____

Cases for Part 5

1. Mrs. Jacobs' Salad Dressing

It is well known in Broussard County that Idabelle Jacobs is a great cook. She has created many recipes that have won Blue Ribbons at the State Fair. Idabelle is best known, however, for her delicious salad dressing.

For a number of years, friends and retailers have been urging Idabelle to sell her dressing commercially. Today she borrowed $25,000 from the Bank of Broussard to produce and market her product. As a consequence, she will be facing the competitors now on the market in the local area. Jacobs' salad dressing can best be described as a rich, garden-fresh, home-style dressing. It costs about the same to produce as competing products.

Question

What should the pricing objective for this firm be? Defend your position.

2. *Liberty Chime and Bell Corporation*

Ralph Bolt, Director of Market Development for Liberty Chime and Bell Corporation, has been asked by Walt Hadband, the company president, to estimate demand after the firm implements a price level change.

Liberty markets carillon chimes and single-hung bells made of bronze all over the United States. Its products are used in churches, public buildings, and carillons. There are other manufacturers of similar products which can be used if Liberty's bells are unsatisfactory. Costs of labor and material have risen to the point where some adjustment must be made. Mr. Hadband has considered a 10 percent price increase, but before announcing the change, he wants to know if sales will decline dramatically.

Question

Can Mr. Bolt provide a reliable estimate of the demand change to Mr. Hadband? How should he go about estimating demand?

3.   *Gunnar Thorwaldsen, Freelance Viking (A Saga of Tenth-Century Norway)*

Gunnar Thorwaldsen, a journeyman knight and freelance shipbuilder from up near Trondheim, has developed a revolutionary new ship which he thinks will revolutionize the manly art of Viking, that periodic quest for slaves and plunder every right-thinking tenth-century Norseman deems his right and obligation. His ship has a unique underwater hull shape which allows it to hold the sea in even the heaviest storms but still draws so little water that it can be grounded on a gradually sloping beach to allow the passengers to depart for a little raiding and pillaging.

Thorwaldsen estimates that he can build his "Viking Special" for around 3,000 kroner (or the equivalent). This includes both fixed and variable costs. Since Gunnar expects to sell his ships to the better class of Vikings, their materials and workmanship must be of the best quality, and the expected lifetime of each vessel (assuming it is not lost at sea, taken by pirates, or burnt by irate victims) will be at least ten years.

The shape of the hull of Gunnar's ship is determined by a special soaking and caulking process which he himself developed and performs in secret. He fully expects it will be at least fifteen years before anyone else can figure out how he manages to create this secret configuration.

Question

Should Gunnar adopt a skimming or a penetration pricing policy?

4. *Monkmeyer Drop Forging Company*

Ted Monkmeyer, President of Monkmeyer Drop Forging Company, feels that his firm has a problem. Distributors are treating the Monkmeyer line of specialty wrenches very casually, and don't seem to be making a very active effort to promote their sale. Jan Stockwell, Mr. Monkmeyer's new Executive Assistant, has suggested a course of action she thinks will go a long way toward solving the problem. Ms. Stockwell believes that Monkmeyer should raise the retail price, thereby increasing the amount of discount per item received by both retailers and wholesalers.

Gene Nolan, Sales Manger for Monkmeyer, is displeased with Jan's proposal. He favors the use of promotional allowances given for specific purposes. Mr. Nolan would use cooperative advertising and PMs.[1]

Questions

a.   Discuss the advantages and disadvantages of each proposal.

b.   If you were the Director of Marketing for Monkmeyer Drop Forging, which of the two alternatives would you choose? Why?

---

[1] PMs, or "Push Monies" are payments made directly to sales clerks and wholesaler salespeople. They are usually figured as a certain percentage of sales. They are sometimes called "spiffs."

5. *Donald M. Landsdowne, Attorney at Law*

Donald M. Landsdowne is an attorney practicing in the state of North Carolina. Mr. Landsdowne specializes in personal injury cases in which he typically represents the plaintiff and is compensated for his services with a percentage of whatever judgment his client receives. Mr. Landsdowne is a very conscientious and thorough practitioner, and his services are considered to be among the best. He has traditionally charged as his fee 40 percent of any awards he was able to get for his clients.

In recent years, there has been an influx of attorneys into the legal profession, and sheer numbers have made the industry very competitive. Mr. Landsdowne has just learned that a number of his fellow attorneys have reduced their fees on personal injury cases to 35 percent, and some are even accepting 30 percent of the award. He is concerned about what to do. He knows that his reputation is well established in this field, and even with the increase in competition he hasn't noticed any diminishment of his caseload. He is concerned because he feels that if he reduces his fees he will be working for less than he is worth. Most of his cases come to him by referral (from people he has successfully represented in the past), anyway.

Question

What should Mr. Landsdowne do?

Name _____   Instructor _____

Section _____   Date _____

Creating a Marketing Plan:
How Much Is Too Much? (And How Little Is Not Enough?)

The information contained in this episode will help you complete Parts III.A. and III.B. of your marketing plan for Latebri Industries. You may wish to review the material in Part Four of the text to refresh your memory before attempting to complete Part III.A.

Episode Five

"OK," said Terry, "let me get this straight. We're going to offer 'minimum downtime' computer service aimed primarily at business users of PCs here in the New Essex area. We're going to be open 24 hours a day, and we'll repair any brand of PC that walks in the door. We're going to offer maintenance contracts on the machines, and we'll pick up and deliver equipment for servicing if desired. I see. That makes me happy. What about you, Brian?"

"I'm fine, too, Ter," Brian said, "I can see where I'm going to be spending a lot of time doing preventive maintenance for people who own those units with the built-in 'computer viruses.' You know, I'll bet we're one of the few service firms in town with people who know how to create the right diagnostics to track those little devils down. It should be fun!"

"Right, fellas," spoke up Laura, "but you know we've got to get down to brass tacks on price sooner or later. You guys have fun just going out there and playing around with all those different brands of machines, but if we don't make some money around here, it's not going to be long before we won't be able to pay the rent. Come look at these figures I've put together. They outline some price information I got my hands on." She handed a copy of the information contained in Tables P5-1 and P5-2 to Brian and Terry.

"Very interesting," muttered Terry, reading the charts he had been handed. "We've really got a wide range of prices here, don't we? It looks like the most common local hourly price is around $80 or $90 an hour."

"Yes," replied Brian, "but there are 10 firms charging only $75. I wonder if they know something we don't know—or maybe it's that we know something they don't—like how to fix computers!"

"Well," smiled Laura, "I've run some figures and if they are right, we can make money according to our plans at any hourly rate equal to or greater than $75. That price would put us in a very competitive position as far as the other computer repair places are concerned."

Table P5-1: Typical IBM Personal Computer Component Service Prices

| Component | Value New | Price for the Average Service Repair | | | |
		Carry-in	Mail-in	On-site	Courier
CPU, 512K, Keyboard	$2,500	$165	$145	$250	$200
Mono Display	300	28	25	44	35
Double 3.5" Floppy	1,000	75	65	116	93
Printer	600	40	35	65	50
Total	$4,200	$308	$270	$475	$378
Percentage of Original Cost		7.33	6.43	11.31	9.00

Adapted with numerous changes from *Purchasing*, 21 June 1984.

Table P5-2: New Essex Area Repair Price Data (from a Survey of 42 Firms)

Charge per Hour	Number	Percentage Reporting
$150	4	9.5%
$110	4	9.5%
$100	4	9.5%
$ 90	10	23.8%
$ 80	7	16.7%
$ 75	10	23.8%
$ 60	3	7.0%

Mean per-hour charge for repairs: $91.19
Median per-hour charge: $90.00
Modal per-hour charge: $82.50

"Yes, that's true," answered Terry, "but it's still the next-to-the bottom price for the market. I think we're better than that. I think we should ask at least $80 per hour for our services, and there should be a one-hour minimum."

"I'll buy the one-hour minimum," spoke up Brian, "but the average I see in these figures is $91.00 and change per hour. Why don't we want to charge something like that?"

"Let's put that decision off for now," commented Laura. "If we offer maintenance contracts, you know, we're going to have to price them as well. How do you propose we do that?"

"I've got that one solved for you, Laura," responded Terry. "An article I read last night gave some actuarial figures and some prices for maintenance contracts and it said that maintenance contracts that sell cost approximately as much as a 'worst-case' repair."

"You mean a repair that involves the whole system?" asked Brian.

"Yes," answered Terry, "and it looks like that sort of call costs about 10 percent, on average, of what a new system would cost. I think our maintenance contracts should be priced at around 10 percent of the cost of a new system to the client."

Laura responded, "Good thinking, Ter; I've seen that article and I think you're right. Let's work on that sort of price for maintenance contracts. Now let's get back to the per hour price for our standard repair service. What price do you think we should set? Let's vote on it."

Guidelines

a. Outline the company's product/service strategy in your planning notebook. Refer back to the information provided in the earlier parts of this exercise for items which may expand on what you learned in this part. Recognize how this strategy developed to serve the needs of the market and of the entrepreneurial trio.

b. What sort of price structure do you favor for Latebri Industries? Should its hourly rate be $75, $80, $90, or some other amount per hour? This time, the decision is yours to make, and you should be able to justify it if called upon to do so.

Part 6

Distribution Strategy

This section of your text presents an overview of the channel of distribution, marketing intermediaries, and physical distribution. Together those concepts form the basis for the development of distribution strategy.

Distribution strategy, the method used to put the product in the possession of the consumer at the right time and place, is an integral part of marketing strategy. Product, price, and promotion are all related to distribution strategy as part of the marketing mix. Likewise, the method used for distribution has impact on the other components of the marketing mix.

Distribution channels facilitate the sale of the product. A channel may be a single transaction between producer and ultimate user, or it may be an extremely complex set of interrelationships including several successive independent firms taking title to goods or assisting in the transfer of title to those goods. Multiple channels are often used to match product availability to the time and place needs of users. In today's market, "reverse" channels have had to be developed to handle product recalls, warranty service, and returnable containers.

The institutions involved in marketing channels include manufacturers, wholesaling intermediaries, retailers, and facilitating agencies. The marketing channel begins with the producer, who often must actively seek wholesalers and retailers to distribute the product. If the manufacturer has a good reputation or is making an outstanding product, wholesalers and retailers will exhibit interest in buying the product and performing other intermediary functions for the manufacturer. The manufacturer must be prepared to compensate and otherwise motivate them to perform their functions in an effective manner. Producers often have a choice of several alternative channels to use and must devise strategies to gain acceptance of their product by marketing intermediaries as well as by consumers. Other channel decisions that producers must make include the intensity of market coverage. Products may be made available in the marketplace through channels providing intensive, selective, or exclusive distribution. Which of these channels is chosen by the producer depends in large part on consumer buying behavior and the need of the manufacturer to control the quality and consistency of dealer service.

Regardless of the desired level of intensity of distribution, the type of channel used will play a significant role in channel strategy. In addition to the traditional, loosely organized channel, there are three classes of vertical marketing systems (VMS) which can be used. These three types include the corporate, administered, and contractual VMSs. When independent marketing intermediaries are employed, firms involved must be aware of potential legal problems arising from such practices as exclusive dealing, closed territories, and tying contracts.

Wholesaling intermediaries are independent individuals and firms that take title to goods or assist in the passage of titles from manufacturers to retailers or industrial users. Wholesalers actually take title to the goods they intend to sell. They, like most retailers, thus engage in speculative buying in the hope that purchasers will be found. In the usual course of events, wholesalers develop long-term relationships with manufacturers and retailers or industrial users. There are many different types of wholesalers, with each type providing a set of services or functions to the manufacturers and retailers with whom it deals.

Agents and brokers are wholesaling middlemen who perform primarily a selling function. They find buyers for goods, but do not themselves take title to those goods. The two major classes of agents are manufacturers' agents and selling agents. Selling agents function as the marketing department for a firm and sell the whole range of products made by the firm. Manufacturers' agents, who usually have geographically defined territories, represent several firms with noncompeting but complementary lines within that territory.

Retailers, like wholesaling intermediaries, buy for resale. Numerous different types of retailers exist to serve the needs of consumers. Retailing changes in an evolutionary process as products, institutional structures, and consumer buying habits change. Because of this, at any given point in time there may be a number of different forms of retail institutions in existence competing for the same consumer market. Many recent trends in retailing, such as scrambled merchandising, hypermarkets, planned shopping centers, and teleshopping, are evidence that retailers are attempting to provide consumers with increased shopping convenience.

Channel relationships, the internal structure of channels and the way business is done within them, are studied as a separate topic within the marketing field. Channels exist to get the product to the consumer, yet the channel is composed of independent individuals and firms, each with different goals and needs. Channels usually perform smoothly, a fact which surprises many people when they realize the strains and stresses which the conflicting goals of channel members often put on the channel itself.

Physical distribution is the mechanism which facilitates the operation of marketing channels. It is certainly not enough that title is transferred from manufacturer to wholesaler to retailer; it is also necessary that product move from source to ultimate user. Physical distribution serves to move, store, and keep track of the product as it travels from producer through the channel of distribution to the ultimate user. These functions must be performed in a timely, efficient, and effective manner.

A properly structured and effectively functioning marketing channel and physical distribution system are necessary for successful marketing. Many people and institutions are involved in making sure the consumer will get the product on time, in good condition, and at the desired place. Without good distribution strategies, business firms soon find themselves in serious trouble.

Chapter 12
Channel Strategy

Chapter Summary

Distribution channels are made up of marketing institutions and the interrelationships among them responsible for the physical movement and flow of title of goods and services from producer to consumer or industrial user. Wholesalers and retailers are the marketing intermediaries (middlemen) in these channels, who serve to bridge the gap between producer and consumer. Distribution channels create time, place, and possession utility by making products and services available when and where consumers want to purchase them, and by facilitating the transfer of title from producers to ultimate users.

Distribution channels are in a constant state of formation and reformation. At any given time, a host of alternative possibilities exists for makers of consumer and industrial goods and providers of services. Some firms sell directly to the ultimate user, while others use a variety of intermediaries to serve their various market segments. It is not at all unusual for a firm to be a member of multiple channels, particularly if that firm serves numerous market segments. Of some interest is the "reverse channel" used by recyclers for product recall programs and, in some situations, where product-service is necessary.

Channel leadership is based in the relative power possessed by the various members of a given channel. Generally, the most powerful member of the channel will emerge as the channel leader. The sources of a member's power in the channel may stem from the power to reward other members, the power to coerce other members, legitimate power inherent in the role of the member, referent power possessed by a particular member, and expert power arising out of knowledge greater than what the others possess. The marketing intermediary having the greatest control over the operations of a particular channel is known as the *channel captain*. The channel captain may be a manufacturer, a wholesaler, or a retailer, depending on where the power resides in that channel's particular combination of interrelationships. The exercise of power in the channel of distribution often results in conflict among the members of the channel. This conflict may be horizontal in nature (among members of the channel at the same level) or vertical (among members of the channel at different levels). Conflict can be reduced if channel members can be convinced to cooperate with each other rather than compete for realization of the same objectives.

Among the basic channel strategy decisions are the choice of which channel to use, level of distribution intensity to be developed, and whether or not vertical marketing systems are to be employed by the firm. The selection of a distribution channel is affected by characteristics of the market, characteristics of the producer, characteristics of the product itself, and the nature of competition. Distribution intensity decisions involve choosing whether to use intensive, selective, or exclusive distribution. The vertical marketing decision usually involves consideration of the degree to which the manufacturer or one of the marketing intermediaries will assume the duties and obligations of other members of the channel. Three major types of vertical marketing systems exist: in the corporate system, there is single, unique ownership of each stage of the marketing channel; in the administered system, a dominant channel member exercises its power to achieve channel coordination; and finally, contractual systems specify by legal process the exact relationships among channel members. Typical contractual vertical marketing systems include wholesaler-sponsored chains, retail cooperatives, and franchises.

Name _____   Instructor _____

Section _____   Date _____

Key Concepts

The purpose of this section is to allow you to determine if you can match key concepts with the definitions of the concepts. It is essential that you know the definitions of the concepts prior to applying the concepts in later exercises in this chapter.

From the list of lettered terms, select the one that best fits each of the numbered statements below. Write the letter of that choice in the space provided.

Key Terms

a. distribution channel
b. marketing intermediary
c. direct selling
d. direct marketing
e. dual distribution
f. reverse channel
g. facilitating agency
h. channel captain
i. brand hostaging
j. intensive distribution

k. selective distribution
l. exclusive distribution
m. exclusive-dealing agreement
n. closed sales territory
o. tying agreement
p. vertical marketing system (VMS)
q. corporate marketing system
r. administered marketing system
s. contractual marketing system
t. franchise

___d___ 1. Direct communication, other than personal sales contacts, between buyer and seller.

___h___ 2. Dominant and controlling member of a marketing channel.

___o___ 3. Arrangement between a manufacturer and a marketing intermediary that prohibits the intermediary from handling competing product lines.

___J___ 4. Policy in which a manufacturer of a convenience good attempts to saturate the market with the product.

___r___ 5. Vertical marketing system in which channel coordination is achieved through the exercise of power by a dominant channel member.

___e___ 6. Network in which a firm uses more than one distribution channel to reach its target market.

___i___ 7. Situation in which a retailer demands trade promotion funds from a manufacturer in exchange for shelf space.

___p___ 8. Preplanned distribution channel organized to be cost effective and achieve improved distribution efficiency.

_b_ 9. Business firm, either wholesale or retail, that operates between the producer of goods and the consumer or industrial user; sometimes called *middleman*.

_K_ 10. Policy in which a firm chooses only a limited number of retailers to handle its product line.

_N_ 11. Restricted geographical selling region specified by a manufacturer for its distributors.

_F_ 12. Path goods follow from consumer back to manufacturer.

_L_ 13. Policy in which a firm grants exclusive rights to a wholesaler or retailer to sell in a particular geographical area.

_S_ 14. Vertical marketing system characterized by formal marketing agreements among channel members.

_a_ 15. Entity consisting of marketing institutions and their interrelationships that is responsible for the physical and title flow of goods and services from producer to consumer or industrial user.

_m_ 16. Arrangement between a manufacturer and a marketing intermediary that prohibits the intermediary from handling competing product lines.

_o_ 17. Vertical marketing system in which there is single ownership of each stage of the marketing channel.

_g_ 18. Institution, such as an insurance company, bank, or transportation company, that provides specialized assistance for channel members in moving products from producer to consumer.

_t_ 19. Contractual arrangement in which a wholesaler or retail dealer (the franchisee) agrees to meet the operating requirements of a manufacturer or other franchiser.

_C_ 20. Direct sales contact between buyer and seller.

Name_____   Instructor _____

Section _____   Date _____

Self Quiz

You should use these objective questions to test your understanding of the chapter material. You can check your answers with those provided at the end of the chapter.

While these questions cover most of the chapter topics, they are not intended to be the same as the test questions your instructor may use in an examination. A good understanding of all aspects of the course material is essential to good performance on any examination.

True/False

Write "T" for True or "F" for False for each of the following statements.

_T_   1. As we are using them, the terms "jobber" and "distributor" are considered to mean the same thing as the term "wholesaler."

_T_   2. Stores that sell products purchased by individuals for their own use rather than for resale are by definition retailers, even though the goods are sold at wholesale prices.

_F_   3. Distribution channels play a key role in the creation of form, time, place, and possession utility.

_F_   4. Possession utility is created only when title to the goods passes from the producer or the intermediary to the purchaser.

_T_   5. Marketing intermediaries facilitate the exchange process by reducing the number of marketplace contacts.

_T_   6. When products from one source are combined with similar products from other sources for purposes of distribution, the process is called *accumulation.*

_F_   7. Historically, the best distribution channel for most goods has proven to be manufacturer to wholesaler to retailer to consumer.

_F_   8. In general, channels of distribution for industrial goods tend to be longer than those for consumer goods because of geographical concentration of buyers and limited number of purchasers.

_F_   9. Direct channels of distribution are much more important in the consumer market than in the industrial market.

_T_ 10. Small retailers rely on wholesalers to be buying specialists who can ensure a balanced inventory of goods produced in various regions of the world.

_T_ 11. The term "industrial distributor" is commonly used in the industrial market to refer to wholesalers who take title to the goods they sell.

_T_   12. Agent wholesalers are typically used in industries where there are a large number of small producers; their primary function is to bring buyers and sellers together.

_F_   13. The producer to agent to industrial user channel is typically used when the unit of sale of a product is small and the cost of product transportation is relatively high.

_F_   14. Dual distribution occurs when a manufacturer uses more than one wholesaler or retailer in any given market to reach the selected target market segment.

_T_   15. If a state or the federal government should pass a law requiring the use of returnable bottles for beer and soft drinks, it would be forcing the creation of a reverse channel of distribution.

_F_   16. If one member of a distribution channel can exercise power over the other members because of a contractual relationship among them, then that member of the channel has "coercive power."

_T_   17. Retailers are more likely to become channel captains these days as large retail chains assume traditional wholesaling functions and may even dictate design specifications to manufacturers.

_T_   18. Among the bases for retailers' ability to hold brands hostage is the fact that the number of retail stores is declining; in fact, the number of grocery stores now is only slightly more than one-half of the number of grocery stores in business in 1968.

_F_   19. Horizontal conflict within a distribution channel occurs when members of the channel at different levels, such as wholesalers and retailers, disagree.

_T_   20. The use of wholesalers becomes almost mandatory when a manufacturer chooses intensive distribution as a strategy.

_F_   21. Exclusive-dealing agreements, closed sales territories, and tying agreements are illegal per se—that is, illegal in and of themselves.

_F_   22. A tying agreement is a contract between a manufacturer and a wholesaler or retailer which prohibits the retailer or wholesaler from carrying competing products made by other manufacturers.

_T_   23. The most significant form of vertical marketing system is the contractual, accounting for nearly 40 percent of all retail sales.

_F_   24. The Independent Grocers' Alliance (IGA) is an excellent example of a retail cooperative.

_T_   25. Franchising in the United States employs over 7 million Americans, some 6.3 percent of the work force.

Multiple Choice

Circle the letter of the word or phrase that best completes the sentence or best answers the question.

d 26. When marketing intermediaries perform the activities of accumulation, breaking bulk, and assorting, they are participating in a process called
   a. standardizing transactions.
   b. cutting the number of marketplace contacts.
   c. assisting in the search process for goods.
   d. sorting to alleviate discrepancies in assortment.
   e. developing markets through segmentation.

b 27. In recent years, companies like Tupperware have had to modify their channels of distribution because
   a. people have had less use for plastic food storage containers as families have become smaller.
   b. more women have entered the work force and don't want to spend time at evening Tupperware parties.
   c. families have found that it is cheaper and easier to eat out than it is to prepare meals and then have to save the leftovers.
   d. protests from marketing intermediaries created such vertical conflict in the channel that they had to accommodate the needs of their middlemen.
   e. production improvements made it possible and necessary for the company to double sales in order to be profitable.

a 28. In the industrial market, you would expect most installations and accessory equipment to be sold
   a. directly from producer to ultimate user.
   b. to the ultimate user through wholesalers.
   c. through agents who sell to wholesalers who then sell to the ultimate user.
   d. directly through agents to the ultimate user.
   e. by retailers directly to the ultimate user.

d 29. Which of the following lists is composed solely of marketing intermediaries?
   a. manufacturers, industrial users, consumers
   b. agents, railroad companies, retailers
   c. retailers, banks, insurance companies
   d. agents, wholesalers, retailers
   e. wholesalers, retailers, consumers

a 30. The so-called "traditional" channel of distribution for consumer goods involves
   a. distribution by a producer through wholesalers and retailers to the consumer.
   b. distribution by a producer through retailers to the consumer.
   c. only a producer and the ultimate user of the product.
   d. manufacturers, agents, wholesalers, and retailers.
   e. distribution by producers to the user through wholesalers and agents.

b 31. Which of the following would be a reverse channel of distribution?
  a.   A manufacturer ships high-style clothing directly to a retailer.
  b.   A supermarket receives returnable bottles from consumers and ships them back to the bottling plant to be sterilized and refilled.
  c.   A manufacturer of industrial installations custom-designs a metal stamping plant for Kaiser Industries.
  d.   The Electromatic Corporation supplies the state of Delaware with a complete traffic control system for the city of Wilmington.
  e.   Your little brother sets up a stand in front of the house and, using lemons and sugar he's filched from the pantry, becomes a small businessman selling lemonade to passersby.

d 32. A dual distribution system is best exemplified by
  a.   the use of insurance companies to absorb some of the risks of doing business.
  b.   creation of a channel of distribution to handle the return of recyclable materials to factories for reprocessing.
  c.   the practice by some social welfare agencies of opening neighborhood offices to be more convenient to their clients.
  d.   the use of its own salesforce and a system of outside jobbers by a manufacturer of mechanics' tools.
  e.   the action of an agent who brings together orange growers and wholesale grocers to create a market for fresh fruit.

b 33. In order for recycling to succeed, which of the following is a basic condition which must exist?
  a.   There must be substantial public interest in recycling and demand for it to be undertaken.
  b.   A substantial and continuous supply of secondary product (recyclable aluminum, reclaimed steel, and so forth) must be available.
  c.   It must be possible to reprocess the material to be recycled, though the process need not be efficient or economic.
  d.   The material to be reprocessed must be metallic or ceramic in nature (like steel or glass).
  e.   Legislation requiring that certain products be reprocessed must be enacted.

c 34. In addition to their use as a device to facilitate recycling, reverse channels of distribution are often used
  a.   for the distribution of services; intangible goods call for a unique relationship between producer and ultimate user.
  b.   in the industrial market for the distribution of high-tech products where a substantial degree of customization is required.
  c.   for the handling of products which have been recalled due to some flaw or which must be returned to the factory for repairs.
  d.   when a very short channel of distribution is called for by some characteristic of the product or the market.
  e.   by making it easier for agencies to facilitate the performance of the services they render.

d 35. Channels which are established by service providers
  a.   tend to be longer than those usually used for tangible goods.
  b.   are usually more impersonal than those used for tangible goods.
  c.   usually include industrial distributors.
  d.   are usually shorter than those used for tangible goods.
  e.   are typically free of horizontal and vertical conflict.

e 36. When members of a channel of distribution agree among themselves to pursue a course of action which they all deem to be in their best interests, they are exercising
  a. reward power over each other.
  b. the power to coerce each other into desired behavior.
  c. legitimate power; after all, they are acting in their mutual best interest.
  d. expert power over each other; they should all certainly know what's best for the group.
  e. referent power; they all want to maintain effective working relationships with each other.

c 37. Of the following statements about channel captaincy, which is most true?
  a. Historically, the role of captain in the channel has tended to be filled by the retailer, though in recent years wholesalers and manufacturers have increased their influence.
  b. Although the influence of wholesalers in the channel of distribution has been on the increase in recent years, they are still largely in the shadow of producers and retailers.
  c. Retailers are increasingly assuming the role of channel captain; their control of shelf slots in their stores contributes to their power, as do the size and volume of retail chains.
  d. Manufacturers seldom fill the role of channel captain; the intense competition among them precludes any single one becoming particularly powerful.
  e. Wholesalers exercise perhaps the greatest amount of power of all possible participants in the distribution channel because only they have the ability to bring producer and user together.

a 38. Brand hostaging occurs when
  a. retailers force a manufacturer to pay trade promotion money or be denied shelf space for its brand.
  b. the brand manager of a particular brand is kidnapped by industrial terrorists and held incommunicado in a small room until large inventories of the product are turned over to competitors.
  c. manufacturers refuse to supply retailers with a preferred product unless the retailers agree to buy quantities of a less desirable item.
  d. retailers are so dependent on manufacturers' brands that they are willing to pay a premium price to get them.
  e. shelf spacing is shifted from one brand to another though each brand sells at the same price.

e 39. Which of the following is an example of vertical channel conflict?
  a. conflict between two or more wholesalers
  b. conflict among a group of retail florists
  c. conflict among drug, variety, and discount stores, all of which sell the same brand name products
  d. conflict between company-owned and independently owned retail outlets in the same chain
  e. conflict between manufacturers and retailers which occurs when the retailers develop private brands

b 40. The basic antidote to channel conflict is
   a. strict enforcement of all legal and contractual provisions of the relationship among the members of the channel.
   b. effective leadership of the channel by the channel captain to create the spirit of being members of the same organization among members of the channel.
   c. for those members of the channel who don't agree with the way things are going to abandon that channel and start their own.
   d. creation of an integrated, single-company controlled channel from production to retail sale to prevent any conflict.
   e. dissolution of the channel by the channel captain; conflict can never be overcome, only contained.

b 41. A firm with a broad product line is usually able to sell directly to retailers or industrial users because
   a. it has enough items in its line to publish a catalog.
   b. larger total sales permit selling costs to be spread over a variety of products.
   c. it can afford more sales representatives than a limited line producer can.
   d. buyers like to do business with big companies that can easily satisfy their needs.
   e. it does not need a large number of customers to survive.

C 42. Among the market factors which determine the structure of a distribution channel is/are
   a. the perishability of the product.
   b. the product's requirements for regular service.
   c. whether the product is designed for the consumer or the industrial market.
   d. the fact that a producer who is financially strong can hire its own salesforce.
   e. the fact that the single-product firm often discovers that direct selling is an unaffordable luxury.

a 43. Some firms are forced to develop unique distribution channels because
   a. independent marketing intermediaries do not adequately promote their offerings.
   b. there is such a small market for their offerings that intermediaries refuse to handle them.
   c. they wish to hold onto the lion's share of the profits from their products.
   d. their products are so unique that no one exists to deal in them.
   e. they have such a bad reputation as suppliers that intermediaries will not handle their products.

b 44. The idea that convenience goods and industrial supplies with typically low unit prices frequently are marketed through relatively long channels of distribution is an example of
   a. a producer factor affecting the choice of a channel of distribution.
   b. a product factor affecting the choice of a channel of distribution.
   c. a competitive factor affecting the choice of a channel of distribution.
   d. a market factor affecting the choice of a channel of distribution.
   e. a promotional factor affecting the choice of a channel of distribution.

a 45. Which of the following is most true of exclusive distribution?
   a. Some market coverage may be sacrificed by choosing this policy, but the loss is offset by the image of quality and prestige which is created.
   b. Mass coverage and low unit prices make the use of wholesalers almost mandatory with this policy.
   c. The firm reduces total marketing costs and establishes better working relationships within the channel by choosing this policy.
   d. Adoption of this policy allows the consumer to buy the product with a minimum of effort.
   e. Cooperative advertising can be used for mutual benefit and marginal retailers can be avoided.

e 46. An exclusive-dealing agreement
   a. restricts the geographical territory of each of a producer's distributors.
   b. requires that a dealer who wishes to become the exclusive dealer for a producer's products also carry other products of that producer.
   c. is legal if the producer's or dealer's sales volume represents a substantial percentage of total sales in the market area.
   d. prohibits the distributors from opening new facilities or marketing the manufacturer's products outside their assigned territories.
   e. prohibits a marketing intermediary from handling competing products.

a 47. Tying agreements are illegal when
   a. they lessen competition.
   b. they are horizontal in nature.
   c. they limit the geographical territory in which the product may be sold.
   d. they tie the marketing intermediary to the producer or service provider by not allowing that intermediary to carry competing products.
   e. they are required by producers as assurance that the marketing intermediary will devote total concentration to the producer's product line.

d 48. Goodyear Tire and Rubber Company manufactures tires and sells them at wholesale and retail through a system of company-owned distributors and stores. Such an arrangement is known as
   a. an administered marketing system.
   b. a wholesaler-sponsored voluntary chain.
   c. a retail cooperative.
   d. a corporate marketing system.
   e. a contractual marketing system.

b 49. If a group of retailers were to start its own wholesaling operation by purchasing ownership shares in it and agreeing to buy a minimum percentage of its inventory from it, it would have created
   a. a corporate marketing system.
   b. a retail cooperative.
   c. a wholesaler-sponsored voluntary chain.
   d. an administered marketing system.
   e. a franchise system.

c 50. Franchising has become such an enormous industry that
   a. over 10 percent of the U.S. work force is employed in the industry.
   b. there are over one million franchised outlets in the United States, employing over four million people.
   c. total sales by franchises now exceed the gross national product of the United Kingdom.
   d. in some industries, franchises account for the total sales of the industry.
   e. success is practically guaranteed for the individual who buys into a franchise operation.

Name _____ Instructor _____

Section _____ Date _____

Applying Marketing Concepts

Joyce Stall was recently appointed marketing manager at Electro Industries, which manufactures amplifiers and speakers for use with electric guitars and other musical instruments. This small Iowa company has traditionally distributed its goods through a regional wholesaler in Sioux City who sold to retailers in Iowa, Nebraska, Kansas, and Illinois.

One of Ms. Stall's first projects was to test the feasibility of selling Electro's products by direct mail promotion to musicians around the country. She discovered a great deal of interest in the company's well-designed, high-quality products, but realized that the company budget would be stretched quite thin if national marketing and distribution were undertaken. Despite the budgetary limits, management has decided to risk expansion and has assigned Joyce the task of creating an efficient, low-cost channel for the Electro line.

____ 1. Ms. Stall should immediately hire a large sales staff to sell Electro products directly to retailers.

____ 2. If Electro sold through wholesalers to retailers and also sold directly to consumers using a door-to-door salesforce, the firm would be using dual channels.

____ 3. Since the "consumer is king," the consumer is the channel captain in the direct marketing channel.

____ 4. It is possible that the new channel will cause vertical channel conflict to occur.

____ 5. Electro's past channel and the new one would be classified as corporate vertical marketing systems.

6. If Ms. Stall decides to approach the market through a limited number of selected retailers, she will be engaged in
    a. the use of a reverse channel.
    b. closed circuit selling.
    c. intensive distribution.
    d. selective distribution.
    e. exclusive distribution.

7. If Joyce decides to use a single wholesaler to distribute the Electro line to all retailers, she will be using
    a. an industrial distributor.
    b. a buying agent.
    c. a channel captain.
    d. an exclusive distributor.
    e. a corporate marketing system.

8. If Ms. Stall sells Electro products only to middlemen who agree not to carry competitive products, she would be using
    a. franchising.
    b. exclusive dealing.
    c. exclusive distribution.
    d. horizontal marketing systems.
    e. a retail cooperative.

9. Which of the following best describes the channel that Electro has been using?
    a. producer to wholesaler to industrial user
    b. producer to consumer
    c. producer to agent to retailer to consumer
    d. producer to wholesaler to retailer to consumer
    e. service provider to consumer

10. If Ms. Stall elects to develop the marketing channel her feasibility study investigated, she will be using which of the following channel designs?
    a. producer to wholesaler to industrial user
    b. producer to consumer
    c. producer to agent to retailer to consumer
    d. producer to wholesaler to retailer to consumer
    e. service provider to consumer

The Merriman Company, a retailer located in Little Rock, Arkansas, is in the process of analyzing its relationships with its various suppliers and customers. Company management has discovered, as it expected, that most purchasing of soft goods (clothing, piece goods, furs) by the company is directly from the manufacturer of the item. Some of Merriman's other lines, however, are bought in a very different manner. Household electrics, if the quantity to be bought is large enough, can often be purchased directly from the producer. If the order is small or if repair parts are needed, however, a local industrial distributor is often the source of products from the same manufacturers. Merriman people also seem to be spending an inordinate amount of time handling goods which have been returned to the store for shipment back to manufacturers for repair under warranty or because a recall order was issued. The company also found that, in recent years, the furniture department, which has its own separate building and has always been somewhat autonomous in its operations, has gone heavily into office furniture and supplies, and sells more furniture, fixtures, and supplies to local businesses than it does household furnishings to the company's traditional customers. Executives realize that times have changed, but are somewhat puzzled by all these relationships, and to top it all off, they have been approached by a group of several other medium-sized retailers with the proposal that they all get together and set up their own captive wholesaling operation to sell to themselves, so they can buy in larger overall quantities and save some money.

11. Merriman typically purchases soft goods
    a. through a "traditional" consumer goods channel.
    b. through a channel direct from producer to retailer.
    c. wherever it can get them at the best price.
    d. only during peak seasons.
    e. from wholesalers specializing in soft goods.

12. Merriman's purchases of household electrics indicate the presence of
    a. collusion, which probably violates the Sherman Act.
    b. much confusion in Merriman's buying department.
    c. a dual distribution system for this class of product.
    d. the inadequacy of Merriman's inventory control system.
    e. a high level of demand for this merchandise in Little Rock.

13. The time Merriman personnel is spending handling merchandise to be sent off for repair or some other manufacturer adjustment should tell you that
    a. Merriman must handle very inferior goods; quality merchandise simply shouldn't be giving that much trouble.
    b. the channel of distribution from those manufacturers to Merriman must be somehow in disarray.
    c. times have changed a lot; in past years it would have been the retailer's responsibility to make good on these items.
    d. Merriman has become involved in reverse channels of distribution; these typically appear under such conditions.
    e. Merriman's New York buying group needs to be made aware of the deficiencies in the goods it is shipping.

14. Merriman's furniture department
    a. appears to have become a wholesale operation in office furnishings and supplies and probably should be set up that way, with the retail furniture and home furnishings department separated from it.
    b. seems to be one of the most efficient parts of the Merriman operation.
    c. is acting as a producer rather than as a marketing intermediary.
    d. is engaging in direct distribution, acting as agent for a broad range of manufacturers.
    e. serves primarily as the base for a reverse channel of business equipment and supplies.

15. If Merriman joins with the other retailers to create the wholesale operation, they will have created a
    a. wholesaler-sponsored voluntary chain.
    b. franchise.
    c. corporate marketing system.
    d. administered marketing system.
    e. retail cooperative.

Name _____   Instructor _____

Section _____   Date _____

Questions for Thought

The questions which follow are designed to help you become familiar with the main concepts in this chapter through interpretation in your own words. They are meant to be answered in a few sentences or a paragraph at most.

1. Explain the role distribution channels play in marketing strategy.

2. Discuss some of the more common types of distribution channels.

3. What are the bases of power in the distribution channel? How does a firm get to be channel captain?

4. Discuss the major channel strategy decisions a firm may have to make.

5. Outline and discuss the concept of the vertical marketing system.

Name _____   Instructor _____

Section _____   Date _____

Experiential Exercises

1. When we think of channels of distribution, we automatically think of the distribution of products. Services must be distributed, too. In fact, the distribution of services is often more difficult than the distribution of products, because keeping an inventory of the ability to render service can be a very chancy thing.

    Services are distributed by public-sector organizations such as fire and police departments and by private-sector operations specializing in such activities as transportation, entertainment, and financial investments.

    For this assignment, select a service industry or a service component of a product provided by a retailer, wholesaler, or specific service provider, and examine the distribution channel or system for that service. What problems in distribution does the provider face? Use the outline below to format the information you get by talking with industry employees, consultation of library sources, and/or conversations with customers of the industry.

    Service you've selected (describe):

    a. What channels are used to provide this service?

    b. How does distribution of this service differ from distribution of the typical product?

    c. Do allocation problems occur with the service? How do companies handling the service cope with those problems?

    d.   How would you change the channel to improve the distribution of the service?

2.   The purpose of this exercise is to investigate the extent to which dual (or an even more extended case, multiple) distribution exists in the market for a single, extremely common product. Consider the simple wall-mounted light switch.

    a.   Discuss the channel of distribution which might bring such a switch to a consumer for do-it-yourself installation.

    b.   What channel of distribution do you suppose an institution like your college or university uses to buy the same switch? How does this differ from the consumer channel?

    c.   When a home is being newly constructed, the electrical contractor purchases switches to install in the job. How and where does this individual buy them and how did they get there?

    d.   The unhandy consumer may have to bring in an electrician to replace a switch in the event that one burns out in his or her home. Examine the channel of distribution that this switch is likely to follow.

Compare your analysis of each of the above channels with those of your classmates. Don't be surprised if there are significant differences in the channels which you have isolated for each of the product users we've mentioned.

3. Channels of distribution develop and change as markets for innovative products develop and change. Using library sources, interviews with knowledgeable people, and perhaps even your own experience, research the development of the channel (or channels) of distribution for home computers.

   a. In the beginning, who were the makers of home (or personal) computers, and how were the computers distributed?

   b. As the market for these units developed, how and when did new producers/intermediaries enter the market and what happened to some of the older members?

   c. At the present time, what does the structure of the channel look like for this class of product? What do you predict it will ultimately develop to resemble?

Name_____   Instructor _____

Section _____   Date _____

Computer Applications

Review the discussion of decision tree analysis in Chapter 12 of the text. Then use menu item 2 titled "Decision Tree Analysis" to solve each of the following problems.

1. Belinda's Feline Fashions is a ten-store chain of pet stores specializing in products for cat owners (or, some would say, products for people who are owned by cats). Belinda Gilliam operates her mini-chain from a headquarters in Dayton, Ohio. Over the last ten years the firm has grown so that sales are now averaging $2 million per year. Ms. Gilliam has been approached by CatFancy, a leading producer of cat care products. It has proposed that BFF become an exclusive intermediary for its products. The arrangement would be that BFF would have geographical exclusivity in its market area but would have to carry only the CatFancy line. The offer looks good to Ms. Gilliam because the CatFancy line is of excellent quality, well-advertised, and has a strong consumer preference. She is of the opinion that her sales would increase by 10 percent if she took the offer.

    Ms. Gilliam, when carefully questioned, indicated that she was "quite sure" (70 percent) that her opinion would be vindicated if she took the CatFancy offer. She did indicate that there was a "remote chance" (30 percent) that sales would decline 10 percent with only the CatFancy line to sell.

    a.   Should Ms. Gilliam accept the CatFancy offer?

    b.   Mel Moffett, Ms. Gilliam's accountant, disagrees with her. He thinks that there is a 90 percent chance that BFF sales would decline by 10 percent because of the loss of customers loyal to brands that would have to be dropped from BFF's line if the offer is accepted. If he is right, should Ms. Gilliam accept the offer?

2. Steve Geraci, who owns an auto parts store in Pullman, Washington, has been approached by a salesman from the Spokane Auto Supply Company, a large wholesaler-sponsored voluntary chain. On the face of it, the deal the chain is offering looks pretty good, and Steve is considering dropping the independent wholesaler from whom he's been buying. The brands carried by Spokane Auto Supply are all well known with reputations for good quality. The salesman concluded his presentation with the comment that Steve "should be able to increase sales by 45 percent" over his current $2 million.

    Steve, however, is no dummy. He has talked to several other firms which have gone with Spokane Auto Supply and feels that there's only a 50 percent chance that he will achieve the 45 percent increase the salesman promised. The other side of the coin is that there is a 50 percent chance that his volume will drop by 50 percent if he goes with the voluntary chain. It seems that deliveries by Spokane Auto Supply are often slow and unreliable, and customers don't like waiting for delivery.

a. Should Steve continue to buy from the independent wholesaler or should he switch to Spokane Auto Supply?

b. Judy Collara, Steve's partner, disagrees with his assessment of the Spokane Auto Supply deal. She believes that the only risk of not achieving the 45 percent increase in sales depends on whether National Auto Supply decides to open a store in Pullman. She knows it has been studying the feasibility of such an action for a long time and that there is an 80 percent probability that it'll move into town in the next year. If that happens, sales will drop by 50 percent if she and Steve stay with the independent wholesaler. If, on the other hand, they switch to Spokane Auto Supply, sales will drop only 20 percent. If Judy is right, what should they do?

Chapter 12 Solutions

Key Concepts

1. d	5. r	9. b	13. l	17. q
2. h	6. e	10. k	14. s	18. g
3. o	7. i	11. n	15. a	19. t
4. j	8. p	12. f	16. m	20. c

Self Quiz

1. T	11. T	21. F	31. b	41. b
2. T	12. T	22. F	32. d	42. c
3. F	13. F	23. T	33. b	43. a
4. F	14. F	24. F	34. c	44. b
5. T	15. T	25. T	35. d	45. a
6. T	16. F	26. d	36. e	46. e
7. F	17. T	27. b	37. c	47. a
8. F	18. T	28. a	38. a	48. d
9. F	19. F	29. d	39. e	49. b
10. T	20. T	30. a	40. b	50. c

Applying Marketing Concepts

1. F	6. d	11. b
2. T	7. d	12. c
3. F	8. b	13. d
4. T	9. d	14. a
5. F	10. b	15. e

Chapter 13

Wholesaling

Chapter Summary

The previous chapter introduced the concept of the channel of distribution and the roles of wholesalers. This chapter will focus exclusively on wholesaling. Wholesaling involves the activities of persons or firms that sell mainly to retailers or to other wholesalers or industrial users, and only in insignificant amounts to ultimate consumers. A true wholesaler takes title to the products it sells. The term *wholesale intermediary* is a broader term that describes not only wholesalers but also agents and brokers that perform important wholesaling activities without taking title to the goods. Wholesaling intermediaries provide time, place, and ownership utilities by performing the marketing functions of buying, selling, storing, transporting, risk taking, financing, and supplying market information.

Wholesaling intermediaries are essential to the efficiency of the distribution channel because they reduce the number of buyer-seller transactions required for the channel to function. If, for example, three manufacturers sold directly to eight retailers, twenty-four transactions would be required to satisfy market demand. If a single wholesaler entered the channel of distribution, the number of transactions would be reduced to eleven.

To avoid confusion, wholesalers, as we have defined them above, are often characterized as "merchant wholesalers." The two major subclasses of merchant wholesalers are full-function merchant wholesalers, such as rack jobbers, and limited-function merchant wholesalers, such as truck wholesalers, cash-and-carry wholesalers, drop shippers, and mail-order wholesalers. Full-function wholesalers are typical of the drug, grocery, and hardware industries, while limited-function wholesalers are found in the coal, lumber, cosmetics, jewelry, sporting goods, and general merchandise areas.

Agents and brokers, or agent wholesaling intermediaries, include commission merchants, auction houses, brokers (with various specialties such as real estate, financial instruments, and certain foods), selling agents, and manufacturers' agents. None of these various intermediaries takes title to the goods in which they deal.

Wholesaling strategy is formulated just like all other marketing strategy. First, a target market is identified and specified in terms of product line, customer size, customer needs, and/or promotional strategy to be employed. Then, a marketing mix is developed. Wholesalers generally rely on adjustments to the width, length, and depth of the product (service) assortment to provide a product/ service strategy. Pricing is more a function of the number and type of services offered than it is of any other variable in the strategy, while distribution strategy is often a function of the typical form of operation of that particular class of wholesaling intermediary. The promotional strategy of the ordinary wholesaling intermediary features an emphasis on personal selling, with advertising and other promotional methods taking a lesser part than they do in retailing.

Name _____   Instructor _____

Section _____   Date _____

Key Concepts

The purpose of this section is to allow you to determine if you can match key concepts with the definitions of the concepts. It is essential that you know the definitions of the concepts prior to applying the concepts in later exercises in this chapter.

From the list of lettered terms, select the one that best fits each of the numbered statements below. Write the letter of that choice in the space provided.

Key Terms

a. wholesaler
b. wholesaling intermediary
c. sales branch
d. public warehouse
e. sales office
f. trade fair
g. merchandise mart
h. merchant wholesaler
i. rack jobber
j. cash-and-carry wholesaler

k. truck wholesaler
l. drop shipper
m. mail-order wholesaler
n. agents and brokers
o. commission merchant
p. auction house
q. broker
r. selling agent
s. manufacturer's agent

_i_ 1. Full-function merchant wholesaler that markets specialized lines of merchandise to retail outlets and provides the services of merchandising and arrangement of goods, pricing, maintenance, and stocking of display racks.

_g_ 2. Permanent exhibition facility in which manufacturers rent showrooms to display products for visiting retail and wholesale buyers, designers, and architects.

_c_ 3. Establishment maintained by a manufacturer that serves as a warehouse for a particular sales territory, thereby duplicating the services of independent wholesalers; carries inventory and processes orders to customers from available stock.

_j_ 4. Limited-function merchant wholesaler that performs most wholesaling functions except financing and delivery.

_d_ 5. Independently owned storage facility that stores and ships products for a rental fee.

_e_ 6. Manufacturer's establishment that serves as a regional office for salespeople but does not carry inventory.

_l_ 7. Limited-function merchant wholesaler that receives orders from customers and forwards them to producers, who ship directly to the customers.

_s_ 8. Agent wholesaling intermediary who represents a number of manufacturers of related but noncompeting products and receives a commission based on a specified percentage of sales.

_h_ 9. Independent wholesaling intermediaries that may or may not take possession of goods but never take title to them.

_p_ 10. Establishment that brings buyers and sellers together in one location for the purpose of permitting the buyers to examine merchandise before a purchase.

_g_ 11. Agent wholesaling intermediary that does not take title to or possession of goods and whose primary function is to bring buyers and sellers together.

_h_ 12. Wholesaling intermediary that takes title to the goods it handles.

_f_ 13. Periodic show at which manufacturers in a particular industry display wares for visiting retail and wholesale buyers.

_m_ 14. Limited-function merchant wholesaler that utilizes catalogs instead of a salesforce to contact customers in an attempt to reduce operating expenses.

_o_ 15. Agent wholesaling intermediary that takes possession of goods when they are shipped to a central market for sale, acts as the producer's agent, and collects an agreed-on fee at the time of sale.

_k_ 16. Limited-function merchant wholesaler that markets perishable food items; also sometimes known as a "truck jobber."

_a_ 17. Wholesaling intermediary that takes title to the goods it handles; also known as "jobber" or "distributor."

_r_ 18. Agent wholesaling intermediary responsible for the total marketing program of a firm's product line.

_b_ 19. Broad term describing wholesalers, agents and brokers that perform important wholesaling activities without taking title to the goods.

Name _____   Instructor _____

Section _____   Date _____

Self Quiz

You should use these objective questions to test your understanding of the chapter material. You can check your answers with those provided at the end of the chapter.

While these questions cover most of the chapter topics, they are not intended to be the same as the test questions your instructor may use in an examination. A good understanding of all aspects of the course material is essential to good performance on any examination.

True/False

Write "T" for True or "F" for False for each of the following statements.

F   1.   There is no wholesaling activity in the market for services.

T   2.   The 416,000 wholesaling establishments listed in the most recent Census of Wholesale Trade were responsible for sales of almost $2 trillion in that reporting year.

T   3.   A marketing institution can continue to exist only so long as it performs a service that fulfills a need.

F   4.   Wholesalers successfully transfer the risk-taking function to other members of the channel of distribution, bearing little of it themselves.

T   5.   Some, but not all, wholesalers assume the inventory function and its associated costs for manufacturers, benefitting through the convenience afforded by the availability of local inventories.

T   6.   Wholesalers can reduce costs at their level of the channel of distribution by making large-volume purchases from the manufacturer.

T   7.   If a single wholesaler is introduced into a channel of distribution containing five manufacturers and ten retailers, the number of transactions required to satisfy the channel's needs will be reduced from fifty to fifteen.

F   8.   Wholesalers must be very careful to protect their positions in the channel of distribution by concealing from manufacturers any information they may have about market acceptance of the manufacturers' products.

F   9.   Wholesalers often apply leverage to their retail customers by selling them goods for cash while themselves benefitting from credit advanced by manufacturers.

F   10.   Marketing functions can be eliminated in the channel of distribution if the members of the channel are willing to forgo their performance.

F 11. It is not unusual for a wholesaler to earn as little as 1.5 percent net profit as a percentage of net sales.

F 12. When a wholesaler has a high rate of inventory turnover, its profit as a percentage of net sales will generally be higher than that of a wholesaler whose turnover rate is low.

T 13. More than half of all industrial goods are sold directly by manufacturers to users and slightly less than one-third are marketed through manufacturer-owned channels.

F 14. The basic distinction between a manufacturer's sales office and a sales branch is that the sales office carries inventory and the sales branch does not.

T 15. A warehouse receipt issued by a public warehouse can be used as collateral for a bank loan.

T 16. One of the attractions of using a trade fair as a selling tool is that the cost of making a face-to-face contact there is only about 44 percent of the cost of a personal sales call.

T 17. When they serve the industrial market, full-function merchant wholesalers usually market machinery, inexpensive accessory equipment, and supplies.

F 18. Rack jobbers are identified as limited-function merchant wholesalers because they have restricted their activities to certain very narrowly defined types of merchandise.

F 19. Truck wholesalers first appeared in the U.S. in the 1930s when retailers began to drive their own trucks to wholesale outlets to make purchases and thus save the cost of delivery to their stores.

T 20. Drop shippers typically operate in industries where products are bulky and customers typically make their purchases in carload lots.

F 21. Brokers can serve as a reliable channel for manufacturers seeking regular, continuing service because their ability to "make a market" places them in a unique position in the wholesale marketplace.

T 22. If a manufacturer decides to use a selling agent to handle its merchandise, it should realize that, in the typical situation, the selling agent will assume full control of the manufacturer's marketing program.

F 23. Manufacturers' agents differ from selling agents in that a manufacturer's agent takes the entire output of its principal, whereas the selling agent usually is only one of a number of such intermediaries being used by that manufacturer.

F 24. Costs of operations (as a percentage of total sales) are highest for merchant wholesalers and lowest for brokers.

F 25. Despite structural changes in the wholesaling market, merchant wholesalers still do the lion's share of the business (58%), followed by agents and brokers (31%), and manufacturers' sales offices and branches (11%).

Multiple Choice

Circle the letter of the word or phrase that best completes the sentence or best answers the question.

e 26. Wholesaling involves the activities of persons or firms that
   a. sell in significant amounts to ultimate consumers.
   b. deal largely with retailers.
   c. sell primarily to industrial users.
   d. do the majority of their business with other wholesalers.
   e. participate in any or all of b, c, and d above.

a 27. In the most technical sense, the term "wholesaler"
   a. should be applied only to merchant wholesale intermediaries.
   b. applies across the board to all those institutions that are intermediaries in the channel of distribution.
   c. can be applied only to full-service marketing intermediaries.
   d. should be used only to describe a firm that deals in industrial goods.
   e. cannot be used to describe a firm that does not offer credit to its customers.

b 28. In justification of the existence of wholesaling activities, it can be mentioned that
   a. only about 10 percent of all goods reaching consumers comes directly from the manufacturer without intermediary involvement.
   b. marketing institutions continue to exist only as long as they perform a service that fulfills a need.
   c. there are almost two million wholesaling intermediaries in this country.
   d. some discount firms claim lower prices because they buy directly from manufacturers.
   e. wholesalers often provide utility of form, time, place, and possession as part of their service package.

c 29. When a wholesaler assumes the inventory carrying function and its associated costs for a manufacturer,
   a. it is inevitable that costs at retail will go up because someone has to pay for these additional services.
   b. the cost of distribution must go up because wholesalers are usually smaller than the retailers they serve.
   c. the wholesaler benefits from the convenience offered by local inventories and the manufacturer benefits from reduced cash needs.
   d. a certain amount of "slack" is introduced into the distribution system, allowing for somewhat less efficient warehouse management at the wholesale level.
   e. the number of contacts between wholesalers and their customers is reduced.

b 30. In a channel of distribution including six manufacturers and seven retailers, the presence of a single wholesaler would reduce the number of transactions necessary to satisfy the channel from 42 to
   a. 26.
   b. 13.
   c. 9.
   d. 7.
   e. 6.

d 31. The marketing function being performed by wholesalers when they provide their customers with new product specifications and communicate to manufacturers about the market acceptance of their offerings is
  a. buying.
  b. financing.
  c. risk taking.
  d. providing market information.
  e. reducing market contacts between manufacturers and end users.

b 32. Credit offered by wholesalers to their customers allows
  a. the wholesaler to control the operation of the customers through threats to cut off credit if wholesaler policies aren't heeded.
  b. the customers to use "leverage," spending a minimum amount of money on inventory investment and maximizing return on invested funds.
  c. manufacturers to manipulate the channel of distribution by demanding cash payments from wholesalers but not from customers who are retailers or end users.
  d. for better information transfer from the customers to the wholesaler and thus to the manufacturer.
  e. a large number of customers to default on their accounts, thus running up the cost of distribution.

a 33. Which of the following states the fundamental principle of marketing which applies to channel decisions?
  a. You can eliminate some of the members of a marketing channel, but you can't eliminate the marketing functions which must be performed.
  b. When a particular member of a marketing channel is eliminated, the cost of channel operation is always reduced.
  c. Channels of distribution operate in such a way that it is virtually impossible to change the structure of an existing channel.
  d. Eliminating independent wholesalers from a marketing channel should increase profit margins of other channel members by at least 10 percent.
  e. The structure of a marketing channel is such that changes in the structure often result in changes in the functions which must be performed.

a 34. The relationship between turnover rate and median level of net profits of wholesalers is generally
  a. inverse: the higher the rate of turnover, the lower the percent profit.
  b. direct: the higher the rate of turnover, the higher the percent profit.
  c. indeterminate: there is no apparent relationship between the rate of turnover and percent profit.
  d. a function of the individual firm: no substantive evidence exists upon which to arrive at a general conclusion.
  e. determined by the wholesaler's customers: you can't generalize by product class or type of operation.

d 35. Sales offices and branches, as identified in your text, are examples of
  a. independent merchant wholesaling intermediaries.
  b. independent agent wholesaling intermediaries.
  c. retailer-owned cooperatives or buying offices.
  d. manufacturer-owned facilities.
  e. brokers used only in certain industries.

e 36. Independently owned storage facilities which will also package goods in small quantities to fill orders for their customers and even handle billing for them are
   a.   merchandise marts.
   b.   trade fairs.
   c.   drop shippers.
   d.   selling agents.
   e.   public warehouses.

d 37. An independently owned, permanent facility which provides space in which manufacturers rent showrooms and maintain permanent exhibits of their product offerings is a
   a.   sales branch.
   b.   trade fair.
   c.   public warehouse.
   d.   merchandise mart.
   e.   brokerage house.

e 38. The yearly gathering at High Point, North Carolina, during which furniture manufacturers display their wares for visiting retail and wholesale buyers, is an example of a
   a.   manufacturer's agency.
   b.   retail buying office.
   c.   public market.
   d.   merchandise mart.
   e.   trade fair.

b 39. Which of the following is a full-function merchant wholesaler?
   a.   a truck wholesaler
   b.   a rack jobber
   c.   a drop shipper
   d.   a commission merchant
   e.   a manufacturer's representative

c 40. The cash-and-carry wholesaler
   a.   markets perishable food items, promoting them aggressively to customers; operating costs are relatively high at about 15%.
   b.   receives orders from customers but has them filled by producers who ship direct; carries no inventory.
   c.   operates in a manner which often precludes its use by large-scale grocery stores; more successful in Great Britain than in the U.S.
   d.   specializes in bringing buyers and sellers together; operates in industries with numerous small buyers and sellers.
   e.   relies on catalogs to do the selling job; usually serves small customers in outlying locations.

c 41. Which of the following product assortments would you expect to find being handled by a drop shipper?
   a.   bread, tobacco, potato chips, and candy
   b.   hardware, cosmetics, jewelry, and sporting goods
   c.   coal, lumber, and industrial chemicals
   d.   health and beauty items, housewares, paperback books, and phonograph records/cassettes
   e.   tobacco, used cars, artworks, livestock, and furs

C   42.   Which of the following merchant wholesalers makes no effort to anticipate customer needs, carries no inventory, and provides no delivery services to its customers?
a.   the rack jobber
b.   the truck wholesaler
c.   the drop shipper
d.   the mail-order wholesaler
e.   the cash-and-carry wholesaler

a   43.   Of the wholesale intermediaries listed below, the one with the lowest cost structure as a percent of sales is
a.   the broker.
b.   the drop shipper.
c.   the rack jobber.
d.   the cash-and-carry wholesaler.
e.   the mail order wholesaler.

a   44.   Commission merchants
a.   are prevalent in the marketing of agricultural products, commonly handling grain, produce, and livestock.
b.   operate largely in industries characterized by large numbers of small buyers and sellers, like real estate.
c.   are often referred to as "independent marketing departments" because they can be responsible for a firm's total marketing program.
d.   are conventionally called "manufacturer's reps" in the trade and represent a number of related but noncompeting product lines.
e.   are responsible for over 30 percent of the sales of all agent wholesaling intermediaries.

d   45.   From 1929 to 1982, the share of the wholesale market held by merchant wholesalers
a.   has increased significantly from 53% to over 78%.
b.   has declined from 21% to only 11%.
c.   has increased from 24% to 31%.
d.   has increased only slightly from 53% to 58%.
e.   has increased from 78% to almost 90%.

e   46.   If a wholesaling intermediary identifies itself as a "food broker," one immediately recognizes that it has identified its target market in terms of
a.   the size of the average customer it hopes to serve.
b.   the needs its customer mix is expected to have.
c.   the promotional strategy it expects to employ.
d.   the aggregate volume it expects to generate from sales.
e.   the product line it plans to carry.

e   47.   For the most part, a wholesaling intermediary's product/service strategy is a function of
a.   its financial capacity and the expertise of management.
b.   whether it is to be organized as a merchant or agent.
c.   competitive interaction between it and other wholesaling intermediaries of whatever description.
d.   the decision of whether or not inventory is to be kept by the intermediary.
e.   its choice of target market.

b 48. A wholesaler's pricing strategy is to a large part determined by
    a.   the nature of competition in that segment of the market.
    b.   the extent of the services it renders.
    c.   the demands of its customers; those who can't compete on price will not survive.
    d.   its promotional budget; those who promote a lot must charge more.
    e.   the seasonality of the merchandise it sells.

c 49. In general, the primary ingredient of a wholesaling intermediary's promotional program is going to be
    a.   advertising.
    b.   sales promotion.
    c.   personal selling.
    d.   specialties, like calendars and imprinted pencils.
    e.   free merchandise given to sweeten the sales pot.

d 50. From the point of view of pricing strategy, which of the following wholesaling intermediaries would you expect to charge the most to its customers?
    a.   selling agents
    b.   manufacturer's agents
    c.   drop shippers
    d.   rack jobbers
    e.   auction houses

Name_____ Instructor _____

Section _____ Date _____

Applying Marketing Concepts

Millie Woodhouse is the owner and chief executive of Woodhouse Computer Peripherals, a newly formed company manufacturing stands that hold materials being input into computers at a special angle so that eye and back strain on the part of the computer operators is minimized. The Woodhouse Wonder was shown at a recent computer trade show with remarkable success, and Millie got so many orders at that show that she has decided to "go national" with her innovation. This decision has raised some real questions about the best way to approach the problem of distribution, and Millie's background in computer science and industrial design hasn't really prepared her to address these basically marketing-oriented decisions.

Several people have approached Ms. Woodhouse, asking to represent her at the wholesale level. Each of them has indicated that he or she can solve her marketing problem. These people include:

a. Lambert McKinney, an outgoing, seemingly vital individual, who has proposed to represent Woodhouse Peripherals in the Great Southwest. He claims to know the owners of every computer store in the area personally, as he has been selling computer furniture, accessories, and supplies in the area for a number of years. He would expect a 12 percent commission.

b. The Divine/Delbert Company, a large firm with 25 sales representatives nationwide, who has offered to take over marketing of the Woodhouse Wonder. Woodhouse Peripherals wouldn't even need a marketing department. LaDonna Divine, the vice-president of the company, has indicated, however, that Divine/Delbert would not carry any inventory or be responsible for anything but selling the product. Like Mr. McKinney, the company would work for a commission on the quantity of product sold.

c. Bar Harbor Industries, a Maine firm primarily serving the New England area, who offered to buy and stock the Woodhouse Wonder. It would then sell this merchandise to retail outlets located in its trading area.

d. Lagonda Daimler, an old college chum of Millie's, who has also offered to help. A marketing major in school, he is currently employed as a salesman for a consumer goods firm. He has told Ms. Woodhouse that she should hire him to sell the company's product; he would then travel the country hiring additional salespeople to work from regional sites. Each site would carry a supply of Woodhouse Wonders for delivery to retail buyers in its sales area. Daimler expects to be the national sales manager.

Ms. Woodhouse talked about these offers with a relative who was the marketing manager for a large furniture company. His advice, which seemed very sound to Millie, was: "Decide which of these outfits will do the best job for what you can afford to pay. Then go ahead and make some decisions."

____ 1. An important function a selling agent would often perform is assuming responsibility for Woodhouse's marketing program.

____ 2.   Limited-function wholesalers perform more services for their customers than full-function wholesalers.

____ 3.   A brokerage firm may or may not take title to the goods it sells.

____ 4.   Merchant wholesalers may or may not take title to the goods they sell.

____ 5.   Cash-and-carry wholesalers may not perform the function of financing.

6. Lambert McKinney is a
    a. full-function wholesaler.
    b. commission merchant.
    c. broker.
    d. limited-function wholesaler.
    e. manufacturers' agent.

7. The Divine/Delbert Company is a
    a. full-function wholesaler.
    b. commission merchant.
    c. broker.
    d. selling agent.
    e. manufacturers' agent.

8. Bar Harbor Industries is a
    a. full-function wholesaler.
    b. commission merchant.
    c. broker.
    d. limited-function wholesaler.
    e. selling agent.

9. Lagonda Daimler is offering to set up a series of
    a. sales offices.
    b. sales branches.
    c. auction houses.
    d. public warehouses.
    e. drop shippers.

10. If Daimler had offered to travel the country soliciting orders for the Woodhouse Wonder which he would then purchase on his own account and have shipped directly to his customers by Woodhouse Peripherals, he would be acting as a
    a. company employee.
    b. drop shipper.
    c. cash-and-carry wholesaler.
    d. rack jobber.
    e. broker.

Alabama Outdoor Sports of Gadsden sells hunting and fishing supplies in several different ways. The company publishes a semiannual catalog which it mails to any retailer with which it has done more than $500 worth of business over the last six-month period. Orders from the catalog may be placed by phone or mail. The company also operates a fleet of ten trucks which it dispatches on weekly routes to regular customers (over $2000 in business over the last six months) in its operating area. These trucks carry a selection of the most popular items in the Outdoor Sports line for immediate delivery and the drivers can take orders for any other item a customer needs for delivery on the next trip. If an account is sufficiently large ($10,000 in volume in the last six months), Outdoor Sports will even dispatch a truck to make immediate delivery of any order and will carry the balance owed on open account for 30 days. Certain items in the Outdoor Sports line are now handled by a special division of the company which visits all customers at least once a month and replenishes their stock of outdoor magazines, hunting and fishing handbooks, and maps and charts. The company calls this operation its "soft lines" division.

____ 11. Even though it operates in several ways, Outdoor Sports remains a merchant wholesaler.

12. In serving its smaller customers (more than $500 but less than $2000 in sales), the company acts like a
    a. drop shipper.
    b. cash-and-carry wholesaler.
    c. mail-order wholesaler.
    d. broker.
    e. rack jobber.

13. Outdoor Sports handles its middle-sized accounts ($2000-$10,000) like a
    a. truck wholesaler.
    b. manufacturers' agent.
    c. drop shipper.
    d. commission merchant.
    e. selling agent.

14. Outdoor Sports' large accounts are handled as if the company was a
    a. manufacturers' sale branch.
    b. drop shipper.
    c. limited-function wholesaler.
    d. full-function wholesaler.
    e. commission merchant.

15. In terms of the way it operates, the "soft lines" division of Outdoor Sports is
    a. a trade fair.
    b. a merchandise mart.
    c. a drop shipper.
    d. a rack jobber.
    e. a public warehouse company.

Name_____   Instructor _____

Section _____   Date _____

Questions for Thought

The questions which follow are designed to help you become familiar with the main concepts in this chapter through interpretation in your own words. They are meant to be answered in a few sentences or a paragraph at most.

1. Wholesaling intermediaries create utility and perform marketing functions. Outline the types of utility they provide and the functions they perform.

2. Discuss, giving specific examples, how wholesaling intermediaries improve channel efficiency.

3.   What are the characteristics which differentiate merchant wholesalers from agents and brokers?

4.   Give an example of how each of the various sorts of merchant wholesalers might appropriately be used.

5.   Discuss the roles of the various sorts of agents and brokers in the marketplace.

Name_____   Instructor _____

Section _____   Date _____

Experiential Exercises

1. The purpose of this exercise is to familiarize you with the wholesalers located in your area.

    Using the yellow pages of the telephone directory and a map of a city in your area, plot the locations of wholesalers in the various categories listed below. Use the space provided to explain any patterns you find. If the yellow pages prove inadequate for the task, consult the city directory or contact the city's Chamber of Commerce and inquire where a directory of local wholesalers might be obtained.

    a.   Plumbing fixtures and supplies

    b.   Fresh and frozen meats

    c.   Major appliances

    d.   Fresh fruits and vegetables

2. The purpose of this exercise is to help you understand how an agent wholesaling intermediary operates. The exercise requires an in-depth investigation of such an intermediary.

    Visit an agent (or broker) wholesaling intermediary in your area and obtain the answers to the following questions.

    a. What type of intermediary have you chosen?

    b. In what lines of products does this firm deal? List them.

    c. Roughly, how many firms does this agent represent?

    d. Approximately how many customers does this outlet serve on a regular basis?

        What types of firms are these? Describe them.

        Does this intermediary sell to other wholesale intermediaries?

    e. Describe the geographical limits of the agent's trade area. You may use miles from a base location or political boundaries such as county lines to define the area.

    f. What major functions does this intermediary perform for its customers?

        For its principals?

g. How many salespeople does this intermediary normally employ?

h. What other information were you able to obtain about the subject company?

Name _____   Instructor _____

Section _____   Date _____

Computer Applications

Review the discussion of inventory turnover in Chapter 13 of the text. Then use menu item 10 titled "Inventory Turnover" to solve each of the following problems.

1. Joseph Meringer is a rack jobber in Pocatello, Idaho, who services drug stores and pharmacies throughout the state. At the beginning of the year a physical inventory determined that he had 1,800,000 items with a total value at retail of $2,646,000. At year's end he had 2,364,000 items worth $3,121,272. His sales were $24,000,000. What was Joseph's turnover rate for the year?

2. In a discussion at a cocktail party the other evening, Joe Smith mentioned that his wholesale firm maintained an average inventory at retail of some $2,600,000. A nosy friend recalled that he had read recently where Joe's company had annual sales for 1988 of $29,250,000. Curious but not very expert, the friend has come to you to compute the turnover rate for Joe Smith's company. What is that rate?

Chapter 13 Solutions

Key Concepts

1.	i	6.	e	11.	q	16.	k
2.	g	7.	l	12.	h	17.	a
3.	c	8.	s	13.	f	18.	r
4.	j	9.	n	14.	m	19.	b
5.	d	10.	p	15.	o		

Self Quiz

1.	F	11.	T	21.	F	31.	d	41.	c
2.	T	12.	F	22.	T	32.	b	42.	c
3.	T	13.	T	23.	F	33.	a	43.	a
4.	F	14.	F	24.	F	34.	a	44.	a
5.	T	15.	T	25.	F	35.	d	45.	d
6.	T	16.	T	26.	e	36.	e	46.	e
7.	T	17.	T	27.	a	37.	d	47.	e
8.	F	18.	F	28.	b	38.	e	48.	b
9.	F	19.	F	29.	c	39.	b	49.	c
10.	F	20.	T	30.	b	40.	c	50.	d

Applying Marketing Concepts

1.	T	6.	e	11.	T
2.	F	7.	d	12.	c
3.	F	8.	a	13.	a
4.	F	9.	b	14.	d
5.	T	10.	b	15.	d

Chapter 14

Retailing

Chapter Summary

The channel of distribution impacts on the ultimate consumer at the retail level. For most consumers, in fact, the channel of distribution is the retailers with whom they do business. Consumers are little aware of wholesalers and manufacturers. Manufacturers and wholesalers, on the other hand, are very aware of the existence of both ultimate consumers and retailers. It is through the retailers that the other levels of the channel are able to make contact with the ultimate consumers who are, for many of them, their ultimate market. Retailers, like wholesalers, engage in the creation of time, place, and possession utility through the services they provide. These services—convenience of location, timely business hours, salesperson assistance, store layout, product assortment on hand, and returns policy—are often more valuable than the product itself in developing consumers' image perceptions of products, services, and even stores themselves.

So what is retailing and how is it carried out? In a nutshell, retailing is "all of the activities involved in the sale of products and services to the ultimate consumer." The majority of all retail sales takes place in retail stores, but nonstore retailing, such as telemarketing (selling by telephone), mail-order selling, vending machine operation, and direct marketing all have their place in the retailing mix.

The structure of retailing and the relationships among retail institutions are in a state of constant evolution. This process has been summarized in the "wheel of retailing" concept, which theorizes that new types of retail institutions gain a foothold in the marketplace by offering their customers lower prices through reduction or elimination of services. Once they have demonstrated their capacity to survive, however, these institutions typically add services and raise prices, thus providing the incentive for the next innovation in low-price retailing. Strategy planning by retailers involves first, as always, the choice of a target market and development of a product strategy. Customer service strategy must then be developed, followed by decisions concerning how pricing is to be accomplished and administered. Retailers must decide on how they are going to apply markups (the difference between what they've paid for a good and the price they ask for it) and markdowns (reductions from the original asking price to be taken if goods don't sell at that price).

Many retailers survive or fail simply because of their choice of store location or distribution strategy. In these areas, they must act in a manner consistent with the image they have chosen to create. Consumers are disturbed by incongruities of location or method of distribution: they expect certain behaviors from retailers based on store locations and the manner of reaching them. To disappoint consumers is very dangerous.

Categorizing retailers can be a very difficult task because there are at least five bases one can use. One may look at (1) the amount of shopping effort consumers expend to get to the retailer, (2) the customer services the retailer provides, (3) the product lines carried by the outlet, (4) where the retail transactions take place, and (5) the form the retailer's ownership takes. Thus, retail institutions may be divided, like consumer goods, into convenience, shopping, and specialty categories. They may be graded on a spectrum of services rendered all the way from self-service to full-service. Using product lines carried, they may be referred to as limited-line stores (carrying extensive selections from only one or two product lines), specialty stores (carrying a very large assortment of goods from only part of a single product line), and general merchandise stores (carrying a wide variety of merchandise from a large number of lines). The general merchandise stores include department stores, variety stores, discount outlets, off-price retailers, hypermarkets, and catalog retailers, among others. If we examine where the retail transaction takes place, we discover that retailers may be engaged in either in-store or nonstore retailing. While most retail sales in the U.S. take place in stores, nonstore retailing accounts for a significant percentage of the sales of certain types of goods and services. Finally, retailers may be classified by ownership. The major types of ownership classifications include corporate chains, independent retailers, independents who have gotten together to form retail cooperatives, and independent members of wholesaler-sponsored voluntary chains or franchises.

Scrambled merchandising is a relatively new occurrence in retailing. It refers to the practice of carrying dissimilar product lines in an attempt to generate higher levels of sales volume. The increasing prevalence of this practice has made it more difficult to classify retailers meaningfully.

Name_____   Instructor _____

Section _____   Date _____

Key Concepts

The purpose of this section is to allow you to determine if you can match key concepts with the definitions of the concepts. It is essential that you know the definitions of the concepts prior to applying the concepts in later exercises in this chapter.

From the list of lettered terms, select the one that best fits each of the numbered statements below. Write the letter of that choice in the space provided.

Key Terms

a. retailing
b. wheel of retailing
c. retail image
d. markup
e. markdown
f. planned shopping center
g. selling up
h. suggestion selling
i. atmospherics
j. limited-line store
k. general merchandise retailer

l. variety store
m. department store
n. mass merchandiser
o. discount house
p. off-price retailer
q. outlet mall
r. hypermarket
s. home shopping
t. chain store
u. scrambled merchandising

__G__ 1. Retail sales technique of convincing a customer to buy a higher-priced item than he or she originally intended.

__M__ 2. Large retail firm that handles a variety of merchandise including clothing, household goods, appliances, and furniture.

__O__ 3. Store that charges lower-than-normal prices but may not offer typical retail services such as credit, sales assistance, and home delivery.

__K__ 4. Establishment that carries a wide variety of product lines, all of which are stocked in some depth.

__F__ 5. Group of retail stores planned, coordinated, and marketed as a unit to shoppers in a geographical trade area.

__H__ 6. Form of retail selling that attempts to broaden the consumer's original purchase with related items, special promotions, and holiday or seasonal merchandise.

__N__ 7. Store that stocks a wider line of goods than a department store but usually does not offer the same depth of assortment.

__E__ 8. Amount by which the seller reduces the original selling price of a product.

_g_   9. Shopping center consisting entirely of off-price retailers.

_p_ 10. Retailer that sells designer labels or well-known brand name clothing at less than typical retail prices.

_u_ 11. Retailing practice of carrying dissimilar product lines in an attempt to generate additional sales volume.

_d_ 12. In pricing strategy, amount added to the cost of an item to determine its selling price.

_s_ 13. Use of cable television to merchandise a product via telephone order.

_i_ 14. Combination of physical store characteristics and amenities provided by the retailer that results in developing a retail image and attracting customers.

_j_ 15. Retail establishment that offers a large assortment of one-product lines or just a few related product lines.

_a_ 16. All activities involved in the sale of products and services to the ultimate consumer.

_L_ 17. A retail firm that offers an extensive range and assortment of low-price merchandise.

_t_ 18. Group of retail stores that are centrally owned and managed and handle essentially the same product lines.

_c_ 19. Consumers' perception of the store and the shopping experience it provides.

_b_ 20. Hypothesis stating that retailers generally gain a competitive foothold by offering lower prices through reduction or elimination of services. Once established, they add services, raise prices, and become vulnerable to new low-price outlets.

_r_ 21. Giant mass merchandiser of soft goods and groceries that operates on a low-price self-service basis.

Name_____ Instructor _____

Section _____ Date _____

Self Quiz

You should use these objective questions to test your understanding of the chapter material. You can check your answers with those provided at the end of the chapter.

While these questions cover most of the chapter topics, they are not intended to be the same as the test questions your instructor may use in an examination. A good understanding of all aspects of the course material is essential to good performance on any examination.

True/False

Write "T" for True or "F" for False for each of the following statements.

T 1. Retailers often intermediate in the channel of distribution by obtaining information from customers and transmitting it to manufacturers and other channel members.

T 2. One of the earliest retailers on the North American continent was the Hudson's Bay Company.

F 3. General stores were doomed by the fact that their habit of carrying a large assortment of items from a small number of product lines made them vulnerable to competition from limited-line and specialty outlets.

F 4. Suburban shopping center developments, convenience food stores, and vending machines are excellent examples of the "wheel of retailing" in action.

F 5. One of the most pronounced trends in retailing today is that of decreased market segmentation.

T 6. The retailing innovation of the 1980s has been the development of the off-price retailer.

F 7. In an attempt to counter competition from specialty and discount stores, many department stores have eliminated high-overhead, low-profit lines such as women's clothing, sportswear, jewelry, cosmetics, and linens.

T 8. Retailers often use the results of marketing research to reevaluate product strategy, sometimes tailoring the product assortments of specific stores to their immediate markets.

T 9. The basic objective of providing services such as gift wrapping, alterations, bridal registries, and interior designers is to attract and retain target customers.

F 10. K-mart's use of Martha Stewart as a shoppers' consultant is designed to make customers feel more comfortable shopping at K-mart stores.

T 11. The retailer is the member of the marketing channel who is directly responsible for the prices consumers pay.

_T_   12.   The amount of markup used by a retailer is typically determined by the number and types of services it provides and the rate of inventory turnover.

_F_   13.   The higher the rate at which a retailer turns over inventory, the greater the markup required for covering costs and generating a profit will be.

_F_   14.   The markup on selling price for a product a retailer purchases for $.60 and sells for $1.20 is 100%.

_T_   15.   If you know the selling price and cost of a good, you can compute the markup based on both selling price and cost.

_F_   16.   To determine the markup percentage on selling price of a good, one approach is to divide the amount added to cost to get the selling price by the cost itself.

_T_   17.   The prices retailers initially ask for the goods they carry are based in part on the cost of those goods and in part on the retailer's judgment of the amounts consumers will be willing to pay for the items.

_T_   18.   If a good is to be marked down, the markdown percentage may be determined by dividing the dollar amount of the markdown by the new or "sale" price.

_F_   19.   The smallest of the types of planned shopping centers is the community shopping center, which usually contains only 10-30 stores.

_T_   20.   Most specialty stores are independent, small-scale operations handling merchandise such as baked goods, furs, and millinery.

_F_   21.   It isn't a regional shopping center unless it has at least 500,000 square feet of shopping space.

_T_   22.   If "selling up" is used indiscriminately, customers will become dissatisfied with that retailer and potential repeat sales will be substantially diminished.

_F_   23.   Convenience retailers typically include furniture stores, appliance retailers, gasoline stations, and some barber shops.

_F_   24.   Many people are quite surprised to learn that supermarket profit margins are usually in the range of 8-9 percent of sales.

_T_   25.   Direct-response retailing is the modern approach to what used to be known as mail-order retailing, using cable TV as well as the more traditional catalog.

Multiple Choice

Circle the letter of the word or phrase that best completes the sentence or best answers the question.

b 26. Professor McNair's "wheel of retailing" concept
   a. postulates that new types of retailers gain a foothold in the marketplace by entering at a fairly high price level and offering a complete service package.
   b. seems to fit the development of such outlets as department stores, chain stores, and supermarkets.
   c. applies most appropriately to the development of suburban shopping centers, convenience stores, and vending machines.
   d. theorizes that, after a new type of marketing institution has established itself in the market, it changes its ways of operating by reducing prices and services until an opportunity is created for a new kind of institution to enter the marketplace.
   e. relates best to the demise of the general store in the U.S.

C 27. A store's or other retail outlet's "retail image" is
   a. the owner's perception of the store and the shopping experience it provides.
   b. its suppliers' perceptions of the store's operating philosophy, place in the market, and profitability.
   c. consumers' perceptions of the store and the shopping experience it provides.
   d. competitors' perceptions of the store and the market niche it occupies.
   e. always consistent with the expectations of the owner, competitors, and shopping consumers.

d 28. One of the most dominant trends in modern retailing is
   a. the tendency for retailers to concentrate their efforts in one or another part of the country and to avoid the national market.
   b. a strong pull toward combining market segments into larger, less homogeneous targets for marketing effort.
   c. for firms to abandon the markets in which they have been most strongly entrenched for the longest periods of time and to strike out into new fields of endeavor.
   d. for firms to shift their strategy to target more narrowly defined markets, increasing the level of market segmentation.
   e. the thrust toward segmentation on highly ethnic grounds.

a 29. Of the following services, which is most specifically designed to build demand for a particular line of merchandise?
   a. K-mart's use of Martha Stewart to promote its kitchen, bed, bath, and home decorating service
   b. provision of a bridal registry service by a department or jewelry store
   c. complimentary coffee provided by a department store to customers who are there when the store's doors open in the morning
   d. a gift wrapping service offered free of charge
   e. provision of rest rooms, lounges, and drinking fountains for use by a store's customers

d   30. If a retailer purchases a refrigerator from its supplier for $350 and offers it for sale for $650, the markup on selling price for this item, rounded to the nearest whole percent, is
    a.   24 percent.
    b.   30 percent.
    c.   35 percent.
    d.   46 percent.
    e.   54 percent.

b   31. Jones Brothers Floor Tile Company just bought an odd lot of some really nice Italian ceramic tile. The tile cost 65 cents per square foot and the brothers usually mark up their merchandise 35 percent on selling price. What should be the asking price on this tile (rounded to the nearest cent)?
    a.   88 cents per square foot
    b. $1.00 per square foot
    c. $1.22 per square foot
    d. $1.64 per square foot
    e. $2.00 per square foot

c   32. The Market has overbought fresh cauliflower and is going to take a markdown on it so it sells before going bad. If the original price was $1.29 per head and a markdown to $0.89 per head is taken, what is the percent markdown (round to the nearest percent)?
    a.   31 percent
    b.   37 percent
    c.   45 percent
    d.   69 percent
    e.   73 percent

b   33. A neighborhood shopping center is usually characterized by
    a.   a market size of 20,000-100,000 persons; the facility is usually anchored by a branch of a local department store.
    b.   a size of 5-15 stores serving 5,000-50,000 persons.
    c.   the presence of some professional offices, such as those of physicians, dentists, and attorneys.
    d.   a theme park on site, somewhat like a mini-Disney World.
    e.   at least 400,000 square feet of shopping area.

a   34. When a salesperson in a store suggests that a new tie certainly would go well with that new shirt you just bought, he or she is practicing
    a.   suggestion selling.
    b.   selling up.
    c.   use of atmospherics.
    d.   franchising.
    e.   simple selling.

e   35. When a store focuses its merchandising efforts on accessible locations, long store hours, rapid checkout service, and adequate parking facilities, it would be reasonable to assume, considering classification by shopping effort, that the store is
    a.   a shopping store.
    b.   a variety or specialty store.
    c.   a mass merchandiser, like an off-price retailer.
    d.   a department store.
    e.   some kind of convenience store.

d 36. Using classification by level of service provided as a base, how would a store that focuses on fashion-oriented shopping goods and specialty items and offers a high level of service be classed?
   a. a hypermarket
   b. a self-service store
   c. a specialty store
   d. a full-service retailer
   e. a self-selection store

c 37. Specialty stores
   a. typically handle only specialty goods (from the point of view of shopping effort).
   b. practice scrambled merchandising to a substantial extent.
   c. typically carry convenience and shopping goods.
   d. are run primarily by large chains; independents are rare.
   e. tend to be very large-scale operations in both physical size and sales volume.

e 38. Using product lines carried as the basis for classification, supermarkets are
   a. specialty stores.
   b. single-line stores.
   c. mixed merchandise marketers.
   d. convenience stores.
   e. limited-line stores.

e 39. When one considers that profit margins in supermarketing average only about 1 percent of sales, one recognizes
   a. why the supermarket industry seems to be dying out; there's certainly no money to be made in it.
   b. why supermarkets are constantly pleading with government for tax breaks and special concessions to help them stay in business.
   c. why the number of supermarkets is decreasing year by year.
   d. why supermarkets are becoming even more selective about the merchandise they carry and are reducing the number of items made available to the public month by month.
   e. how important rapid inventory turnover is to a supermarket if it is to produce sufficient return on investment to justify its continued operation.

a 40. A general merchandise retailer specializing in designer labels and well-known brand name clothing bought on special and offered to the public at prices reflecting the savings realized is a(n)
   a. off-price retailer.
   b. department store.
   c. discount house.
   d. hypermarket.
   e. catalog retailer.

e 41. In recent years, the discount house concept has been revitalized by those stores requiring customers to purchase memberships and operating on a no-frills, cash-and-carry basis. These stores are called
   a. factory-direct retail stores.
   b. variety stores.
   c. micromarkets.
   d. mass merchandisers.
   e. warehouse clubs.

42. The biggest growth area in the field of direct-response selling is
    a. mail-order merchandising through catalogs.
    b. sales at the catalog-order desks of retail stores.
    c. the use of cable TV networks to sell merchandise which is ordered directly over the phone.
    d. sales of Slim Whitman records and tapes on broadcast TV.
    e. sales by product demonstration in the home.

43. Discount houses, off-price retailers, and hypermarkets are all examples of
    a. mass merchandisers.
    b. department stores.
    c. catalog retailers.
    d. specialty stores.
    e. small-scale independent retail merchants.

44. Mass merchandisers have made a place for themselves in the retail marketplace by emphasizing
    a. low prices for not so well-known products, high turnover of goods, and reduced services.
    b. low prices for well-known brand name products, high turnover of goods, and reduced services.
    c. high prices for well-known brand name products, low turnover of goods, and a high level of quality service.
    d. low prices for well-known brand name goods, high turnover of goods, and a high level of quality service.
    e. low prices for well-known brand name goods, low inventory turnover, and a high level of quality service.

45. Department stores have been vulnerable to competition from mass merchandisers, among others, because
    a. they have relatively high operating costs, averaging from 45-60 percent of sales.
    b. they have been slow to adapt to conditions in the marketplace, often refusing to take competitive action from motives of tradition.
    c. their suburban locations isolate them from the real bases of their markets.
    d. their bare-bones approach to merchandising has turned a lot of people off to the way they do business.
    e. of their refusal to modernize their central city locations to provide the convenience factors people are looking for.

46. The hypermarket
    a. originated in Germany and has spread throughout Europe and the Middle East.
    b. usually features over 200,000 square feet of selling space stocked with a wide selection of grocery items and general merchandise at discount prices.
    c. differs from a supermarket primarily in the merchandise carried; it's not so different in size and operating philosophy.
    d. has not as yet had marked success in any market in which it has thus far been introduced. It may be a blind alley in retail evolution.
    e. is another name for the warehouse club type of retail store.

c 47. Chain stores of one sort or another account for approximately what percent of all retail sales?
   a. 35 percent
   b. 44 percent
   c. 52 percent
   d. 66 percent
   e. 72 percent

d 48. The nation's largest retail chain, with some $44 billion in 1986 sales, is
   a. K-mart Corporation of Troy, Michigan.
   b. The Kroger Grocery and Baking Company of Cincinnati, Ohio.
   c. Wal-Mart Stores of Bentonville, Arkansas.
   d. Sears, Roebuck and Company of Chicago, Illinois.
   e. Schwegmann Brothers Giant Supermarkets of New Orleans, Louisiana.

d 49. Even though only 7 percent of all U.S. retailers has sales in excess of $1 million annually, that 7 percent accounts for
   a. almost one-third of all retail sales.
   b. nearly one-half of all retail sales.
   c. slightly more than one-half of all retail sales.
   d. almost two-thirds of all retail sales.
   e. nearly three-fourths of all retail sales.

e 50. Scrambled merchandising refers to
   a. the fact that most retailers are so disorganized that they do not know what their merchandise inventory includes, much less how much of each item is on hand.
   b. the practice of allowing merchandise normally housed in one department to be shifted to another department for a special sales event, thus "scrambling" the inventory.
   c. the practice of buying up stock from failed stores and mixing it in with fresh stock purchased for normal inventory, a questionable practice at best.
   d. the habit which many consumers have gotten into of failing to replace merchandise which they have decided not to buy back on the proper shelves, dumping it instead any old place in the store, and thus scrambling the merchandise.
   e. the practice of carrying dissimilar lines in an attempt to generate additional sales volume.

Name_____ Instructor _____

Section _____ Date _____

Applying Marketing Concepts

Sportsman's Paradise is an independently owned retail store that sells rifles, shotguns, ammunition, and associated equipment for use by both hunters and competitive shooters. In addition, it also offers a complete line of hunting and shooting clothes, a gun repair service, and an extensive array of gun safety, target shooting, and self-defense classes.

____ 1. Because of its combination of merchandise and services, Sportsman's Paradise practices scrambled merchandising.

____ 2. Sportsman's Paradise is a good candidate to engage in direct selling.

____ 3. Sportsman's Paradise's product lines would be easy to market via teleshopping.

____ 4. If the store added a line of snow skis, it would be engaging in scrambled merchandising.

____ 5. In order to compete with the large chain stores, Sportsman's Paradise should carry exclusive lines, provide superior service, and stress its knowledge of local market conditions.

6. This store would be classed as a
    a. specialty store.
    b. general merchandise store.
    c. department store.
    d. limited-line store.
    e. discount house.

7. If a store like Sportsman's Paradise requires convenient access by at least 150,000 people to survive, which of the following locations would be most advantageous for it?
    a. neighborhood shopping center
    b. community shopping center
    c. suburban shopping center
    d. regional shopping center
    e. central business district

8. If this store sold only rifles, it would be an example of a
    a. specialty store.
    b. general merchandise store.
    c. department store.
    d. limited-line store.
    e. mass merchandiser.

9. If Sportsman's Paradise hired an interior designer to make the interior of the store resemble a hunting lodge, it would be attempting to use
   a. distribution to attract a target market.
   b. product/service strategy to attract buyers.
   c. retail image to attract a target market.
   d. location to attract customers.
   e. product/service strategy to attract new customers.

10. Sportsman's Paradise is thinking about publishing a catalog and taking orders, where legally permitted, by phone and mail. It would send the ordered merchandise to the customer by mail or by private carrier. What type of nonstore retailing would this be?
   a. catalog retailing
   b. direct-response retailing
   c. automatic merchandising
   d. off-price retailing
   e. direct selling

Joy and Larry Fein have operated Fein's corner market for over 30 years. During all that time, they have operated their store the way they thought their customers would want them to. They open the doors at seven in the morning and close at ten at night, seven days a week. Their parking lot is large and well lighted, and they make sure there are never more than three people in line at the cash register. They have always been very proud of the fact that their store kept away from what they referred to as faddish merchandise and stuck to the basics. Good quality meats, breads, dairy products, and standard fruits and vegetables. And everything in the store, without exception, was Kosher. Of course, not all their clientele was Jewish, hence they remained open on the Sabbath with the help of their non-Jewish employees.

11. In terms of the shopping effort required to shop at Fein's, the store is a
   a. shopping store.
   b. convenience store.
   c. specialty store.
   d. self-selection store.
   e. full-service retailer.

12. Looking at the product lines carried by Fein's we would have to come to the conclusion that the store was
   a. a specialty store.
   b. a limited-line store.
   c. a general merchandise store.
   d. a general store.
   e. a variety store.

13. Considering their pride in their resistance to carrying lines of merchandise dissimilar to the basics of grocerydom, it should be concluded that the Feins
   a. have resisted the temptation to go into scrambled merchandising.
   b. should move with the times and broaden their merchandise assortment.
   c. have accommodated themselves to the inevitable pressures of the need to make a profit by adding lines which scrambled their merchandise assortment.
   d. have successfully practiced selling up on their customers.
   e. know how to apply suggestion selling.

14. Fein's corner market, as far as we know, is
    a. a member of a corporate retail chain.
    b. a member of a wholesaler-sponsored voluntary chain.
    c. a member of a retail cooperative.
    d. an independent retail institution.
    e. a subsidiary of a holding company.

15. The fact that all the merchandise at Fein's is completely Kosher indicates that the Feins
    a. have applied geographic segmentation to the marketplace to choose a market segment.
    b. have used psychographic segmentation to the marketplace to choose a market segment.
    c. have segmented the market demographically.
    d. have applied segmentation by end use to their marketplace.
    e. have done little, if any, segmentation of the market.

Name_____ Instructor _____

Section _____ Date _____

Questions for Thought

The questions which follow are designed to help you become familiar with the main concepts in this chapter through interpretation in your own words. They are meant to be answered in a few sentences or a paragraph at most.

1. It has been said that the development of retailing institutions is an evolutionary, rather than a revolutionary, process. Discuss the evolution of retailing in the United States.

2. Discuss the elements and development of a retailing strategy.

3. Retailers can be classified using any one of five different bases. Discuss.

4. The concept of scrambled merchandising is a rather new one in the field of retailing, yet it seems quite popular. Outline and discuss this concept.

Name _____   Instructor _____

Section _____   Date _____

Experiential Exercises

1. Planned shopping centers have become so common in the United States that we often take them for granted. In this exercise you will examine planned shopping centers from a professional point of view.

   a. Using a map of a city near your campus or home, carefully plot the location of every planned shopping center. Next, scale the distance by road between each center. Now answer the following questions.

      1. What are the logical reasons for the location of each planned shopping center?

      2. If you were to build a neighborhood shopping center in or near the city, where would you build it? Why?

   b. Visit a planned shopping center and draw a plan showing the location of each retail store in the center. (If the center being visited has more than 100 stores, draw a plan of only one section or level of it.) Show all parking areas and walkways. Select a group of four stores immediately adjacent to each other and classify them according to the bases that follow.

Store Name	Customer Effort	Services Provided	Product Lines	Ownership
1.				
2.				
3.				
4.				

c. If you were able to rent space in the shopping center you visited, what kind of store would you open? Why? In what part of the center would you prefer to rent? Why?

2. The purpose of this exercise is to familiarize you with the use of scrambled merchandising by various retail outlets. You will examine several stores with different basic product mixes and attempt to determine the degree to which they are involved in scrambled merchandising.

Visit four retail stores convenient for you to reach. Each store should have a different basic product mix than the others. Some suggested stores might be a supermarket, a hardware store, a pharmacy, a camera store, a furniture store, or even a toy store. For each store, acquire the following information. Be prepared to ask store personnel enough questions to complete each of the questions which follow.

Store 1: Store name

_____

Basic product line

_____

Dissimilar lines carried

_____

Approximate percentage of selling space devoted to unrelated lines

_____

Logic behind carrying the unrelated lines

_____

Store 2: Store name

_____

Basic product line

_____

Dissimilar lines carried

_____

Approximate percentage of selling space devoted to unrelated lines

_____

Logic behind carrying the unrelated lines

_____

Store 3:   Store name

_____

Basic product line

_____

Dissimilar lines carried

_____

Approximate percentage of selling space devoted to unrelated lines

_____

Logic behind carrying the unrelated lines

_____

Store 4:   Store name

_____

Basic product line

_____

Dissimilar lines carried

_____

Approximate percentage of selling space devoted to unrelated lines

_____

Logic behind carrying the unrelated lines

_____

a. Are there any similarities, store to store, in the information you have gathered? Are they a function of:

Customer effort considerations?

Services offered?

Store ownership?

Product lines carried?

b. How would you say these stores are dissimilar in their approaches to scrambled merchandising? Are the dissimilarities a function of:

Customer effort considerations?

Services offered?

Store ownership?

Product lines carried?

Name_____   Instructor _____

Section _____   Date _____

Computer Applications

Review the discussion of markups and markdowns in Chapter 14 of the text. Then use menu item 11 titled "Markups" to solve problem 1. Use menu item 12 titled "Markdowns" to solve problem 2.

1. Melanie Scott imports native art from Paraguay and markets it to young, upwardly mobile people. Twice a year, Melanie flies down to Paraguay to meet with local artists and purchase items she thinks her customers will like. As soon as she returns from each of these trips, she publishes a catalog in which each item she has bought is pictured and described along with its price. Most of the products she sells are marked up 70% of the selling price. On her last trip, she discovered a new studio in Villarrica whose artists were producing truly exceptional work. She immediately contracted to take their entire yearly output of sculptures (only 150 units) at a price of $200 each. Because of their exceptional quality, Melanie feels she can get twice her normal markup on cost for these sculptures.

    a.   What is Melanie's normal markup on cost?

    b.   What will be the catalog price for these sculptures?

2. Ellis Pellissier, whose home-appliance store is located in a neighborhood suffering from a severe economic downturn, has been experiencing trouble getting people into the store. He just completed an inventory revealing that he had 35 color TVs in stock for which he had paid $250 each. Ellis has been trying to sell the TVs at a markup of 70% on cost. He has decided to have a big sale and to try and move the TVs at $10 over cost.

    a.   What is Ellis' normal retail price for the TVs?

    b.   What is the markdown percentage for the big sale?

Chapter 14 Solutions

Key Concepts

1. g	6. h	11. u	16. a	21. r
2. m	7. n	12. d	17. l	
3. o	8. e	13. s	18. t	
4. k	9. q	14. i	19. c	
5. f	10. p	15. j	20. b	

Self Quiz

1. T	11. T	21. F	31. b	41. e
2. T	12. T	22. T	32. c	42. c
3. F	13. F	23. F	33. b	43. a
4. F	14. F	24. F	34. a	44. b
5. F	15. T	25. T	35. e	45. a
6. T	16. F	26. b	36. d	46. b
7. F	17. T	27. c	37. c	47. c
8. T	18. T	28. d	38. e	48. d
9. T	19. F	29. a	39. e	49. d
10. F	20. T	30. d	40. a	50. e

Applying Marketing Concepts

1. F	6. d	11. b
2. F	7. d	12. b
3. F	8. a	13. a
4. T	9. c	14. d
5. T	10. b	15. c

Chapter 15
Physical Distribution

Chapter Summary

Physical distribution includes a broad range of activities aimed at the efficient and effective movement of finished goods from the place of production into the hands of the consumer. Although the temptation is to think of physical distribution as being the same as transportation, this is not true. Though transportation is an important element, physical distribution also includes customer service, inventory control, materials handling, packaging, order processing, the selection of warehouse sites, and warehouse operation. The term *logistics* may be used synonymously with physical distribution. These eight elements are interrelated and must be balanced so that the physical distribution system operates smoothly and is not suboptimized. *Suboptimization* refers to concentrating effort to create efficient operation in one or a few of the elements of a system, while other elements are allowed to operate inefficiently.

The ultimate goal of physical distribution specialists is to produce a specified level of customer service while minimizing the costs involved in moving and storing product as it makes its way through the channel of distribution from point of production to point of final sale. The objective of the physical distribution function is to focus on reducing total distribution costs to minimize the degree of suboptimization. The distribution department of a firm is one of the classic examples of the application of the systems approach to business activity.

In recent years, the transportation industry in the United States has experienced substantial deregulation. Whereas in prior years members of the industry were inhibited by law from exercising creativity in solving shippers' problems, they are now free to develop unique solutions when the need arises. The transportation carriers most affected by deregulation have been railroads, air carriers, and motor freight operators.

The five types of carriers available to shippers are railroads, motor carriers, water carriers, pipelines, and air carriers. Each of these has its advantages and its disadvantages as a choice for a particular shipper. Railroads, the most-used medium of transportation, are flexible in handling products and are widely available, but are only average when it comes to speed, dependability in meeting schedules, and cost. Moreover, they do not offer the availability of frequent shipment. Motor carriers are relatively high in cost, but are fast, dependable, allow for frequent shipments, and are very widely available. Water carriers, despite their slow speed, low shipment frequency, and limited availability, compete because of their very low cost. Pipelines, though they account for a substantial quantity of goods shipped, rank low on availability, flexibility, and speed. Like water carriers, though, they are quite inexpensive to use. Air transportation is the highest cost medium available for transportation, but offers very fast and dependable schedules.

Name _____   Instructor _____

Section _____   Date _____

Key Concepts

The purpose of this section is to allow you to determine if you can match key concepts with the definitions of the concepts. It is essential that you know the definitions of the concepts prior to applying the concepts in later exercises in this chapter.

From the list of lettered terms, select the one that best fits each of the numbered statements below. Write the letter of that choice in the space provided.

Key Terms

a. physical distribution
b. system
c. suboptimization
d. customer service standards
e. class rates
f. commodity rate
g. storage warehouse

h. distribution warehouse
i. economic order quantity (EOQ) model
j. just-in-time inventory system
k. stockout
l. materials handling
m. unitizing
n. containerization

____   1.   Organized group of components linked according to a plan for achieving specific objectives.

____   2.   Inventory control system designed to minimize inventory at production plants.

____   3.   Broad range of activities concerned with the efficient movement of finished products from the end of the production line to the consumer.

____   4.   Standard transportation rates established for shipping various commodities.

____   5.   Facility designed to assemble and then redistribute products to facilitate rapid movement of products to purchasers.

____   6.   Technique for determining the optimal order quantity for each product. Optimal point is determined by balancing the costs of holding inventory and the costs involved in placing orders.

____   7.   Process of combining as many packages as possible into one load, preferably on a pallet, in order to expedite product movement and reduce damage and pilferage.

____   8.   Special transportation rate granted by carriers to shippers as a reward for either regular use or large-quantity shipments.

____   9.   Inventory item that is unavailable for shipment or sale.

___ 10. Process of combining several unitized loads of products into a single load to facilitate intertransport changes in transportation modes.

___ 11. Condition in which individual objectives are achieved at the expense of broader organizational objectives.

___ 12. All activities involved in moving products within a manufacturer's plants, warehouses, and transportation company terminals.

___ 13. Quality of service that a company's customers will receive.

___ 14. Traditional warehouse in which products are stored prior to shipment.

Name_____ Instructor _____

Section _____ Date _____

Self Quiz

You should use these objective questions to test your understanding of the chapter material. You can check your answers with those provided at the end of the chapter.

While these questions cover most of the chapter topics, they are not intended to be the same as the test questions your instructor may use in an examination. A good understanding of all aspects of the course material is essential to good performance on any examination.

True/False

Write "T" for True or "F" for False for each of the following statements.

_____ 1. Improving customer service through more efficient physical distribution can mean substantial cost savings to system users.

_____ 2. The terms *transportation* and *physical distribution* can be used interchangeably.

_____ 3. The cost of physical distribution represents almost half of total marketing costs.

_____ 4. Traditionally, managers have attempted to reduce costs by improving the efficiency of goods production.

_____ 5. The activity of warehousing creates utility of place while the activity of transportation creates utility of time.

_____ 6. A loyal customer can be worth as much as $100,000 to a company in repeat purchases over his or her lifetime.

_____ 7. Each component of a system operates independently of every other component in the system.

_____ 8. Suboptimization occurs when a specified level of customer service is achieved while the total cost of physically moving and storing products as they go from the point of production to the point of ultimate purchase is minimized.

_____ 9. Among the most powerful tools for influencing people's perceptions of overall quality is customer service.

_____ 10. Increasing the level of a company's customer service standards will typically cost the company more money.

_____ 11. American Airlines customer service standards require that 95 percent of all passengers purchasing tickets at a booking counter should not have to wait more than five minutes.

_____ 12. The single largest expense item in physical distribution is the cost of inventory control systems.

_____ 13. In transportation, class rates are sometimes called special rates and are the standard rate for every commodity moving between any two places.

_____ 14. Common carriers are for-hire carriers that serve the general public with regulated rates and services.

_____ 15. Although their share of the market has dropped from over 60 percent in 1940 to only 37 percent in 1986, the railroads are still America's single largest transportation medium on the basis of ton-miles carried.

_____ 16. Motor carriage represents the most efficient mode of transportation for bulky commodities over long distances.

_____ 17. Motor freight lags behind only the railroad medium in the number of ton-miles of freight haulage it handles every year.

_____ 18. One of the factors which limits the use of the pipeline medium is its speed; the average pipeline shipment moves along at a rate of only three to four miles an hour.

_____ 19. United Parcel Service, Federal Express, and the U.S. Postal Service are examples of freight forwarders.

_____ 20. A make-bulk center is a type of distribution warehouse that consolidates several small shipments into one big one and delivers it to its destination.

_____ 21. The economic order quantity (EOQ) model is based on a trade-off between the cost of goods bought by a company and the cost of processing orders for those goods.

_____ 22. Shrink packaging involves binding a unitized load in a special plastic which shrinks when it cools after heating, thus securing the elements of the load together.

_____ 23. While warehousing and materials-handling costs are typically subject to economies of scale, delivery costs, on the other hand, rise as the distance between warehouse and customer increases.

_____ 24. America's "just-in-time" inventory system is an adaptation of the Soviet "Krasny Krim" system which involves moving inventory to production facilities only as it is needed.

_____ 25. Paperwork alone represents over 12 percent of U.S. foreign trade cost.

Multiple Choice

Circle the letter of the word or phrase that best completes the sentence or best answers the question.

26. According to your text, in a recent year physical distribution costs have amounted to
    a. some $450 billion or 12 percent of the gross national product.
    b. at least $750 billion, more than the cost of national defense.
    c. around $650 million, approximately 21 percent of the gross national product.
    d. more than $1 trillion, up 20 percent in the last two years.
    e. less than $250 billion, a decrease of 15 percent from previous years.

27. A term which can be used interchangeably with *physical distribution* is
    a. logistics.
    b. transportation.
    c. inventory adjustment.
    d. customer satisfaction standardization.
    e. suboptimization.

28. One of the major reasons for the increased attention to physical distribution activities by management is
    a. recognition of their effect on production efficiency in factories.
    b. the realization that transportation is the primary source of competitive advantage in today's markets.
    c. the importance of reducing the cost of every aspect of the physical distribution process.
    d. recognition of their role in providing customer service.
    e. that these activities have been neglected for many years, and as a result the system is on the brink of collapse.

29. The study of physical distribution is one of the classic examples of
    a. high comedy in the field of business management.
    b. the systems approach to business problems.
    c. errors magnified by the efforts made to correct them.
    d. a complex analysis reduced to simplistic terms.
    e. examination of a process going nowhere at a faster and faster rate.

30. The objective of an organization's physical distribution system is
    a. to deliver the goods faster and better than the competition.
    b. to satisfy all the firm's customers all the time with the best quality products delivered in the most rapid fashion from a storage facility operated at the highest level of efficiency.
    c. to develop the most modern, high-tech transportation network in the firm's marketplace so as to reduce competition and improve customer service.
    d. to serve each manager with the minimum-cost profile of the distribution function under his or her supervision.
    e. to establish a specified level of customer service while minimizing the costs involved in physically moving and storing product as it moves from the point of production to the point of ultimate sale.

31. Suboptimization frequently occurs in physical distribution because
    a. every manager of a physical distribution task attempts to minimize cost of his function, not of the whole system.
    b. there is too much emphasis on customer service and not enough emphasis on reducing the cost of each physical distribution function.
    c. too ambitious a level of customer service is chosen as a standard, thereby driving up operations costs.
    d. inventory management fails, causing the system to run out of stocks of important goods just when they're needed most.
    e. firms find themselves operating outdated, old-fashioned warehouses and can't afford to develop better, more efficient facilities.

32. Which of the following would be a valid customer-service standard?
    a. All shipments will be sent motor freight unless another mode is specified by the customer.
    b. Shipment will be made open-account to firms rated BAA or better by Dun and Bradstreet; all others must pay cash with their order.
    c. Ninety percent of all orders will be filled within 24 hours after receipt; all orders will be filled within 48 hours after receipt.
    d. Returns will be accepted only with prior approval by our management and then only if it can be proven that the goods were bought from us within the last 15 days.
    e. We dry-store merchandise ordered from us for 72 hours after we receive the order; after that, it is returned to stock and the customer is charged 15 percent for restocking.

33. The largest single expense item in physical distribution is
    a. the cost of warehousing, amounting to 34 percent of the whole cost of the physical distribution process.
    b. materials handling; the increased sophistication of this process has driven its cost up to 41 percent of the total.
    c. order processing; the volume of orders pouring into the distribution system has driven the cost of this function up to 26 percent of the total.
    d. transportation; despite new media and new forms of organization in the field, it still costs more than 37 percent of the total.
    e. inventory control; increased hijacking, pilferage, and other forms of "shrinkage" have driven the cost of this function up to 32 percent of the total.

34. In transportation, this type of rate allows the shipper and the carrier to negotiate a rate to be charged for a particular service. Such a rate is called
    a. a class rate
    b. a contract rate.
    c. a special rate.
    d. a commodity rate.
    e. an insider rate.

35. The current trend toward deregulation of the nation's transportation media began with the
    a. Motor Carrier Act.
    b. Airline Deregulation Act.
    c. Staggers Rail Act.
    d. Celler-Kefauver Act.
    e. Stanford-McCauley Amendment to the Sherman Act.

36. If a freight carrier offers its services to the public, operates under a regulated system of rates and services, and must seek approval from a regulatory body to operate, it is
    a. a contract carrier.
    b. a designated carrier.
    c. a private carrier.
    d. a common carrier.
    e. a bulk carrier.

37. The standard measure of traffic volume for transportation media is
    a. the hundredweight (cwt.).
    b. the "short box" (an 8' x 10' container).
    c. the palletload (a 48" x 60" x 42" cubic measure).
    d. 78,600 pounds (the weight limit on U.S. secondary roads).
    e. the ton-mile (one ton moved through a distance of one mile).

38. Despite the shrinkage which their portion of U.S. freight volume has suffered over the last 40 years, railroads still dominate carriage of freight by a ratio of about
    a. 4 to 1.
    b. 3 to 1.
    c. 2 to 1.
    d. 3 to 2.
    e. 4 to 3.

39. The Seaboard Railroad's Orange Blossom Special is an excellent example of a
    a. piggyback operation.
    b. unit train.
    c. run-through train.
    d. train whose name might be the basis for the name of a movie or a novel, but never a song.
    e. train on a processing route.

40. Motor carriage's primary advantage over the other transportation media is
    a. its ability to move bulky commodities efficiently over long distances.
    b. its capacity to safely carry natural gas and oil products at a very low cost.
    c. relatively fast, consistent service for both large and small shipments.
    d. speed; motor carriage is nearly twice as fast as the next fastest medium.
    e. its ability to handle the paperwork involved in effectively shipping goods.

41. For which of the following cargo lists would water carriage be the most likely choice?
    a. finished lumber, coal, automobiles, industrial chemicals
    b. clothing, food products, furniture and fixtures, machinery
    c. minerals and ores, bulk chemicals, petroleum products
    d. natural gas, coal slurries, crude oil, jet fuel
    e. cut flowers, microchips, medical instruments, precision tools

42. If you sought to ship a product by the least-cost method, the obvious choice would be
    a. railroad.
    b. motor freight.
    c. pipeline.
    d. air freight.
    e. water carrier.

43. A traditional warehouse most often used by firms facing seasonal fluctuations in the supply of or demand for their products is
    a. a make-bulk center.
    b. a storage warehouse.
    c. an automated warehouse.
    d. a distribution warehouse.
    e. a break-bulk facility.

44. The economic order quantity model is based on the premise that
    a. the total cost of inventorying goods will be at a minimum when the costs of holding goods and those of ordering goods are together at a minimum.
    b. the total cost of inventorying goods will be minimized if a single order is placed for the entire year's requirement.
    c. the more orders placed, the less the total cost of maintaining an inventory.
    d. the fewer goods held in inventory at any given time, the less total inventory cost.
    e. it isn't holding cost or ordering cost that's important, it is the actual cost of buying goods that runs up inventory costs.

45. If a product which a customer has ordered is not available for shipment or sale, one has
    a. a credit check condition.
    b. to make a credit to a sales account.
    c. to record the Universal Product Code of the item.
    d. to compensate by using a different transportation method.
    e. a stockout condition.

46. Automated warehouses are capable of
    a. providing major savings for high-volume distributors such as grocery chains.
    b. reducing labor costs and worker injuries.
    c. lowering the amount of pilferage, fires, and breakage.
    d. all of the above.
    e. none of the above.

47. Freight forwarders are considered to be transportation intermediaries because they
    a. buy shipping services at the LTL or LCL rate and charge their clients the TL or CL rate for them.
    b. buy shipping services at the TL or CL rate and charge their clients the LTL or LCL rate for them.
    c. buy shipping services at the TL or CL rate and charge their clients a price between that rate and the LTL or LCL rate for them.
    d. serve carriers by booking shipments for them; they do the paperwork and the carriers just move the goods.
    e. serve as arbitrators in the event of a conflict between a shipper and a common carrier.

48. Which of the following is a legitimate example of a supplemental carrier?
    a. Norfolk Southern Railroad Company
    b. Purolator Courier Company
    c. Flying Tigers Airlines
    d. United Gas Pipeline Company
    e. Canal Barge Company, Inc.

49. Containerization involves
   a. combining as many packages as possible into one load, preferably on a pallet.
   b. properly packing each item of a shipment into its own carton or container.
   c. recording the exact contents of each package that is part of a shipment.
   d. combining several unitized loads; a standardized shipping container is typically used.
   e. moving products within a manufacturer's plant and warehouses; special "tote boxes" are used.

50. Container ships have delivered an impetus to exporting because
   a. they are so fast; a container ship can be offloaded in less than 24 hours while a regular vessel takes up to two weeks.
   b. they can vary their routes very easily while at sea; goods can be shipped before they are actually sold.
   c. they facilitate the smuggling of contraband into foreign countries; no one ever looks into the sealed containers when they arrive at the port.
   d. it is easier to insure the cargoes against loss; Lloyd's much prefers the seaworthiness of container ships to that of conventional vessels.
   e. they are so flexible; a ship carrying grain today can be carrying industrial chemicals or livestock tomorrow.

Name _____   Instructor _____

Section _____   Date _____

Applying Marketing Concepts

I/O Systems, Inc., is a chain of retail stores catering to personal computer users. The company stocks the input and output devices necessary for the use of these machines—keyboards, modems, printers, print buffers, cable assemblies, diskettes, various types of paper products, and parts and supplies for all the equipment it sells. The history of I/O Systems has been short but exciting. Founded only eight years ago as one small store in a medium-sized midwestern city, the company now has over 200 stores nationwide. This rapid growth has brought not only the expected profits but also problems. The main problem facing I/O's founder and chief executive, Art Mosse, is the challenge of physical distribution.

The company has over 300 suppliers. At the present time, these suppliers receive orders from and ship directly to each I/O store. Store managers handle all shipping and materials-handling problems themselves. Mr. Mosse realizes that such a system is not appropriate for a company of this size. Suppliers charge more for small shipments to the stores than they would for large shipments to a company warehouse. Moreover, if the company buys in large quantities, it can secure quantity discounts it is not currently receiving. There is also a problem with delivery; shipments are often lost or late in arriving at the company's stores. In recent months, the store managers have begun to complain about having to inspect incoming shipments for defects, do paperwork on returns to suppliers, and handle special orders, all of which are very time-consuming. Main office personnel, in the meantime, are complaining about their lack of control of buying activities at the local stores and their total inability to keep track of inventory. To top it all off, sales are being lost because of too many stockouts in the retail stores.

Something must be done! Mr. Mosse has received several suggestions from other members of management, from lower-level employees who work in the affected divisions of the company, and even from a certain number of irate customers. He has disregarded many of the suggestions from customers as being too personally painful or physically impossible (leaping from high windows *does* hurt; we won't discuss the physical impossibilities). To others he has given substantial thought. One of the more interesting suggestions involves setting up a central, automated warehouse to receive all supplier shipments. From that location, goods could be shipped to the stores by common carrier. A second suggestion is to set up several automated warehouses rather than one, to cut down on delivery time.

Before a meaningful decision can be made, a number of questions must be answered. Two of these are: Should the company buy a fleet of trucks or use common carriers? Should all buying, returned goods, and so forth be coordinated by the main office?

____ 1. To have an integrated physical distribution system, I/O should consider using the EOQ model of inventory control.

____ 2. Because avoiding stockouts is so important to a firm like I/O Systems, the just-in-time system of inventory control would probably not be a very good choice for it.

____ 3. Automated warehouses are probably quite feasible for the needs of a firm like I/O Systems.

_____ 4. Freight forwarders should be used by I/O Systems, especially if the company does buy a fleet of trucks.

_____ 5. The Motor Carrier Act of 1980 could be of benefit to the company if it decides to use common carriers.

6. What type of warehouse is the company thinking of installing?
   a. a storage warehouse
   b. a distribution warehouse
   c. a make-bulk facility
   d. a manufacturing warehouse
   e. a bonded warehouse

7. A key function of the warehouse the company is thinking of building is
   a. unitizing.
   b. containerizing.
   c. breaking bulk.
   d. long-term storage.
   e. making bulk.

8. If the company uses a common carrier to deliver orders to the individual stores, what type of rate would it be charged?
   a. a class rate
   b. a commodity rate
   c. a special rate
   d. a negotiated rate
   e. a flat rate

9. If I/O Systems were to install a physical distribution system, a basic systems orientation would require the inclusion of certain features, while others would remain optional. Which of the following would constitute an optional feature in such a system?
   a. order processing
   b. inventory control
   c. intermodal coordination
   d. customer service
   e. materials handling

10. If the company is losing sales due to stockouts in stores, then
    a. customer service standards are not being met.
    b. the stores are too far from the suppliers.
    c. the company needs to hire better store managers.
    d. customers are demanding too much; the company should take a "if we don't have it, you probably don't need it" posture.
    e. a careful analysis of the salespersons' activity sheets is in order; they're probably over-selling some lines.

Melrose Manufacturing Company, a maker of farm machinery located in the community of Bugtussle, Texas, is facing something of a crisis in its operations. It has been approached by a representative of a foreign country which wants to buy 5,000 of the firm's mule-drawn earth augers. Melrose knows nothing whatsoever about international trade. In addition, the company is in no position to lay in the supplies and materials to build 5,000 of the machines. In a good year, it might sell 500 of them in the domestic market. The foreign country said it'd send an inspector to approve the machines as they came off the production line and pay for them on the spot. Melrose would be expected to prepare the machines for shipment, for which the foreign nation would compensate it. Each machine has overall dimensions of seven feet in width, six feet, eight inches in height, and nine feet, six inches in length. They would all be going to the same destination, the capital of the foreign nation, Blagoveshchensk. This city is several hundred miles from the ocean and the highway system between it and the port of Chimutsk is appalling. It does, however, have good road connections with the interior of the country and an excellent airport. The nation's rail system is uniformly good.

____ 11. If Melrose undertakes this job itself, it should be prepared to allocate 36 hours of employee time to preparing the paperwork to go along with each shipment of augers.

____ 12. If the earth augers are shipped in containers, there is increased danger of damage to them because they cannot be seen through the solid walls of the container.

____ 13. All of the activities of preparing the augers for shipment up to the time they're turned over to a transportation company constitute warehousing from Melrose's point of view.

14. In recognition of Melrose's total ignorance of international distribution,
   a. it should probably turn this deal down; there is no practical way to satisfy its customer.
   b. it should get in touch with a good foreign freight forwarder; such people specialize in just this sort of thing.
   c. it probably needs to get in touch with the U.S. State Department.
   d. it should send one of its people off to the state university to take a course in foreign trade.
   e. there is little to be said; such ignorance inevitably leads to business failure.

15. Faced with an apparent shortage of funds to undertake this foreign contract, Melrose looks like
   a. an excellent candidate for just-in-time inventory management; the customer's willingness to pay as machines come off the production line means Melrose can minimize inventory investment at no penalty to itself.
   b. it may have to undertake only a part of the contract or subcontract it out to someone who is better funded.
   c. a company that cannot seize an opportunity when it presents itself.
   d. it may be in financial trouble and a likely candidate for a takeover bid by a larger, better-funded firm.
   e. just another small-time country manufacturer that doesn't know what it's doing.

16. The best way to prepare the augers for shipment would probably be
    a. to crate each of them individually; their dimensions are so large no other method makes sense.
    b. to unitize each machine on its own pallet; that way each machine would be complete on arrival.
    c. to containerize the machines in the largest standard container (40 feet in length); since all the machines are going to the same destination, this is the sensible way to solve the problem, shipping four machines per container.
    d. in whatever fashion is most convenient; after all, they now belong to the foreign government and damages are its problem.
    e. to turn them over to the foreign government at the end of the production line and let it worry about it.

17. A recommended shipping route for these products would be
    a. from Bugtussle to Dallas by truck; then to Blagoveshchensk by air freight.
    b. from Bugtussle to Houston by truck; then to Chimutsk by container ship; and from Chimutsk to Blagoveshchensk by truck.
    c. from Bugtussle to Houston by truck; then to Chimutsk by container ship; and from Chimutsk to Blagoveshchensk by rail.
    d. from Bugtussle to Houston by truck; then to Jacksonville, Florida, by train; from Jacksonville to Chimutsk by container ship; and then to Blagoveshchensk by truck.
    e. from Bugtussle to Los Angeles by train; then to Yokohama by unscheduled steamer (not container ship); to Port Moresby, Papua-New Guinea, by sailing schooner; from Port Moresby via Bombay to Chimutsk by outrigger canoe; then to Blagoveshchensk by yak caravan.

Name _____ Instructor _____

Section _____ Date _____

Questions for Thought

The questions which follow are designed to help you become familiar with the main concepts in this chapter through interpretation in your own words. They are meant to be answered in a few sentences or a paragraph at most.

1. How does the process of physical distribution contribute to the effectiveness of a firm's marketing strategy?

2. Discuss the major components of an effective physical distribution system.

3. How may the problem of suboptimization be solved in the area of physical distribution?

4. How has deregulation affected the use of railroads by firms involved in physical distribution? Motor freight? How has air freight been affected?

5. Compare the five major transportation media on the bases of relative speed, individual dependability, frequency of shipment, availability, and flexibility in dealing with shippers' needs. Is there one medium which is always the best choice?

Name_____ Instructor _____

Section _____ Date _____

Experiential Exercises

1. The purpose of this exercise is to familiarize you with the workings of the transportation system and its interrelationship with the other features of the physical distribution system.

    Visit the nearest office of firms in as many of the transportation media as you can conveniently reach: a railroad company, a motor freight carrier, an airline company, a barge or steamship line, and a pipeline company. (If you are in an isolated location, this may be a major task. Persevere and do the best you can.)

    a. Ask a representative of each company what kind of service it renders from your location. Are there regularly scheduled arrivals and departures? How frequently? To and from what locations? Note below the information you receive.

        Medium:

        Services offered:

        Schedule:

        Locations:

        (Repeat format for each medium. Use additional paper as needed.)

    b. Ask to see the company's "tariff schedule." What does this document reveal?

c.   Ask a representative of each company if there are any special services it renders at your location. Note these below.

d.   Comment on the similarities and the differences you have observed in the methods of operation, quoting of tariffs, and other features of the firms you have visited.

2.   Visit a storage warehouse and a distribution warehouse located near your home or school. (Many public warehouses, particularly those operated by "transfer and storage" companies, are storage warehouses. Warehouses operated by wholesale grocery companies, hard goods wholesalers, and other vendors to local retailers are often distribution warehouses. Check your *Yellow Pages* and make some phone calls before embarking on your visits.)

a.   Discuss the differences in physical characteristics between the two types of warehouses.

b. How does the level of activity compare between the storage warehouse and the distribution warehouse?

c. Discuss the similarities and the differences you have observed between the materials-handling equipment and activities at the two types of facility.

d. Discuss the niche which each of these warehouses occupies in the physical distribution process.

Name _____ Instructor _____

Section _____ Date _____

Computer Applications

Review the discussion of economic order quantity (EOQ) in Chapter 15 of the text. Then use menu item 12 titled "Economic Order Quantity" to solve the following problem.

Luis Ramirez-Bientempo must determine the EOQ for the ink used in the printing plant where he works. He has talked with the head press operator and the maintenance department and has learned that last year's consumption of ink was 82,600 pounds. The ink averaged $.50 per pound in price. It costs the company 25 percent of cost to carry ink in inventory for a year, and placing an order costs $103. It is estimated that current year's consumption of ink will be 97,500 pounds.

a. Calculate the EOQ for ink for this year.

b. Calculate the EOQ for ink for *last year*, assuming all costs and prices were the same then as they are now.

c. Determine the correct order size for this year if the supplier of the ink decides that all orders must be in even increments of 1,200 pounds (a palletload).

Chapter 15 Solutions

Key Concepts

1.	b	6.	i	11.	c
2.	j	7.	m	12.	l
3.	a	8.	f	13.	d
4.	e	9.	k	14.	g
5.	h	10.	n		

Self Quiz

1.	T	11.	F	21.	F	31.	a	41.	c
2.	F	12.	F	22.	T	32.	c	42.	e
3.	T	13.	F	23.	T	33.	d	43.	b
4.	T	14.	T	24.	F	34.	b	44.	a
5.	F	15.	T	25.	F	35.	b	45.	e
6.	T	16.	F	26.	c	36.	d	46.	d
7.	F	17.	F	27.	a	37.	e	47.	c
8.	F	18.	T	28.	d	38.	d	48.	b
9.	T	19.	F	29.	b	39.	a	49.	d
10.	T	20.	T	30.	e	40.	c	50.	a

Applying Marketing Concepts

1.	T	6.	b	11.	T	16.	c
2.	T	7.	c	12.	F	17.	c
3.	T	8.	a	13.	F		
4.	F	9.	c	14.	b		
5.	T	10.	a	15.	a		

Part Six Puzzle

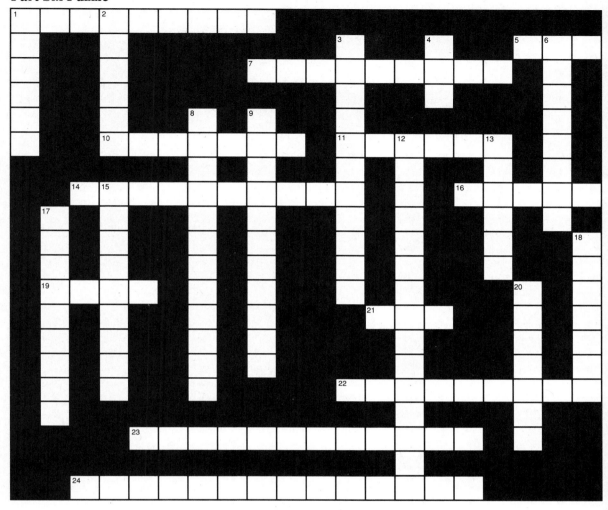

ACROSS CLUES

1. type of VMS in which there is single ownership of each stage of the marketing channel
5. optimal amount to order given the cost structure of ordering versus holding goods on hand
7. activities involved in the sale of products and services to the ultimate consumer
10. in distribution, relationships among institutions to facilitate getting goods to users
11. organized components linked by plan to achieve objectives
14. also called a jobber or distributor, this intermediary takes title to goods it sells
16. kind of limited-function merchant wholesaler which sells perishable food items; also wagon jobber
19. type of distribution in which a firm uses more than one channel to reach its target market

21. acronym describing preplanned distribution channel organized for cost effectiveness
22. standard transportation rate established for shipping various commodities
23. warehouse facility designed to assemble and redistribute products rapidly
24. path goods follow from consumer back to manufacturer

DOWN CLUES

1. groups of retail stores centrally owned and managed, selling essentially the same products
2. in warehousing, an independently owned storage facility which stores and ships for a fee
3. manufacturer-owned facility that carries inventories and processes orders from available stock
4. inventory control system designed to maintain minimum on-hand product at production locations

6. type of retailer that sells designer labels or well-known brand name clothing at low cost
8. word which describes channel position of retailers and wholesalers
9. consumer's perception of store and the shopping experience it provides
12. accomplishing individual objectives at the expense of broader organization objectives
13. the amount added to the cost of an item to determine its selling price
15. demand by retailers for promotional funds in return for shelf space for a brand of goods
17. periodic show at which manufacturers display wares for intermediary buyers
18. traditional warehouse in which products are stored prior to shipment
20. dominant and controlling member of a marketing channel

Name_____   Instructor _____

Section _____   Date _____

Cases for Part 6

1. Leonhardt Farms, Inc.

Roy Leonhardt, owner and Chief Executive of Leonhardt Farms, a large head vegetable operation near Fresno, California, is considering a suggestion made to him by his son, Roy Jr., a recent graduate of Cal State. Junior has suggested that the family corporation, now one of the largest independent growers of lettuce and cabbage on the West Coast, abandon its long-standing relationship with the Greengrocer Wholesale Food Brokerage Company and handle its own distribution. Junior contends that Leonhardt's own railroad sidings and truck fleet are adequate to handle outbound shipments and that the special services available from the railroads, like diversion in transit, will make it possible for Leonhardt to process orders that come in during the picking season even after the lettuce and cabbage have been shipped.

Roy Sr. is not so eager to abandon the relationship between the farm and Greengrocer. Greengrocer has always been very efficient in preselling Leonhardt's output before it was harvested, and paid promptly. Roy Sr. never had to bother with worrying about the mechanics of getting the goods where they were needed. He simply shipped in carload lots where Greengrocer told him to. Now he was concerned. Junior seemed so confident in their ability to handle this new state of affairs.

Question

Before making a decision, what are some additional factors that Mr. Leonhardt had better consider before implementing Roy Jr.'s plan?

2.　*Aquaplane Industries, Incorporated*

Aquaplane Industries, a well established boat builder with yards in Jacksonville and Pensacola, Florida, and Brownsville, Texas, builds and sells 20- to 34-foot pleasure boats designed specifically for salt water use. Since the company's beginning in 1956, sales have grown steadily during periods of economic growth and have been stable during downturns of the economy. Recently, however, John Massa, Sales Manager for Aquaplane, has been under pressure from Harbie Mellner, the company president, to increase sales and profits. John believes this can best be done through the company's existing marketing channels. After analyzing his firm's distribution pattern, Massa has come to the conclusion that increased sales through marinas, the company's only distributors, are unlikely.

An additional marketing channel for Aquaplane has been suggested by Rick Mingus, a volume used-car dealer in a major Gulf Coast city. Mingus wants to sell Aquaplane boats on his used-car lots because "for many middle-class customers the choice is between a second car and a boat." Mingus has pledged to promote Aquaplane boats aggressively and, in return for an exclusive dealership, to carry no competing line of boats.

John realizes that marketing channels do change over time, and he is interested in experimenting with new channel arrangements. Perhaps this new channel would increase sales and profits for Aquaplane.

Questions

a.　What factors constitute important considerations for Aquaplane's decision?

b.　What steps should be included in the selection of a new marketing channel?

c. Should Massa accept Mingus' offer?

3. *Mimi's Mart*

Mimi Delachaise, owner of Mimi's Mart, a medium-sized supermarket located in Plaisance, a growing southern city of 15,000, has enjoyed ten years of successful operation. Recently, however, her dreams of an uncomplicated existence were rudely disrupted when Market Giant Stores, a national discount supermarket chain, announced plans to build a store in a new shopping center located at the southern edge of Plaisance.

Market Giant is an efficient chain that sells on a high-volume, low-price basis. Not only does Market Giant sell national brand merchandise at low prices, it also has an excellent house brand, Market Gold. Market Gold is a fast-selling line of food products that is always priced a few cents less than national brands. Market Giant also stocks an economy brand called Mighty Good that attracts some buyers.

Ms. Delachaise realizes that Mimi's Mart can't compete on a price basis. She is hoping, however, that the fine, friendly service and excellent reputation of her store will keep her customers from leaving to shop at Market Giant.

Garrison Alidont, general manager of Alidont Grocery Supply Company, has proposed that Ms. Delachaise join his organization. Alidont pointed out that this organization, a voluntary chain of 35 independent supermarkets, buys in quantity and obtains discounts similar to those enjoyed by Market Giant. In addition, his organization has its own line of branded merchandise, Gourmet Delight, which is comparable in quality and price to Market Gold. Alidont has pledged to Ms. Delachaise that if she joined his chain she could "compete with Market Giant in every way."

Questions

a. What benefits can a voluntary chain provide a retailer?

b. Should Ms. Delachaise accept Mr. Alidont's invitation to join his voluntary chain?

4. *Printemps du Nord*

Printemps du Nord, a Montreal-based, medium-priced department store, is considering opening an outlet in Duquesne City, a town of some 300,000 located in a northern state of the United States.

Two locations are under serious consideration by Printemps. The first would be in a new, medium-sized shopping center located at the opposite end of town from a five-year-old, existing center which contains the flagship location of Duquesne City's only home-owned department store chain.

The new shopping center will contain a department store (which could be Printemps), a grocery store, a hardware store, a variety store, a drug store, a discount department store, a bank, and about 30 specialty shops. The developer of the new shopping center has asked Printemps to be the department store. It is understood that if Printemps does not accept, the home-owned chain will probably take that location.

Some of Printemps' people are in favor of the new shopping center location. Their enthusiasm is tempered, however, by the belief that if the branch is not profitable in four years, there could be financial problems.

The other location being examined by Printemps is in the central business district of Duquesne City. Even though the home-owned department store closed its downtown location five years ago to move to the shopping center, there is another department store in the CBD which is doing well. In addition, the federal government is planning a major office complex downtown, and there are strong rumors that a major New York corporation is shifting its corporate headquarters to a location in downtown Duquesne City.

Printemps officials are somewhat turned off to the new shopping center because there will be a discount department store located there. They feel the discounter will provide serious competition. Printemps, because it offers higher levels of service and a repair facility for appliances, can't match the prices of the discount operation. The shopping-center developer can't be talked out of that feature of the center.

Question

What action do you think Printemps du Nord should take?

5. Milkmaid Manufacturing Company

Milkmaid Manufacturing Company makes mechanical milking machines sold through dealers. It is thinking of changing its distribution system. Currently, each dealer maintains a small inventory of one or possibly two of the bulky milkers and storage units. Final assembly of milker/storage units takes place at one of four strategically located Milkmaid warehouses before shipping to dealers. Common carriers are used to ship the units from the main plant to the regional warehouses and from the regional warehouses to the dealers.

There have been problems with this system of late. Carrier service has at times been poor. Some deliveries have been late and others have arrived in damaged condition. Melrose Morton, marketing manager for Milkmaid, has been searching for alternatives that will reduce dealer complaints and, if at all possible, reduce physical distribution expense. You have been called in to render your expert opinion.

Questions

a. What alternative transportation arrangement would you suggest Milkmaid consider? Should it buy or lease its own trucks, use a contract carrier, or possibly resort to some sort of intermodal transportation?

b.   What do you think of Milkmaid's assembly and storage warehouses? Is there a better way to provide for storage and assembly?

6.   *Wilson Publishing Company*

Wilson Textbook Company published college textbooks used throughout the United States and Canada. Textbooks are ordered by college bookstores as soon as professors place orders for their courses. All orders are filled from the company plant located at River Falls, Ohio.

Every term a number of professors are late ordering books. This creates a flurry of activity at the beginning of every semester. Recently, the number of late orders has been growing, and delivery of some texts has been as late as two weeks after the beginning of classes. Needless to say, complaints from professors and students have increased in number and virulence. The management of Wilson, however, sees no way to solve the problem as long as professors continue to place late orders.

Questions

a.   What changes would you suggest be made in Wilson's distribution system?

b. Should Wilson attempt to advise professors to order early? Can company salespeople obtain accurate order estimates? In other words, can the order-processing system be improved?

Name_____   Instructor _____

Section _____   Date _____

Creating a Marketing Plan: Let's Find a Place to Hang Our Hats

The information which you will receive in this episode should allow you to complete Part III.C. of your marketing plan.

Episode Six

"If I ever have to look at another dump like that last one, I'll quit!" was Laura's vehement comment after she and Brian drove away from the address the commercial real estate agent had given them. She and the guys knew what they needed: a place of about 2,000 square feet, part warehouse/service area, part office, located near the center of the concentration of businesses in New Essex. The problem seemed to be that the places they felt they could afford suffered from one or more fatal flaws, like inadequate wiring or lack of security—after all, the place was going to be full of computers, test equipment, and components.

"Let's try one more place, 'L,'" said Brian, ever optimistic. "Now that we've established our credit with MicroDevices and KLB, we can get going as soon as we get a place. It was rare luck that we were able to buy those two service vans the telephone company ordered but never had delivered. I doubt that we could have found such nice machines anywhere else for the price. It's a good thing your uncle is in the automobile business and knew about them."

"That's true. I guess I can't expect everything to go smoothly all the time. Didn't you say you had seen an ad in today's paper for a place that it sounded like we could use?" asked Laura.

"Yes," replied Brian, "it's right around the next corner. Let's take a look." They turned the corner and parked next to a nicely maintained concrete block building. "I see there's someone here," said Laura, pointing to a small van parked next to the open side door of the structure.

"Maybe we can get in and take a look," was Brian's reply, "or maybe whoever's there can tell us something about the place." They approached the open door.

Thirty minutes later they emerged in the company of an older man. "The place is just perfect, Mr. Cressy. We'll have our attorney call yours tomorrow to iron out the details, but I think we've got a deal," said Laura, shaking hands with the older man. "Very good, Ms. Claire," was his response. "I think you'll find the building and the location are perfect for your plans."

Later, back at Laura's house, where Terry was waiting, the threesome sat down to organize their thoughts. Terry passed out sheets of paper to the other two and said, "Here are the suppliers we've arranged to buy from and the lead times from each one. Obviously, we're going to have to stock more deeply on parts from some of these people than from others."

Table P6-1: Suppliers, Items Supplied, and Lead Times

Supplier	Items Supplied	Lead Time
Action Electronics	Mechanical parts	7 days
KLB Corporation	Electronic parts	7 days
New Haven Electronics	Electronic parts	7 days
LL Melwer	Electronic devices	7 days
NPN Electronics	Mechanical parts	7 days
Data Exchange	Printer parts	14 days
MicroDevices	Electronic devices	30 days
Okidata	Printer parts	30-90 days
Epson	Printer parts	30-90 days
NEC	Printer parts	30-60 days
Star Micronics	Printer parts	30-60 days
Panasonic	Printer parts	30-45 days
Data Products	Printer parts	30 days

"Why do these printer people take so long to fill orders?" asked Brian. "I guess because all those parts are imported, and maybe they make less money from selling them than they do from selling finished goods," replied Terry. "Anyway, those lead times are what they told me, so I guess we'd better proceed accordingly."

"Right, let's order the stuff we're going to need to have on hand when we open the doors. I suppose we'd better plan for the full length of time for replenishment on those printer parts, so get what you think we'll need for the longest lead time when you order," Laura told Terry. "You guys get on home now, and we'll meet again tomorrow morning to get the lease finalized with the lawyer."

Guidelines

Review the requirements of Part III.C. of your marketing plan, and, using the information in this episode, complete that part of the plan.

Part 7

Promotional Strategy

Promotion and promotional strategy are the subjects of this section of your text.

Promotion is one of the most dynamic and most severely criticized aspects of marketing. It can be defined as the marketing function of informing, persuading, and influencing the consumer's purchase decision. Its elements include personal and nonpersonal selling (subdivided into advertising, sales promotion, and public relations). Effective promotional strategy requires that these elements be properly mixed.

One of the most important tasks facing the marketing manager is the integration of the promotional plan into the overall marketing plan. Promotional objectives must be consistent with the overall marketing objectives. One or more of the five basic objectives of promotion form the basis for a promotional strategy. Promotional objectives are achieved through a promotional budget. Since it is difficult to measure the revenue return of promotion, traditional methods of allocating a promotional budget are based on sales volume, competitive action, and promotional objectives.

Nonpersonal selling includes advertising, sales promotion, and public relations. *Advertising*, which can be defined as a nonpersonal sales presentation usually directed to a large number of potential customers, is an important part of modern business. The two basic types of advertising—product and institutional—can be further classified into informative, persuasive, and reminder categories.

Sales promotion is the name applied to assorted nonrecurrent and somewhat extraordinary nonpersonal selling efforts. There are six basic types of sales promotion: point-of-purchase advertising; specialty advertising; trade shows; samples, coupons, and premiums; contests; and trading stamps.

Public relations activities are often used to supplement other promotional efforts in the marketing mix. Publicity about a firm's products or services is often used to supplement other means of personal and nonpersonal promotion.

Personal selling practitioners, a vital part of the promotional mix, have evolved from the old-time peddler to today's professional salesperson. The sales process usually follows seven steps beginning with prospecting and qualifying and ending with follow-up after the sale has been made. The content and emphasis of the sales presentation depend on whether the sales practitioner is responsible for order processing, creative selling, or missionary sales. A personal salesforce means sales management. Someone must recruit, train, organize, supervise, pay, and evaluate sales practitioners and act in a boundary-spanning role between them and upper-level management.

Chapter 16
Introduction to Promotion

Chapter Summary

Promotion, in its broadest sense, is the function of informing, persuading, and influencing the consumer's purchase decision. Promotion interacts with the other elements of the firm's marketing mix to provide utility for consumers and to help in the achievement of organizational objectives. Marketing managers set the goals and objectives of the promotional strategy to be consistent with overall organizational objectives and the goals of the marketing organization. The various elements of promotional strategy—personal selling, advertising, sales promotion, publicity, and public relations—are blended into a coherent promotional plan which becomes part of the marketing strategy for reaching untapped market segments. The system is completed by a feedback mechanism which includes marketing research and field reports from company personnel. This mechanism serves to identify any deviations from the marketing strategy and suggests modifications and improvements.

Promotion and communication are closely related concepts. If communication is defined as "the transmission of a message from a sender to a receiver," then marketing communications are messages that deal with buyer-seller relationships. The concept of marketing communication is broader than that of promotional strategy because it includes word-of-mouth advertising and other forms of unstructured communication.

Promotion has as its basic objectives (1) the provision of information, (2) stimulation of demand, (3) differentiation of the product, (4) accentuation of the product's value, and (5) stabilization of sales. To achieve these objectives, a blend of the components of the promotional mix must be created which will effectively reach the firm's target market(s) and serve to achieve the organization's objectives. The marketing manager adjusts the blend of personal and nonpersonal selling to best effect the desired result.

Developing a promotional mix is a complex task calling for skill and talent. There is an explicit relationship among the elements of promotion and the type and value of the product or service being promoted, the nature of the marketplace, the stage of the product life cycle, and the funds available to do the job. Timing of a promotional campaign is also crucial to its success or failure. Thus, as the promotional mix is examined for various classes of products, one will find that personal selling predominates when the products being sold are destined for industrial use, when they are of high unit value, and during the transaction phase of the purchase decision process. Advertising tends to be the promotional tool of choice when consumer goods are being promoted, when the goods are of low unit value, during the latter stages of the product life cycle, and pre- and posttransaction in the purchase decision process.

Promotion may attempt to push a product through the channel of distribution by relying on personal selling to convince members of the channel to handle the product being promoted, or it may try to pull the product through the channel by promoting directly to end users through mass media advertising and sales promotion. The technique used depends on the nature of the product, the characteristics of the market segment being sought, and the budget available to do the job.

Promotion is not a free good. All of the elements of the promotional mix must be purchased in the market and paid for in one way or another. A number of methods have been developed to arrive at a dollar figure to budget for promotional expenses. The percentage-of-sales method, for example, bases the budgeted amount on a proportion of either past or forecast sales. The fixed-sum-per-unit method allocates a certain amount of money for promotion to each unit produced or sold. Historical or forecast figures can be used. Another method of budgeting for promotion is to simply meet competition's expenditures on either a dollar-for-dollar or percentage basis. The task-objective approach, an approach preferred by many marketing-oriented managers, first defines realistic goals for the promotional campaign and then determines the amount of activity required to achieve each objective.

Promotion is not free from criticism. Some of its critics claim that it makes no social contribution, that advertisements are insults to intelligence, that promotion forces people to buy things they don't need, and that most promotion activity is unethical. Marketers cannot deny all of these criticisms, but it is certainly not true that all promotion is a waste. One must be very careful when one defines one's terms. Most of the bases for criticism of promotion are relative and are stated in terms such as "too much" or "too little," both of which reveal that they are matters of opinion. It can certainly be demonstrated that promotion has social, business, and economic importance in a society where freedom of choice is seen to be a desirable goal for which to strive.

Name _____   Instructor _____

Section _____   Date _____

Key Concepts

The purpose of this section is to allow you to determine if you can match key concepts with the definitions of the concepts. It is essential that you know the definitions of the concepts prior to applying the concepts in later exercises in this chapter.

From the list of lettered terms, select the one that best fits each of the numbered statements below. Write the letter of that choice in the space provided.

Key Terms

a. promotion
b. marketing communications
c. AIDA concept
d. promotional mix
e. personal selling
f. advertising
g. sales promotion

h. public relations
i. publicity
j. pulling strategy
k. pushing strategy
l. percentage-of-sales method
m. fixed-sum-per-unit method
n. task-objective method

_n_ 1. Promotional budget allocation method in which a firm defines its goals and then determines the amount of promotional spending needed for achieving them.

_g_ 2. Marketing activities other than personal selling, advertising, and publicity that stimulate consumer purchasing and dealer effectiveness.

_b_ 3. Transmission from sender to receiver of messages dealing with buyer-seller relationships.

_i_ 4. Stimulation of demand by disseminating commercially significant news or obtaining favorable media presentation not paid for by an identified sponsor.

_c_ 5. Traditional expansion of the steps an individual must take prior to making a purchase decision.

_a_ 6. Informing, influencing, and persuading the consumer's purchase decision.

_e_ 7. Interpersonal influence process involving a seller's promotional presentation conducted on a person-to-person basis with the prospective buyer.

_h_ 8. Firm's communications and relationships with its various publics.

_j_ 9. Effort by a seller to stimulate demand by final users, who will then exert pressure on the distribution channel to carry the good or service.

_m_ 10. Budget allocation method in which promotional expenditures are a predetermined dollar amount for each sales or production unit.

_d_ 11. Blend of personal selling and nonpersonal selling created by marketers in an attempt to achieve promotional objectives.

_F_ 12. Paid, nonpersonal communication through various media by business firms, nonprofit organizations, and individuals that are in some way identified in the message and hope to inform or persuade members of a particular audience.

_L_ 13. Budget allocation method in which the funds allocated for promotion during a given time are based on a specified percentage of either past or forecast sales.

_K_ 14. Effort by a seller to members of the marketing channel to stimulate personal selling of the good or service.

Name_____   Instructor _____

Section _____   Date _____

Self Quiz

You should use these objective questions to test your understanding of the chapter material. You can check your answers with those provided at the end of the chapter.

While these questions cover most of the chapter topics, they are not intended to be the same as the test questions your instructor may use in an examination. A good understanding of all aspects of the course material is essential to good performance on any examination.

True/False

Write "T" for True or "F" for False for each of the following statements.

F   1.   For communication to be effective, it is only necessary that the message be understood by the sender.

T   2.   In E. K. Strong's acronym, AIDA stands for attention, interest, desire, and action.

T   3.   Feedback to a communication may take the form of attitude change, purchase, or even nonpurchase of a good or service.

F   4.   According to a recent study of food preferences, yogurt has become America's third best-liked food, ranking behind only chocolate ice cream and corn-on-the-cob.

F   5.   Noise in the communications process always results from some sort of mechanical or electronic failure in the communications equipment.

T   6.   The primary objective of most promotional efforts is to increase the demand for a specific product or service.

F   7.   *Heterogeneous demand* means that consumers regard a firm's output as virtually identical to its competitors' products.

F   8.   The demand curve for products with a "prestige" image may be more responsive to price differences than that of a competitor without a quality reputation.

T   9.   Even today, the number of people employed in personal selling, the original form of promotion, approximates 6 million in the United States.

T 10.   If a nonpersonal promotion is designed to stimulate demand for a product or service by obtaining favorable presentation of it on radio, TV, or the stage without having to pay, it is considered publicity.

F 11.   Personal selling is generally the most effective form of promotion when for a product there is a very large number of buyers scattered over a broad area.

T   12. In the introductory stage of the product life cycle, personal selling is heavily emphasized to inform the marketplace of the merits of the new product or service.

T   13. Low-unit-value products are typically promoted using a heavy proportion of advertising in the promotional mix.

F   14. A pulling promotional strategy relies on personal selling to convince members of the channel of distribution to spend extra time and effort promoting the vendor's product.

F   15. Industrial firms generally spend more of their promotional budget for advertising than personal selling, while the reverse is true for consumer goods companies.

T   16. Promotion is subject to diminishing returns; that is, at some point in time an increase in promotional spending will fail to produce a corresponding increase in sales.

F   17. The ideal method of allocating a promotional budget is to increase the budget until no further money is available to be spent for promotion; in other words, to use every penny you can lay your hands on for promotion.

T   18. The use of scanner sales data as a research tool promises to revolutionize evaluation of consumer promotions.

T   19. Criticisms of advertising which focus on words such as "tasteless" and "obnoxious" ignore the fact that no commonly accepted set of values exists within our social framework. In other words, there's no such thing as "bad taste"; there's only your taste and my taste.

F   20. Probably the most common way to set promotional budgets, the fixed-sum-per-unit method applies a predetermined money allocation to each unit of sale or production.

T   21. A traditional method of allocating promotional outlays involves simply meeting competition dollar for dollar or on a percentage basis; it is thought that this method merely preserves the status quo—everybody keeps his/her market share but nobody moves ahead.

F   22. During the pretransactional period of the purchasing process, personal selling is probably more important than advertising.

T   23. Among the indirect methods of evaluating the effectiveness of advertising are recall and readership measurements.

T   24. The U.S. government spends about $300 million a year on advertising and ranks among the country's top 30 users of advertising media.

F   25. The cost of promotion inevitably increases the prices consumers pay for goods.

Multiple Choice

Circle the letter of the word or phrase that best completes the sentence or best answers the question.

e 26. An effective message must
   a. be understood by the receiver.
   b. stimulate the receiver's needs and suggest an appropriate method of satisfying them.
   c. be understood by the sender.
   d. gain the receiver's attention.
   e. achieve all of the above objectives.

b 27. The AIDA concept proposed by E. K. Strong more than 60 years ago explains
   a. why Giuseppe Verdi gave his opera this peculiar name.
   b. the steps an individual must go through before making a purchase decision.
   c. the relationship among ability, intelligence, dedication, and activity in the marketing process.
   d. the structural relationships among variables in the development of the promotional mix.
   e. the various components of the promotional process: advertising, indoctrination, description, and acceptance.

d 28. In the process of communication, the translation of the message into understandable terms is known as
   a. feedback.
   b. decoding.
   c. transmission.
   d. encoding.
   e. transfer.

c 29. When a receiver responds to a message through a change of attitude, by making a purchase, or even by not making a purchase, the phenomenon is called
   a. reaction to media saturation.
   b. development of potential customers.
   c. feedback in the communications process.
   d. message transfer from source to end user.
   e. human variability, usually type "A."

a 30. Of the following, which is most correctly an example of noise in the marketing communications process?
   a. An advertisement is incorrectly assumed to be a news program by a viewer who tunes in a little late.
   b. A viewer of the President's State of the Union message refuses to believe a word of it because he/she is a member of a different political party.
   c. An individual isn't watching when a promotional message appears on television.
   d. Viewers laugh off a tornado alert because they've never been through a twister and don't believe in the danger.
   e. A commercial is presented at the right time, to the right audience, using the correct advertising medium.

c 31. A newspaper advertisement which emphasizes such items as the description of products being offered for sale, the prices at which they're being offered, and the store's hours of business is most likely designed to
   a. differentiate the products offered from competitive products in the same marketplace.
   b. lay emphasis on the product's value.
   c. provide information about the availability and cost of the products being advertised.
   d. stabilize sales of the products over a period of time.
   e. promote the business rather than the products themselves.

b 32. If promotion is successful in shifting the demand for a product or class of products, the result can be
   a. the creation of a situation such that price must be lowered to retain the existing level of sales for the product.
   b. an increase in sales without a corresponding decrease in price.
   c. a decline in sales volume despite a lowering of the price.
   d. stabilization of sales volumes and prices across the industry.
   e. erratic changes in sales volumes that seem to have no relationship to price levels.

a 33. If a promotional program is designed to create a "prestige" image for a product or store, it is designed to
   a. make the demand curve for the product or store less responsive to price differences than that of a less prestigious offering.
   b. increase demand for the product or store being promoted.
   c. stabilize sales of the product or for the store, correcting for seasonal or cyclical problems it may be having.
   d. reduce the demand for the product or store; after all, only upper-class buyers seek out prestige offerings.
   e. shift the burden of promotion from advertising to personal selling.

d 34. The original form of promotion, the one with the longest history, is
   a. advertising; advertising messages have even been found on the walls of the ruins of Pompeii.
   b. public relations; the Phoenicians were always very careful to keep on good terms with their customers and competitors.
   c. sales promotion; it is recorded that the ancient Greeks often offered premiums and prizes to employees who sold more than their quota.
   d. personal selling; presumably the very first exchanges in trade were made by two individuals acting face-to-face.
   e. publicity; no one knows for sure when publicity began, but Pepsi bottles at least three thousand years old have been found at stage level in the ruins of the Greek theatre at Catharsis.

e 35. Advertising, sales promotion, and public relations are all
   a. paid communications through various media that include identification of the sponsor and that hope to inform or persuade members of a particular audience.
   b. examples of promotion through mass media such as newspapers, television, radio, magazines, and billboards.
   c. particularly appropriate methods of promoting products that rely on sending the same promotional message to large audiences.
   d. nonrecurrent promotional methods used on an irregular basis.
   e. examples of forms of nonpersonal selling.

a 36. A firm's communications and relationships with its various publics define
   a. public relations.
   b. publicity.
   c. advertising.
   d. sales promotion.
   e. personal selling.

b 37. The major disadvantages of this form of promotion are that there is considerable waste in its use, it is difficult to demonstrate product, sales are hard to close, and it is difficult to measure results. This promotional tool is
   a. personal selling.
   b. advertising.
   c. sales promotion.
   d. public relations.
   e. publicity.

c 38. The fact that highly standardized products with minimal servicing requirements are less likely to depend on personal selling than are technically complex custom products is an example of the way
   a. the nature of the market influences the promotional mix.
   b. the stage in the product life cycle affects the promotional mix.
   c. the nature of the product affects the promotional mix.
   d. the product's price affects the promotional mix.
   e. the funds available for promotion affect the promotional mix.

e 39. Reminder advertising typically begins to appear in the
   a. introductory stage of the product life cycle.
   b. early part of the growth stage of the product life cycle.
   c. later part of the growth stage of the product life cycle.
   d. early maturity stage of the product life cycle.
   e. later part of the maturity stage of the product life cycle.

d 40. If a manufacturer begins advertising a new good to consumers before that good has even become available to wholesale and retail intermediaries in the channel of distribution, it is probably using a
   a. pushing strategy to secure distribution at the wholesale level of the channel.
   b. thrust-off promotion to get the product adopted by the members of the channel before the public becomes aware of it.
   c. mixed-bag strategy designed to create the proper atmosphere for product introduction to the consumer market.
   d. pulling strategy to develop end-user demand so that final consumers will force retailers and wholesalers to stock the product.
   e. forced-choice program to make channel members decide which of two competing products they're going to stock.

d 41. Which of the following combinations of sales promotion techniques is increasing in popularity with food marketers as a means of gaining consumer support?
   a. extensive use of newspaper inserts and cents-off coupons
   b. consumer advertising using interactive home computing equipment and production of self-sponsored TV programs
   c. increasingly elaborate point-of-purchase displays and manufacturer salesmen "pitching" the product in the stores
   d. sponsorship of special events and unusual sampling settings, such as out-of-store locations
   e. mechanized promotions such as robots serving the product and use of comparison tests loaded in favor of the sponsor's product

a 42. Evidence suggests that sales initially lag behind promotion
   a. for structural reasons—stocking retail shelves, low initial production, and lack of buyer knowledge.
   b. because promotional efforts are often misdirected in the beginning, aiming at markets that don't develop.
   c. because the promotional budget is too small to support a sufficiently high level of sales in the beginning.
   d. because diminishing returns are typical during this period of product availability—spending more on promotion doesn't yield greater sales.
   e. for no apparent reason; there are insufficient data on which to base any conclusions.

C 43. The ideal method of allocating a promotional budget is
   a. to try and get every nickel you can lay your hands on and spend it largely on advertising.
   b. to spend equally on advertising, sales promotion, and personal selling.
   c. to increase the promotional budget until the cost of each additional increment equals the additional revenue received.
   d. to match what the competition spends either dollar for dollar or percent for percent.
   e. to allocate a fixed sum for advertising and when it's gone, it's gone.

b 44. The most common way of establishing promotional budgets is most likely the
   a. marginal analysis method.
   b. percentage-of-sales method.
   c. fixed amount available method.
   d. fixed-sum-per-unit method.
   e. method described by Svoboda in *Alligators and Advertising*.

a 45. Effective use of the task-objective method of budget allocation depends on
   a. realistically defining the communication goals the promotional mix is expected to achieve.
   b. having available a very large sum of uncommitted funds to support the promotional program.
   c. understanding the necessity for a concentration of funds on advertising and the lesser importance of personal selling.
   d. retarding the promotional expenditure flow until results are apparent.
   e. carefully hoarding monies from one year to the next until they can be most effectively spent.

46. Advertising is considered to be more important than personal selling during which phases of the purchasing process?
    a. the pretransactional and the transactional
    b. the transactional and the posttransactional
    c. the pretransactional and the posttransactional
    d. the transactional
    e. the pretransactional

47. Given the availability of technology and an appropriate method, most marketers would prefer to measure promotional effectiveness using
    a. standard statistical tools, such as mean difference testing.
    b. direct-sales-results tests which would reveal the impact of every dollar spent on advertising on sales.
    c. indirect evaluation of effectiveness, using such devices as recall and readership analysis.
    d. sales inquiries and studies of attitude change caused by promotion.
    e. traditional methods based on the expertise of company executives.

48. A person who always buys Kraft Mayonnaise and rushes to stock up when the product goes on sale would be categorized, using the most recent UPC scanning analyses, as
    a. a person who is not promotion sensitive.
    b. an individual who buys only brands that are on sale.
    c. a family shopper who buys on-sale brands he or she would not ordinarily buy.
    d. a packrat who buys anything on sale, even if he or she will never use it.
    e. a consumer who is loyal to a particular product and stocks up when the product goes on sale.

49. Comments such as "most advertisements assume I'm an idiot" and "advertising is almost always in bad taste" relate to
    a. the importance of advertising to the economy.
    b. advertising's role in perpetuating undesirable stereotypes.
    c. advertising's importance in the business sphere.
    d. relationships we've all noticed between advertising and mental capacity.
    e. perceptions of the social importance of advertising.

50. Promotion can be said to be economically important because
    a. it provides employment for thousands of people.
    b. it increases sales volumes, thus lowering per-unit cost.
    c. it subsidizes the communications and entertainment media.
    d. it performs all of the functions outlined above.
    e. none of the above constitutes a valid reason to call promotion "important" in any fashion.

Name_____   Instructor _____

Section _____   Date _____

Applying Marketing Concepts

It's always a bit intimidating to report for work at a new place for the first time, and John Forrester admitted to himself that he felt a little uneasy about his new job at Springhill Industries, a well-known maker of small computers. Replacing a promotions manager who has been in the job for 25 years is always tough. It didn't take John long, however, to get into the swing of things and settle down to a long, close look at the company's promotional program. Some things were pretty much as he expected them because Springhill was an industrial supplier and followed pretty conventional promotional practices insofar as advertising and personal selling were concerned. He was somewhat disturbed when he discovered, however, that there was no mechanism by which the comments and actions of customers were reported back to his department. He made a note to check on that, as well as on his observation that many of the company's promotional pieces— advertisements, catalogs, and mailers—were badly written and difficult to understand; he even had trouble figuring some of them out. He also worried about the company's relationship with the local community. Fences surrounding the plant bore signs saying "No Trespassing—Keep Out" and the main gate, which was policed by armed guards, was even more intimidating with its "Stop— Show Identification—Authorized Personnel Only" sign. Such isolation seemed a bit much to John, as did the fact that Springhill had no athletic teams playing in the local junior or adult leagues.

1. Springhill Industries' promotional program probably
   a. puts more emphasis on personal selling than on advertising.
   b. puts more emphasis on advertising than on personal selling.
   c. emphasizes personal selling and advertising equally.
   d. uses neither personal selling nor advertising.
   e. relies on publicity to carry the burden of promotion.

2. That John was worried that there was no way for him to know customers' comments and actions indicates he was concerned
   a. about the effectiveness of his sales promotion program.
   b. about the degree to which his advertising money was being wasted on fancy artwork by the layout department.
   c. that feedback from the marketplace was not being used to make adjustments to the company's programs and practices.
   d. that his position in the company was isolated from the decision makers at headquarters.
   e. that salespeople weren't doing their jobs in the field properly.

3. Difficulty in understanding an advertising message, catalog entry, or the terms of a mailer means
   a. that Springhill Industries must be on the verge of failure.
   b. very little; these sorts of things are used merely to get the customer's attention.
   c. that someone in the production department probably wrote the catalogs.
   d. that there is a very real danger that enough noise will be created in the communications channel to defeat the intent of the communication.
   e. that someone has probably been trying to do two jobs at once: write advertising and learn to read.

4. Springhill Industries' seeming isolation from the local community is probably evidence
   a. of a weakness in its public relations program.
   b. of the fact that it's got something to hide at its plant location.
   c. that the president of the company really did say "Bah, humbug!" last Christmas when approached by the local Church Fund.
   d. of the low level of competitiveness in the small computer market these days.
   e. of good legal thinking; the company certainly doesn't want to have to worry about paying for injuries to unauthorized persons on its grounds. It's better to shoot them for trespassing before they can hurt themselves.

Primate Manufacturing Company, a new manufacturer of android personal computing machines, has retained you as its promotion manager. At present, Primate PCs are sold to wholesalers in units of six to a case, which is the standard unit for sales and cost analysis purposes. Promotional expenditures are allocated on a per-case basis at the rate of $18 per case shipped.

5. Which of the following promotional budgeting techniques is Primate Manufacturing using?
   a. percentage of sales
   b. fixed-sum-per-unit
   c. meeting competition
   d. task-objective method
   e. spend what you have

6. If 10 percent of total sales had been the promotional allocating rule, the method would have been
   a. percentage of sales.
   b. fixed-sum-per-unit.
   c. meeting competition.
   d. task-objective method.
   e. marginal analysis method.

Name _____   Instructor _____

Section _____   Date _____

Questions for Thought

The questions which follow are designed to help you become familiar with the main concepts in this chapter through interpretation in your own words. They are meant to be answered in a few sentences or a paragraph at most.

1. Relate the process of communication to the application of promotional strategy.

2. Discuss the primary determinants of the promotional mix.

3. How does the promotional mix relate to the marketing mix?

4. Discuss the various ways in which a promotional budget may be developed.

5. Discuss some of the more common criticisms of promotion and make a defense against each of them.

Name_____   Instructor _____

Section _____   Date _____

Experiential Exercises

1. The importance of the various promotional tools differs depending on which phase of the purchasing process the product's buyer has reached. Review your text concerning the roles advertising and personal selling play during the pretransactional, transactional, and posttransactional phases of this process and then:

   a. List three products and develop a promotional device for them to reach people during the posttransactional period.

      1. (Example) Automobile. Send the proud new purchaser of the BMW 735iL a letter congratulating him/her on his/her good taste in buying such a fine machine. Specifically mention the name of the "representative" who will be handling warranty service of the car (should any be required) with a telephone number and address.

      2.

      3.

   b. Using the three products from part a, show how your use of promotion would differ in the pretransactional stage.

      1. Automobile

2.

3.

c.   How do the objectives of promotion differ among the three stages of the purchasing process?

2.   Social customs, holidays, and special occasions provide many opportunities for unique promotional approaches. We are all familiar with the custom of giving gifts on birthdays, erecting decorated evergreen trees for Christmas (and in some cases, Hanukkah), and shooting fireworks on the Fourth of July. In this exercise, you will look a bit more closely at these social institutions.

a.   List three customs, holidays, or special occasions not mentioned above and relate them to some special good or service that is called for. Confine your occasions to those normally celebrated in the U.S. Then show some types of promotion which could be used to promote the events.

Custom	Good or Service	Promotion
1.		
2.		
3.		

b. Create your own three special occasions, holidays, or customs that would call for parties, gift-giving, or human sensitivity. Show products or services that would be required and suggest promotions that could be applied to each.

Custom	Good or Service	Promotion
1.		
2.		
3.		

Name _____   Instructor _____

Section _____   Date _____

Computer Applications

Review the discussion of the alternative methods of allocating promotional budgets in Chapter 16 of the text. Then use menu item 13 titled "Promotional Budget Allocations" to solve each of the following problems.

1. Albertsen's, a chain of bakeries in a large midwestern city, has allocated $300,000 for its 1991 promotional budget. The allocation was based upon using the same percentage of sales as had been used during 1990. During 1990, the chain generated sales of $4,000,000 and spent a total of $240,000 on promotion. How much sales revenue does Albertsen's expect to produce in 1991?

2. Giovanni Bianco, director of marketing for Vinos Finos, Inc., is working up his 1992 promotional budget. His historical sales and promotional figures are as follows:

Year	Sales for Year	Spent on Promotion
1987	$1,240,000	$ 87,600
1988	$1,360,000	$ 97,720
1989	$1,440,000	$104,400
1990	$1,480,000	$105,520
1991	$1,504,000	$112,800
1992	$1,550,000(est.)	?

Bianco has also discovered sales and promotional outlay figures on his three biggest competitors for 1991. During that year, Vins Superieurs sold about $1,640,000 worth of wine on a promotional budget of $95,120; Vinhos Portugesas sold about $2,800,000 with a promotional budget of $170,800, and Winos Northamericanos did about $3,000,000 on a promotional expenditure of $180,000.

a. What percentage of 1991 sales should Bianco include in his 1992 promotional budget if he bases it on the percentage of sales used in 1991? How many dollars would go for promotion?

b. Suppose Mr. Bianco decides to use the average percentage over the last five years as the basis for his 1992 promotional budget. What percentage would be included? And how many dollars would that be?

c. Suppose he based his budget for promotion on the average of the percentage expenditures of his three closest competitors. What percentage would he use? How many dollars would be appropriated for promotion?

3. Jomo Kallakaw, manager of the Finest Kind Seafood Market and Florist Shop, has decided to budget a fixed sum per unit to determine the correct promotional budget for 1992. He is going to base the exact amount on the average for other seafood markets/florist shops in his area. Available data revealed the following:

Shop	Per Unit Promotional Expenditure*
A	$17
B	$28
C	$35
D	$45
E	$50

*A unit is 12 dozen of anything--cod or roses, it doesn't matter.

Jomo expects 1992 sales to be 2,500 units. How much should he allocate per unit to promotion in 1992? What will his total promotional budget be?

4. The Okaloosa Company of Belzoni, Mississippi, was founded by the Indian tribe of the same name to develop the tribe's native ability to build prefabricated wooden structures. The firm's growth has been substantial, and the high quality of the finished product and its genuine "American" design has won it high praise from architects and buyers alike. Jack Whitelaw, tribal chief and business manager of the company, is working on the promotional budget for 1992. Sales and promotional expenditure records since 1986 are summarized below:

Year	Sales	Promotion as a Percent of Sales
1986	$ 5,000,000	4.0
1987	$ 6,200,000	4.6
1988	$ 7,600,000	5.0
1989	$ 8,400,000	5.2
1990	$10,800,000	5.4
1991	$11,900,000	5.5

The sales forecast for 1992 is $12,800,000. The firm's four major competitors have sales and promotional budgets as follow:

Competitor (Tribe)	Annual Sales (Est.)	Promotional Budget (Est.)
Calcasieu	$ 7,600,000	$319,200
Choctaw	$ 8,400,000	$596,400
Chickasaw	$13,400,000	$670,000
Catahoula	$18,400,000	$993,600

a. What percentage of 1992 sales should the Okaloosa Company include in its 1992 promotional budget if the budget is based on the percentage allocated for 1991 sales? How many dollars would be earmarked for promotion?

b. Suppose the average percentage spent over the last six years is to be the percentage allocated in 1992. What percentage would be allocated? How many dollars?

c. Jack Whitelaw is concerned that perhaps meeting competition is a better idea than simply spending to one's own average. He wonders if perhaps he should base spending for promotion on the average percentage outlays of his four major competitors. What percentage would be used if this were done? How many dollars would this be?

Chapter 16 Solutions

Key Concepts

1. n	6. a	11. d
2. g	7. e	12. f
3. b	8. h	13. l
4. i	9. j	14. k
5. c	10. m	

Self Quiz

1. F	11. F	21. T	31. c	41. d
2. T	12. T	22. F	32. b	42. a
3. T	13. T	23. T	33. a	43. c
4. F	14. F	24. T	34. d	44. b
5. F	15. F	25. F	35. e	45. a
6. T	16. T	26. e	36. a	46. c
7. F	17. F	27. b	37. b	47. b
8. F	18. T	28. d	38. c	48. e
9. T	19. T	29. c	39. e	49. e
10. T	20. F	30. a	40. d	50. d

Applying Marketing Concepts

1. a
2. c
3. d
4. a
5. b
6. a

Chapter 17

Advertising, Sales Promotion, and Public Relations

Chapter Summary

For many organizations, advertising represents the most important form of nonpersonal promotion. Advertising may be used at any level of the channel of distribution and, using different media, by advertisers with very large or very small promotional budgets. The history of advertising is assuredly a long one, traceable back certainly to the days of ancient Rome, when visual symbols were used on signs to tell a largely illiterate population the nature of the business carried on at a location. Advertising in one form or other has been around since the earliest beginnings of the exchange process. It probably predates writing and its origins lie in the calls and chants of itinerant vendors of goods and services.

Advertising in the modern American economy generally falls into one of two categories: product advertising or institutional advertising. Product advertising aims at selling a good or service, while institutional advertising promotes any concept, idea, philosophy, or goodwill for an industry, company, organization, person, locality, or government agency. Both product and institutional advertising may be further broken down into informative, persuasive, and reminder-oriented categories. Advertisers may choose from a wide range of media to carry their messages. Newspapers, magazines, outdoor advertising, and direct mail constitute the print media while radio and television are the basic broadcast media. Alternative media not easily classed as either print or broadcast are also available, ranging from transit advertising to ads included in prerecorded videocassettes. Each medium possesses its own set of advantages and disadvantages: newspapers dominate the local scene, for example, while at the national level television is the preferred medium.

It is extremely important to be able to measure the effectiveness of advertising. This is accomplished by pretesting and posttesting. Pretesting, which is undertaken before the ad is run, includes such devices as sales conviction tests and blind product tests. Posttests, which include readership tests, unaided recall tests, inquiry tests, and split runs, are done after the advertisement has been used.

The advertising department of the firm is usually a staff group reporting to the chief marketing executive. Among the jobs which an advertising department may be called upon to do are research, artwork and design, copywriting, and media analysis. Many advertising departments also handle their firms' sales promotion function. Outside the firm, independent advertising agencies are available to provide the creativity and objective point of view which a firm's in-house advertising department may not be able to give. Specialist firms such as these may be used for creative services, account management, research, or promotional services.

Advertisements do not spring full-blown from the back rooms of companies or advertising agencies. Their creation involves a keen awareness of their purposes: (1) to gain attention and interest, (2) to inform, persuade, and/or remind, and (3) to lead eventually to buying action. From an initial idea, a potential advertisement develops into a thought sketch, then into a rough layout. The layout is modified and refined until the final version of the ad is ready for production.

Sales promotion, perhaps the most difficult of the elements of the promotional mix to accurately define, is nonetheless a very important part of a firm's promotional effort. Among the tools of sales promotion are (1) point-of-purchase advertising (displays erected in stores), (2) specialty advertising (give-away items bearing the advertiser's name), (3) trade shows (large-scale product demonstrations), (4) samples (actual product given away), (5) coupons (one-time price reductions), (6) premiums (gifts given with a product purchase), (7) contests, and (8) trading stamps.

Public relations (the firm's relationships and communications with its various publics) involves customers, employees, stockholders, suppliers, government, and society in general. The most visible and promotional component of public relations is publicity, the dissemination of newsworthy information about a product or company. Often used in new-product introductions, publicity properly handled can have enormous value to the organization.

Name_____   Instructor _____

Section _____   Date _____

Key Concepts

The purpose of this section is to allow you to determine if you can match key concepts with the definitions of the concepts. It is essential that you know the definitions of the concepts prior to applying the concepts in later exercises in this chapter.

From the list of lettered terms, select the one that best fits each of the numbered statements below. Write the letter of that choice in the space provided.

Key Terms

a. advertising
b. positioning
c. product advertising
d. institutional advertising
e. informative advertising
f. persuasive advertising
g. reminder advertising
h. advocacy advertising
i. media scheduling
j. advertising agency

k. comparative advertising
l. retail advertising
m. cooperative advertising
n. pretesting
o. posttesting
p. sales promotion
q. point-of-purchase advertising
r. specialty advertising
s. public relations
t. publicity

_e_ 1. Promotion that seeks to announce the availability of and develop initial demand for a product, service, organization, person, place, idea, or cause.

_m_ 2. Sharing of advertising costs between the manufacturer and the retailer of a good or service.

_c_ 3. Nonpersonal selling of a good or service.

_o_ 4. Assessment of advertising copy after it has been used.

_g_ 5. Promotion seeking to reinforce previous promotional activity by keeping the name of the product, service, organization, person, place, idea, or cause in front of the public.

_i_ 6. Timing and sequencing of advertisements.

_d_ 7. Promoting a concept, idea, philosophy, or goodwill of an industry, company, organization, place, person, or government agency.

_t_ 8. Stimulating demand by placing significant news about or obtaining a favorable presentation for a product, service, place, idea, person, or organization without the sponsor paying for it.

_q_ 9. Displays and other promotions located near the site of the actual purchasing decision.

_j_ 10. Marketing specialist firm used to assist advertisers in planning and implementing advertising programs.

_b_ 11. Developing a marketing strategy aimed at a particular market segment and designed to achieve a desired position in the prospective buyer's mind.

_s_ 12. Firm's communications and relationships with its various publics.

_f_ 13. Competitive promotion that seeks to develop demand for a product, service, organization, person, place, idea, or cause.

_h_ 14. Paid public communication or message that presents information on a point of view bearing on a publicly recognized, controversial issue.

_r_ 15. Sales promotion technique that involves the use of articles such as key rings and ballpoint pens that bear the advertiser's name, address, and advertising message.

_L_ 16. Nonpersonal selling by stores that offer goods or services directly to the consuming public.

_n_ 17. Assessment of an advertisement's effectiveness before it is actually used.

_K_ 18. Nonpersonal selling efforts that make direct promotional comparisons with leading competitive brands.

_a_ 19. Paid, nonpersonal communication through various media by business firms, nonprofit organizations, and individuals who are identified in the message and hope to inform or persuade members of a particular audience.

_p_ 20. Marketing activities other than personal selling, advertising, and publicity that enhance consumer purchasing and dealer effectiveness.

Name _____ Instructor _____

Section _____ Date _____

Self Quiz

You should use these objective questions to test your understanding of the chapter material. You can check your answers with those provided at the end of the chapter.

While these questions cover most of the chapter topics, they are not intended to be the same as the test questions your instructor may use in an examination. A good understanding of all aspects of the course material is essential to good performance on any examination.

True/False

Write "T" for True or "F" for False for each of the following statements.

_F_ 1. Since the end of World War II, advertising and related expenditures have risen at roughly the same rate as the gross national product.

_T_ 2. The nation's three leading advertisers—Procter and Gamble, Philip Morris, and Sears—spend more than $1 billion per year on advertising.

_T_ 3. The nursery rhyme "Hot Cross Buns" had its origins in a shouted advertising slogan.

_F_ 4. The first advertising agency in the United States was organized by George P. Rowell in 1844.

_F_ 5. The average American is exposed to some 3,000 advertising messages every day.

_T_ 6. Advertising attempts to condition the consumer to adopt a favorable viewpoint toward the promotional message.

_F_ 7. Advertisers are often less concerned with the technical aspects of advertisement construction than they should be, concentrating instead on the more basic steps, such as market analysis.

_T_ 8. Positioning strategy is applied primarily to products which are not leaders in their particular industries.

_F_ 9. Institutional advertising is concerned with reinforcing previous promotional activity by keeping the name of the subject of the previous effort before the public.

_F_ 10. Advocacy advertising is sometimes known as institutional advertising.

_T_ 11. The objective of media selection is to achieve adequate media coverage without going beyond the identifiable limits of the potential market.

_F_ 12. Most newspaper advertising revenues come from national advertisers, while television derives the bulk of its revenues from local sources.

F   13. Cable television cannot be considered a broadcast medium because it only reaches 18 percent of U.S. households.

F   14. Among the disadvantages of the television medium is its lack of impact, flexibility, and prestige.

T   15. Radio is a low-cost advertising medium with a high factor of immediacy.

T   16. Magazines are divided into three basic categories—consumer, farm, and business publications.

T   17. Effective use of an advertising agency requires a close relationship between the advertiser and the agency.

F   18. The volume of comparative advertising in the U.S. is surprisingly large, accounting for an estimated 41 percent of all radio and television commercials.

T   19. Retail stores seldom use advertising agencies, preferring to create their own advertising in-house.

F   20. Posttesting is generally more desirable than pretesting of advertising because of the potential cost savings.

T   21. Sales promotional techniques may be used by all members of a marketing channel: manufacturers, wholesalers, and retailers.

F   22. Specialty advertising began when early automobile vendors began giving their customers free keychains as a souvenir of their visit to the showroom.

T   23. Premiums are items given free or at reduced cost when another item is purchased.

T   24. Public relations is an efficient indirect communications channel for promoting products, although its objectives typically are broader than those of other components of promotional strategy.

F   25. Publicity may be looked upon as an entirely cost-free medium for promotion of a company's products or services.

Multiple Choice

Circle the letter of the word or phrase that best completes the sentence or best answers the question.

b 26. In ancient Rome, a sign hanging on a building showing a boy being whipped indicated
    a. that the building housed a jail.
    b. that the building contained a school.
    c. that the structure housed a slave market.
    d. that the owner of the building had been imprisoned for beating his employees.
    e. that the edifice contained a temple to Apollo, who, in his human form, had often suffered the pain of the whip.

a 27. Marketers use a positioning strategy
   a. to distinguish their good or service from the competition.
   b. to prevent the intrusion of new products or services into the market.
   c. to avoid making direct comparisons between one product and another.
   d. to enhance a dominant share of the market.
   e. as a desperate move when a product market is dying.

d 28. Mita Copiers, by stressing the fact that its company makes "copiers . . . just copiers," is
   a. positioning its offering on the basis of a price/quality comparison.
   b. telling us who the users of its product should be—people who want copies . . . just copies.
   c. weakening its case for technical expertise; its foundation is too narrow so it can't be much good.
   d. positioning an aspect of its marketing mix in direct opposition to the leading competitors, all of whom make other things in addition to copiers.
   e. probably trying to make the point that copiers are difficult to produce.

c 29. Advertising which seeks to develop initial demand for a product, service, organization, person, place, idea, or cause is called
   a. product advertising.
   b. persuasive advertising.
   c. informative advertising.
   d. reminder advertising.
   e. comparative advertising.

b 30. Advertising which promotes a concept, idea, philosophy, or the goodwill of an industry is known, in general, as
   a. persuasive advertising.
   b. institutional advertising.
   c. selective advertising
   d. public information.
   e. standards advertising.

e 31. Advocacy advertising is really a special form of
   a. corporate product advertising.
   b. informative institutional advertising.
   c. reminder life-cycle advertising.
   d. informative political advertising.
   e. persuasive institutional advertising.

c 32. The most popular of all media choices, bringing in 29 cents of every dollar spent on advertising in the U.S., is
   a. television, today's hottest medium.
   b. radio, now in a period of active resurgence.
   c. newspapers, an old standby with local users.
   d. direct mail, one of the most active modern media.
   e. outdoor advertising, which billboards the nation's roads and highways.

a 33. Which advertising medium offers the advantages of immediacy, low cost, flexibility, practical and low-cost audience selection, and mobility?
   a. radio
   b. television
   c. newspapers
   d. magazines
   e. direct mail

b 34. Some of the disadvantages of using the newspaper medium as an advertising vehicle are
   a. lack of flexibility found in other media and long lead time between ad placement and appearance.
   b. short life span, relatively poor reproduction quality, and haste in reading.
   c. high cost, loss of control of the promotional message, and public distrust of the medium.
   d. consumer resistance to the medium and high per-person acquisition cost.
   e. the necessity for an extremely brief message and lack of aesthetics in the eyes of the public.

d 35. The shorter the repurchase cycle for a product or service, the more likely it is that
   a. advertising expenditures will rise and fall during the year.
   b. advertising will be a relatively unimportant part of the promotional mix.
   c. a company will rely on direct mail promotion rather than more traditional media.
   d. the media schedule chosen will be consistent throughout the year.
   e. competitors will not react to media changes by a single member of the market.

d 36. Outdoor advertising is particularly effective
   a. in rural locations where the message can be seen at a great distance.
   b. when placed along lightly traveled arteries so that people can pay more attention to the advertising and less to driving.
   c. when fairly large blocks of print are used to communicate the desired information.
   d. in metropolitan and other high-traffic areas.
   e. when placed so that foot traffic is forced to detour around the billboards to get where it's going.

b 37. Within most businesses, the advertising function is usually set up as
   a. a line department reporting directly to the chief executive officer of the company.
   b. a staff department reporting to the vice-president or director of marketing.
   c. a home-office department housed in the engineering division.
   d. a staff department with responsibility directly to the president of the firm.
   e. a functional division of the company with its own vice-president and an equal voice in company policymaking with all other divisions.

c 38. When a firm uses an advertising agency,
   a. the agency should be kept at arms' length; it is, after all, serving its own purposes and not necessarily those of the company using it.
   b. it should expect the cost of advertising to go up; after all, the agency has to be paid for its services.
   c. the agency is typically paid by the media, not the firm, in the form of a 15 percent discount off the price of advertising placed.
   d. it may lose some of the creativity it may have been able to get from its own people; agency people don't know the product line or the company as well as its own employees.
   e. it must choose from over 100,000 such independent marketing specialists here in the United States.

39. The final step in the advertising process is
    a. choice of a medium to carry the message.
    b. definition of a target market to appeal to.
    c. retention of an advertising agency to develop the program.
    d. deciding on the positioning of the product with respect to the competition.
    e. development and preparation of an actual advertisement.

40. In an advertisement, the part of the ad that actually names the sponsor and may even tell you the company's address and phone number is called the
    a. headline.
    b. subhead.
    c. upper body.
    d. lower body.
    e. signature.

41. According to the authors of your text, a condition that should be eliminated is that too many advertisers fail to do this in their advertising. They fail to
    a. suggest how readers can buy the product if they want it.
    b. tell the reader what the product actually is.
    c. identify themselves and establish their credibility.
    d. gain our attention with their message.
    e. include a headline; all ads must have a headline.

42. One of the things that users of comparative advertising must be certain about is that they
    a. are the industry leader; followers don't do well with comparative advertising.
    b. make comparisons that can't be checked; you can say anything as long as no one can disprove it.
    c. are able to prove their claims; comparative advertising that can't be backed up has been known to produce lawsuits.
    d. not mention specifically what they are comparing with their product; that way, nobody can squawk even if the point of the comparison is obvious.
    e. make no comparisons that have any meaning; the public won't know the difference, anyway.

43. The primary advantage of using big-name personalities as product spokespeople is that they may
    a. improve product recognition in an environment filled with competing advertising.
    b. allow a company to pay less attention to trends; their credibility is inherent and doesn't vary with fashion.
    c. create a whole new level of interest in the company, as did John Houseman's commercials for McDonald's.
    d. create interest in the company, especially when the personality has no apparent relationship with the product.
    e. allow the company to be less creative; using personalities lets them carry the load so the rest of the program can slide a little.

d 44. The basic problem with retail advertising is that
   a. it varies widely in its effectiveness.
   b. consumers are often suspicious of retail price ads.
   c. source, message, and shopping experience affect consumer attitudes toward these ads.
   d. retail stores often treat advertising as a secondary activity, rarely using advertising agencies.
   e. it accounts for such a sizable portion of annual advertising expenditures.

e 45. When a manufacturer pays a part of a retailer's cost of advertising the manufacturer's products, it is practicing
   a. demonstrative advertising.
   b. comparative advertising.
   c. retailer-sponsored advertising.
   d. testimonial advertising.
   e. cooperative advertising.

a 46. When interviewers from McCann-Erickson ask heavy users of a product which of two alternative advertisements would convince them to purchase it, they are conducting a
   a. sales conviction pretest.
   b. blind product pretest.
   c. dummy ad test.
   d. recognition pretest.
   e. aided recall test.

b 47. Burke Marketing Research Corporation posttests advertisements by
   a. conducting readership or recognition tests on people who have read magazines containing the ads.
   b. telephoning people the day after a television commercial has aired and testing its effectiveness.
   c. using unaided recall tests to determine an ad's impact.
   d. including an inquiry card with the ads so people can respond directly to the ad.
   e. splitting runs on cable television and using recall tests as a follow-up.

c 48. Looked at from the point of view of dollars spent on the activity,
   a. advertising and sales promotion are virtually tied on a year-to-year basis for the amount spent on each.
   b. advertising accounts for roughly twice as much promotional spending each year as sales promotion.
   c. sales promotion actually leads advertising in terms of the dollars spent on each.
   d. public relations and sales promotion together still don't approach the dollar value of advertising each year.
   e. sales promotion lags behind both advertising and public relations in yearly expenditures.

e 49. The practice during the Middle Ages of giving wooden pegs inscribed with artisans' names to prospective customers so they could use them to hang up their armor has led to the modern practice called
   a. couponing.
   b. sampling.
   c. trade show promotion.
   d. public relations.
   e. specialty advertising.

e

50. Anheuser-Busch's TIPS (Training and Intervention Procedures for Servers of Alcohol) program is an example of a
   a. publicity program aimed at building consumer support for bartenders.
   b. contest for barroom bouncers, in which they demonstrate the methods by which they practice their craft.
   c. sampling program where liquor retailers are given product to be distributed free to their best salespeople.
   d. multimedia promotional package designed to be shown at trade shows.
   e. public relations program aimed at educating retailers in how to handle intoxicated patrons.

Name _____   Instructor _____

Section _____   Date _____

Applying Marketing Concepts

Your job as national advertising manager for Kumquat Soap has become a source of great frustration to you. You know that your product is superior to any other cleansing and beauty soap on the market and that the addition of genuine kumquat oil (kumquats, for those unfamiliar with them, are small, very tart citrus fruits with a light, delightfully scented, and highly concentrated oleoresin in their peel) makes your product an excellent deodorant and antiperspirant. It is also a totally natural product, containing only organically produced ingredients. But your firm is so small (less than 1 percent of the market) that you can't afford to buy advertising like Procter and Gamble, Lever Brothers, Colgate, or any of the other "big guns" of the industry. Faced with this problem, you are considering how best to use your rather modest advertising budget.

1. Convinced that your very modest share of the market is due to the fact that the majority of the population doesn't know of your product, you feel that you must use your advertising to tell consumers who and what you are. The type of advertising to use in this instance would be
   a. product advertising.
   b. persuasive advertising.
   c. advocacy advertising.
   d. reminder advertising.
   e. informative advertising.

2. Very aware that your unique selling proposition requires the use of an advertising medium which will be highly selective, speedy in effect, highly personalized, and capable of delivering a complete message, you choose as your major medium
   a. local newspapers.
   b. direct mail.
   c. specialty magazines.
   d. outdoor advertising.
   e. radio.

3. Convinced that part of the reason your market share is so small is because very few people have ever tried your product, you authorize your local sales representatives to stand near the display of your product in local stores and give away miniature bars of Kumquat Soap you've had made up. This promotional technique is
   a. the form of sales promotion known as sampling.
   b. point-of-purchase advertising.
   c. pretesting: recipients of the free bars get to pretest them before buying your soap.
   d. sales promotion by means of specialty advertising.
   e. sales promotion through the use of a premium.

4. Upon reflection, you decide that one way to improve your competitive position would be by advertising your product in such a way as to point out its obvious superiority to Zest, Dial, Irish Spring, and other well-known bath soaps, each of which would be mentioned by name. This type of advertising is called
   a. competitive advertising.
   b. compulsive advertising.
   c. comparative advertising.
   d. "cause" advertising.
   e. corporate advertising.

5. Further thought convinces you that making a frontal attack on all the major soap companies might not be the best way to develop Kumquat's market. You consider, however, creating an advertising program for Kumquat which will stress the soap's all-natural formulation. Such a program would position your product against the competition by its
   a. applications.
   b. product class.
   c. attributes.
   d. user characteristics.
   e. competitive position.

Elmo Leopold has been assigned the task of putting together his firm's advertising plan for next year. He has struggled mightily to figure out what was done by the firm last year. Almost eight million dollars was spent, but Mr. Leopold isn't sure what happened to the money. The firm set no specific promotional objectives, though it did spend a lot on audience analysis reports and research aimed at identifying the characteristics of readers of advertisements for the company's products.

6. Mr. Leopold will probably be unable to come to any conclusions concerning the success of last year's advertising program because
   a. no audience analysis was undertaken.
   b. no objectives were set.
   c. pretesting was done incorrectly.
   d. media choices were improperly made.
   e. the budget was too small for analysis.

7. The research which was done to identify the characteristics of the firm's audience was
   a. a pretest of the company's advertising.
   b. a wise use of a portion of the advertising budget.
   c. budgeted as a test of the achievement of advertising objectives.
   d. a posttest of advertising effectiveness.
   e. the perfect test of the validity of promotional objectives.

Name _____   Instructor _____

Section _____   Date _____

Questions for Thought

The questions which follow are designed to help you become familiar with the main concepts in this chapter through interpretation in your own words. They are meant to be answered in a few sentences or a paragraph at most.

1. Identify the major types of advertising which one might expect to find in any medium.

2. Choosing media requires trading one set of advantages and disadvantages for another. Outline the major advertising media, mentioning the advantages and disadvantages of each.

3. Discuss some of the methods developed to measure the effectiveness of advertising.

4. Sales promotion may be accomplished by any of several methods. Discuss these various methods.

5. Discuss some of the contributions made by public relations and publicity to an organization's promotional strategy.

Name_____ Instructor _____

Section _____ Date _____

Experiential Exercises

1. Some products lend themselves better to advertising in one medium than in another.

    a. For each of the media mentioned below, list a product or products frequently advertised in that medium. Then explain why you think that medium is commonly chosen for the product you listed.

        1. Medium: Newspapers

            Product: Foods

            Why: Consumers who cook can compare prices from the ads and take the newspaper with them when shopping.

        2. Medium: Magazines

            Product:

            Why:

        3. Medium: Television

            Product:

            Why:

        4. Medium: Radio

            Product:

            Why:

5. Medium: Direct Mail

Product:

Why:

6. Medium: Outdoor

Product:

Why:

b. For each of the products you listed in part a, indicate what type of sales promotion might be used and how it would best be implemented.

	Product	Sales Promotion	How Used
1.	Food	Coupon	Place in newspapers to encourage product sale.
2.			
3.			
4.			
5.			
6.			

2. Your text lists six major types of advertising. Each of these types of advertising lends itself to a different application. Find three advertisements that you think are particularly good examples of different types of ads. List below why you think these examples are particularly good.

   a. Type of advertisement:

   Sponsor:

   Why it is particularly appropriate:

   b. Type of advertisement:

   Sponsor:

   Why it is particularly appropriate:

   c. Type of advertisement:

   Sponsor:

   Why it is particularly appropriate:

3.   Every student of marketing should have the opportunity to determine whether or not he or she is creative. In this exercise you will create a one-page advertisement for a particular product or service.

a.   Choose a product or service about which you have some knowledge, either from work experience or as a consumer.

Product chosen:

b.   Create an advertisement for this product or service by cutting out parts (headlines, illustrations, copy) from existing magazine advertisements and pasting them together. Use a standard 8.5 by 11.5 inch piece of paper as your base. As you cut out the parts of ads to use, make note of the name of the magazine from which you are cutting each part, the date of that issue, type of product or service being advertised, and what you used from that ad. (You will soon begin to notice that certain magazines and certain types of ads seem to go together.)

c.   What types of people would you expect to read your ad? What psychographic or demographic characteristics would you expect them to have?

d.   Categorize your advertisement. Have you attempted to sell the product, the company, a cause, or a government agency? Did you position your product, and if so, how?

Name _____   Instructor _____

Section _____   Date _____

Computer Applications

Review the discussion of the cost-per-thousand criterion in Chapter 17 of the text. Then use menu item 14 titled "Advertising Evaluations" to solve each of the following problems.

1. Gustave Longchamps manages the Consumer Products Division of Firebrand Manufacturing Company. He is in the process of narrowing the number of magazines being considered for the 1992 advertising campaign, and has reduced the list to eight possibilities. Longchamps has considered the magazines' readership characteristics and also the percentage of the readers of each magazine whom he feels exactly match the perfect Firebrand customer.

Magazine	Four-Color Page Rate	Total Readers (in millions)	Percentage Firebranders
Flameout	$11,500	3.2	17%
Airman	$17,500	4.0	21%
Liftoff	$13,000	3.6	21%
Aeronaut	$36,000	19.6	11%
Balloonist	$28,000	10.6	13%
Franklin's	$ 7,500	2.4	27%
Spacetime	$34,500	15.2	16%
Outthere	$26,000	8.4	19%

a. Which of the eight magazines has the lowest CPM if total readers are considered? Which has the highest CPM?

b. Which of the eight magazines has the lowest CPM if only target market readers are considered? Which has the highest?

2. Louise Anglaterra is in charge of magazine advertising for The Boulders, a resort on Monte Sano, just outside Huntsville, Alabama. She is examining the figures on six major national magazines as candidates for this year's advertising.

   a. Given the information below, which magazine has the lowest total CPM? The lowest CPM for male readers? For female readers?

Magazine	Four-color Page Rate	Total Readers (in hundreds)	Men (in hundreds)	Women (in hundreds)
Travel News	$36,375	11,375	3,473	7,902
Leisure Time	$45,187	9,335	5,575	3,760
Outdoors	$32,675	7,300	4,220	3,080
Movin' On	$46,200	18,940	8,790	10,150
MountainTops	$27,750	5,365	4,045	1,320
Vacationspot	$40,367	7,180	3,645	3,535

3. After reviewing the readership profiles for the six magazines included in problem 2, Louise has developed the following estimates of the percentages of male and female readers of each magazine who exactly match the profile of The Boulders' target customers:

Magazine	Percentage of Readers in Target Market Male Readers	Female Readers
Travel News	49	21
Leisure Time	32	34
Outdoors	24	22
Movin' On	26	38
MountainTops	34	16
Vacationspot	22	29

   a. Which of the six magazines has the lowest CPM for male readers who match the target profile? The highest?

b.   Which magazine has the lowest CPM for female readers who match the target profile? The highest?

4.   Aksel Nordhoff is an advertising buyer specializing in radio for Bingham, Bongham, Bopham, and Bashem, an advertising agency specializing in heavy-duty saturation advertising. Aksel wants his message to reach people between the ages of 18 and 49 in the Mobile, Alabama, area during drive time, while they're going to and from work. He has narrowed the choices to four stations, each of which offers the format he thinks will attract his target listeners.

Radio Station	Cost for 30-Second Spot	Total Listeners All Ages	Ages 18-34	Ages 35-49
KRGA	$190	25,000	6,500	6,000
KABB	$200	28,000	5,600	7,000
KMOB	$250	42,000	16,800	12,600
KKIK	$290	70,000	21,000	17,500

a.   Which of the four stations has the lowest overall CPM? Which is the most expensive on a CPM basis?

b.   Which of the four stations has the lowest CPM for listeners aged 18-34? Which is most expensive for this group?

c.   Which of the four stations will reach Mr. Nordhoff's target customers at the lowest CPM?

Chapter 17 Solutions

Key Concepts

1. e	6. i	11. b	16. l
2. m	7. d	12. s	17. n
3. c	8. t	13. f	18. k
4. o	9. q	14. h	19. a
5. g	10. j	15. r	20. p

Self Quiz

1. F	11. T	21. T	31. e	41. a
2. T	12. F	22. F	32. c	42. c
3. T	13. F	23. T	33. a	43. a
4. F	14. F	24. T	34. b	44. d
5. F	15. T	25. F	35. d	45. e
6. T	16. T	26. b	36. d	46. a
7. F	17. T	27. a	37. b	47. b
8. T	18. F	28. d	38. c	48. c
9. F	19. T	29. c	39. e	49. e
10. F	20. F	30. b	40. e	50. e

Applying Marketing Concepts

1. e	5. c
2. b	6. b
3. a	7. d
4. c	

Chapter 18

Personal Selling and Sales Management

Chapter Summary

Personal selling, which is any promotional presentation conducted on a person-to-person basis with the potential buyer, is an inherent function of any enterprise. There are, at present, some 8 million people employed full-time at this activity in the United States. For the average firm, selling expenses often equal 10 to 15 percent of sales. Advertising costs seldom exceed 3 percent of sales for the same firm. Personal selling is likely to be the major component of the firm's promotional mix when consumers are geographically concentrated, when orders are typically large, when the products or services involved are expensive, technically complex, and require special handling, when trade-ins are involved, when channels of distribution are short, and when the number of potential buyers is relatively small.

The actual personal selling activity may be accomplished in any of three ways. The first, field selling, involves making sales calls to customers at their homes or businesses and providing demonstrations of the product or information about it. Over-the-counter or retail selling, the second type of personal selling activity, involves providing product information to the customer and arranging for completion of the sales transaction at the retail location. Finally, telemarketing, which is personal selling conducted entirely by telephone, is used to reduce the substantial cost involved in maintaining a salesforce to call on customers at their homes or places of business. It may be done outbound (when salespeople contact customers) or inbound (when customers call to get information and make purchases).

Personal selling involves the successful completion of three basic tasks. When an order is handled in a routine manner—the sales setting is such that the need is made known to and is acknowledged by the buyer—order processing takes place. If persuasion must be used to make the prospect see the value of the good or service, then the selling is said to be *creative*. Missionary selling, which is indirect in nature, involves making goodwill calls and providing technical or operational assistance to customers.

The process of selling involves seven steps: (1) the sales practitioner *prospects*, seeking likely candidates to become customers for his or her product or service; these prospects are *qualified* by determining that they have both the authority and the money to make a purchase; (2) the practitioner then *approaches* likely customer candidates, making initial contact with them; (3) if the contact proves successful, the sales practitioner makes a *presentation* of the product or service being offered, describing its usefulness to the prospective customer; (4) a *demonstration* may take place, allowing the potential buyer to see the product in action; (5) if the prospect exhibits sales resistance, the practitioner *handles the objections* to purchase which may arise; (6) and hopefully *closes* the sale. The process isn't over, however, because, in the interest of customer satisfaction, (7) *follow-up* is undertaken, contacting the customer to make sure he or she is happy with his or her purchase.

The personal selling function, like every other activity in business, must be managed. Sales managers connect the salesforce with the other aspects of the firm's internal environment, as well as with the environments outside the firm. Thus, sales managers represent their salespeople to top management, to the other functional units of the firm such as the research department, and to outsiders including trade groups, customers, competitors, suppliers, and regulatory agencies. On a concrete or day-to-day basis, sales managers recruit and select salespeople, operate training programs, create a viable selling organization, supervise the activities of the salesforce, provide motivation and compensation to their people, and exercise the authority and responsibility for evaluation and control of salesforce performance.

Name_____ Instructor _____

Section _____ Date _____

Key Concepts

The purpose of this section is to allow you to determine if you can match key concepts with the definitions of the concepts. It is essential that you know the definitions of the concepts prior to applying the concepts in later exercises in this chapter.

From the list of lettered terms, select the one that best fits each of the numbered statements below. Write the letter of that choice in the space provided.

Key Terms

a. personal selling
b. field selling
c. over-the-counter selling
d. telemarketing
e. order processing
f. creative selling
g. missionary sales
h. prospecting
i. qualifying
j. approach

k. precall planning
l. presentation
m. canned approach
n. closing
o. follow-up
p. sales management
q. boundary-spanning role
r. commission
s. salary
t. sales quota

_l_ 1. Describing a product's major features and relating them to a customer's problems or needs.

_o_ 2. Postsales activities designed to assure that a person who has made a recent purchase will become a repeat customer.

_h_ 3. Personal selling function of identifying potential customers.

_q_ 4. Sales manager's role of linking the salesforce with the other elements of an organization's internal and external environments.

_p_ 5. Planning, organizing, staffing, motivating, compensating, evaluating, and controlling a salesforce to ensure its effectiveness.

_s_ 6. Fixed compensation payments made periodically to an employee.

_g_ 7. Indirect selling by specialized salespeople promoting the firm's goodwill, often by assisting customers in use of the product.

_e_ 8. Identifying customer needs, pointing them out to customers, and completing orders; typical of selling at the wholesale and retail levels.

_C_   9. Type of personal selling conducted in retail and some wholesale locations in which customers come to the seller's place of business.

_j_   10. Sales practitioner's initial contact with a prospective customer.

_f_   11. Personal selling in which a considerable degree of analytical decision making on the buyer's part results in the need for skillful proposals of solutions for the customer's needs.

_n_   12. Point in personal selling at which the salesperson asks the customer to make a purchase decision.

_b_   13. Sales presentations made at prospective customers' homes or places of business on a face-to-face basis.

_t_   14. Level of expected sales for a territory, product, customer, or salesperson against which actual results are compared.

_k_   15. Use of information collected during prospecting and qualifying and during previous contacts with the prospect to tailor the approach and presentation to match the customer's needs.

_a_   16. Interpersonal influence process involving a seller's promotional presentation conducted on a person-to-person basis with the buyer.

_m_   17. Memorized sales talk used to ensure uniform coverage of the selling points management has deemed important.

_d_   18. Promotional presentation involving use of the telephone on an outbound basis by salespeople or an inbound basis by customers who initiate calls to obtain information and place orders.

_r_   19. Incentive compensation directly related to the sales or profits achieved by the salesperson.

_i_   20. Determining that a prospect has the needs, income, and purchase authority necessary to become a potential customer.

Name_____   Instructor _____

Section _____   Date _____

Self Quiz

You should use these objective questions to test your understanding of the chapter material. You can check your answers with those provided at the end of the chapter.

While these questions cover most of the chapter topics, they are not intended to be the same as the test questions your instructor may use in an examination. A good understanding of all aspects of the course material is essential to good performance on any examination.

True/False

Write "T" for True or "F" for False for each of the following statements.

_F_   1.   Expenditures for advertising almost always exceed expenditures for personal selling in the average American firm.

_T_   2.   In the nineteenth century, salespeople selling both to consumers and marketing intermediaries were called "drummers."

_F_   3.   Selling offers a simple, uncomplicated form of employment for today's college graduate; minimal company and product knowledge are all that are typically required for success.

_T_   4.   It is not at all unusual to find representatives of major banking institutions making field sales calls these days; deregulation of their industry has resulted in a more competitive marketplace in which marketing-oriented thinking has become the rule, rather than the exception.

_T_   5.   Over-the-counter selling typically involves providing product information and arranging for completion of the sales transaction.

_F_   6.   A salesperson who is assigned to answer the phone and take orders or answer customers' questions is involved in outbound telemarketing.

_F_   7.   Selling is no longer truly a profession; it has devolved into a mechanical activity largely dependent on computers for any meaningful creativity.

_F_   8.   The first step in order processing is to point out to the customer his or her need for the sales practitioner's product or service.

_T_   9.   Most sales positions, even many of the most creative, involve a certain amount of order processing.

_T_   10.   Newly introduced products often require a lot of creative selling.

_T_   11.   In many instances, missionary salespeople neither contact the actual users of the products they are selling nor take orders.

F   12.   The first step in the selling process is making the approach to the prospective customer.

F   13.   One of the most exciting things about prospecting is the high likelihood that the activity will offer an immediate payback.

T   14.   Effective "precall planning" gives the sales practitioner valuable information about the prospect's purchasing habits, attitudes, activities, and opinions.

T   15.   The canned approach to sales presentation has largely been abandoned with the realization that each purchase decision is unique and requires a unique treatment.

T   16.   Objections raised by prospects in the selling process typically involve the product's features, its price, or services to be offered by the selling firm.

T   17.   Despite the fact that closing should be the natural conclusion of an effective sales presentation, a surprising number of sales practitioners find it difficult to actually ask for an order.

F   18.   The "If-I-can-show-you . . ." closing technique warns the prospect that a sales agreement should be concluded now because some important feature of the deal being offered, such as price or availability, will soon be changed.

F   19.   One of the problems with recruiting people to become sales practitioners is the low degree of job security offered by this kind of employment.

F   20.   A salesforce organized along product lines would have specialized salesforces for each major type of customer served.

T   21.   The concept of "span of control" refers to the number of sales representatives who report to the first level of sales management.

F   22.   It has been found that sales practitioners are best motivated by financial compensation to the exclusion of almost any other form of professional encouragement.

T   23.   A straight salary compensation plan gives management more control over how sales personnel allocate their efforts, but it reduces the incentive to expand sales.

F   24.   According to a recent survey, the most common method of compensating sales practitioners is straight commission.

F   25.   The *process* area of the work environment refers to the sales practitioner's technical ability: knowledge of the product, customer, and company, as well as selling skills.

Multiple Choice

Circle the letter of the word or phrase that best completes the sentence or best answers the question.

d 26. The average firm's selling expenses (percentage of sales spent on personal selling activities) are likely to fall into which of the following ranges?
   a.   1 to 3 percent
   b.   3 to 5 percent
   c.   5 to 10 percent
   d.   10 to 15 percent
   e.   15 percent or more

b 27. Peddlers sold the necessities of civilized life and a few luxuries to the farmers and settlers of the vast North American continent primarily during the
   a.   sixteenth and seventeenth centuries.
   b.   eighteenth century.
   c.   nineteenth century.
   d.   twentieth century.
   e.   late nineteenth and early twentieth century.

c 28. A sales practitioner whose job consists primarily of making sales calls on customers at their homes or places of business is involved in
   a.   creative sales.
   b.   over-the-counter sales.
   c.   field selling.
   d.   missionary work.
   e.   demand selling.

e 29. A selling approach conducted entirely over the telephone is most correctly known as
   a.   field selling.
   b.   under-the-counter selling.
   c.   creative selling.
   d.   order processing.
   e.   telemarketing.

a 30. Today's sales practitioner should be most concerned with
   a.   helping customers select the correct products for meeting their needs.
   b.   selling whatever is available; after all, life must go on.
   c.   generating the greatest possible number of commission dollars for his or her own welfare.
   d.   being visible to upper management; after all, the goal is advancement within the firm.
   e.   processing orders as quickly and efficiently as possible.

a 31. When a sales practitioner helps a customer identify his or her needs, points out those needs to the customer, and completes the order for the customer, that sales practitioner has
   a.   engaged in order processing.
   b.   completed a creative selling assignment.
   c.   engaged in sales engineering.
   d.   acted as a missionary to that customer.
   e.   functioned as a "drummer" in the classic sense of the word.

C 32. Which of the following statements is true concerning the sales activity of prospecting?
   a. Previous customers of the company seldom make good prospects for new sales.
   b. Prospecting is easy; a good sales practitioner should never spend more than 10 percent of his or her time prospecting.
   c. Prospecting can be very frustrating because there is no immediate payback from doing it.
   d. Once a good client base has been established, the sales practitioner can stop prospecting; sales will come from the referrals existing clients will provide.
   e. Advertising almost never serves as a useful vehicle for new customer prospecting.

b 33. The process of qualifying a sales prospect
   a. involves gathering relevant information about the prospect to make initial contact go more smoothly.
   b. is the task of making sure that the prospect really is a potential customer.
   c. is used less frequently by retail sales practitioners than it is by wholesalers' and manufacturers' sales representatives.
   d. involves making the initial contact with the prospect.
   e. is considered by many sales management experts to be the very essence of the sales process.

e 34. When a sales practitioner describes a product's major features to a prospective customer, pointing out its strengths and citing illustrative successes, he or she is
   a. making an approach to that prospective customer.
   b. demonstrating the product.
   c. following up on a closing which someone else made.
   d. seeking to qualify the prospective customer.
   e. making a presentation of that product.

d 35. The traditional approach to sales presentations pioneered by the National Cash Register Company during the late 1800s is
   a. the semiprepared approach; the sales representative familiarizes himself or herself only with basic product knowledge and expects natural selling talent to carry the presentation.
   b. the "never-take-no-for-an-answer" approach; the name of this approach really says it all.
   c. the professional approach; the sales practitioner approaches the prospect in a thoroughly professional manner, ready to deal with any questions and problems that individual has.
   d. the canned approach; a memorized sales talk is delivered to the prospect covering management's view of the significant points of the product.
   e. the basic approach; the sales professional deals with basics first, getting technical only when the prospect asks for such a treatment of the product.

b 36. The key to a successful product demonstration is
   a. impact; the demonstration must be really impressive.
   b. planning; the demonstration must go off like it's supposed to or the effort is totally wasted.
   c. novelty; the prospect should be shown the product in a new and different way.
   d. effect; some practitioners say that the demonstration should sell the product all by itself.
   e. detail; the demonstration should show the product in every possible use or application.

C 37. The professional sales practitioner uses a prospect's objections
   a. as a device to abruptly end the sales presentation; it has been found that if prospects are left to "stew" for a little while, they often exhibit heightened interest.
   b. as a lever to manipulate the prospect into buying what the salesperson has to offer.
   c. as a cue for providing additional information to the prospect.
   d. to acquire additional information from the prospect about his or her background and history.
   e. as a basis for a different type of presentation, the "overkill," which hammers objections down.

e 38. The moment of truth in selling is the
   a. approach; a good approach is everything.
   b. qualifying process; wasting time with unqualified prospects really reduces selling productivity.
   c. presentation; without a good presentation, you have no hope of gaining the customer's confidence.
   d. demonstration; as has been said so many times, "a demonstration is worth a thousand pictures."
   e. closing; you will certainly never sell anything without eventually asking for the order.

a 39. When a sales practitioner asks a prospect, "Well, do you want the red Cadillac or the blue one?," he or she is using what kind of closing technique?
   a. the alternative-decision technique
   b. the If-I-can-show-you technique
   c. the standing-room-only technique
   d. silence; some people react positively to it
   e. an extra-inducement close

d 40. The successful sales practitioner seeks to ensure that today's customers will be future customers through effective
   a. handling of prospect objections; a convinced customer is a repeat customer.
   b. sales presentations; a customer well sold is a repeat customer.
   c. use of closing techniques; a customer who believes it was all his or her own idea will come back again.
   d. follow-up; this postsales activity often determines whether a person will become a repeat customer.
   e. prospecting; a customer from the beginning is a customer for life.

a 41. The linking of the salesforce with other elements of the internal and external environments of the firm by sales managers is a
   a. boundary-spanning role which they normally occupy.
   b. task which many sales managers avoid.
   c. new development in the field of organization theory.
   d. most unusual occurrence, not normally found in American business.
   e. unique phenomenon which occurs only in retail environments.

e 42. The initial step in building an effective salesforce is
   a. organizing the sales practitioners in a format consistent with the firm's needs.
   b. training sales personnel in correct selling techniques.
   c. motivating sales personnel to persist in their selling efforts.
   d. compensating sales personnel fairly and equitably.
   e. recruiting and selecting a group of qualified personnel.

C 43. Which of the following is a true statement concerning selling as a profession?
  a. Advancement for salespeople seldom occurs laterally to a more responsible position in some other functional area of the firm.
  b. The earnings of successful sales practitioners are somewhat lower than those of successful people in other professions.
  c. Economic downturns affect personnel in sales less than they do people in most other employment areas.
  d. Sales practitioners seldom operate as "independent" business people but usually as part of a selling team.
  e. Sales practitioners derive satisfaction in their profession largely from their incomes and seldom from helping customers satisfy their wants and needs.

b 44. In the selection of sales personnel, which of the following is usually the last step before all information is analyzed and a hiring decision made?
  a. an in-depth interview
  b. a physical examination
  c. aptitude and intelligence testing
  d. reference checks
  e. filling out the application

d 45. A sales organization which markets large numbers of similar but separate products that are of a very technical or complex nature and sold through different marketing channels would probably be organized
  a. geographically.
  b. along customer lines.
  c. using engineering specialties as a base.
  d. by product class.
  e. according to the sizes of the various customers of the firm.

e 46. The most common method(s) of compensating sales practitioners is/are
  a. straight commission, no salary.
  b. straight salary, no commission.
  c. a salary plus bonus plan.
  d. a salary plus commission program.
  e. c and d; the percentage of firms using them is about the same.

a 47. According to Johnson, Kurtz, and Scheuing as cited in your text, the optimal span of control for first-level managers supervising technical or industrial sales practitioners is
  a. around 6 sales practitioners to each supervisor.
  b. usually 8 sales personnel to each supervisor.
  c. ordinarily 9 or 10 sales operatives to each supervisor.
  d. 11 or 12 sales employees to each supervisor.
  e. as many as 20 sales employees to each supervisor.

b 48. Each aspect of sales performance for which a standard exists should be measured separately. This helps to prevent
  a. confusion on the part of the evaluated individual as to how the evaluation was conducted.
  b. the halo effect, in which the rating on one factor is carried over to other performance variables.
  c. evaluation of the process of selling rather than the achievements of the sales operative.
  d. personality, rather than performance, becoming the basis for evaluation.
  e. the bad news being transmitted back to the sales employee through unauthorized channels.

C 49. Motivation of sales personnel
    a.   generally avoids appealing to emotional needs.
    b.   is seldom designed to provide psychological encouragement.
    c.   often takes the form of debriefings and information sharing.
    d.   relies almost entirely on monetary rewards.
    e.   has been shown to be effected only with financial incentives.

d 50. Of all of the functions performed by the sales manager, it is felt that the most difficult probably
    a.   are recruitment and selection.
    b.   is training the salesforce to the standard required.
    c.   involves the supervision of all those sales practitioners.
    d.   are the evaluation and control of salesforce performance.
    e.   is the motivation of the independently spirited sales employees.

Name _____   Instructor _____

Section _____   Date _____

Applying Marketing Concepts

During your last semester in school, you go over to your school's placement office and sign up to interview with firms seeking people with your qualifications. You are somewhat surprised to discover that there appear to be quite a few positions available with local companies, primarily wholesalers, that call for sales skills but indicate that no outside work will be required. A number of other positions call for degrees in finance or marketing, and show that "business development" is the area for which personnel are being sought. A little investigation reveals that the accounting firms and financial institutions listing these positions are among the most aggressive in the area, seeking new commercial accounts in an active fashion. You sign up for several of these interviews, and are somewhat surprised when you are told that a number of these companies have specified that a person must have had certain courses before they can even be interviewed. Either because of good planning or dumb luck, it happens that you have taken all the required courses, and interview with a number of these firms. They all require a seemingly endless stream of paperwork. First, there is the placement office form to fill out, then each company seems to want you to fill out a "personal data sheet," and finally there is the interview. You wonder who the people interviewing you are. They seem to know the company and its products quite well, and indicate that if you were to be chosen to fill an open position, you would be working for them. After your third interview in two days, you decide to go somewhere quiet and think about this whole process. It seems very detailed and confusing.

1. The positions with local wholesalers calling for selling skills but no outside work are probably
   a. missionary sales positions.
   b. positions as sales trainers.
   c. over-the-counter sales positions.
   d. creative selling positions.
   e. field sales positions.

2. The positions with the accounting firms and financial institutions are most likely
   a. portfolio analysts' positions.
   b. openings for staff accountants in the auditing division.
   c. related to sector analysis or loan profitability.
   d. field sales positions in the commercial accounts area.
   e. missionary sales positions designed to build public image.

3. If the interviewing process is considered to be a sales opportunity for the companies interviewing (selling the idea of working for them), then their requirement that you have a degree in a particular major and/or have taken particular courses would be part of the
   a. prospecting and qualifying process.
   b. approach to the prospect.
   c. presentation of company advantages.
   d. preapproach planning.
   e. follow-up step in sales.

4. If one of the firms with whom you have interviewed is interested in you, what do you suppose will happen next?
    a. You will be asked to report to a doctor's office for a physical examination.
    b. You will be called in for a second interview.
    c. The company will make you take a battery of placement tests.
    d. You will be hired immediately.

5. The people with whom you had your first interview are probably
    a. professional interviewers who do this sort of thing all the time.
    b. people who occupy the same position you would and have been told to find a successor so they can be transferred.
    c. sales managers for the companies in the local area, doing part of their job.
    d. representatives of your college filling in for people who work for the interviewing companies.
    e. staff people from the interviewing companies who have nothing better to do.

You have gone to your computer supply store to buy a box of data diskettes. A helpful clerk has assisted you in finding the type of disks you need and you are in the process of walking to the cash register to pay for them. On the way, the clerk stops at a display of storage boxes for computer diskettes and asks if you have a problem storing your diskettes neatly and conveniently. Though you say you've never had a problem—your old shoe box works just fine—he shows you how this "diskfile" has little partitions in it which separate the diskettes and can even be locked for privacy.

6. The clerk's demonstration of the "diskfile" is an example of
    a. order processing.
    b. creative selling.
    c. telemarketing.
    d. closing.
    e. prospecting.

7. The clerk's assistance to you in finding diskettes to meet your needs and ringing up the sale is an example of
    a. order processing.
    b. creative selling.
    c. missionary selling.
    d. passive selling.
    e. qualifying.

8. The position occupied by this sales clerk would be classified as
    a. field selling.
    b. missionary selling.
    c. telemarketing.
    d. over-the-counter sales.
    e. merchandising.

The salesforce at Oleander Mills is divided into two groups: the consumer products group and the industrial products group. Sales representatives in the consumer products group are paid a base salary plus 10 percent of their gross sales after they have met a minimum sales volume requirement for the month, which is set on a month-by-month basis. The industrial sales practitioners are also salaried, but receive an additional payment each month based on the number of new accounts they open. This amount is based on management's estimate of the ultimate volume each account will deliver. The amount the sales representative sold to the account in opening it does not matter.

9. The salesforce at Oleander Mills is organized along
   a. product lines.
   b. customer lines.
   c. geographical lines.
   d. a combination of geographical and customer lines.
   e. a combination of product and geographical lines.

10. Sales representatives in the consumer products group are compensated on a
    a. straight salary basis.
    b. salary plus commission basis.
    c. salary plus bonus basis.
    d. straight commission basis.
    e. basis no one understands.

11. Sales representatives in the industrial products group are paid
    a. a straight commission.
    b. salary plus commission.
    c. straight salary.
    d. salary plus bonus based on new business.
    e. commission plus bonus.

Name _____   Instructor _____

Section _____   Date _____

Questions for Thought

The questions which follow are designed to help you become familiar with the main concepts in this chapter through interpretation in your own words. They are meant to be answered in a few sentences or a paragraph at most.

1. Personal selling may be of greater or lesser importance in the promotional mix depending on a number of factors. Discuss the factors which affect the relative importance of personal selling in this context.

2. Discuss how each of the three basic sales tasks may be performed by field sales personnel, over-the-counter sales representatives, and telemarketers. Make sure you show your understanding of the differences among these three varieties of sales practitioners.

3. Outline the steps in the sales process.

4. Discuss the functions performed by sales managers. Include an explanation of the boundary-spanning role they play.

Name_____   Instructor _____

Section _____   Date _____

Experiential Exercises

1. In this exercise, you will experience the sales process from the sales professional's point of view. Your instructor may decide to conduct this exercise in class as a role-playing exercise, so be prepared to participate should the need develop.

    The product you are to sell is Copymatic. Like its predecessor, Vegamatic, Copymatic is the device of a thousand uses. It makes perfect copies of any document laid on its top platform, operates from three "D" size flashlight batteries which will last for up to 100 hours, and its compact size of 8.5 by 11.0 by 1.5 inches (almost exactly the size of your study guide—happy coincidence!) makes it quite portable. The device costs $395 complete and is warranted for one year. It can copy on any handy piece of paper, has no moving parts, requires no ink, and is disposable after it has produced a guaranteed minimum of 10,000 copies.

    a. From among your friends, acquaintances, and business contacts, create a prospect list. Qualify each prospect on the basis of need for Copymatic and ability to pay.

    b. Devise an approach strategy to use in bringing Copymatic to the attention of qualified prospects. What kinds of preapproach planning do you intend to do? How will the approach be made?

c.   Write (using a separate piece of paper, if necessary) a sales presentation for Copymatic. As a part of your presentation, demonstrate Copymatic's many remarkable properties.

d.   How would you handle the objection: "Yes, it's a great little machine, but I really don't need one."

e.   Copymatics are sold only for cash. Create a close that minimizes the difficulties of asking for "cash on the barrelhead" but at the same time asks for the order.

f.   Create a follow-up program to keep Copymatic owners happy.

2. Personal selling is an interpersonal activity, conducted on a face-to-face basis. As such, it implies human relationships with all of the variability that the species can produce.

Operators of retail stores whose employees have face-to-face contact with the general public are well aware of the problems associated with customer-employee interaction. Because of high employee turnover and a low level of prior preparation, such employees are often ill-suited for direct contact with the man-off-the-street. Attitude, dress, mannerisms, and even such things as vocal accents all affect the promotional process in a face-to-face situation.

a. Make a list of five *do's* and five *don'ts* for the employees of a small retail store, such as a fast-food restaurant, that would help minimize face-to-face promotional problems between customer and employee.

Do	Don't
1.	
2.	
3.	
4.	
5.	

b. List three things that you would do to motivate employees in that same fast-food restaurant. These motivational tools can be used weekly, monthly, quarterly, or with whatever frequency you think will work best.

Motivational Tool	How Will It Help?
1.	
2.	
3.	

3. A prospect's objections can actually help sell the product. Name a consumer product, list an objection a customer might have to buying it, give possible answers to the objections, and tell how this process may have helped sell the product.

Example:

Product: A new automobile

Objection: "I can't say I'm crazy about the color of this car."

Answer: "This is only one of many colors available; here, let's look at the color chart for this model."

How it helped: The objection was really a request for additional information about color availability. The customer needs to know about all of the colors that are available.

Your turn at bat:

Product:

Objection:

Answer:

How it helped:

Name _____   Instructor _____

Section _____   Date _____

Computer Applications

Review the discussion of the workload method used to determine the required number of sales professionals in Chapter 18 of the text. Then use menu item 15 to solve each of the following problems.

1. Melvin Taylor is vice-president for sales of National Auto Supply. He uses three classifications for his firm's 3,000 commercial accounts. There are 400 firms in class A, 1,060 in class B, and 1,540 in class C. He would like to have his sales personnel call on each class A account at least 26 times a year, each class B account 20 times, and each class C account 15 times. Each sales call on a class A or B account should last 25 minutes, but a call on a class C account should be over in 12 minutes. Each of Mel's sales professionals works a 40-hour week, 48 weeks a year. Fifty percent of selling time is spent calling on established accounts, 30 percent on travel, and 20 percent on nonselling activities. How many sales employees should National Auto have?

2. Elaine Morel is a Baton Rouge-based manufacturer's agent in the business forms business. She has 2,900 established customers, of whom 500 are classed type A, 650 type B, and the remainder, 1,750 strong type C. Each type A account is contacted once a month and a sales call lasts one hour. Type B accounts are contacted once every two months for 40 minutes per call. The less profitable type C accounts receive four calls per year for 35 minutes each. There are unplanned or "fill-in" calls which add another 5 percent to the total. Ms. Morel's average sales representative works a 40-hour week for 46 weeks a year. Sixty percent of his/her time is spent working established accounts, with the remainder being equally divided among calls on new prospects, travel, and nonselling activities. How many sales practitioners are needed to cover Ms. Morel's market?

3. SunFun Swimming Pool Supply Company, a wholesaling operation out of International Falls, Minnesota, currently serves retail accounts all over the midwest. Fifteen percent of the firm's accounts are type A, another 25 percent are type B, and the remainder are type C. Type A accounts receive a weekly sales call lasting 35 minutes; type B accounts are called on every other week for 25 minutes; and type C accounts are visited every month for 20 minutes apiece. The nature of the pool supply business in the upper midwest is such that 20 percent must be added to the time total for unplanned calls on customers. Each SunFun sales representative works 48 weeks per year (many pools become ice-skating rinks for a substantial portion of the year, and SunFun sells those lines, too) for an average of 40 hours each week. About 45 percent of each sales rep's time is spent on established accounts, with 25 percent spent on calling on new prospects, 20 percent traveling, and 10 percent on selling activities. At present, the company has 2,200 active accounts.

a.   How many sales representatives does SunFun need?

b.   If sales calls on type C accounts are increased from 12 to 24 per year, what impact will this have on the number of sales representatives needed?

c.   Mr. Gunnar Sjoblom, sales manager for SunFun, thinks he needs to make a reallocation of his salesforce's time to contact more potential accounts. He is considering reducing the amount of time spent by each sales professional to 35 percent of total time on the job. How would this change affect the number of sales representatives needed?

Chapter 18 Solutions

Key Concepts

1. l	6. s	11. f	16. a
2. o	7. g	12. n	17. m
3. h	8. e	13. b	18. d
4. q	9. c	14. t	19. r
5. p	10. j	15. k	20. i

Self Quiz

1. F	11. T	21. T	31. a	41. a
2. T	12. F	22. F	32. c	42. e
3. F	13. F	23. T	33. b	43. c
4. T	14. T	24. F	34. e	44. b
5. T	15. T	25. F	35. d	45. d
6. F	16. T	26. d	36. b	46. e
7. F	17. T	27. b	37. c	47. a
8. F	18. F	28. c	38. e	48. b
9. T	19. F	29. e	39. a	49. c
10. T	20. F	30. a	40. d	50. d

Applying Marketing Concepts

1. c	6. b	11. d
2. d	7. a	
3. a	8. d	
4. b	9. a	
5. c	10. b	

Part Seven Puzzle

ACROSS CLUES

4. informing, persuading, influencing consumer's purchase decision
8. basically the same as advertising except not paid for by sponsor
9. fixed compensation payments made periodically to employees
10. acronym for attention-interest-desire-action explaining purchase behavior
12. advertising seeking to reinforce previous ads by keeping the name of the product before the public
13. selling done in the homes or businesses of prospects on a face-to-face basis
14. postsales activity designed to help make a one-time purchaser a repeat customer
16. includes displays, trade shows, demonstrations, and other nonrecurrent sales efforts
17. interpersonal process involving selling presentation conducted face-to-face with a prospect
19. strategy of promoting to members of a channel to stimulate personal selling of a good
20. promotional strategy designed to create a certain position for a product in the prospect's mind
21. type of advertising designed to let people know that a product is available

DOWN CLUES

1. in marketing, transmission from sender to receiver dealing with buyer-seller relationship
2. acronym for point-of-purchase advertising or other activity
3. blend of personal and nonpersonal selling used by firm to reach its promotional objectives
5. firm's communications and relationships with its various publics
6. approach to selling using memorized sales talk to ensure coverage of main selling points
7. paid, nonpersonal communication by identified sponsor to inform or persuade audience
11. percentage-of-sales and task-objective are two ways to develop a promotional one
15. strategy which stimulates final user demand to exert pressure on distribution channel to deliver
18. nonpersonal selling by stores that sell direct to the consuming public

Name _____   Instructor _____

Section _____   Date _____

Cases for Part 7

1. *Financial Management Services*

Financial Management Services, a broad-spectrum financial and retirement planning firm, is seeking a new way to access potential clients. In the past, the firm has relied on advertisements in the financial section of the newspaper, outlining the benefits offered by financial planning and the advantages of working with a firm like FMS. Recently, responses to this advertising have been on the decline, and the sales staff at FMS is wondering how it might create some new way of prospecting for clients. In the past, the newspaper ad was quite successful in generating qualified leads, partly because of its placement in the financial section of the newspaper but also because of the way it was written, carrying a direct appeal to people with substantial assets.

FMS doesn't believe that the number of people who are in need of its services has decreased, but the number of firms offering similar services has increased markedly. None of the new firms has the expertise or breadth of experience of FMS, however.

Question

Suggest several ways in which FMS can generate more qualified prospects for its sales practitioners.

2. *Mountain Brook Farms*

Mountain Brook Farms, a pork processor located in Monticello, Iowa, is one of the country's premier producers of specialty sausages. It manufactures not fewer than 43 varieties of this product. Over the last three years, sales have leveled off but expenses have continued to increase.

Until now, Mountain Brook Farms has budgeted promotion on the basis of a percentage of sales. The marketing manager, Annemarie Metzger, feels that Mountain Brook's method of promotional budgeting may be a prime factor causing static sales.

Question

From Ms. Metzger's viewpoint, what could Mountain Brook do to help remedy this situation? What changes would your solution involve? If necessary, use numbers to illustrate your answer.

3. *Miller Major Appliance Corporation*

As the name implies, the Miller Corporation is a major producer of home appliances. The company's sales staff sells to wholesalers and distributors throughout the United States and Canada. Because of the nature of its selling job, it has traditionally been paid a straight salary.

Miller is thinking about adding a new division which will sell directly to property developers—builders specializing in construction of condominiums, tract homes, and apartment complexes. This would be "package selling" in which Miller would furnish all the electrical appliances for the development: stoves, refrigerators, water heaters, dishwashers, garbage disposals, washing machines, clothes dryers, and heating and cooling systems. Some of these items would not be made by Miller but would be part of the package through arrangement with other manufacturers and would bear the Miller name.

One consideration in establishing the new division is the salesforce. Miller believes the creative type of sales practitioner is appropriate in this case.

Question

What type of compensation plan might be most effective for the new division? Why?

4.   *Central Shoe Company*

Central Shoe Company is a large manufacturer of shoes and related leather goods and is known as a leader in its industry. The firm's research and development department is particularly effective.

Just over a year ago, Central first placed on the market a revolutionary type of shoe. Made of real leather, a special treatment made the product scuff- and scratch-proof, and it never had to be waxed or polished. For six months, Central had this segment of the market to itself, but within the last six months, several other firms have begun to market shoes with all the advantages of the Central shoe.

Central's advertising program for the last year has centered on informing the public of the availability of the new shoes. Management now feels that the basic objective of its advertising should change.

Question

What new objective for advertising should be established? Give some examples of ads that might be used to accomplish the new objective.

Creating a Marketing Plan: Now Let's Get the Message Out "We're Here!"

Episode Seven is designed to provide you with information which will let you complete Part III.D. of your marketing plan.

Episode Seven

When we left the intrepid entrepreneurs, they were in the process of arranging for quarters into which to move their new business. It is now several weeks later, and most of the mechanics of setup have been accomplished. The firm now has a business address, all of the appropriate licenses and permits, a stock of repair parts, a service area equipped with testing and repair equipment, and two well equipped vans capable of doing field repairs or transporting equipment which can't be repaired in the field back to the service facility.

The problem now is to let people know that the firm exists, and that it is eager to provide the high-quality service its owners have made their objective. The three partners have met to discuss the promotional means they're going to use to get their message across.

"Well, I think it's obvious that we need a display ad in the *Yellow Pages*," said Terry. "As I said before, there are all these repair firms which have listings, but only a very few ads. I think we need something to tell our target market we're out there to serve it."

"Good thought," replied Brian, "but the next edition of the *Yellow Pages* doesn't come out for four months. What are we going to do in the meantime? I propose we advertise in the business section of the newspaper; just a small ad once a week, and we can offer a free "preventive maintenance check" as a get-acquainted deal."

"Now I know why you wanted those stickers with our name, address, and phone number printed on them," commented Laura. "You plan on sticking those on any piece of machinery we get our hands on!"

"And on any other logical surface that would give us a shot at being the first firm they think of when the office PC goes on the blink," laughed Brian. "I propose that, for the time being, at least two of us act as a salesforce and get out there dropping off business cards and stickers at every business whose door we can get through. How about it?"

"Real good," remarked Laura, "but I've been thinking; why just try to let these people know who we are? Why not generate cash flow as soon as possible by selling them maintenance contracts right off the bat? I've written up a little promotional piece that we can drop off along with our business cards when we call on people. See, it tells them a little about the three of us—let's face it, we've got pretty good credentials, and if we don't toot our own horn, who's going to toot it for us—along with some of the costs of having computers repaired versus what we planned to charge for complete maintenance contracts. I think we can generate some business that way. I've even had the back page printed with some important computer facts that will let them spot problems they can correct without calling us. That may keep them from throwing the brochure away."

"Super job!" was Terry's comment. "And though it may be a little bit off the track, let me volunteer to do something which may seem a little strange but I think will do us a world of good. I'm going to hire my niece—she's your cousin Erin, Brian—to come over on Saturday mornings and work on the grass and shrubs around this building. Have you noticed what dumps most of our competitors' facilities are? I don't see any reason why we shouldn't have a good looking place. And I think we should spend time keeping the inside neat, too."

"Not off the track at all, Ter," said Laura. "People do react to the appearance of a place, and we have to expect our customers to come by here to drop off and pick up the equipment we haven't gone and gotten from them. They might as well get a good impression of us from our store as well as from our work. Besides, this isn't a bad neighborhood for a commercial street. We might as well get along with our neighbors, too. I know Erin loves to work in the yard. Maybe we can get her to plant some of those flowering shrubs she put in around your aunt's house."

Guidelines

Examine the suggestions the partners have made and use them and your own ideas to complete Part III.D. of the marketing plan.

Part 8

Marketing in Special Settings

This section of your text covers the two topics of international marketing and the marketing of services.

The United States is deeply involved in international marketing. Some American firms are heavily dependent on foreign customers for sales and revenues, while others depend on imports as a source of raw materials and component parts. Though this country is one of the world's largest importers and exporters, foreign trade still accounts for only a relatively small proportion of this country's GNP.

Understanding the international market involves understanding the differences among buyers from country to country. The environments of marketing differ as one moves from culture to culture, affecting perceptions of the nature of the marketplace.

Entry into the world market may be made by direct or indirect exporting, foreign licensing, overseas marketing, and foreign production and marketing. Companies operating in the international sphere may use a global or a multinational marketing strategy.

Alternative product/promotional strategies for international markets include straight extension, promotional adaptation, product adaptation, dual adaptation, and product invention. Which of these is used depends on the characteristics of the environment into which the marketing mix is being entered.

Services are intangible tasks that satisfy consumer and industrial user needs when efficiently developed and transmitted to chosen market segments. About half of all consumption spending goes for the purchase of services and 75 percent of new jobs in this country are in that area.

Services possess five key elements: (1) they are intangible; (2) they are inseparable from the provider; (3) they are perishable; (4) standardization of services is difficult; and (5) buyers often participate in their development and distribution. Buyers of services behave differently from buyers of goods in three important respects: their attitudes, needs and motives, and purchase behavior.

Though the growth of the service market has been substantial in recent years, development of effective marketing programs has been slow. Of late, however, most service firms seem to have become marketing-oriented.

Chapter 19

Global Dimensions of Marketing

Chapter Summary

Substantial numbers of U.S. businesses are seeking new markets outside this country. Some are so deeply involved in international undertakings that a large share of their revenues and profits is generated in foreign countries. Firms in the product market aren't the only ones to have international interests; service firms such as Manpower, Incorporated, have significant operations in the foreign sphere. Chase Manhattan Bank operates in more than one hundred countries and earns 20 percent of all its profits from foreign operations.

U.S. companies sell into the foreign market, but they also buy from it as well. Raw materials, component parts, and finished goods of foreign origin enter the United States in great volume every day. No longer are these products confined to the rather limited lines of days gone by, like automobiles, electronic devices, and steel. In a recent visit to the supermarket, this writer noticed jams and jellies from Hungary, spaghetti (three brands) from Italy, cheese from Switzerland, Italy, and the Netherlands, salami from Denmark, and beer from any number of nations.

In recent years, firms worldwide have shown increased interest in entering the foreign market by acquisition of foreign properties. CBS Records was sold to Japan's Sony Corporation in 1988 for $2 billion, primarily to give Sony a U.S.-based stable of talent to produce the records, tapes, and other entertainment software needed to balance Sony's hardware line. Firms may enter the international market for other reasons, though. Technological breakthrough is not confined to a single or even a few countries. Remarkable progress in videophotography has been made in Israel, for example. A foreign firm entering into a relationship with an Israeli firm in the forefront of this technology can reap the benefits in its home market. Foreign involvement may help a firm combat the entry into its home market of foreign firms or products that constitute a threat to it. Black and Decker's awareness of Makita's success in the power tool market in Europe gave it the forewarning to develop a competitive strategy which helped forestall Makita's use of the extremely successful tactics which had gained it 20 percent of the European power tool market in three short years.

Involvement in foreign markets is important to a nation for two major reasons. First, international trade expands the size of the domestic market and makes possible significant economies of scale in distribution and production. Second, it creates jobs because each billion dollars of exports this nation generates for itself means about 25,000 jobs for its workforce.

Involvement in foreign trade may be by means of exporting or importing; through foreign licensing of company patents, proprietary techniques, or processes; by active involvement in overseas marketing of domestically produced products; and by producing and marketing goods abroad. Any of these activities may be affected by differences between environmental factors in the domestic market and those abroad. Cultural, legal, social, and economic factors may all affect how a firm may participate in the international market.

There are, of course, differences in how firms approach international marketing strategy. Some take a global view, applying domestic techniques worldwide with little or no modification. These firms are fewer in number than those who use a multinational approach, however. The multinationalists employ marketing programs tailored to the characteristics of buyers from each of the foreign markets in which they operate. A further examination of the implications of globalism versus multinationalism reveals five possible product/promotional strategies which may be applied internationally. These are: (1) straight extension, or introducing the same product sold at home into a foreign market using the same promotional strategy; (2) promotional adaptation, which introduces the same product into a foreign market but uses a different promotional strategy; (3) product adaptation, in which the product is altered but the same promotional strategy is used; (4) dual adaptation, which features changes in both the product and its promotion; and (5) product invention, in which an entirely different product and promotional strategy is developed for the foreign market.

At present, the U.S. is a very attractive market for foreign firms. The country's large population, its affluence as expressed in terms of discretionary income, political stability, general acceptance of foreign investment, and a reasonably healthy economy all make it a desirable place to have an involvement. In addition, recent declines in the value of the dollar relative to foreign currencies have made this country attractive to foreign marketers.

Name _____   Instructor _____

Section _____   Date _____

Key Concepts

The purpose of this section is to allow you to determine if you can match key concepts with the definitions of the concepts. It is essential that you know the definitions of the concepts prior to applying the concepts in later exercises in this chapter.

From the list of lettered terms, select the one that best fits each of the numbered statements below. Write the letter of that choice in the space provided.

Key Terms

a. exporting
b. importing
c. infrastructure
d. exchange rates
e. friendship, commerce, and navigation (FCN) treaties
f. tariff
g. General Agreement on Tariffs and Trade (GATT)
h. import quota
i. embargo
j. exchange control

k. dumping
l. foreign licensing
m. joint venture
n. multinational corporation
o. global marketing strategy
p. multinational marketing strategy
q. straight extension
r. product adaptation
s. promotional adaptation
t. dual adaptation
u. product invention
v. countertrade

_____ 1. The same product marketed in the home market is introduced in the foreign market using the same promotional strategy.

_____ 2. Trade restriction that limits the number of units of certain products that can enter a country for resale.

_____ 3. Purchasing of foreign products and raw materials.

_____ 4. Firm with significant operations and marketing activities outside its home country.

_____ 5. The development of an entirely different product combined with a new promotional strategy to take advantage of unique foreign opportunities.

_____ 6. International agreements that deal with many aspects of commercial relations among nations.

_____ 7. Agreement by which a domestic firm permits a foreign company to produce or distribute the firm's goods in the foreign country or gives it the right to use the firm's trademark, patent, or processes in a specified geographical area.

_____ 8. International trade agreement that has helped reduce world tariffs.

_____ 9. International strategy wherein product modifications are made for the foreign market but the same promotional strategy is used.

_____ 10. Price of one nation's currency in terms of other countries' currencies.

_____ 11. Strategy in which modifications of both product and promotional strategy are used in the foreign market.

_____ 12. Application of market segmentation to foreign markets by tailoring the firm's marketing mix to match specific target markets in each nation.

_____ 13. Agreement in which a firm shares the risks, costs, and management of a foreign operation with one or more partners who are usually citizens of the host country.

_____ 14. Complete ban on the import of specified products.

_____ 15. Controversial practice of selling a product in a foreign market at a price lower than what it sells for in the producer's domestic market.

_____ 16. Marketing of goods and services in foreign countries.

_____ 17. Standardized marketing mix with minimal modifications that a firm uses in all of its foreign markets.

_____ 18. Method used to regulate the privilege of international trade among importing organizations by controlling access to foreign currencies.

_____ 19. Term used to describe a nation's communications systems (radio, television, print media, telephone), transportation networks (paved roads, railroads, airports), and energy facilities (power plants, gas and electric utilities).

_____ 20. Tax levied against imported products.

_____ 21. Strategy in which the same product is introduced in a foreign market with a unique promotional strategy for the new market.

_____ 22. Form of exporting whereby products and services are bartered rather than sold for cash.

Name _____   Instructor _____

Section _____   Date _____

Self Quiz

You should use these objective questions to test your understanding of the chapter material. You can check your answers with those provided at the end of the chapter.

While these questions cover most of the chapter topics, they are not intended to be the same as the test questions your instructor may use in an examination. A good understanding of all aspects of the course material is essential to good performance on any examination.

True/False

Write "T" for True or "F" for False for each of the following statements.

____ 1. Johnson and Johnson, Gillette, Eastman Kodak, the Coca-Cola Company, and Dow Chemical Company all derive more than 40 percent of their annual earnings from international operations.

____ 2. The more complex a product is, the more likely it is that American marketers will be at a competitive disadvantage with respect to foreign producers.

____ 3. The United States is both the world's largest exporter and its largest importer.

____ 4. The 250 U.S. firms that do the largest amount of exporting account for over 80 percent of U.S. export volume.

____ 5. By the year 2025, world population is expected to have exceeded 8 billion persons.

____ 6. Tokyo, with its population of 14.3 million, remains the world's largest city (i.e., in terms of population).

____ 7. Brazil and South Korea can be classed as "newly industrialized countries."

____ 8. The British firm of Audits, Ltd., pioneered the study of people's buying habits through examination of their garbage.

____ 9. When the dollar's value is high on the exchange market, U.S. products become expensive abroad and foreign products less expensive here.

____ 10. It should always be possible to determine the precise impact of cultural, social, and economic factors before entering a foreign market.

____ 11. Colgate's renaming of its Irish Spring soap "Nordic Spring" when it was introduced in England is an example of the effect of economic differences between this country and Great Britain.

___ 12.   The requirement that all ads for candy in the Netherlands must show a toothbrush is an example of the effect of the legal environment on marketing activities.

___ 13.   Revenue tariffs, when applied, are generally higher than protective tariffs.

___ 14.   The United States has used both import and export quotas in regulating trade with foreign nations.

___ 15.   Indirect exporting occurs when a firm sets up a "front" company to handle the majority of its business abroad, thus avoiding government regulation which would otherwise affect it.

___ 16.   The ultimate degree of company involvement in the international marketing arena is overseas marketing.

___ 17.   Bribery, excessive market control, and domination of the marketplace are some of the reasons that multinational companies are increasingly being viewed as a negative influence on host economies.

___ 18.   Companies using a global marketing strategy change their market approach for each foreign market in which they become involved.

___ 19.   A straight extension marketing strategy is appropriate for products with universal appeal such as Coca-Cola and Levi's Jeans.

___ 20.   The marketing of different blends of coffee combined with different promotional programs in the various markets where those products are sold would be an example of a dual adaptation strategy.

___ 21.   Distribution strategy in entering a foreign market is particularly vulnerable to deficiencies in the transportation infrastructure.

___ 22.   The tried and true pricing strategies which have stood the test of time here in the United States seem to work equally well abroad.

___ 23.   In Japan, penetration pricing seems to work against a product by devaluing it in the eyes of consumers as well as marketing intermediaries.

___ 24.   Countertrading is a form of exporting where products are sold on a bid-asked basis just as is done in the over-the-counter market for stocks and bonds.

___ 25.   In recent years, retail operations in the United States have been favorite targets for foreign acquisition; in fact, A&P and Grand Union Supermarket chains are owned in whole or in part by foreign investors.

Multiple Choice

Circle the letter of the word or phrase that best completes the sentence or best answers the question.

26. When Howard Furniture Company purchases kiln-dried spruce or ash lumber from a Canadian supplier, it is
    a. acquiring goods from a foreign supplier to complement its main product line.
    b. taking advantage of a foreign innovation to improve the quality of its own products.
    c. forestalling foreign competition by getting involved in a market abroad.
    d. buying raw materials from a foreign supplier to use in its domestic operations.
    e. speculating on the increasing scarcity of spruce and ash in the United States by laying in a large supply to beat market fluctuations in the price.

27. A nation with a labor force of 25 million and exports worth $50 billion will have approximately which of the following percentages of its labor force engaged in work to serve its export markets?
    a. 5 percent
    b. 10 percent
    c. 15 percent
    d. 25 percent
    e. 50 percent

28. Even though the United States is one of the world's largest exporters, our exports as a proportion of GNP amount to
    a. less than one-tenth the proportion of exports of the Netherlands.
    b. only one-fifth of Japan's proportion of exports.
    c. twice the proportion exported by the Dominion of Canada.
    d. about one-half the proportion exported by West Germany.
    e. five times as much as is exported by Great Britain.

29. A very significant figure in the context of U.S. business' lack of involvement in the foreign market is the fact that
    a. over 95 percent of all manufacturing firms do not export at all.
    b. the bulk of U.S. exports is arranged for by the customers who wish to buy the product.
    c. the 250 largest U.S. exporters account for over 80 percent of U.S. export volume.
    d. firms such as General Electric, Ford Motor Company, and IBM do not export.
    e. most U.S. exports are the products of firms owned by interests abroad.

30. Nations which trade manufactured goods and services among themselves and export to less developed countries are identified in the text as
    a. newly industrialized countries.
    b. industrial nations.
    c. underdeveloped countries.
    d. subsistence economies.
    e. overdeveloped economies.

31. The French reluctance to pour cold milk over dry cereal illustrates
    a. the difference between the economy of France and that of the United States; in France milk is too costly to be eaten with cereal.
    b. how buyer behavior and common custom differ between two cultures; the French usually see warm milk at the breakfast table because it's used in *café au lait*.
    c. how weird the French really are; most of them prefer to pour a carafe of red wine over their Post Toasties.
    d. the influence of religion on daily behavior; the French consider the eating of cereal and milk a sinful act.
    e. how politics can be involved with even the smallest act; the French still remember the German fondness for cold cereals and balk at the thought of doing anything even remotely German.

32. A nation's population, its per capita income, and its stage of economic development are characteristics of its
    a. social environment.
    b. cultural environment.
    c. political environment.
    d. legal environment.
    e. economic environment.

33. When one examines the state of a nation's highway and railroad system, the availability and coverage of its radio, TV, and newspaper network, and how much energy is available from its generators, gas pipelines, and other utilities, one is scrutinizing
    a. the social environment of the country from an industrial point of view.
    b. the country's ability to deliver social services at an adequate level.
    c. the likelihood for the country to be subject to a revolutionary takeover.
    d. what has come to be known as the infrastructure provided by that nation's economy.
    e. the possibility of getting caught should the necessity for a fast getaway arise.

34. If the exchange rate of a U.S. dollar went from 250 Japanese yen to 200 Japanese yen,
    a. Japanese products should cost only 80 percent of what they cost before the change if paid for in dollars.
    b. American products should cost the Japanese 25 percent more than they did before the change if paid for in yen.
    c. American products should cost only 80 percent of what they cost before the change if paid for in yen.
    d. there would be no change in relative prices; money can't be used as a basis for cost in international trade.
    e. the value of the dollar would effectively increase beyond the capacity of the Japanese to buy American products.

35. Components of the cultural environment in international trade include a nation's
    a. size, per capita income, and stage of economic development.
    b. political stability, system of government, and number of political parties.
    c. legal system, content of specific laws, and operation of the courts system.
    d. participation in such activities as dumping, protective tariffs, and exchange control.
    e. language, educational system, religious attitudes, and value systems.

36. The package of a brand of cookies (biscuits, for the Anglophiles among you) widely distributed in Europe contains on the label a list of the cookies' ingredients in not fewer than seven languages: English, German, French, Italian, Spanish, Dutch, and Danish. The reason for this seeming excess of information
    a. lies in the political environment; the manufacturer of the cookies wants all its customers to feel fairly treated.
    b. is a legal one; many countries require that a product's ingredients be listed on the package in the local tongue.
    c. stems from the desire of the cookie baker to impress all its customers with the purity and wholesomeness of its products.
    d. is so that the value of the cookies may be determined for purposes of setting tariff rates.
    e. has been lost in the dimness of the past; even the baker probably is unaware of why this is done.

37. The body of international law may be found
    a. in the United States Statutes and Code of Federal Regulations for citizens of the United States.
    b. in the statutes, laws, and regulations of the appropriate country of jurisdiction.
    c. in the treaties, conventions, and agreements that exist among nations.
    d. in the Codes of the United Nations.
    e. in the Laws and Regulations of the Admiralty.

38. The function of the Webb-Pomerene Export Trade Act of 1918 is to
    a. exempt from the antitrust laws various combinations of U.S. firms acting together to develop foreign markets.
    b. control the shipment of U.S. goods to foreign countries in ships registered to countries other than the United States.
    c. empower the United States Coast Guard to board, search, and seize vessels found to have contraband materials aboard, regardless of whether they are inbound or outbound.
    d. encourage export of U.S. products by subsidizing American firms actively participating in foreign trade.
    e. establish a U.S. foreign trade commission to negotiate with nations abroad for special privileges for U.S. firms.

39. Taxes levied against imported products, whether assessed on the basis of the amount of product being imported or its market value, are called
    a. embargoes.
    b. import quotas.
    c. exchange taxes.
    d. antidumping penalties.
    e. tariffs.

40. A tax levied against imported goods and whose purpose is to fund the operations of the government of the importing country is called a(n)
    a. protective tariff.
    b. revenue quota.
    c. exchange control.
    d. general agreement on tariffs and trade.
    e. revenue tariff.

41. *Dumping* is the practice of
    a. selling outdated, defective, or contaminated goods in the international market rather than in the home market.
    b. escaping from undesirable foreign contracts by simply dumping on the foreign party to the contract and abandoning the agreement.
    c. taking materials which have been seized by the government under the Contraband Products Act out to sea and dumping them overboard.
    d. selling a product in a foreign market for a price lower than it brings in the home market.
    e. selling merchandise overseas before it has been introduced in the home market in order to prevent foreign competitors from entering the home market once the goods do become available there.

42. The Common Market (or European Community (EC) as its members now prefer to have it called) is perhaps the world's best example of
    a. a mutual defense organization; like NATO, the members of the EC have agreed to immediately come to each other's aid in the event of war.
    b. an internally self-competitive organization; the natural and political boundaries of Europe have made internal competition among nations fierce and effective.
    c. a multinational economic community, integrated with respect to the abolition of internal tariffs and a uniform tariff policy with respect to nonmembers.
    d. an economic union; since 1948, the EC has operated under a single uniform set of regulations regarding foreign trade by its various members.
    e. how a good idea can have unfortunate consequences; the recent collapse of the EC has demonstrated how fragile any treaty-based organization must be.

43. When a firm enters the foreign market only infrequently for the purpose of selling surplus or obsolete inventory, that firm is engaged in
    a. dumping in the foreign market.
    b. indirect exporting to the foreign market.
    c. competitive participation in international trade.
    d. contraband dealings with foreign interests.
    e. joint-venture dealings with foreign principals.

44. When a domestic firm enters into an agreement with a foreign company which allows the foreign company to produce and distribute the domestic company's products or services or to use its trademarks, patents, or proprietary processes in a specific geographical area, the domestic firm has
    a. issued a license to the foreign firm.
    b. formed a joint venture with the foreign company.
    c. engaged in foreign marketing of its products and services.
    d. laid the groundwork for foreign production and marketing by its own people.
    e. forever lost its rights to those assets which it has allowed the foreign company to use.

45. A firm which chooses to use a "global marketing strategy" will
    a. use a standardized marketing mix, with minimal modifications, in every market in which it becomes involved.
    b. alter its products but not its promotional mix as necessary to appeal to the tastes and preferences of its various markets.
    c. alter its promotional mix but not its products as it enters various foreign markets.
    d. modify both its products and its promotional mix for each of the different markets it enters.
    e. be prepared to take whatever actions are necessary to assure itself of success in each of its different markets.

46. A firm which approaches the international market with a product unlike anything it has ever sold in the domestic market is probably applying the
    a. straight extension strategy for entering the international market.
    b. promotion adaptation strategy for entering that market.
    c. dual adaptation strategy for market entry into a foreign market.
    d. product invention strategy in recognition of unique differences between the domestic and foreign markets.
    e. product adaptation strategy for entry into foreign markets.

47. The first decision which must be made concerning distribution strategy for a foreign market is
    a. how the product will be distributed within the foreign market.
    b. the method that will be used to enter the foreign market.
    c. who is going to exercise control over distribution in the foreign market.
    d. what devices will be used to maintain product quality during the distribution process.
    e. whether the product will be packaged differently in the foreign market than at home.

48. Which of the following would be an example of a countertrade?
    a. Cincinnati-Milacron sells computer-controlled milling machines to a West German company; the West Germans pay in U.S. dollars.
    b. General Motors sells jet engines to a British firm; the British pay in pounds sterling.
    c. Turnbull Cone Baking Company sells ice cream cones to a firm in Bolivia; the Bolivians pay by shipping tin ingots to the Turnbull people.
    d. Peerless Valve Company sells water valves to the city of Milan, Italy; the city pays in a combination of U.S. dollars, Italian lire, and West German bearer bonds.
    e. Rolls-Royce ships nine Silver Cloud convertibles to the Pasha of Ranjipur; the Pasha pays in gold.

49. Pricing decisions in the foreign market
    a. can always be approached the same way they are in the United States; this aspect of marketing never varies.
    b. are seldom subject to political constraints; politicians recognize that without profits, products aren't produced.
    c. are relatively free of competitive implications; most foreign economies are much more highly controlled than ours, and competition much less active.
    d. must recognize that a pricing strategy that works in the United States doesn't always work abroad; modifications may have to be made to recognize numerous differences between the foreign market and the U.S. market.
    e. are little affected by the actions of commodity marketing organizations like the Organization of Petroleum Exporting Countries.

50. Foreign-owned assets in the United States are growing at a rate of
     a. $1 trillion (thousand billion) a year.
     b. $750 billion a year.
     c. $500 billion a year.
     d. $250 billion a year.
     e. $100 billion a year.

Name_____ Instructor _____

Section _____ Date _____

Applying Marketing Concepts

Trevolta, Incorporated, is a medium-sized manufacturer of electronic specialties located in Quitman, Mississippi. Founded in 1975, the company has made its name in the United States by producing and marketing "Trevolta Thunder," a line of ultra-high powered audio amplifiers designed for use primarily by rock bands. Some of the Trevolta units are capable of outputs up to 1000 watts with minimal (.01 percent) distortion across the entire audio range. Recognizing the importance of British artists in this field, the company is investigating the possibility of entering the foreign market. It has been approached by the Tannoy Company, Ltd., which has requested the rights to manufacture some of Trevolta's patented antidistortion circuits in Great Britain, selling them under the Trevolta/Tannoy Brand. Tannoy would provide the manufacturing facilities, Trevolta the patents, quality control, and marketing expertise.

The Trevolta management has told Tannoy that it would consider the arrangement, but in the meantime it is exploring other possibilities. It recognizes that should it decide to enter the British market on its own, its product would have to be modified to operate on the 220-volt, 50-cycle electrical current used in that market. There is considerable concern, as well, over whether the British market can be approached the same way as the U.S. market. Data indicate that British rock musicians are both older and less into the mind-jelling amplitude of sound than American players. It has been suggested that any promotion aimed at the British market should stress the low distortion of the Trevolta amplifiers rather than their mind-bending output power. One officer of the company has even suggested that a new line of unitized amplifier-speaker-synthesizer combinations be developed especially for the British market because she believes that British musicians typically play much smaller halls than their American counterparts and would want the more economical, multicapable units.

1. Should Trevolta enter into the arrangement suggested by Tannoy, it would have created a(n)
    a. export contract.
    b. licensing agreement.
    c. joint venture.
    d. shared-rights consortium.
    e. export trade law standard relationship.

2. If Trevolta makes the voltage modifications required by British electrical standards and exports units to that country promoting them in the same way it promotes them in the United States, its strategy will be
    a. straight extension.
    b. dual adaptation.
    c. triple adaptation.
    d. product adaptation.
    e. promotion adaptation.

3. If Trevolta accepts the theory that British rock musicians are older and less explosive than their U.S. counterparts, modifying its promotional program as well as the equipment's electrical supply standards, it will be adopting a
    a. dual adaptation strategy.
    b. marginal entry strategy.
    c. promotion adaptation strategy.
    d. product invention strategy.
    e. product adaptation strategy.

4. Heeding the advice of the executive who proposes the development of a different, multipurpose Trevolta unit for the different requirements of the British market would result in the adoption of a
    a. dual adaptation strategy.
    b. straight extension strategy.
    c. product invention strategy.
    d. product adaptation strategy.
    e. market development strategy.

Aunt Melba's Natchitoches Pie Corporation, of Natchitoches, Louisiana, has been making and selling for over fifty years its variety of the unique fried meat pies for which its section of the state is justly famous. The company operates more than 30 pie stands and drive-through restaurants in Louisiana, Texas, and Arkansas.

Aunt Melba's recently received an inquiry from an Australian engineer working in nearby Shreveport. The engineer, Walter Christie, has apparently become quite fond of the Natchitoches (pronounced Nack-it-tosh) fried pie and believes that it would be quite a success back home in the land down under, where the inhabitants often eat a quick lunch consisting of the famous Australian meat pie. The meat pie is a small pot pie eaten from the hands somewhat like a sandwich. Christie has asked Aunt Melba's for the exclusive rights to distribute its fried pies in his homeland.

The company, realizing that a population of some 14 million people is roughly the same size as the one it now serves, countered by offering to bring Walter into the firm. After a brief training period, he would be sent to Australia to introduce the product to the market. He did not reject the offer outright, but did mention that he wanted a proprietary interest in any such venture.

Further investigation of the Australian market by Aunt Melba's officials proved very interesting. While Australians, particularly in heavily populated New South Wales, do like to eat and run, early efforts by U.S. fast food chains specializing in sandwiches met with considerable resistance. Australians simply did not approve of the skimpy portions of meat and poor quality of bread used in the American sandwiches. One U.S. fast food executive was heard to say, "Australians are very fussy about bread; they will put almost anything in a sandwich—beans, spaghetti, even corn—but if the bread isn't up to snuff, that's the end of it." An executive of another firm commented, "They have a sandwich down there they call 'the lot.' It has everything—the lot—on it: pineapple, meat, egg, potato, whatever. We just couldn't compete with that, so we changed our product."

Armed with those observations, Aunt Melba's executives rethought their position. After all, why should they take a financial risk? Since Walter Christie seemed to have financial backing, they decided to let him have the rights to their fried pie in the Australian market for a number of years, provided he paid them a sizable royalty on sales.

___   5.   It is likely that Aunt Melba's fried pies will have to be modified to be compatible with Australian tastes.

___   6.   It is likely that Mr. Christie and Aunt Melba's will be faced with Australian tariffs and import restrictions.

___   7.   Wealthier countries such as Australia may prove to be prime markets for U.S. products, particularly consumer goods.

___   8.   If Aunt Melba's and Mr. Christie come to terms, there is a real danger that Aunt Melba's will be guilty of dumping.

___   9.   Aunt Melba's is following a global marketing strategy.

___   10.   Mr. Christie's original proposal was in the nature of a request for a joint venture arrangement.

11.   The level of involvement of the firm under Walter's proposal would be
   a.   accidental exporting.
   b.   foreign licensing.
   c.   overseas marketing.
   d.   foreign production and marketing.
   e.   direct exporting.

12.   The level of involvement of the firm under its original counter to Walter would be
   a.   accidental exporting.
   b.   foreign licensing.
   c.   overseas marketing.
   d.   foreign production and marketing.
   e.   direct exporting.

13.   The major barrier to the introduction of American fast food into Australia, as shown in the testimony of the interviewed executives, was
   a.   cultural.
   b.   economic.
   c.   trade restrictions.
   d.   political.
   e.   exchange rate controls.

14.   Which component of the marketing mix seems to present the greatest challenge for firms entering the Australian fast food market?
   a.   distribution
   b.   price
   c.   product
   d.   promotion
   e.   none of the above

Name_____ Instructor _____

Section _____ Date _____

Questions for Thought

The questions which follow are designed to help you become familiar with the main concepts in this chapter through interpretation in your own words. They are meant to be answered in a few sentences or a paragraph at most.

1. Discuss, in general terms, the relationship of marketing environment variables to international marketing.

2. Discuss various methods that a firm might use to enter the international market. How does the global versus multinational strategy decision affect the choice of method?

3. Describe the various product/promotional strategies used in international marketing.

4. Why is the United States such an attractive target market for foreign marketers at the present time?

Name_____   Instructor _____

Section _____   Date _____

Experiential Exercises

1. The purpose of this exercise is to familiarize you with the operation of certain special locations all over the United States called "foreign trade zones." There are over 100 of these special areas in the country, set up by the U.S. government.

    a. Contact the nearest office of the United States Department of Commerce and determine the location of the Foreign Trade Zone nearest your home or college. Inquire about the functions it performs and the firms which use it.

    Location:

    Functions performed:

    Companies using it:

    b. Visit the nearest Foreign Trade Zone (if such a visit is feasible) and notice the special arrangements which allow it to function as it does.

    c. Speak with an official of one of the companies using the FTZ and discuss some of the advantages which its use offers.

2. The purpose of this exercise is to help you understand the importance of imported products to the U.S. market.

Visit a local retail store—department store, discount house, specialty store, limited line store, or supermarket.

a. Select 20 items at random and check to see the name of the manufacturer or importer and the country where they were produced. List the information in the spaces provided.

	Item	Description	Name of Company	Country of Origin
1.				
2.				
3.				
4.				
5.				
6.				
7.				
8.				
9.				
10.				
11.				
12.				
13.				
14.				
15.				
16.				
17.				
18.				
19.				
20.				

b.   What countries seem to have a competitive advantage in the product lines you surveyed?

c.   How many of the products are manufactured or imported by multinational corporations based in the United States? (You may need to use library resources such as *Standard and Poor's Industry Surveys* to answer this question.)

3.   Arrange a meeting with a representative of a firm that is engaged in marketing domestically and internationally. Discuss the differences between marketing in the United States and in at least one foreign country. Use the materials in your text to prepare a set of questions before you meet with the executive. Be sure to cover the strategic areas of product, price, distribution, and promotion. After your meeting write a brief essay about how the company you visited plans and implements its marketing strategy in foreign countries. (Use extra paper if needed.)

Name_____   Instructor _____

Section _____   Date _____

Computer Applications

Review the discussion of the return on investment (ROI) model in Chapter 19 in the text. Then use menu item 8 to solve problem 1.

1. Monolith Industries is considering marketing its line of industrial plastics in a developing country. Market research has estimated that it will cost about $400,000 to gain the right to do business and establish a modest distribution system in the country. Sales potential is expected to be about $16,000,000 and a beginning sales forecast of $4,800,000 has been made. Monolith executives believe that a profit of 25 percent of sales can be made the first year.

    a. Assuming accurate forecasts, what will first year ROI be?

    b. If market entry were to cost $1,200,000 rather than the expected $400,000, what would the ROI be?

Review the discussion of the economic order quantity (EOQ) model. Then use menu item 13 titled "Economic Order Quantity" to solve problem 2.

2. Hunt Veterinary Labs needs to determine the size of shipments of animal health test units to be shipped to its European warehouse facility. The European warehouse manager has been ordering in lots of 20 and averaging 50 shipments per year. Each test unit costs $50 and the cost of processing each shipment is $50. Inventory carrying costs are 30 percent. Sales in Europe last year were 1,120 units and this year they are expected to be 1,300 units.

    a. What was the EOQ for the European warehouse last year?

    b. What will the EOQ for this year be?

    c. If the warehouse manager desires to keep ordering in multiples of 20 units, what is the appropriate order size for this year?

Chapter 19 Solutions

Key Concepts

1. q	6. e	11. t	16. a	21. s
2. h	7. l	12. p	17. o	22. v
3. b	8. g	13. m	18. j	
4. n	9. r	14. i	19. c	
5. u	10. d	15. k	20. f	

Self Quiz

1. T	11. F	21. T	31. b	41. d
2. F	12. T	22. F	32. e	42. c
3. F	13. F	23. T	33. d	43. b
4. T	14. T	24. F	34. c	44. a
5. T	15. F	25. T	35. e	45. a
6. F	16. F	26. d	36. b	46. d
7. T	17. F	27. a	37. c	47. b
8. T	18. F	28. a	38. a	48. c
9. T	19. T	29. c	39. e	49. d
10. F	20. T	30. b	40. e	50. e

Applying Marketing Concepts

1. c	6. F	11. a
2. d	7. T	12. d
3. a	8. F	13. a
4. c	9. F	14. c
5. T	10. F	

Chapter 20

Marketing of Services

Chapter Summary

Some marketers consider there to be little difference between the marketing of services and the marketing of products. Both may be approached in the same manner. First, markets must be investigated and a target market chosen for development. Then, a marketing mix appropriate to the target market must be prepared. Finally, the marketing mix must be taken into the marketplace and, hopefully, will become a success. Yet despite these basic similarities, there are substantial differences between services and products and resulting differences in how they are best marketed. This chapter examines those differences.

Defining exactly what constitutes a service is a difficult task. Often there is intermixture of product and service in the same marketing mix. When one takes one's automobile to a service center for a brake job, one is indeed purchasing brake linings, a certain amount of brake fluid, and perhaps other parts, depending on what is required; but one is also buying the expertise of the individual who does the work and his or her opinion concerning whether new brake cylinders are necessary or whether the brake drums or discs need to be refaced before the job can be called complete and the car safe for driver and passengers. Nonetheless, services must be defined, and a useful definition is one which recognizes that services are intangible tasks which satisfy consumer and industrial-user needs when efficiently developed and distributed to chosen market segments. Perhaps the most important single word in this definition is "intangible," which simply means "nonphysical." In other words, you can't lay hands on a service.

Services are an important component of the economy. Almost 52 percent of all personal consumption spending in the United States is for services. Structurally, service employment now accounts for over three-fourths of all new jobs in this country, and a quarter of the nation's exports.

Five characteristics of services have significant impact on the field of marketing: (1) services are intangible, having no physical existence; (2) services can't be separated from the service provider; (3) services are perishable; (4) standardization of services is a difficult task; and (5) buyers often participate in the development and distribution of services. Users of services have different expectations when they enter the marketplace to purchase a service than they do when they buy physical products, so their behavior is changed. Their attitudes tend to be different, as are their needs and motives, and these differences result in different purchase behavior.

Despite the growing importance of the service industries in the economy, their recognition of the importance of effective marketing has been a slow process. Many authorities, among them Theodore Levitt, feel that this problem was due to their tendency to define their industry too narrowly, resulting in what Levitt identified as "marketing myopia," which is a sort of nearsightedness about one's position in the marketplace. In recent years, it seems that Levitt's writings and musings have been read by a number of service providers who have developed effective marketing programs in a number of industries.

Name _____   Instructor _____

Section _____   Date _____

Key Concepts

The purpose of this section is to allow you to determine if you can match key concepts with the definitions of the concepts. It is essential that you know the definitions of the concepts prior to applying the concepts in later exercises in this chapter.

From the list of lettered terms, select the one that best fits each of the numbered statements below. Write the letter of that choice in the space provided.

Key Terms

a. goods-services continuum   c. services
b. productivity   d. tertiary industries

____ 1. Output produced by each worker.

____ 2. Businesses that specialize in the production of services.

____ 3. Intangible tasks that satisfy consumer and industrial-user needs when efficiently developed and distributed to chosen market segments.

____ 4. Method of visualizing the differences and similarities between goods and services.

Name_____ Instructor _____

Section _____ Date _____

Self Quiz

You should use these objective questions to test your understanding of the chapter material. You can check your answers with those provided at the end of the chapter.

While these questions cover most of the chapter topics, they are not intended to be the same as the test questions your instructor may use in an examination. A good understanding of all aspects of the course material is essential to good performance on any examination.

True/False

Write "T" for True or "F" for False for each of the following statements.

_____ 1. Marketing programs for services typically call for a very different approach than those for products.

_____ 2. Services and goods together often form the "product" component of the marketing mix.

_____ 3. *Most* products have both goods and services components.

_____ 4. One thing that definitively separates goods from services is tangibility; a pure service is never tangible.

_____ 5. Services now account for over 60 percent of the average consumer's expenditures.

_____ 6. The service sector of the economy now provides almost half of the new jobs which appear yearly.

_____ 7. Since personal selling and advertising cannot show the service itself, they must illustrate the benefits the service offers.

_____ 8. Because services are inseparable from service providers, reputations of service vendors are frequently key factors in buying decisions.

_____ 9. Services are perishable because, when stored in inventory, they tend to deteriorate rapidly.

_____ 10. It is often difficult, but never impossible, to standardize offerings among sellers of the same service.

_____ 11. There is often substantial interaction between the service provider and the customer in the production and marketing of services.

_____ 12. A motion picture theatre would typically be classed as a people-based service rather than an equipment-based service.

____ 13.   The element of services which usually differentiates them from one from another is the personal element.

____ 14.   The intangibility of services tends to make buyers rely on objective analyses of services and their sellers when making buying decisions.

____ 15.   Purchase behavior for services may differ from purchase behavior for goods in the amount of prepurchase planning typically undertaken, the influences which are brought to bear on the buyer, and the degree of personal involvement the buyer feels.

____ 16.   The slow adoption of marketing as a business activity by many service marketers can be attributed to their failure to recognize the scope of their businesses—"marketing myopia."

____ 17.   Colin Clark has theorized that, in the highest-level economies, the majority of the labor force is employed in manufacturing.

____ 18.   The association which many people make between service industries, unskilled jobs, and low pay is not borne out by the facts in those areas, where a substantial shift from goods industries to service industries has taken place.

____ 19.   One reason for the rapid growth of business service firms is that they are frequently able to perform the customer's major activities more cheaply than the customer can.

____ 20.   One of the ways in which regulation affects the marketing of services is by increasing the range of competition, thereby reducing its intensity.

____ 21.   According to Theodore Levitt, increased productivity in the service sector of the economy will be achieved, not simply by working harder, but through the application of improved organizations, incentives, technology, and skills to the job.

____ 22.   Direct competition between goods and services seldom occurs because it is impossible to satisfy service needs through the substitution of goods.

____ 23.   Entrepreneurial service providers may find themselves in direct competition with government or its agencies in the provision of certain services.

____ 24.   Close regulation by government has typically meant limited price competition for many services; for others, industry traditions have had the same effect.

____ 25.   Sales promotion is widely used in services marketing, with sampling, demonstrations, premiums, and contests being the favored vehicles.

Multiple Choice

Circle the letter of the word or phrase that best completes the sentence or best answers the question.

26. The development of a marketing program for a service typically begins with
    a. the development of a marketing mix to satisfy a market segment.
    b. investigation, analysis, and selection of a market segment.
    c. the realization that marketing a service is radically different than marketing a physical product.
    d. creation of the service in recognition of universal need for it.
    e. definition of the specific limits of the developer's capacity to perform the service.

27. Which of the following most closely approximates a *pure* service?
    a. having your car washed and waxed by a "detailing" company
    b. repairs made to your television set when a major component fails
    c. purchasing a security package for your home from Westec; the package includes an alarm system as well as periodic visits during the day and night by Westec patrols
    d. buying a set of tires and having them mounted and balanced at a local Firestone store
    e. enjoying a meal at a fine restaurant

28. The leading categories of service expenditures among consumers are
    a. energy and personal care.
    b. medical and business services.
    c. communications and travel.
    d. housing and transportation.
    e. education security.

29. Services are difficult to demonstrate at trade shows, display in retail stores, illustrate in advertisements, and sample because
    a. they are perishable.
    b. they are inseparable from their provider.
    c. they are usually not standardized.
    d. of interaction between buyer and seller.
    e. they are intangible.

30. Which of the following best illustrates the perishability of services?
    a. They do not have features that can be seen, heard, smelled, tasted, or touched.
    b. In consumers' minds, those who provide the service *are* the service.
    c. They cannot be produced ahead of time and stored in inventory in anticipation of periods of peak demand.
    d. Consistency of quality is difficult to achieve even in the services provided by a single seller.
    e. The consumer often plays a major role in the determination of when and how the service is going to be performed.

31. Which of the following is the best example of an equipment-based service?
    a. an accounting practice
    b. a firm of lawyers
    c. a public relations company
    d. a dental practice
    e. an advertising agency

32. One need that services marketers should be able to satisfy better than goods marketers is
    a. the need for consistent, repeatable quality at every purchase.
    b. the desire for personal attention.
    c. the necessity of being there when and where needed.
    d. a feeling of satisfaction that the job has been properly done.
    e. the ability to hold the purchased object in one's hand.

33. Which of the following relationships shows the least effect of what Levitt identified as "marketing myopia"?
    a. the bank president who says, "We provide our customers with security"
    b. the manufacturer who states, "We make furniture"
    c. the executive of the hotel chain who says, "We provide lodging to travelers"
    d. the railroad executive who notes, "We are in the railroad business"
    e. the network TV producer whose opinion is, "We make TV shows"

34. Most explanations of the sharp increases in spending for services and the rapid development of service industries in the United States since World War II are predicated on
    a. a return to a more subsistence-oriented life-style calling for less dependence on manufactured goods and more on individual skills.
    b. a shifting in the American economy from primary industries to secondary industries.
    c. the changes associated with a maturing economy and the by-products of rapid economic growth.
    d. liberation of women from the home and into the workforce, distributing expertise more uniformly across the manufacturing sector of the economy.
    e. a decline in American productivity which has called for additional people to be employed in "cleaning up" the mess we have made of this continent.

35. A shift in the economy away from manufacturing and toward service industries is often incorrectly associated with
    a. an increase in per-capita income in those areas where there has been a shift from manufacturing to services as the economic base.
    b. the use of labor for tertiary production.
    c. technological advances; the rate of consumption of services has little to do with the level of technology.
    d. changes in the distribution of population toward a more urban society.
    e. a low level of skill on the part of employees and commensurately inferior rates of pay.

36. Which of the following is true of the market for business services?
    a. The growth in spending for business services has been less significant than that for consumer services.
    b. Many firms purchase business services because they are unable to perform a particular specialized task which an outside source can provide.
    c. The profitability of business-service providers is questionable; intense competition makes the field marginal.
    d. Many business services provided by outside operations cost more than if the purchasing firm performed the services itself.
    e. Most business services are purchased as a mark of prestige rather than for any economic or practical reason.

37. Which of the following is an example of a service unique to today's culture in the United States?
    a. janitorial services provided by separate companies to business users
    b. personal services such as haircutting and styling in a salon environment
    c. automotive repairs done by dealers at their service facilities
    d. a service which makes third-party apologies for people who fear they have offended others
    e. travel agencies which will book single airfares or package tours on request

38. One of the social/cultural trends occurring in the United States today which is relevant to services marketing is
    a. a shifting of tastes to a preference for services as status symbols.
    b. a declining emphasis on personal security, tightening the market for insurance and investment services.
    c. less consideration of travel and education for reasons of status and more of a view of them as necessities.
    d. lessening of the fear of mortality, reducing demand for medical services and health clubs.
    e. a significant decline in participation in cultural events to "see and be seen" and an increase in real interest in them.

39. Government regulation affects the marketing of services by
    a. increasing the range of competition, thereby reducing its intensity.
    b. increasing the array of options available to the marketer, thereby allowing a more flexible operation of the marketplace.
    c. allowing business decisions to be made for purely business reasons; the regulations clarify everyone's position with regard to possible action by the regulatory agency.
    d. applying to relatively few firms in the service industries, and then usually only the largest which would become visible to federal regulators.
    e. forcing a part of the decision-making process to be aimed at predicting the actions of regulatory agencies.

40. The use of robots in service industries for purposes such as surveillance of prisons, conducting preliminary medical interviews, and serving meals to hospital patients is an example of
    a. how the shortage of human help has forced the use of these stopgap measures to provide basic necessities for people.
    b. how people's expectations have changed; a few years ago, no one would have accepted these concepts.
    c. an effort to improve productivity in the service sector of the economy; using robots instead of humans increases the service output per person employed.
    d. experimentation with technology which may or may not prove to be successful or acceptable.
    e. yet another effort to weaken the bargaining power of unions at the negotiating table.

41. The paradoxical nature of the competitive environment in the market for services is best exemplified by the fact that
    a.   people want services but very often do not wish to pay what they are worth to get them.
    b.   internal competition is fierce for all except the most marginal kinds of services.
    c.   competition often comes not from other services but from goods manufacturers or government-provided services.
    d.   despite uniform ease of entry, some segments of the service market remain almost totally unserved.
    e.   high levels of profitability have not drawn service providers into the service sector in anything like the volume one would ordinarily expect.

42. Which of the following is the best example of a service normally provided only by government?
    a.   communications
    b.   security in one's old age
    c.   medical care
    d.   security of one's person and property
    e.   None of these are services which are exclusive to government.

43. Express Mail is an example of a government service
    a.   which has direct competition from the private sector.
    b.   which was created to serve a market segment too small to profitably be served by commercial interests.
    c.   which has as its main market the government itself.
    d.   provided only to a limited number of users on a preferential basis.
    e.   offered on an experimental basis to develop better communications networks within the nation's communications system.

44. The most commonly used segmentation method applied by service marketers is
    a.   geography.
    b.   psychography.
    c.   demography.
    d.   benefits.
    e.   economy.

45. Dry cleaning, shoe repair, and similar personal services are usually classed as
    a.   shopping services.
    b.   specialty services.
    c.   impulse services.
    d.   emergency services.
    e.   convenience services.

46. Price competition for many services is limited because
    a.   of rapid price increases across the board; over the last 20 years, service prices have risen over 100 percent more than goods prices.
    b.   production, marketing, and administrative costs must be covered regardless of competitive conditions.
    c.   of the involvement of employees in the pricing process.
    d.   of close regulation by federal, state, or local government agencies, as in the case of utilities.
    e.   of the relative scarcity of suppliers compared to the size of the market.

47. The use of variable pricing to overcome the problems associated with the perishable nature of services is best illustrated by
   a.   the traditional pricing structure in the advertising agency business.
   b.   airlines which offer highly discounted fares on heavily competitive routes.
   c.   negotiation of prices and other terms which typically takes place in the marketing of specialized business services.
   d.   the rapid increase in the prices of highly sought-after consumer and professional services.
   e.   the close regulation of most utilities by federal, state, and local governments.

48. If marketing intermediaries are used by service firms in the channel of distribution, they are usually
   a.   merchant wholesalers.
   b.   full-service retailers.
   c.   limited-line retailers.
   d.   agents or brokers.
   e.   specialty wholesalers.

49. Distribution channels for services are typically
   a.   simpler and shorter than those for goods.
   b.   longer and more complex than those for goods.
   c.   less personal and more institutional than those for goods.
   d.   marked by more concern with storage, transportation, and inventory control than are channels for goods.
   e.   characterized by extensive use of sophisticated materials handling equipment.

50. Linking a service to a concrete image or symbol such as the insurance industry has done with its umbrellas, rocks, and blankets is known as
   a.   "creativizing " it.
   b.   "tangibilizing" it.
   c.   "personalizing" it.
   d.   "dehumanizing" it.
   e.   "sensitizing" it.

Name _____   Instructor _____

Section _____   Date _____

Applying Marketing Concepts

John Alberts is a landscape architect who has been in practice some fifteen years. His clients are primarily large business firms, among them Integrity Outdoor Advertising Company, one of the nation's largest owners of billboards and other outdoor advertising displays. John is somewhat concerned because his contract with Integrity will expire soon, and he knows that he will be facing competition to continue the beautification of the land surrounding the company's billboards all over the Southeast. He knows that the executives of the company are very happy with his work, and he feels that they think of him as "their" architect. The other firms competing for the contract have sent in "sales teams" to try and convince Integrity to do business with them, and each executive has mentioned to John what a turnoff the presentations have been, dealing primarily with costs and only marginally with aesthetics. This has made him feel better, because he knows his prices are competitive, and the plantings he has provided to Integrity to carry out his designs have been of only the best stock. Despite this, he knows he's going to have to be prepared to offer his very best as the renewal date approaches.

1. Clients who rent Integrity's billboards are purchasing
    a. a pure service or something very close to it.
    b. something which is predominantly a service with some goods included.
    c. something which mixes products and services in roughly equal proportions.
    d. something which is predominantly a product with a somewhat smaller service component.
    e. a pure good.

2. Given that John provides the plantings which are used in his work of beautifying Integrity's billboard locations, his position on the goods-services continuum is
    a. at the service end; what he does is a pure service.
    b. certainly not a pure service; he is dealing in goods as well.
    c. well toward the goods end of the continuum; his services are a minor part of the total offering he's providing.
    d. at the goods end; his product is purely goods.
    e. at both ends; the services he provides are totally separate from whatever goods may be involved.

3. John is hoping to retain the contract because he feels that he is in a position to provide the one thing that the other competitors don't seem to have,
    a. size and scale of operations.
    b. effective sales personnel who can really hammer home a concept.
    c. the ability to do the job the company wants done.
    d. the ability to cut costs at every opportunity, doing an acceptable job at the lowest expenditure.
    e. a personal relationship with company executives and their trust in his relationship with him.

4. Judging by what you know of John's clients, how would you categorize the nature of his services?
   a. They are directed toward the industrial market and are people based.
   b. They are directed to the consumer market and are equipment based.
   c. They are industrially oriented and equipment based.
   d. They are consumer oriented and people based.
   e. They are consumer based and performed by unskilled workers.

5. John's recognition that he's going to have to "be prepared to offer his very best" as the end of his current contract draws near implies
   a. that he feels he's going to have to bribe Integrity officials to secure renewal of his relationship with them.
   b. that he hopes to hit them with his very best designs just before his contract runs out.
   c. that John knows that he's going to have to negotiate with the Integrity people to secure a renewal of his contract.
   d. that John feels there's little hope his contract will be renewed.
   e. that he hasn't done a very good job for Integrity in the past.

Sally Smith, owner of Sally Forth, Inc., is assessing the progress of her new business venture, shopping for people who don't have time to shop for themselves. A phone call to Sally Forth with a request that a birthday present be bought for a six-year-old nephew and sent to the child's address can be fulfilled the same day the request is made. Sally Smith is quite pleased; she has had to hire five additional shoppers to handle the avalanche of requests for things that people need to buy but can't find time to go out and get. The 20 percent surcharge over the cost of any merchandise purchased doesn't seem to bother many of the people who call to request the service.

6. Sally Forth provides
   a. a consumer service that's equipment based.
   b. an industrial service that's people based.
   c. a consumer service that's people based.
   d. an industrial service that's equipment based.
   e. an industrial service with a product component.

7. The need for a service like Sally Forth grows out of changes in the
   a. economic environment.
   b. social/cultural environment.
   c. political/legal environment.
   d. technological environment.
   e. competitive environment.

8. If intended use were the basis, Sally Forth would be classed as a
   a. consumer convenience service.
   b. consumer specialty service.
   c. diversified consumer service.
   d. general industrial service.
   e. specialty industrial service.

Name _____   Instructor _____

Section _____   Date _____

Questions for Thought

The questions which follow are designed to help you become familiar with the main concepts in this chapter through interpretation in your own words. They are meant to be answered in a few sentences or a paragraph at most.

1.   Using the goods-services continuum, distinguish between goods and services.

2.   Outline the major characteristics of services.

3.   How does buyer behavior in the purchase of services differ from buyer behavior when goods are bought?

4.   Discuss the evaluation of the marketing function in service-oriented industries.

Name _____   Instructor _____

Section _____   Date _____

Experiential Exercises

1. Get a small notebook and, for two days, describe each service that you use. You may ride the bus, get a haircut, cash a check at the bank, or pick up your dry cleaning. You may elect to create a table of uses for very frequently used services, such as speaking on the telephone. At the end of the second day, fill in the information below.

    a. Total number of different services used:

    b. Most frequently used service:

        How many times this service was used:

    c. Pure services used: (List them)

    d. Mixed goods/services used: (List them)

2. Acquire a copy of a Yellow Pages Telephone Directory. Open the directory to a randomly chosen page and, starting with the classification which opens or continues on the left-hand page, decide whether that and the next 99 classifications list companies which provide predominantly goods or predominantly services. Report the results of your efforts below.

    a. Proportion of service providers:

    b. Proportion of goods providers:

Name _____   Instructor _____

Section _____   Date _____

Computer Applications

Use menu item 8 entitled "Return on Investment" to solve problem 1. Problems 2 and 3 may be solved using menu item 16, "Salesforce Determination."

1. A small computer service company in Richmond, Virginia, is considering buying a similar firm in Charlottesville. The asking price for the Charlottesville company is $500,000. The Charlottesville operation currently earns a return of $150,000 on annual revenues of $750,000. What would be the return on investment if this operation were purchased?

2. Leroy Terwilliger, owner and operator of Service Solicitations, a firm specializing in soliciting funds for charitable institutions, has received the assignment of soliciting St. Louis, Missouri, for the American Safe Homes Association. Mr. Terwilliger has determined that St. Louis contains a total of 575,000 households, of which he has classified some 55,000 as type A (high value contributor). Another 120,000 households have been determined to be type B (medium value contributor), and the remaining 400,000 are type C (low value contributor). Mr. Terwilliger estimates that contact with a high value contributor should take 20 minutes if a contribution is to be successfully solicited. It should be possible to realize a contribution from a type B contributor in 15 minutes, and from a type C household in 10. Mr. Terwilliger has twelve weeks to complete the solicitation. If Mr. Terwilliger's solicitors, each of whom works a 36-hour week, spend 50 percent of their time calling on designated accounts, 35 percent traveling, and the remaining 15 percent filling out reports, how many solicitors should Mr. Terwilliger assign to St. Louis?

3. Analytical Services, Inc., provides pathological laboratory services to the Baltimore, Maryland, area. Gene Hitchcock, M.D., the owner and managing director of the company, has realized that he needs to maintain closer ties with some of Baltimore's 2,700 physicians than with others. He has broken down the physician population of Baltimore into three groups. The "A" group, composed mainly of internists and diagnostic practitioners, requires 30 minutes per week to serve each of the 300 members. The "B" group, of whom there are 800, can be handled in 15 minutes per week, while the class C practitioners, making up the remaining 1,600 physicians, can be dealt with in only 5 minutes per week. If Dr. Hitchcock's "physician interface" personnel work 40-hour weeks and can devote 80 percent of their time to dealing with doctors, the remaining 20 percent being devoted to paperwork, how many "physician interface" personnel will be needed to handle the workload?

Chapter 20 Solutions

Key Concepts

1. b
2. d
3. c
4. a

Self Quiz

1. F	11. T	21. T	31. d	41. c
2. T	12. F	22. F	32. b	42. e
3. T	13. T	23. T	33. a	43. a
4. T	14. F	24. T	34. c	44. c
5. F	15. T	25. F	35. e	45. e
6. F	16. T	26. b	36. b	46. d
7. T	17. F	27. a	37. d	47. b
8. T	18. T	28. d	38. a	48. d
9. F	19. F	29. e	39. e	49. a
10. F	20. F	30. c	40. c	50. b

Applying Marketing Concepts

1. a
2. b
3. e
4. a
5. c
6. c
7. b
8. a

Part Eight Puzzle

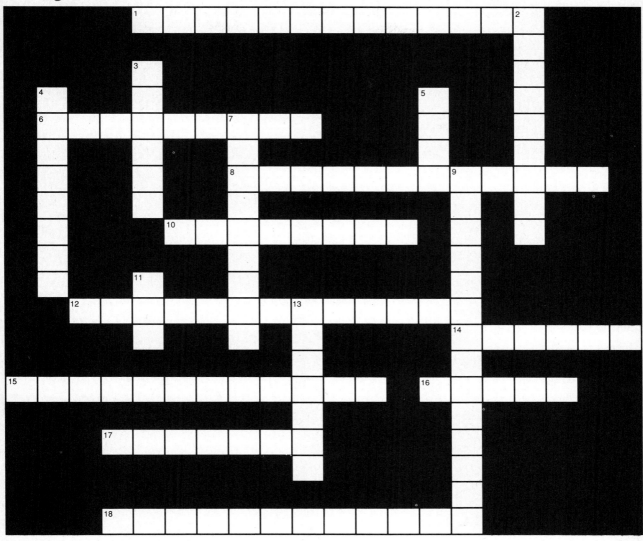

ACROSS CLUES

1. a firm with significant operations and marketing activities outside home country
6. marketing goods and services in foreign countries
8. output produced by each worker
10. industries that specialize in the production of services
12. price of one nation's currency in terms of other nations' currencies
14. tax levied against imported products
15. form of exporting which barters products or services rather than selling them for cash

16. with respect to imports, a trade restriction that limits units of product that can enter country
17. selling a product in a foreign market for less than it sells for in the domestic market
18. agreement in which a firm shares in a foreign operation with partners, usually also foreign

DOWN CLUES

2. permitting a foreign company to produce or distribute a firm's product in a foreign market
3. strategy featuring a standard marketing mix used in all of a firm's foreign markets

4. intangible tasks that satisfy user needs when distributed to chosen market segments
5. acronym for international trade agreement that has helped to reduce world tariffs
7. purchasing of foreign products and raw materials
9. communications systems, transportation networks, and energy facilities
11. treaties dealing largely with commercial relations among nations (acronym)
13. complete ban on the import of certain products

Name_____   Instructor _____

Section _____   Date _____

Cases for Part 8

1. *Magnano Manufacturing Company*

Betty Schultz got off the airplane at Sonno Maggiore, capital of Piulentezza, enthusiastic to get down to business with the local representatives of the National Department of the Post, Telephone, and Telegraph. Though her plane was three hours late, she didn't consider that a major problem. There are always delays in international travel. She was most surprised to discover that her own firm, Magnano Manufacturing Company, had not sent a car to pick her up. Just as she was getting ready to place a call to them on the airport telephone (there was only one), a vehicle screeched up outside and she heard her name being called. It was a company driver who apologized for not being there when she arrived, but stated that they simply had not expected the plane to get in early! Somewhat taken aback, Betty nonetheless allowed the man to claim her luggage and escort her to the company car, a somewhat down-at-the-heels 1958 model. In response to her question about why the company maintained such a disreputable vehicle, his comment was, "Va bene, signorina, it is not good to appear too well off. This is one of the newest and best cars in all of Sonno Maggiore. It is maintained by our own mechanics and will outrun any car in the city, either police car or vehiculo ladro (robber's car)." As he said this he ran yet another stop light and continued on to the Hotel Andare Coricarsi, supposedly Sonno Maggiore's best.

Surprisingly, the hotel was wonderful. The room was large, clean, and beautifully appointed; the service kindly, considerate, and professional; and no one would accept any kind of tip. Dinner that evening was a gastronomic delight, consisting of seven courses of beautifully prepared food, although some of it was a little different from what Betty was used to, and she suspected that if she ever found out what it really was, she might become slightly ill.

She got a good night's rest and was up at the crack of dawn, dressed and ready to go to work. But she couldn't seem to get a dial tone from the telephone, and when she went downstairs, the desk clerk told her that the telephone exchange didn't open until 10 AM. Moreover, he couldn't get her a cab to take her to the office because the cabs didn't start running until around 9:30 (more or less). He suggested she take breakfast in the dining room until he could arrange to care for her needs. Faced with the inevitable, she went into the dining room, which was packed with local businesspeople (most of whom were drinking coffee and carrying on lively conversations). There, lo and behold, was the manager of the local office of Magnano, who saw Betty enter and waved her over to his table. He was most enthusiastic to see her, and explained that his intention was to meet her in the dining room. He knew she'd show up there because, he laughed, there wasn't anywhere else to go at that hour of the morning.

When Betty stumbled in at 1 AM the next morning, she knew she was out of her depth. This was a country where telephones only worked ten hours a day and taxicabs and public transportation didn't come on duty until midmorning. She had been introduced to 20 different and supposedly important people by Magnano's local representative, who seemed more interested in the conditions of their families than of their desire to do business with the company. When she had asked about making appointments with some of these people for business, Sr.

Bientutti, Magnano's local manager, had muttered something about "Maybe next week, or the week after."

Betty was frazzled. She had budgeted four days for this trip, and she could see that whatever was going to happen was going to take a lot longer than that.

Question

What should Betty Schultz do?

2.   *So You Want to Be a World-Class Marketer?*[1]

It is necessary to have knowledge of some seemingly obscure facts if you are to make your way in the world of international marketing.

See how many of the following you can answer. The answers can be found on the next page.

1.   What country prohibits the sale of imported bananas?
   a.   Kuwait
   b.   South Africa
   c.   Germany (FRG)

---

[1]   Adapted from "Global Trivia: A Test for the Worldly Wise," *Across the Board*, September 1985, p. 77 (The Conference Board). Derived from work done by Runzheimer International, a Rochester, Wisconsin management and consulting firm.

2. For each vehicle-mile traveled, what country has the highest pedestrian death rate?
   a. Poland
   b. United States
   c. Germany (FRG)

3. The longest river in the world is the
   a. Amazon.
   b. Nile.
   c. Volga.

4. What city has the largest seaport in the world?
   a. London
   b. New York
   c. Rotterdam

5. What is a rack rate?
   a. the rib section of a slaughtered animal
   b. the undiscounted price of a hotel room
   c. a degree of torture

6. The Japanese drive on which side of the road?
   a. left
   b. right
   c. middle

7. *Kuala Lumpur* means
   a. hello.
   b. goodbye.
   c. muddy river.

8. If you should find yourself in a Flughafen, you are at an airport in what country?
   a. Norway
   b. Germany (FRG)
   c. Luxembourg

9. Among the countries of the world, how does the People's Republic of China rank in terms of area?
   a. second
   b. third
   c. tenth

10. Of which country is Harare the capital?
    a. Zaire
    b. Zambia
    c. Zimbabwe

11. Romaji is
    a. used to bring out the delicate taste of squid.
    b. used to translate Japanese to Roman characters.
    c. the Kentucky Derby winner horsenapped from an Irish stud farm.

12.   What is the currency of Malaysia?
    a.   the baht
    b.   the ringgit
    c.   the rupee

13.   What country uses the dollar as its national currency?
    a.   Liberia
    b.   Australia
    c.   Canada

14.   Which of the following is a major English city?
    a.   Hull
    b.   Cardigan
    c.   Greenock

Ten or more correct makes you a world traveler (or very lucky). Seven to ten right, and you're an average expert on world affairs. Less than seven, you're a typical American.

Answers:

1. c	8. b
2. a	9. a
3. b	10. c
4. c	11. b
5. b	12. b
6. a	13. all
7. c	14. a (the others are in Wales and Scotland)

3.   *Industrial Health Services*

Al Newman is thinking of leaving Industrial Health Services and setting up his own industrial medical clinic. For the last seven years, Dr. Newman has been the medical director and examining physician for Industrial Health Services, a firm which specializes in examining managerial personnel of local businesses.

These examinations are usually carried out in the manager's office. Some firms have their executives examined every two years as a matter of course, others when they are applying for an increase in life or medical insurance benefits for their people.

Over the last seven years, Dr. Newman has gotten to know a number of the high level executives of numerous local firms and feels that they would switch to him rather than remain with IHS should he leave. He knows, however, that IHS is a large firm with a good local and regional reputation in this somewhat specialized field. He is wondering whether the move which he is contemplating would be a wise one.

Questions

a. What are some of the characteristics of the market for services which make Dr. Newman's idea potentially viable?

b. What are some of the characteristics of the market for services that make Dr. Newman's idea potentially risky?

Name _____   Instructor _____

Section _____   Date _____

Creating a Marketing Plan: "So When Do We Start to Get Rich?"

The material provided in this episode should allow you to complete Part III.E. of your marketing plan.

Episode Eight

The three partners, having incorporated their business, have each bought 20,000 shares of the authorized 80,000 shares of Subchapter S common stock for one dollar apiece. They have also secured a $90,000 bank loan at a rate of 9.5 percent to be repaid over five years in monthly installments of $1890.90.

They have established that sales of $180,063 will allow them to break even. Pro Forma Income Statements for the first three years of operation have been prepared and are included in Table P8-1.

Table P8-1: Pro Forma Income Statements for Years 1, 2, and 3 for Latebri Industries, Inc.

Year	One	Two	Three
Revenue	$ 66,568	$120,876	$144,147
Allowances	2,645	4,800	5,724
Net Sales	63,923	116,076	138,423
Cost of Services	24,105	24,675	24,920
Gross Margin	39,818	91,401	113,502
Operating Expenses	104,859	65,149	63,370
Marketing Expense*	14,359	30,031	32,389
Operating Income (Loss)	(79,401)	(3,779)	17,743

*Includes sales commissions, sales staff salaries, and advertising.

The threesome, as sole employees of the firm, will have collected all the commissions and salaries paid by the firm during the first three years. Those amounts are summarized in Table P8-2.

Table P8-2: Salaries and Commissions Paid, First Three Years, for Latebri Industries, Inc.

Year	One	Two	Three
Administrative Salaries	$30,000	$30,000	$30,000
Service Salaries	19,200	19,200	19,200
Sales Commissions	6,745	12,247	14,605
Sales Salaries	11,400	11,400	11,400
Total Amounts	$67,345	$72,847	$75,205

They are, of course, due any dividends which they may elect to pay themselves from profits earned in year three and subsequent years.

Guidelines

Use this information to prepare Part III.E. of your marketing plan. Note that, since this is a start-up business, projections have been made pro forma for a period of three years. Impact of the trio's efforts will be evidenced by the degree to which the projections and reality are similar.

Question

Will it all have been worth it? Considering the future of the company, will the three partners have gotten out of it what they expected to, in your opinion? Remember, the psychic reward of entrepreneurship has some value.

Answers to
Crossword Puzzles

Answers to Part One Puzzle

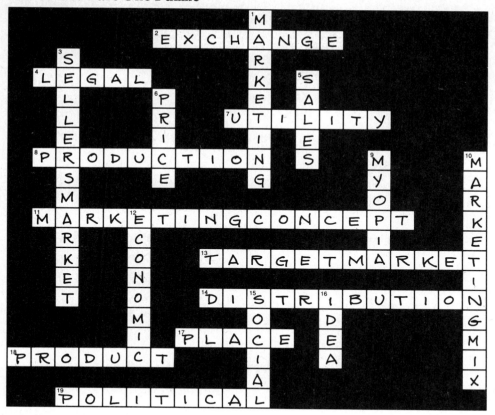

Answers to Part Two Puzzle

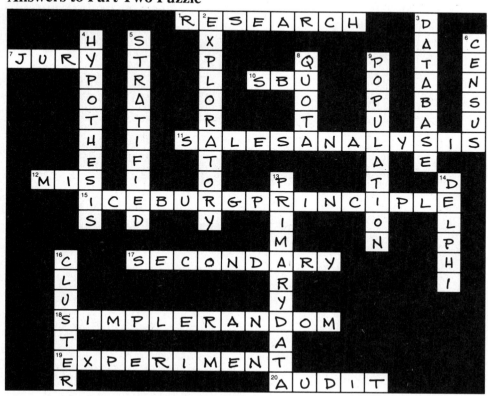

Answers to Part Three Puzzle

Answers to Part Four Puzzle

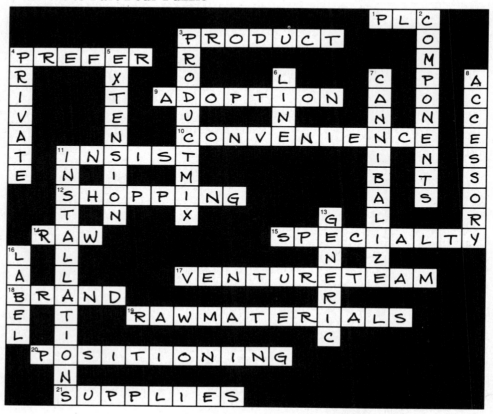

Answers to Part Five Puzzle

Answers to Part Six Puzzle

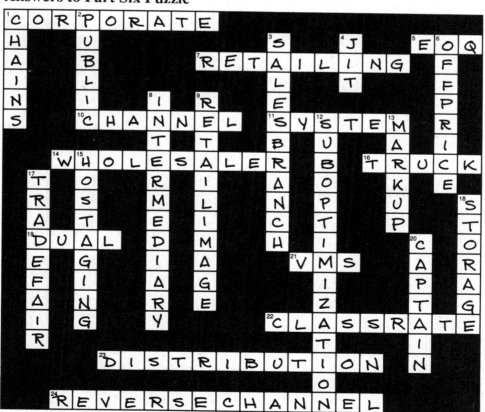

624

Answers to Part Seven Puzzle

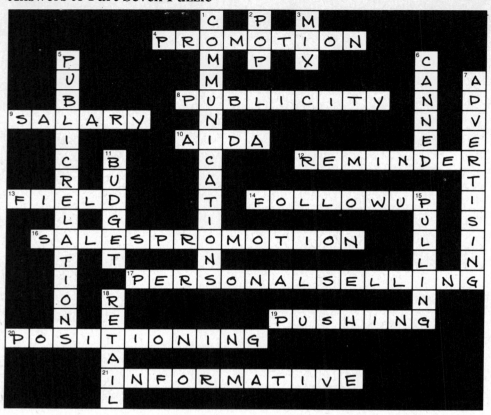

Answers to Part Eight Puzzle

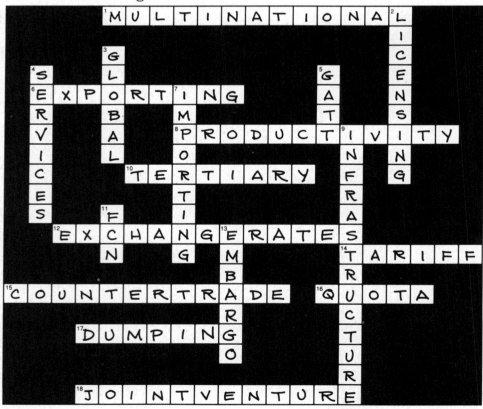